SHONEN JUMP MANGA

DRAGON BALL Z

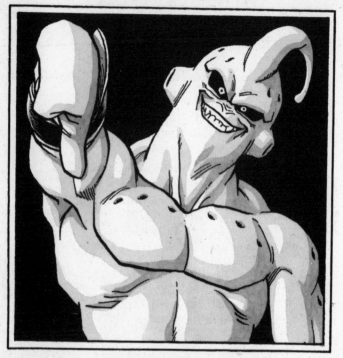

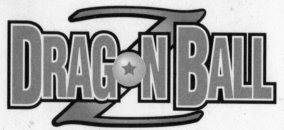

Vol. 25

DB: 41 of 42

STORY AND ART BY
AKIRA TORIYAMA

THE MAIN CHARACTERS

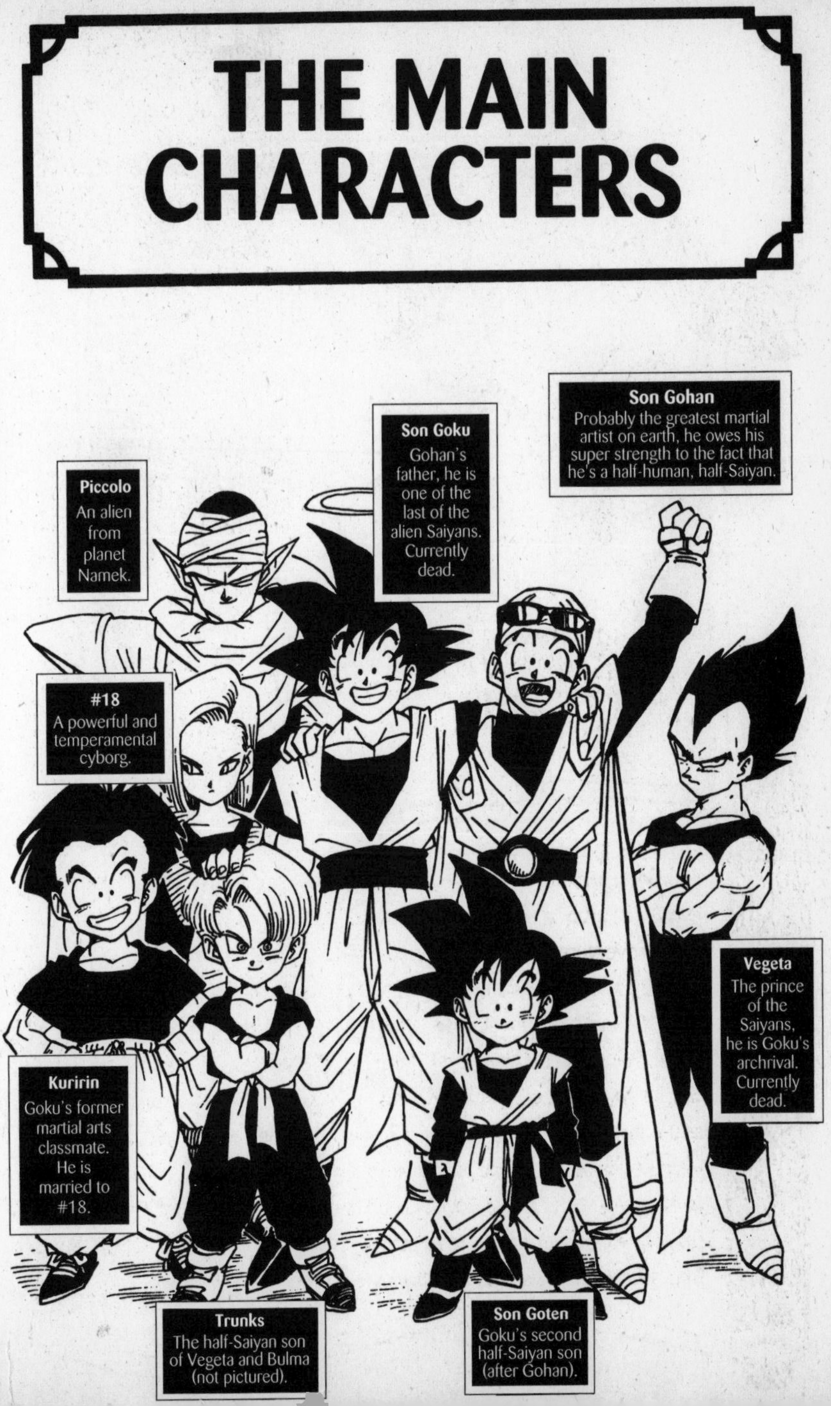

Son Gohan
Probably the greatest martial artist on earth, he owes his super strength to the fact that he's a half-human, half-Saiyan.
Son Goku
Gohan's father, he is one of the last of the alien Saiyans. Currently dead.
Piccolo
An alien from planet Namek.
Vegeta
The prince of the Saiyans, he is Goku's archrival. Currently dead.
#18
A powerful and temperamental cyborg.
Kuririn
Goku's former martial arts classmate. He is married to #18.
Son Goten
Goku's second half-Saiyan son (after Gohan).
Trunks
The half-Saiyan son of Vegeta and Bulma (not pictured).

Hercule
An ordinary wrestler who became world-famous when he took credit for defeating Cell.

Kaiô-shin
The "Lord of Lords," he is the supreme deity of the Dragon Ball universe. He rescued Gohan and spirited him away to an alien planet for training.

The Former Kaiô-shin
An old god who was the "Lord of Lords" 15 generations ago. Gohan's trainer.

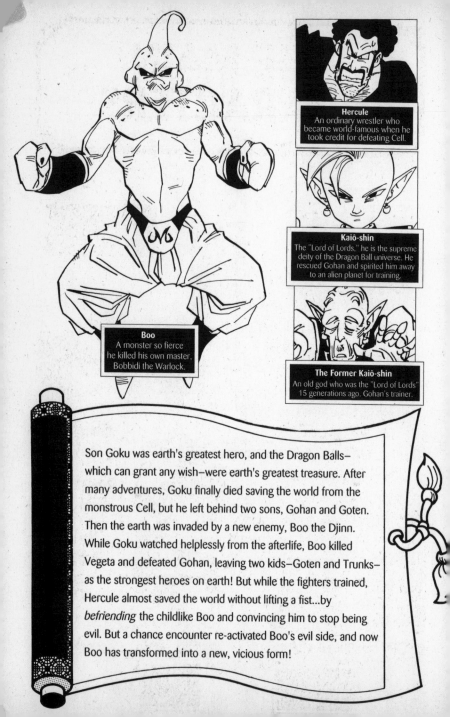

Boo
A monster so fierce he killed his own master, Bobbidi the Warlock.

Son Goku was earth's greatest hero, and the Dragon Balls–which can grant any wish–were earth's greatest treasure. After many adventures, Goku finally died saving the world from the monstrous Cell, but he left behind two sons, Gohan and Goten. Then the earth was invaded by a new enemy, Boo the Djinn. While Goku watched helplessly from the afterlife, Boo killed Vegeta and defeated Gohan, leaving two kids–Goten and Trunks–as the strongest heroes on earth! But while the fighters trained, Hercule almost saved the world without lifting a fist...by *befriending* the childlike Boo and convincing him to stop being evil. But a chance encounter re-activated Boo's evil side, and now Boo has transformed into a new, vicious form!

DRAGON BALL Z 25

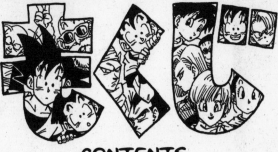

CONTENTS

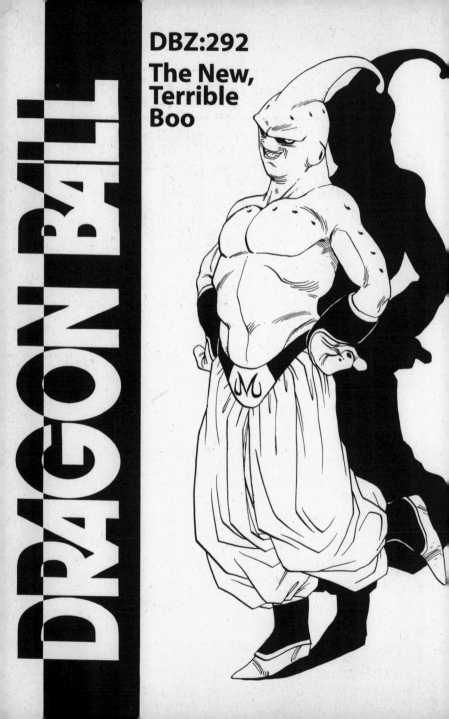

DRAGON BALL

DBZ:292
The New,
Terrible
Boo

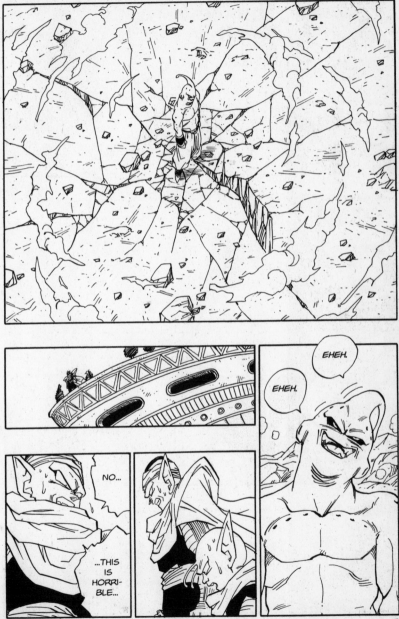

NO...

...THIS
IS
HORRI-
BLE...

EHEH.

EHEH.

READ THIS WAY

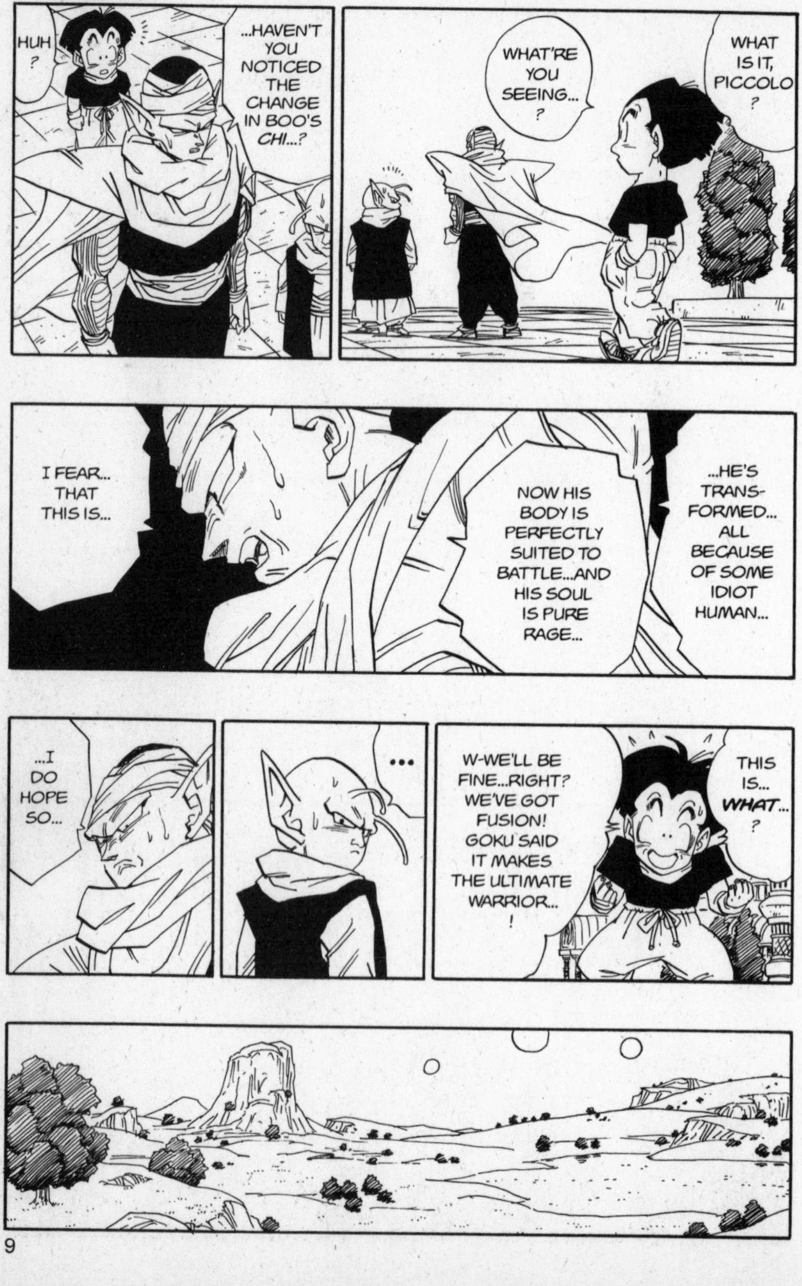

WHAT IS IT, PICCOLO?
WHAT'RE YOU SEEING...?
...HAVEN'T YOU NOTICED THE CHANGE IN BOO'S *CHI*...?
HUH?
...HE'S TRANS-FORMED... ALL BECAUSE OF SOME IDIOT HUMAN...
NOW HIS BODY IS PERFECTLY SUITED TO BATTLE...AND HIS SOUL IS PURE RAGE...
I FEAR... THAT THIS IS...
THIS IS... ***WHAT***...?
W-WE'LL BE FINE...RIGHT? WE'VE GOT FUSION! GOKU SAID IT MAKES THE ULTIMATE WARRIOR...!
...
...I DO HOPE SO...

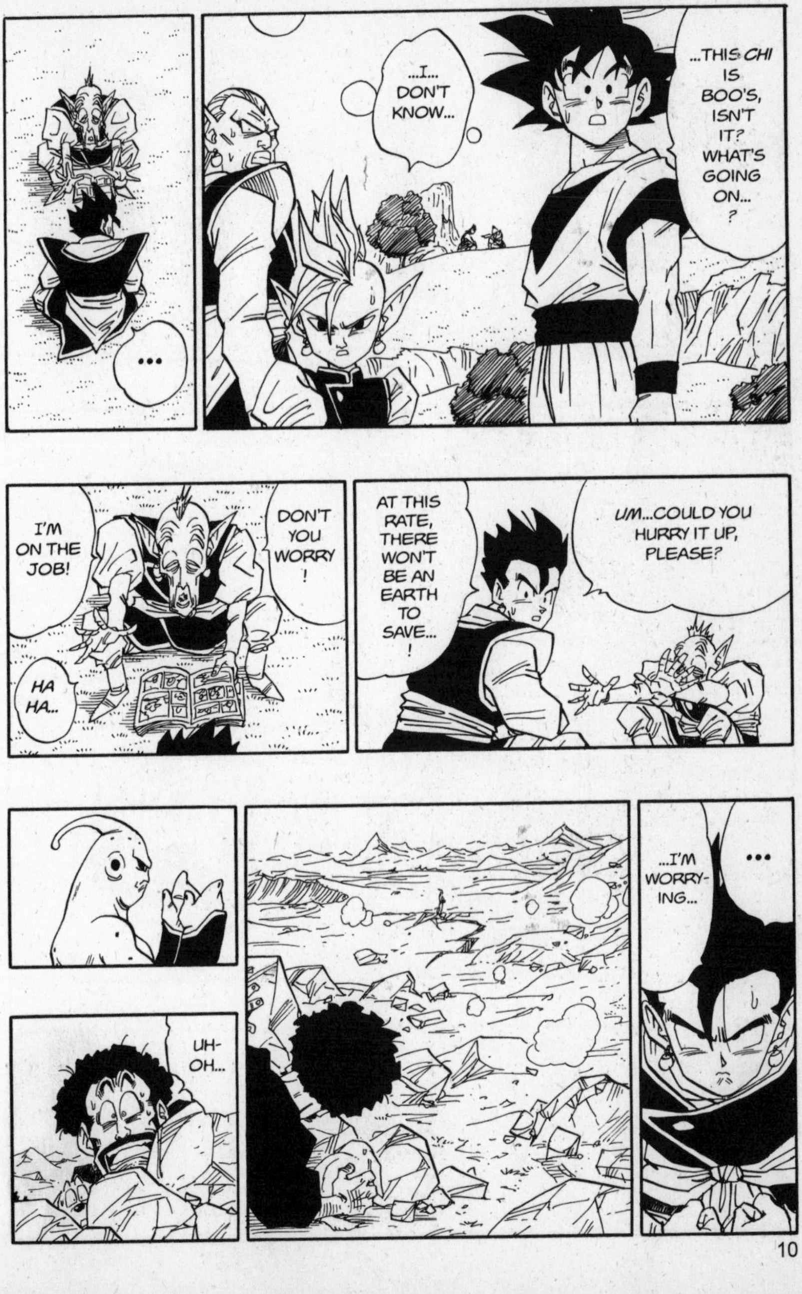
...THIS CHI IS BOO'S, ISN'T IT? WHAT'S GOING ON...?
...I... DON'T KNOW...
...
UM...COULD YOU HURRY IT UP, PLEASE?
AT THIS RATE, THERE WON'T BE AN EARTH TO SAVE...!
DON'T YOU WORRY!
I'M ON THE JOB!
HA HA...
...
...I'M WORRY-ING...
UH-OH...

READ THIS WAY

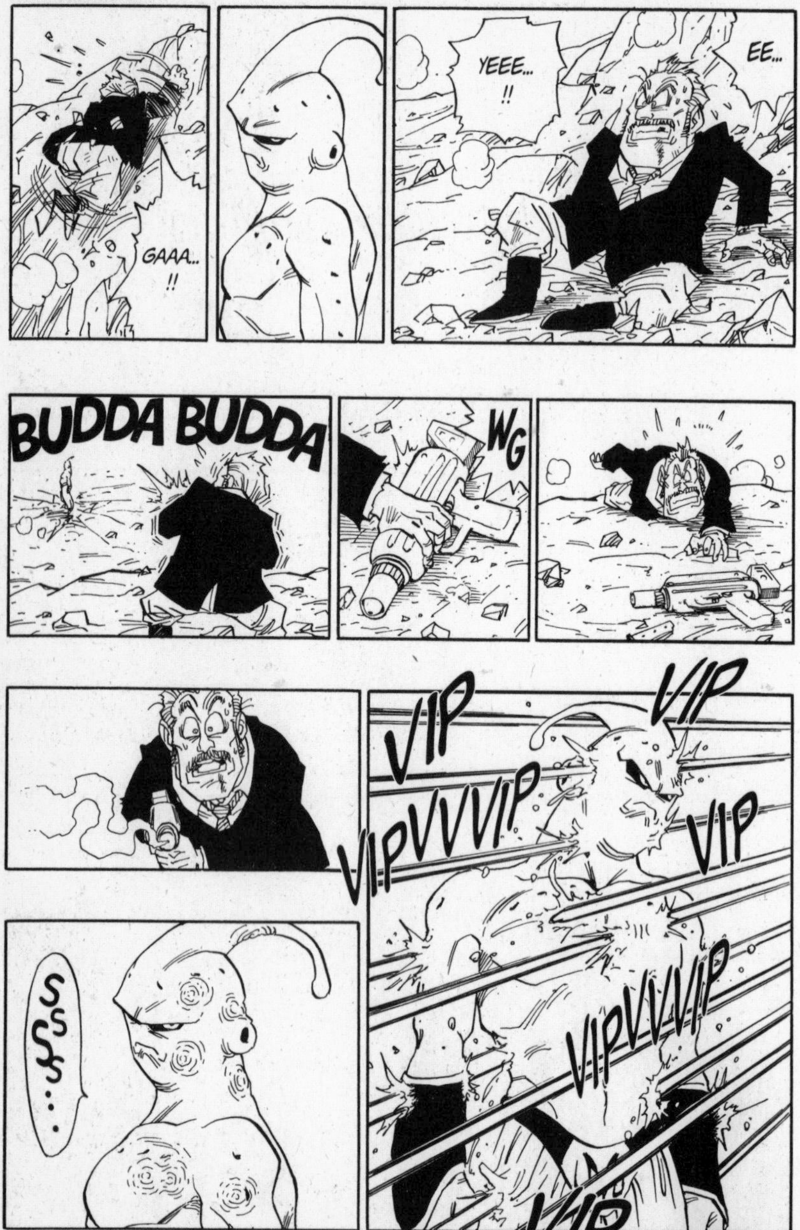

EE...
YEEE... !!
GAAA... !!
WG
BUDDA BUDDA
VIP
VIP
VIPVVVIP
VIP
VIPVVVIP
VIP
SSSS...

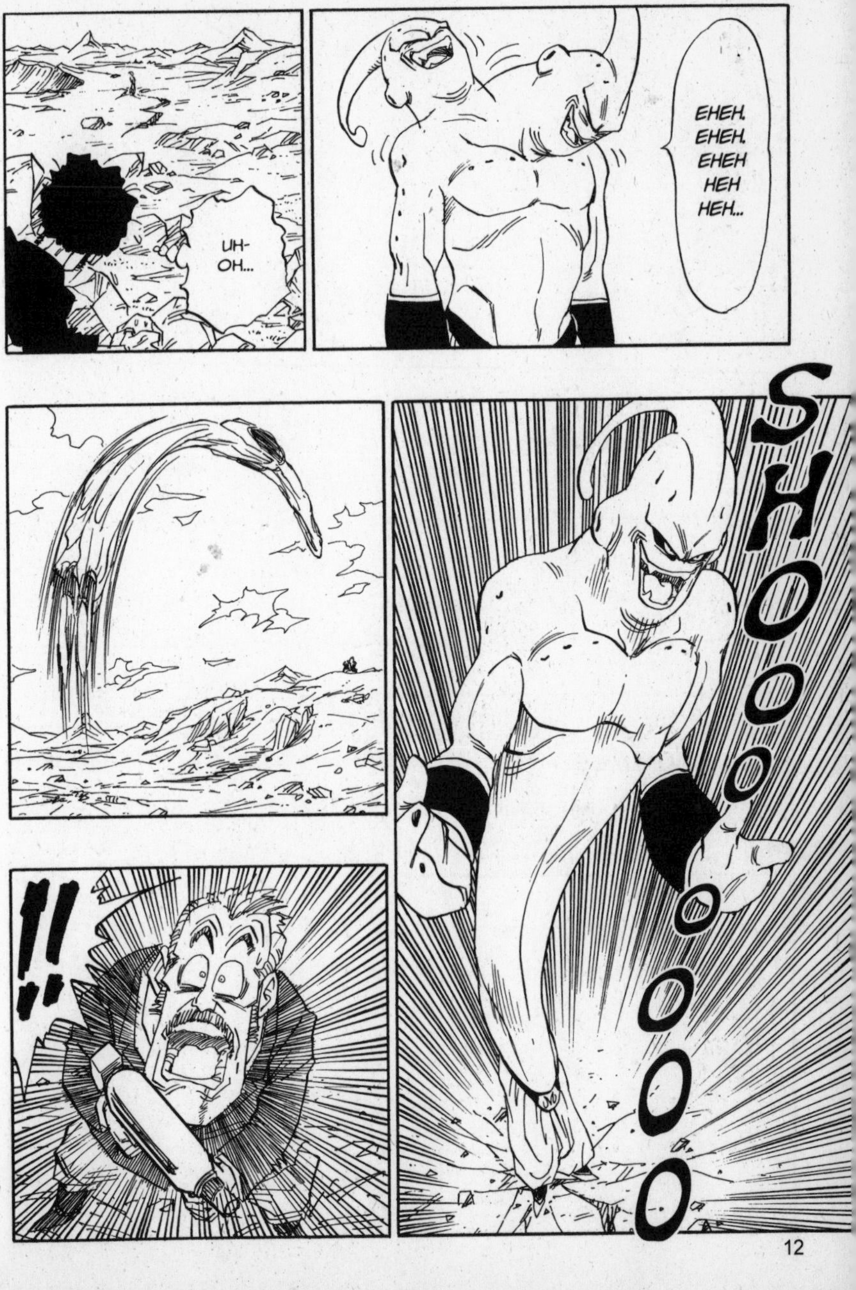
EHEH. EHEH. EHEH HEH HEH...
UH-OH...
SHOOOOOOOOOO
!!

READ THIS WAY

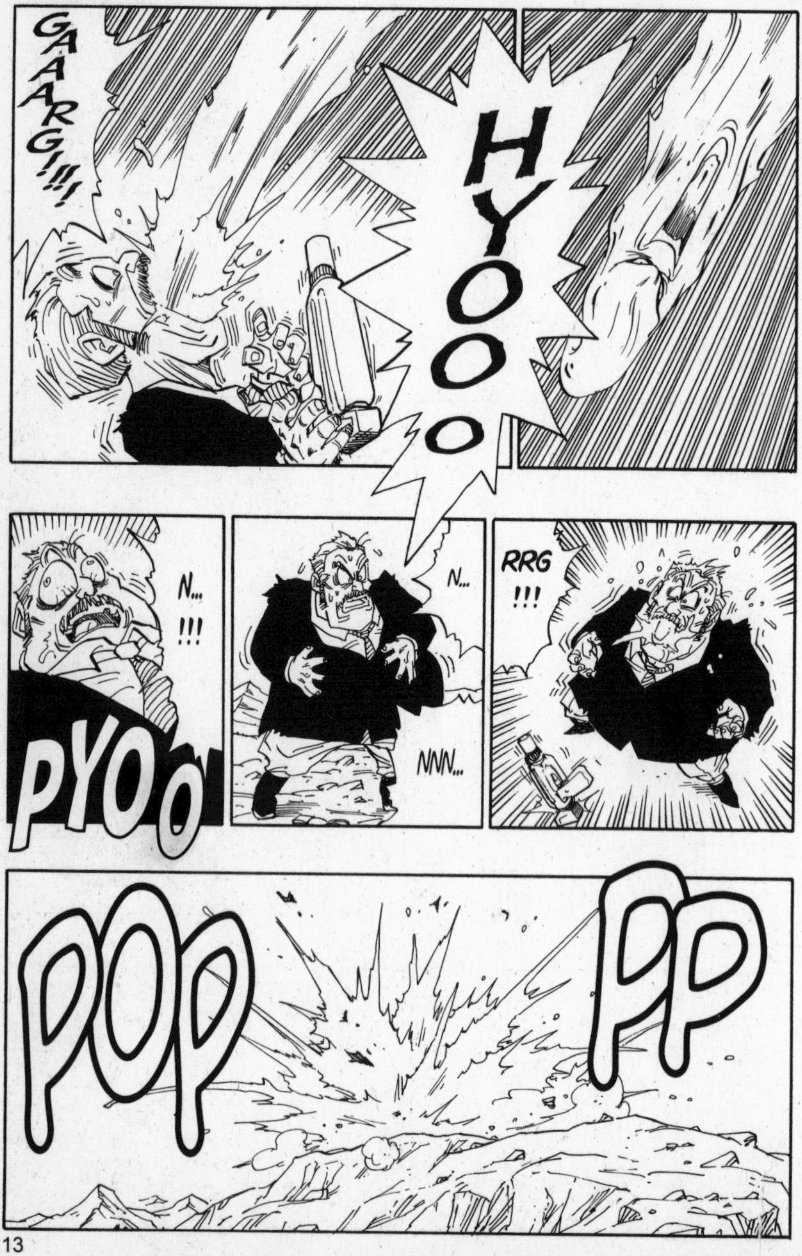

HYOOOO
GAAARG!!!!
RRG
!!!
N...
NNN...
N...
!!!
PYOO
POP
PP

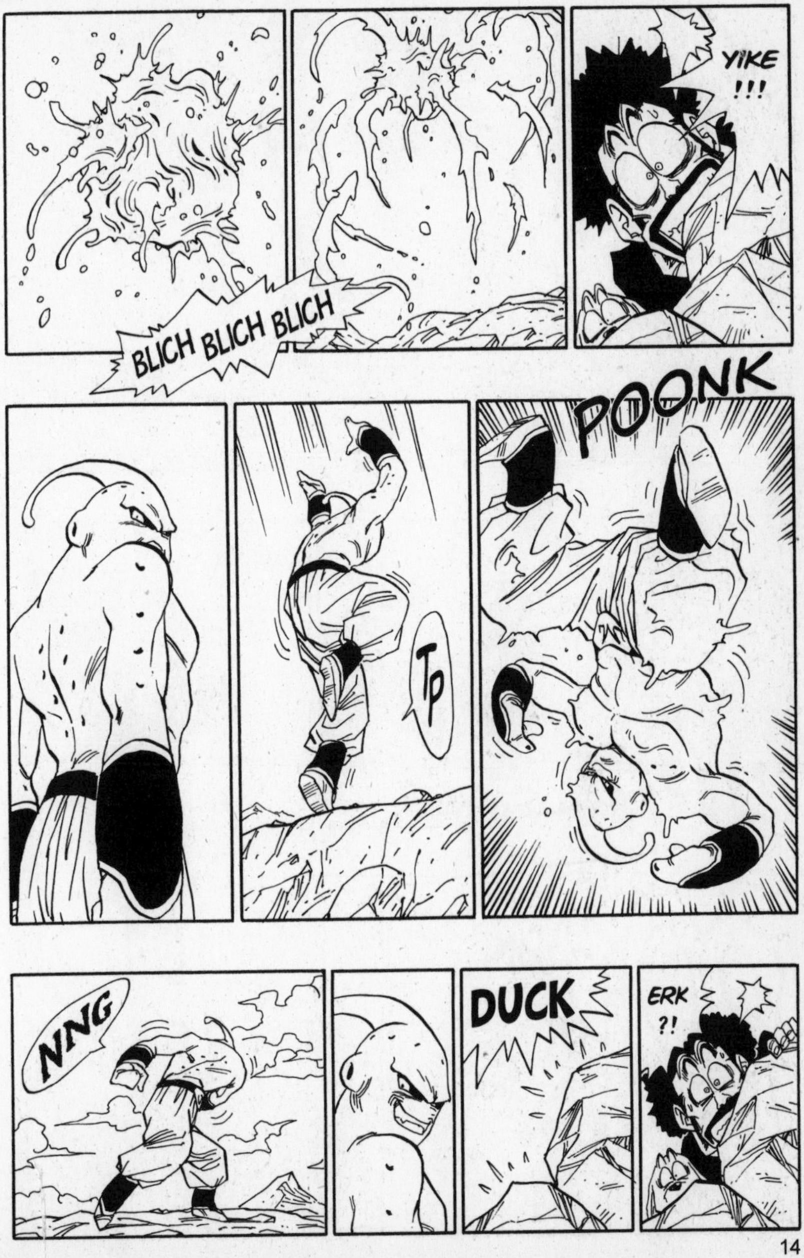
YIKE !!!
BLICH BLICH BLICH
POONK
Tp
ERK ?!
DUCK
NNG

READ THIS WAY

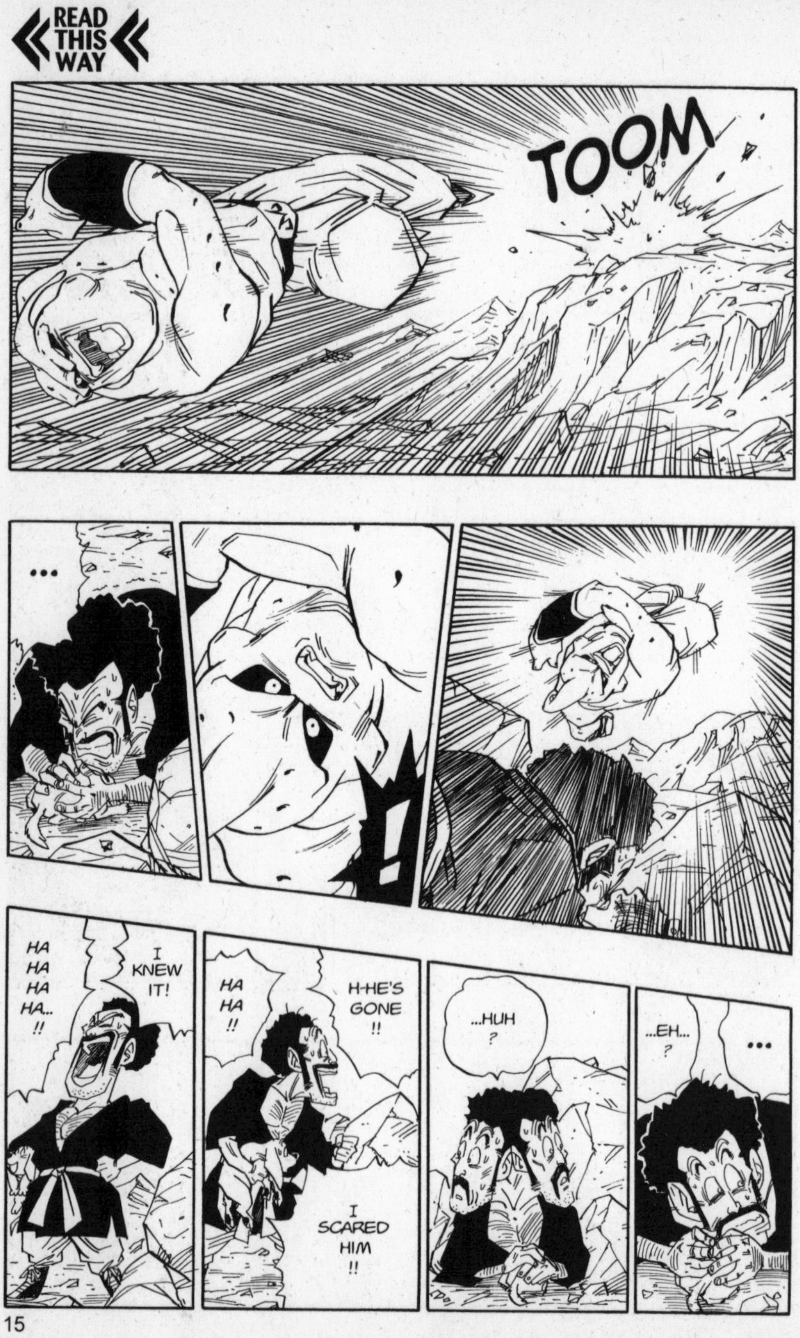

TOOM
...
...
...EH...?
...HUH?
H-HE'S GONE!!
HA HA!!
I SCARED HIM!!
I KNEW IT!
HA HA HA HA...!!

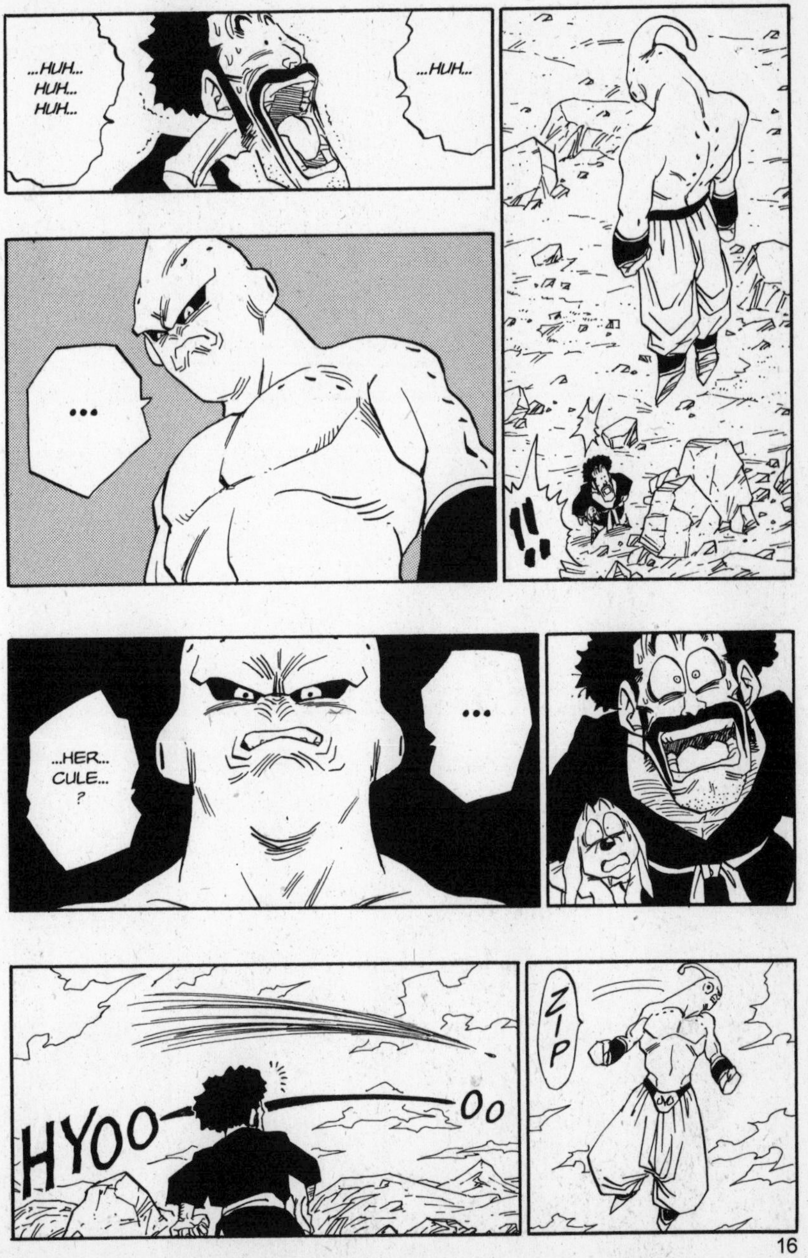

!!
...HUH...
...HUH...
HUH...
HUH...
...
...
...HER...
CULE...
?
ZIP
HYOO—OO

READ THIS WAY

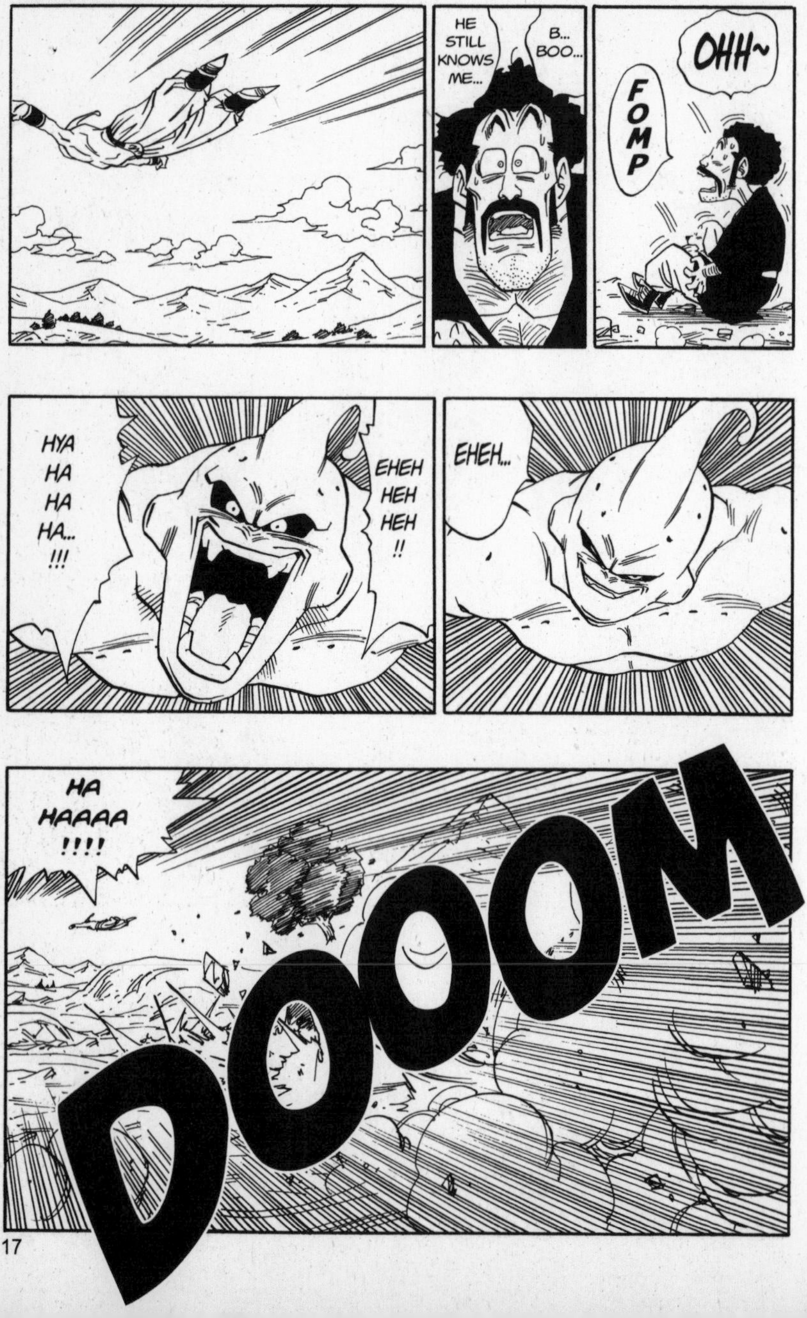

OHH~
FOMP
B... BOO...
HE STILL KNOWS ME...
EHEH...
EHEH HEH HEH !!
HYA HA HA HA... !!!
HA HAAAA !!!!
DOOOM

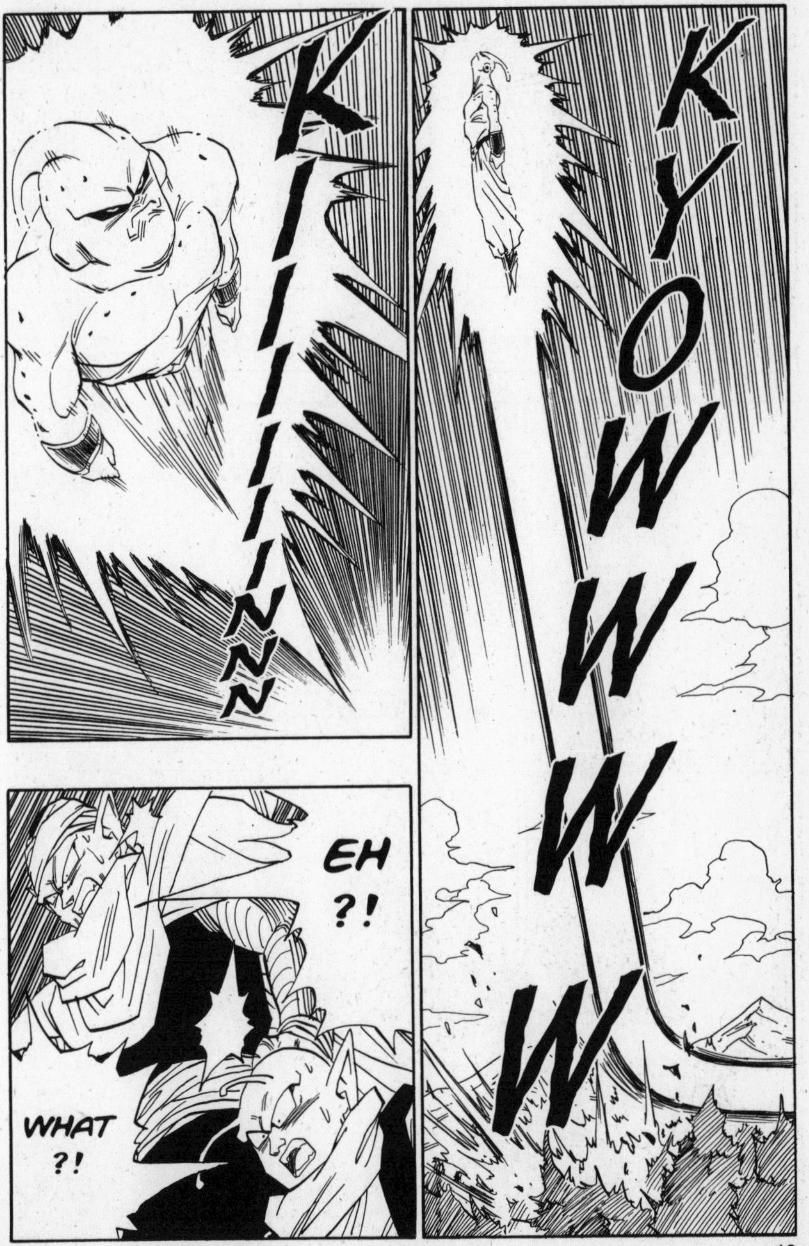
KYOWWWW
K------NNN
EH ?!
WHAT ?!

READ THIS WAY

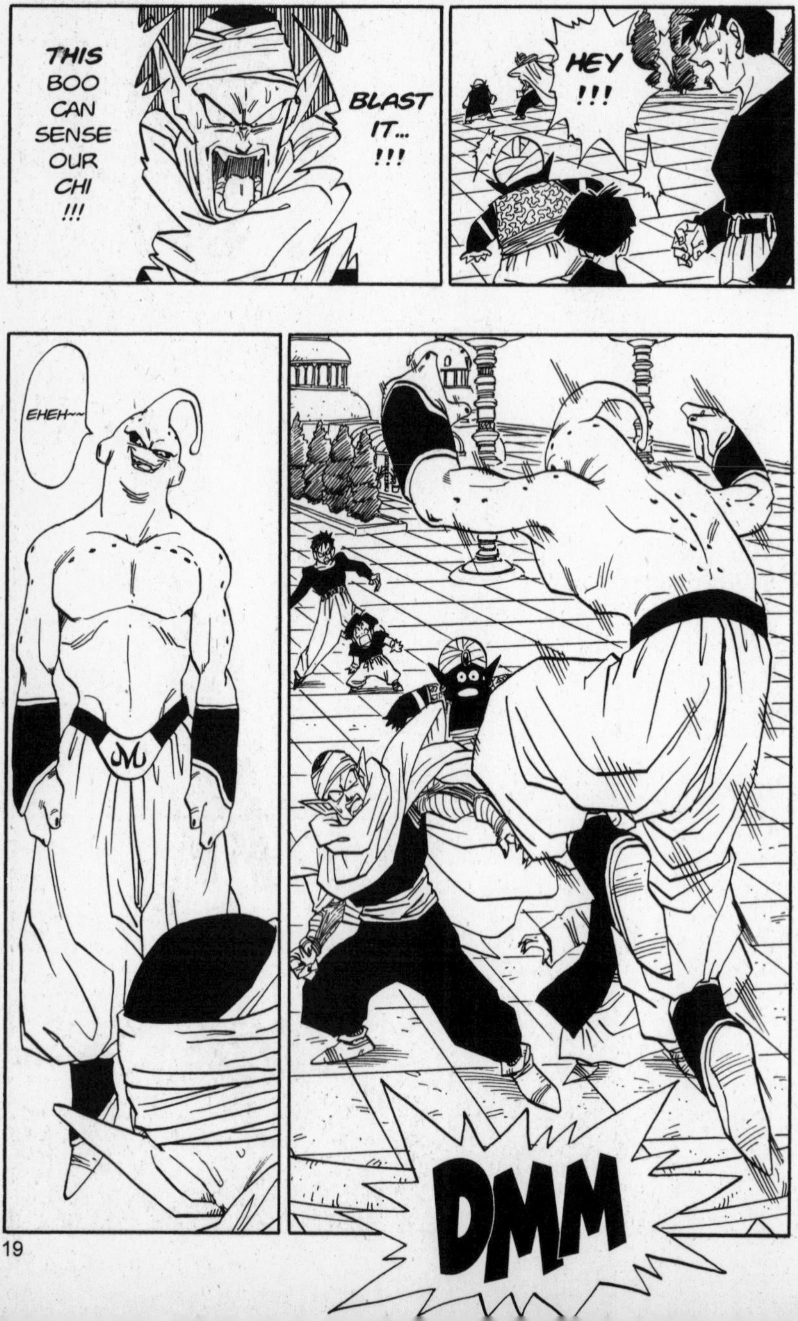

HEY !!!
BLAST IT... !!!
THIS BOO CAN SENSE OUR CHI !!!
DMM
EHEH~~

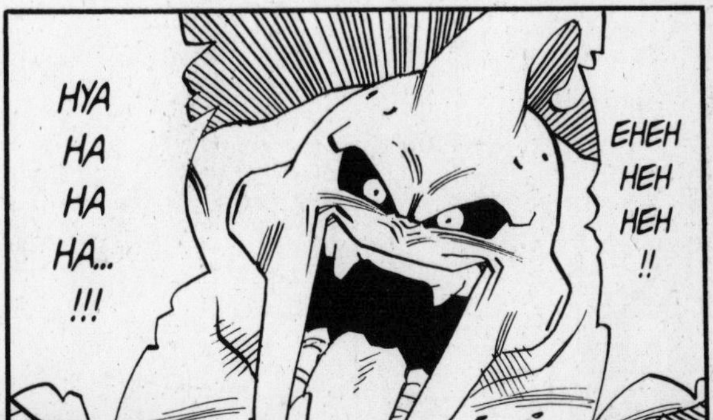
EHEH
HEH
HEH
!!
HYA
HA
HA
HA...
!!!

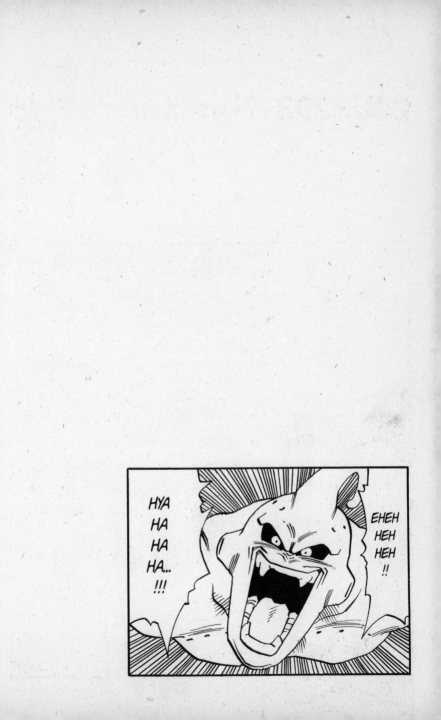

DBZ:293 • Humanity's End

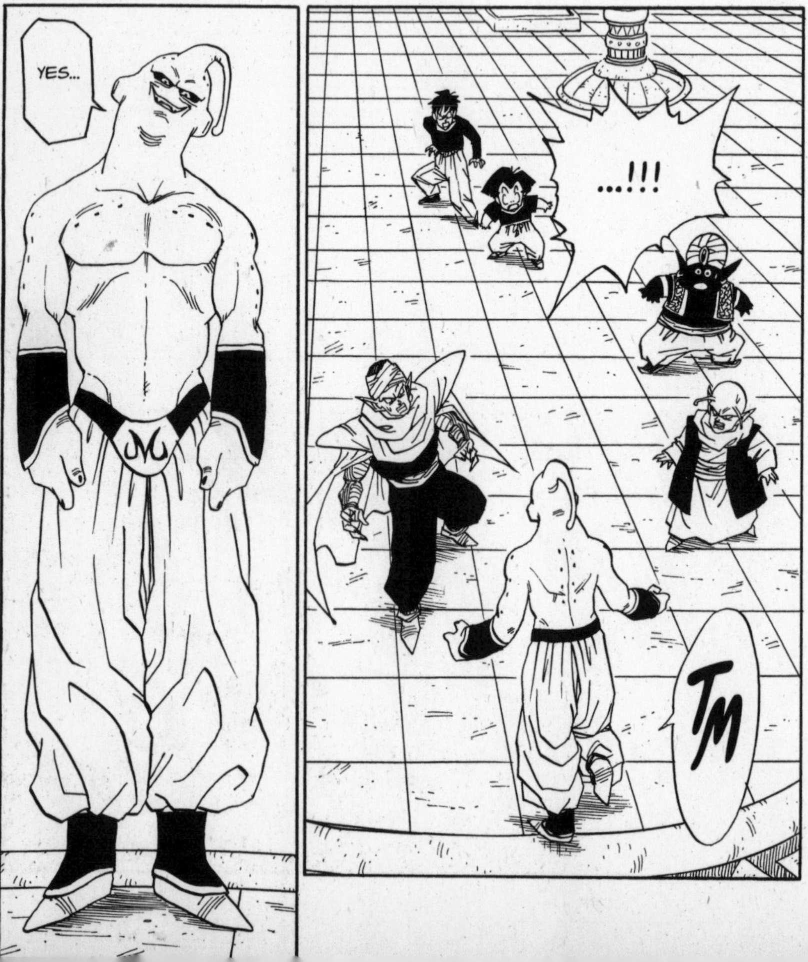
...!!!
TM
YES...

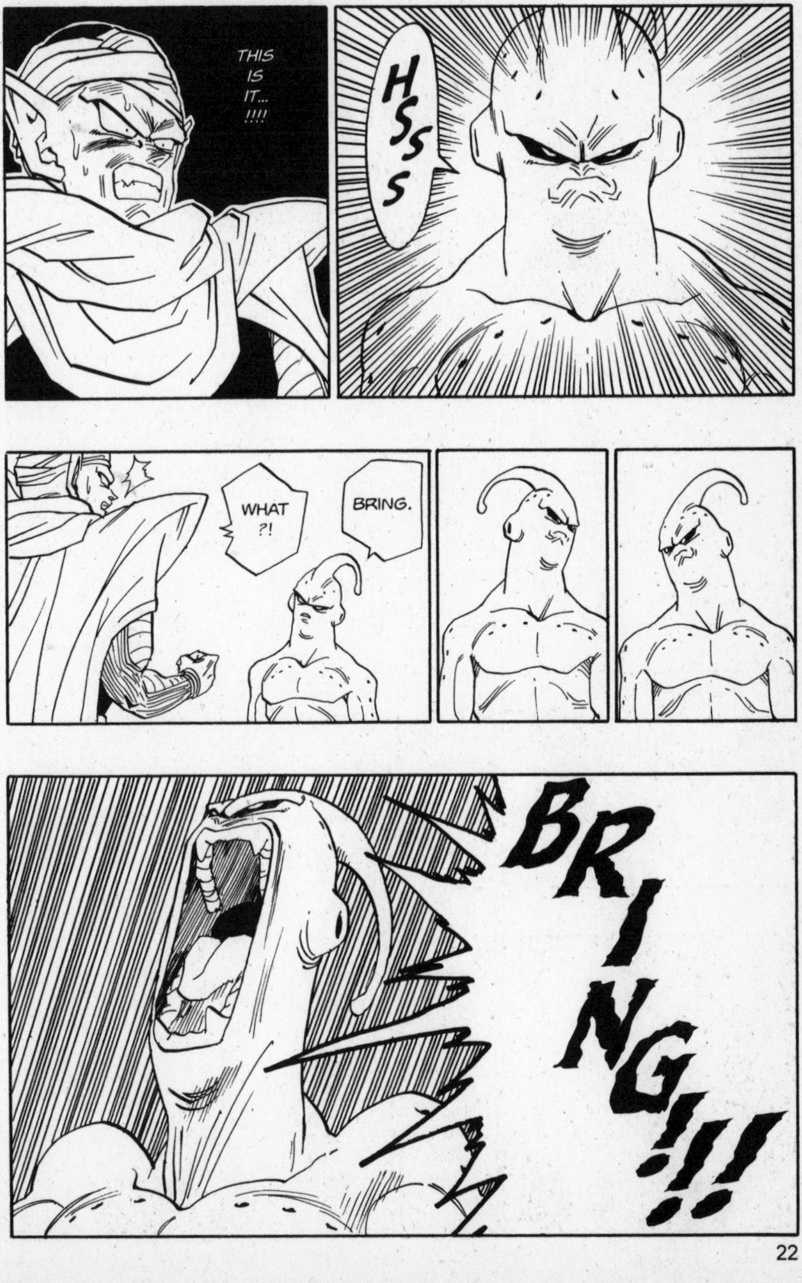
HSSS
THIS IS IT...!!!!
BRING.
WHAT?!
BRING!!!

READ THIS WAY

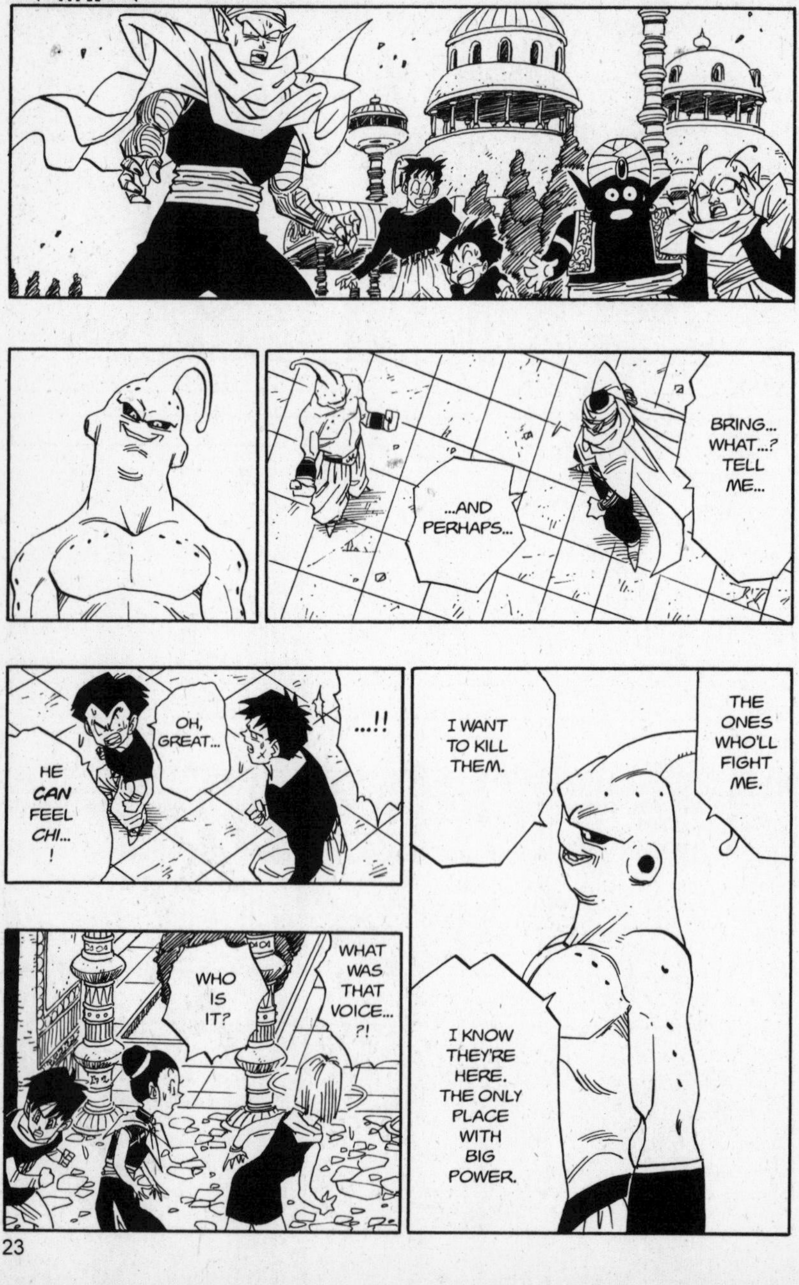
BRING... WHAT...? TELL ME...
...AND PERHAPS...
THE ONES WHO'LL FIGHT ME.
I WANT TO KILL THEM.
I KNOW THEY'RE HERE. THE ONLY PLACE WITH BIG POWER.
...!!
OH, GREAT...
HE *CAN* FEEL CHI...!
WHAT WAS THAT VOICE...?!
WHO IS IT?

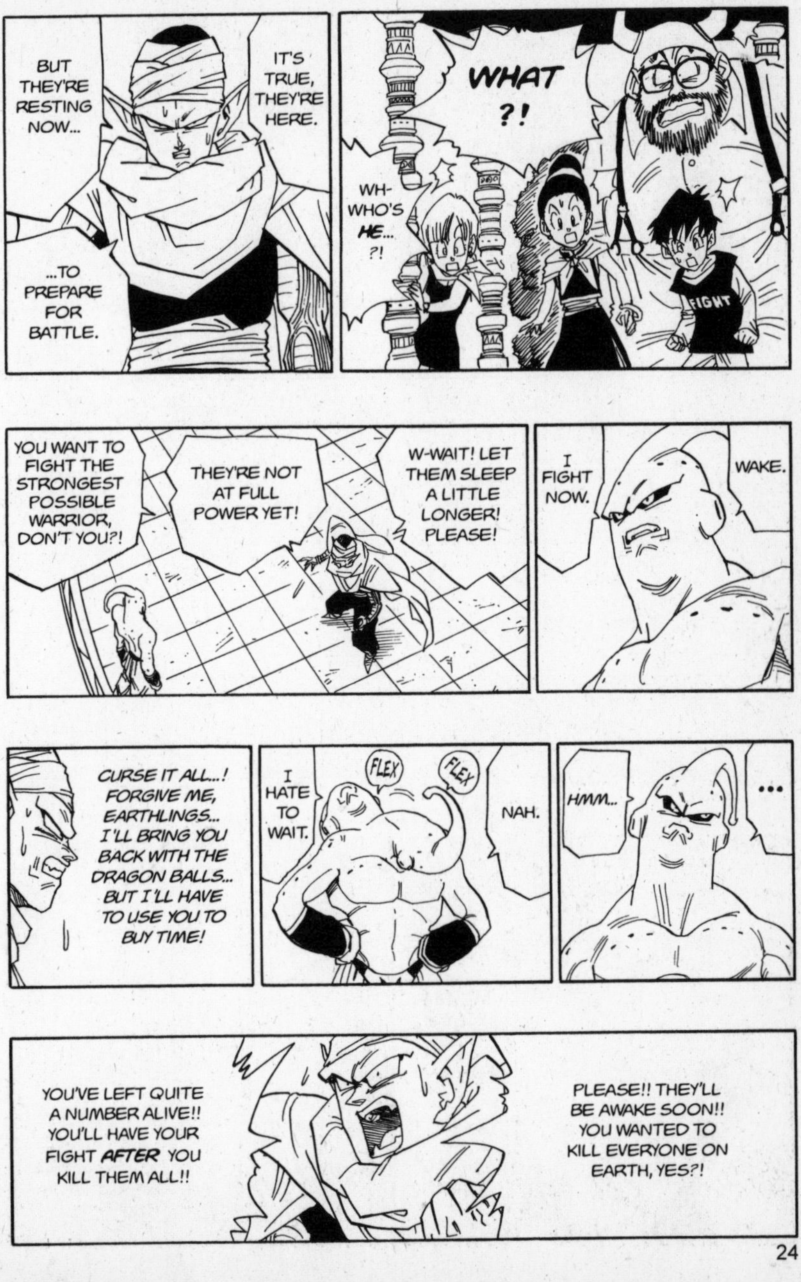
WHAT ?!
WH-WHO'S HE...?!
IT'S TRUE, THEY'RE HERE.
BUT THEY'RE RESTING NOW...
...TO PREPARE FOR BATTLE.
WAKE.
I FIGHT NOW.
W-WAIT! LET THEM SLEEP A LITTLE LONGER! PLEASE!
THEY'RE NOT AT FULL POWER YET!
YOU WANT TO FIGHT THE STRONGEST POSSIBLE WARRIOR, DON'T YOU?!
...
HMM...
NAH.
FLEX
FLEX
I HATE TO WAIT.
CURSE IT ALL...! FORGIVE ME, EARTHLINGS... I'LL BRING YOU BACK WITH THE DRAGON BALLS... BUT I'LL HAVE TO USE YOU TO BUY TIME!
PLEASE!! THEY'LL BE AWAKE SOON!! YOU WANTED TO KILL EVERYONE ON EARTH, YES?!
YOU'VE LEFT QUITE A NUMBER ALIVE!! YOU'LL HAVE YOUR FIGHT ***AFTER*** YOU KILL THEM ALL!!

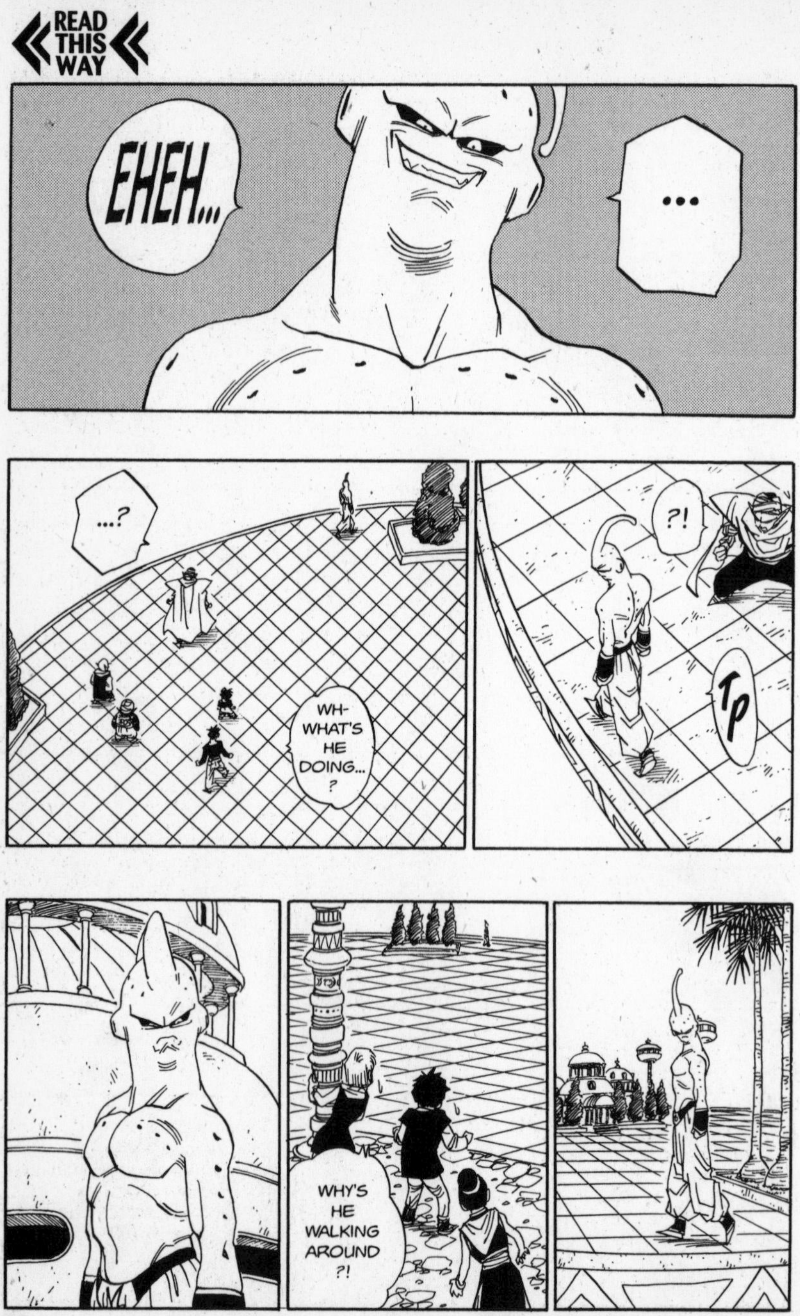
READ THIS WAY
...
EHEH...
?!
TP
...?
WH-WHAT'S HE DOING...?
WHY'S HE WALKING AROUND?!

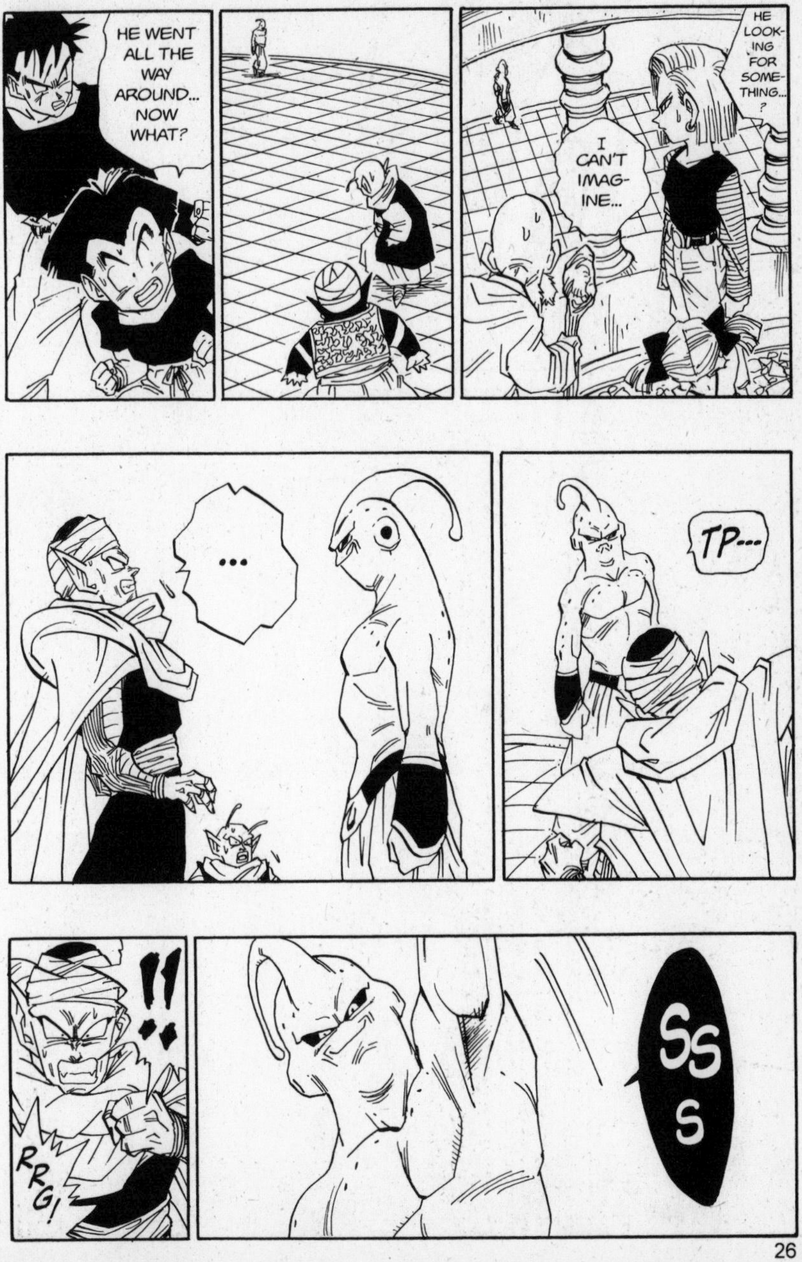
HE LOOKING FOR SOMETHING...?
I CAN'T IMAGINE...
HE WENT ALL THE WAY AROUND... NOW WHAT?
TP---
...
Ss s
!!
RRG!

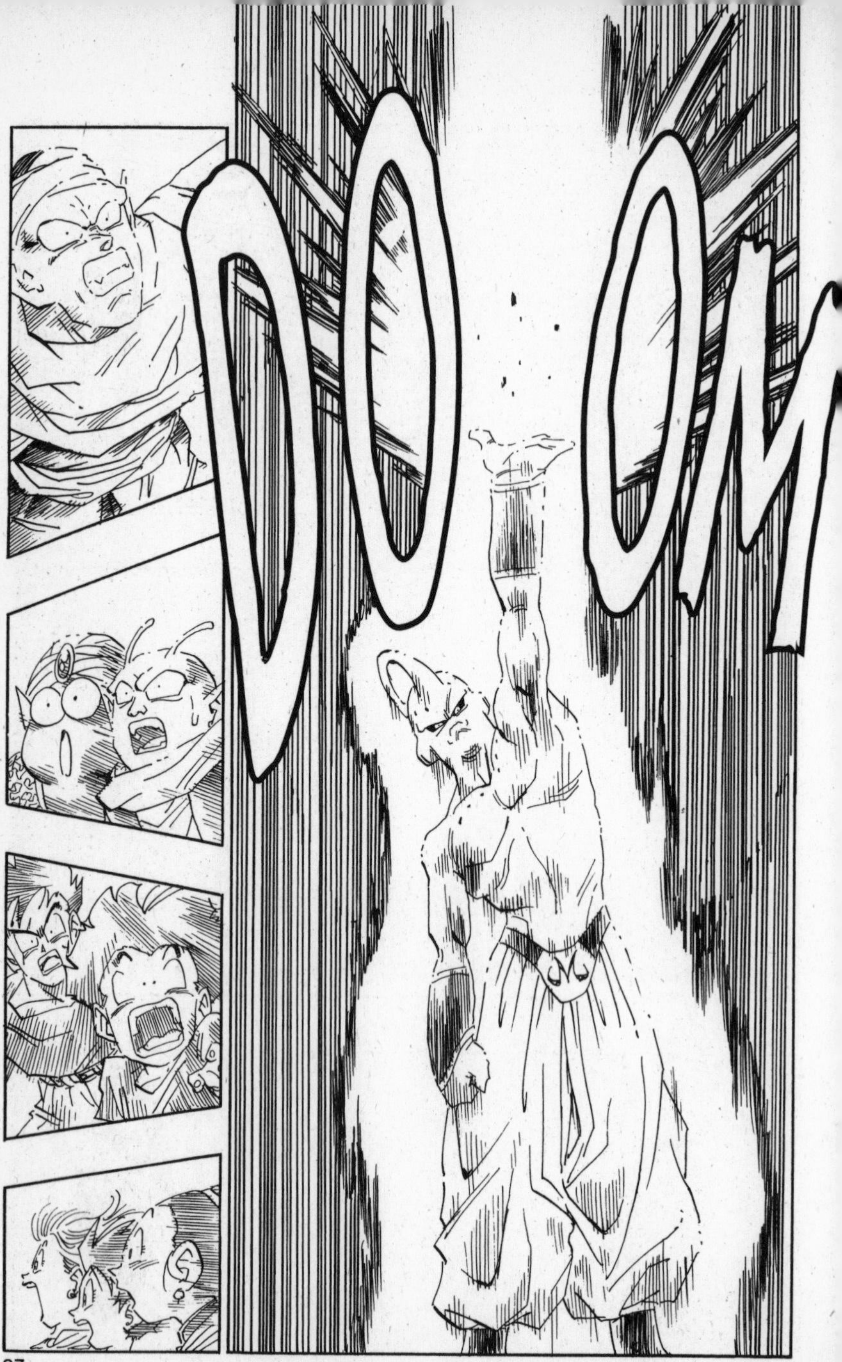
DOOM

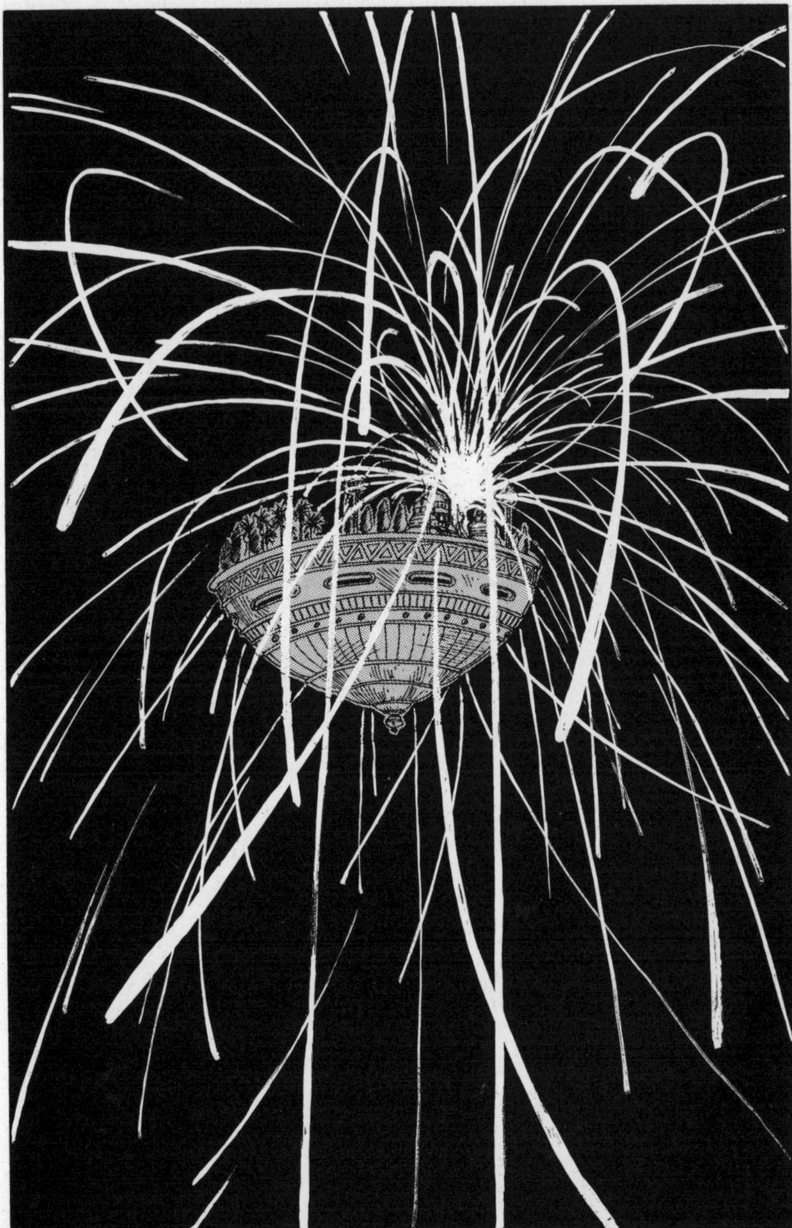

READ THIS WAY

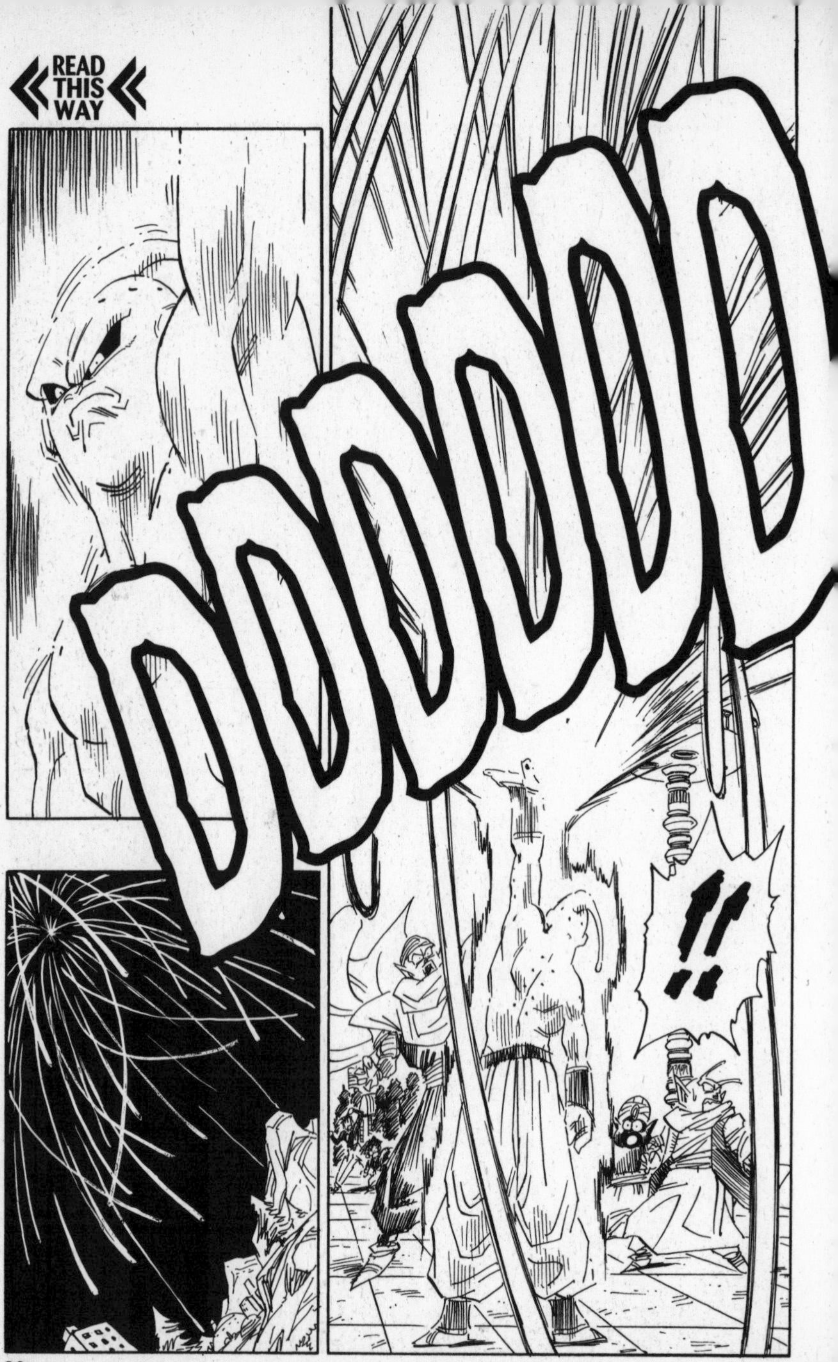
DDDDDD
!!

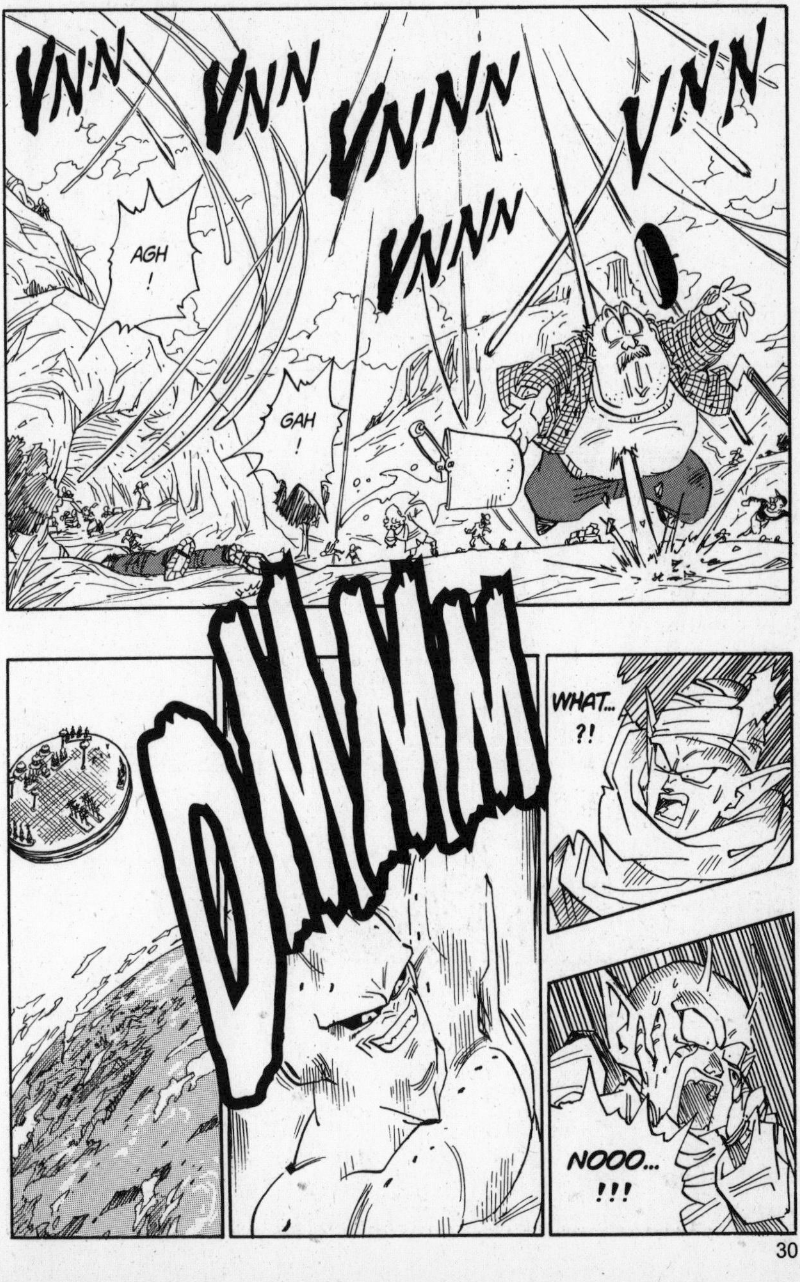
VNN
VNNN
VNNN
VNN
VNN
AGH!
GAH!
WHAT...?!
NOOO...!!!
DMMMM

READ THIS WAY

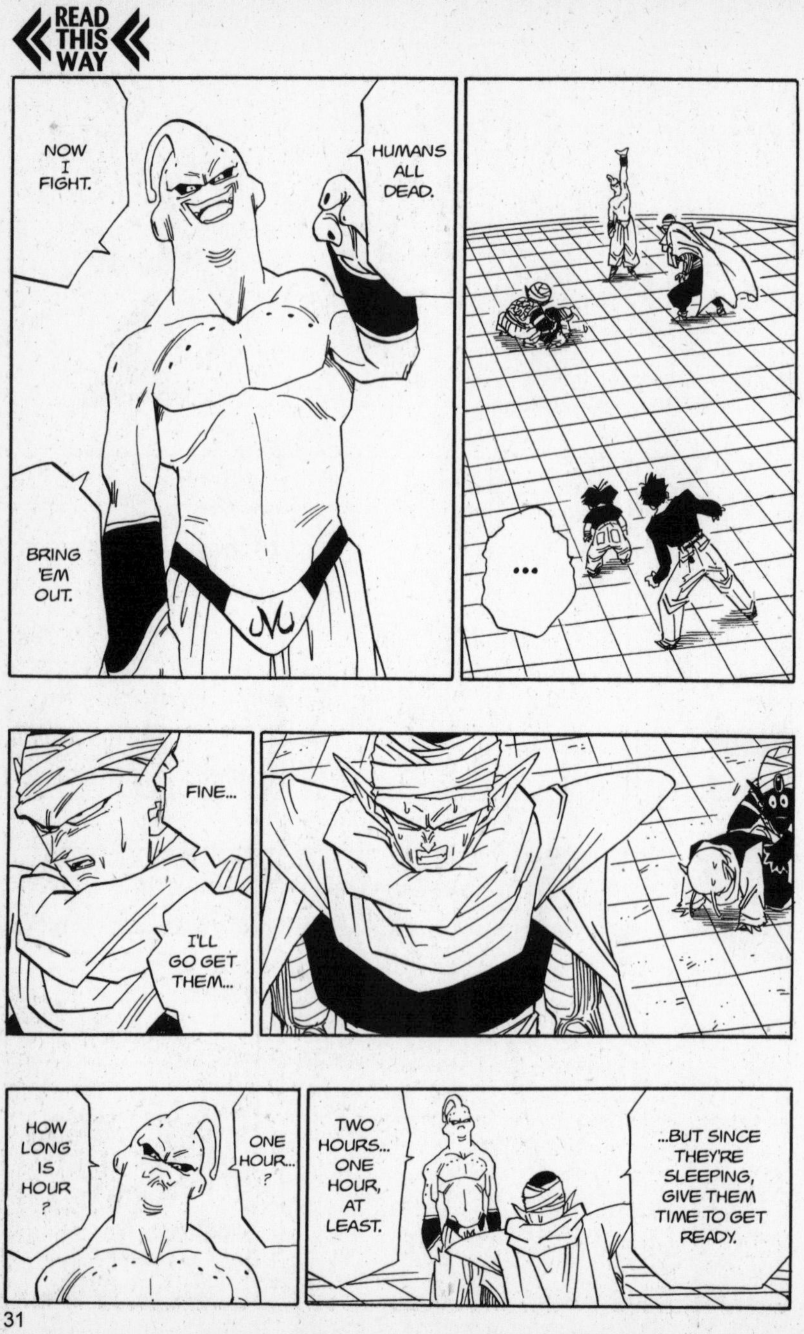
...
HUMANS ALL DEAD.
NOW I FIGHT.
BRING 'EM OUT.
FINE...
I'LL GO GET THEM...
...BUT SINCE THEY'RE SLEEPING, GIVE THEM TIME TO GET READY.
TWO HOURS... ONE HOUR, AT LEAST.
ONE HOUR...?
HOW LONG IS HOUR?

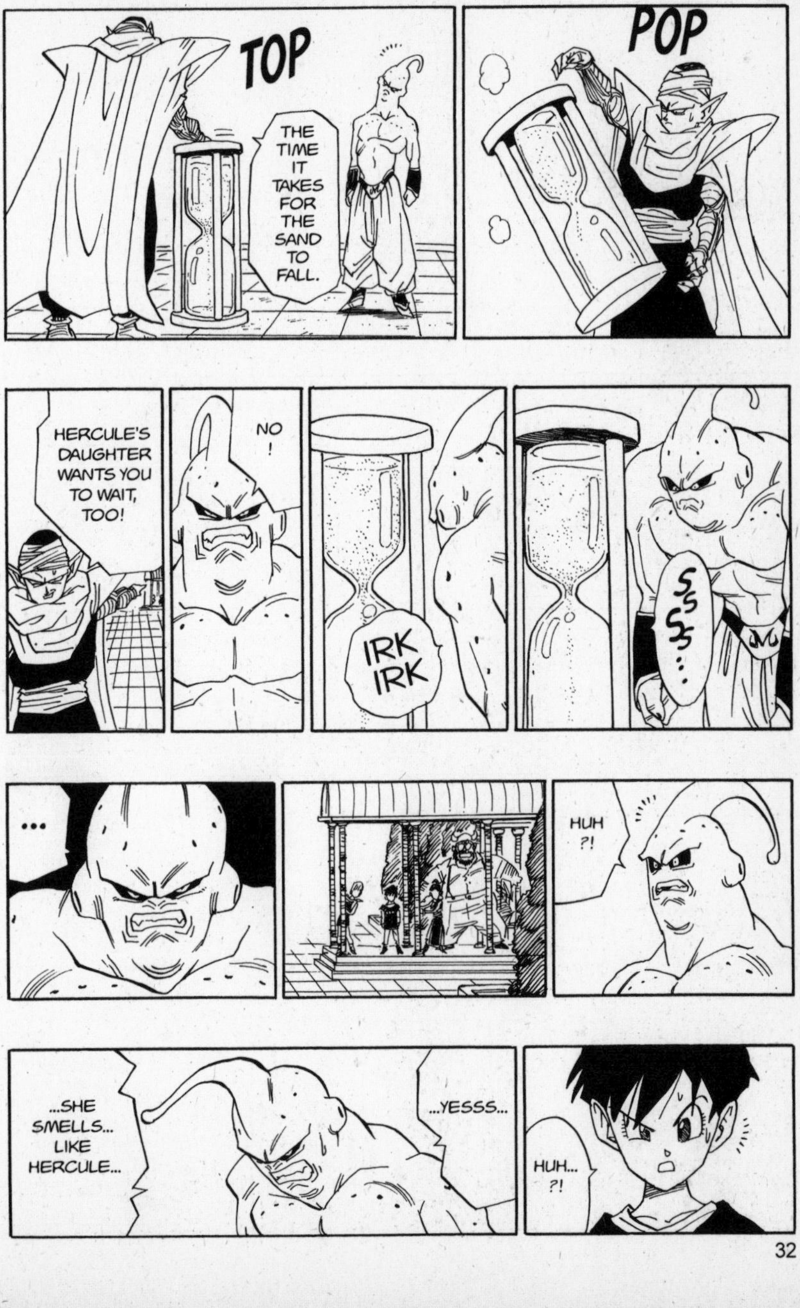
POP
TOP
THE TIME IT TAKES FOR THE SAND TO FALL.
SSSS...
IRK IRK
NO!
HERCULE'S DAUGHTER WANTS YOU TO WAIT, TOO!
HUH ?!
...
HUH... ?!
...SHE SMELLS... LIKE HERCULE...
...YESSS...

READ THIS WAY

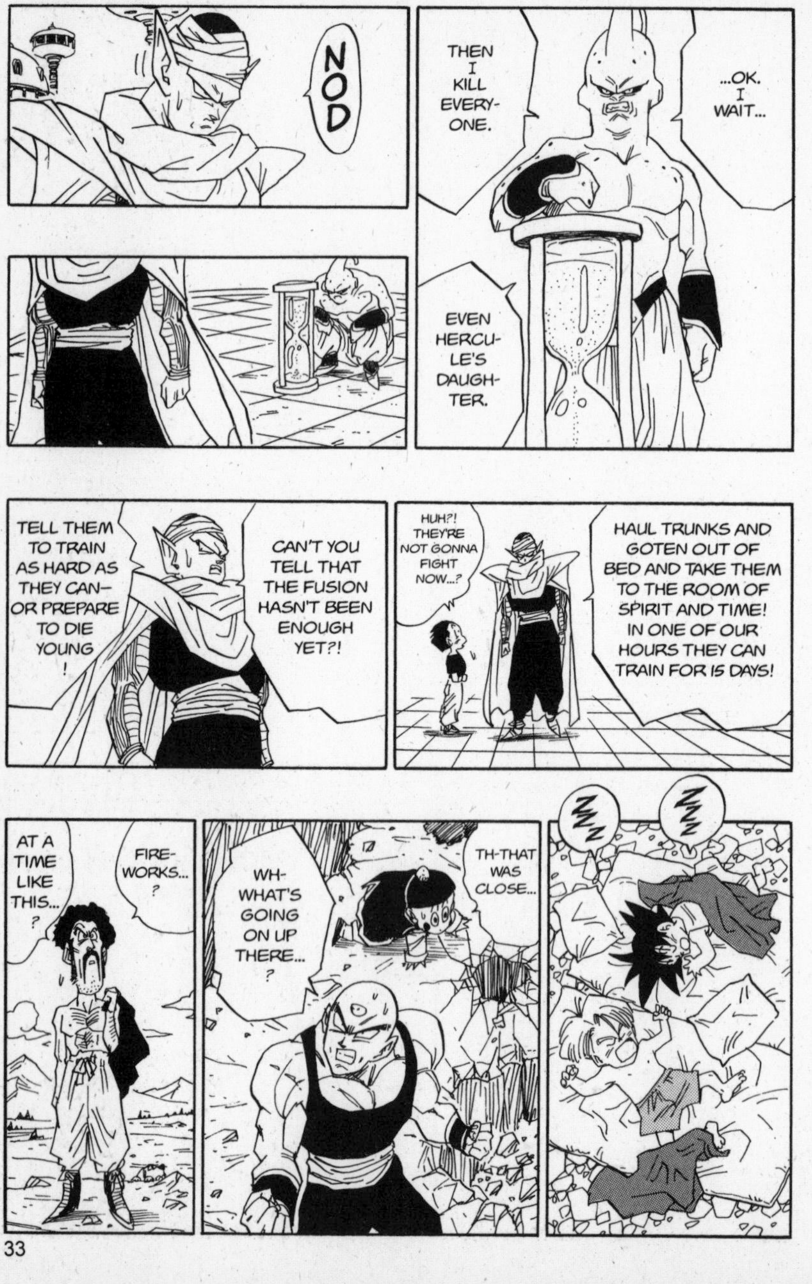
...OK. I WAIT...
THEN I KILL EVERYONE.
EVEN HERCULE'S DAUGHTER.
NOD
HAUL TRUNKS AND GOTEN OUT OF BED AND TAKE THEM TO THE ROOM OF SPIRIT AND TIME! IN ONE OF OUR HOURS THEY CAN TRAIN FOR 15 DAYS!
HUH?! THEY'RE NOT GONNA FIGHT NOW...?
CAN'T YOU TELL THAT THE FUSION HASN'T BEEN ENOUGH YET?!
TELL THEM TO TRAIN AS HARD AS THEY CAN—OR PREPARE TO DIE YOUNG!
ZZZ
ZZZ
TH-THAT WAS CLOSE...
WH-WHAT'S GOING ON UP THERE...?
FIREWORKS...?
AT A TIME LIKE THIS...?

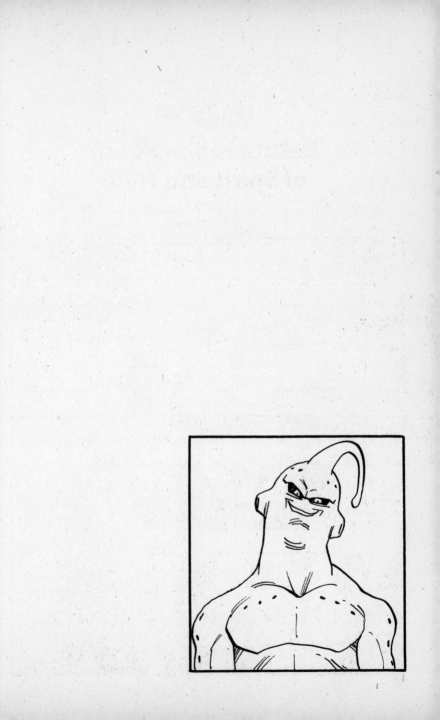

DBZ:294
Return to the Room of Spirit and Time

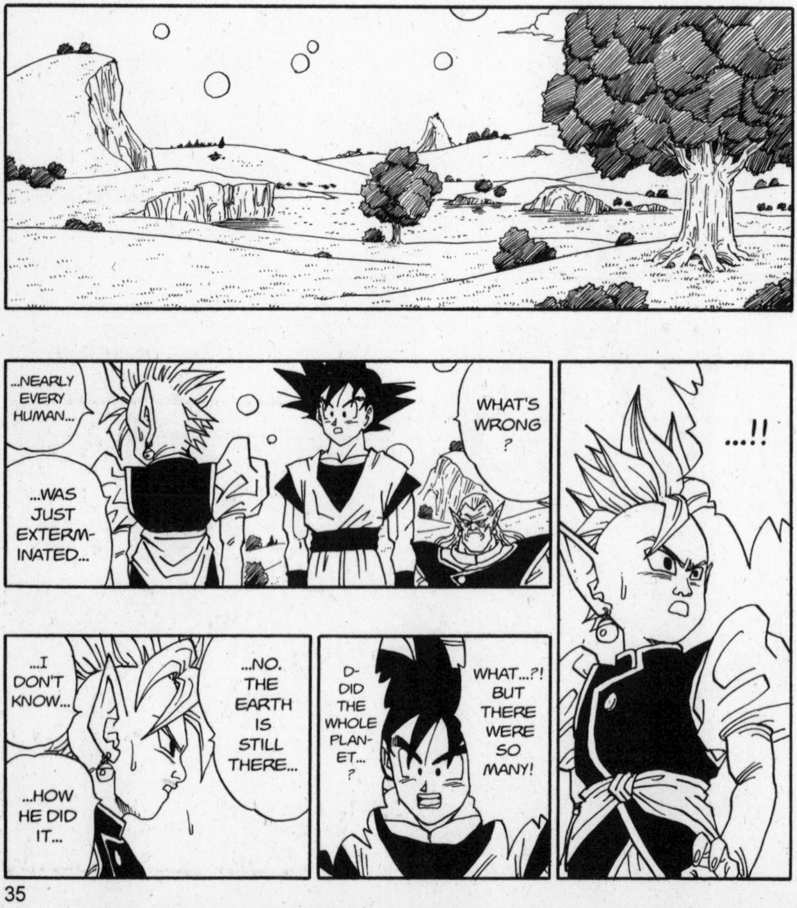
...!!
WHAT'S WRONG?
...NEARLY EVERY HUMAN...
...WAS JUST EXTERMINATED...
WHAT...?! BUT THERE WERE SO MANY!
D-DID THE WHOLE PLANET...?
...NO. THE EARTH IS STILL THERE...
...I DON'T KNOW...
...HOW HE DID IT...

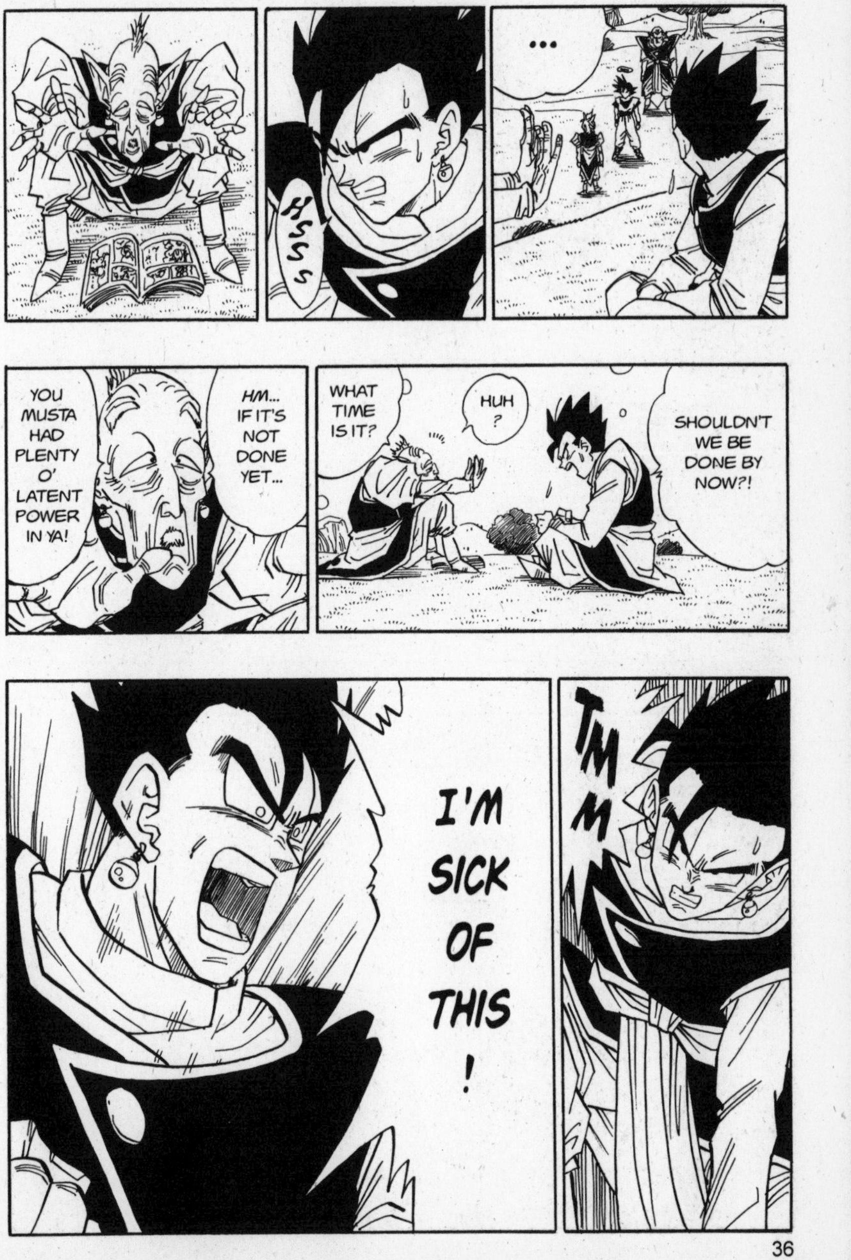
...
HSSS
SHOULDN'T WE BE DONE BY NOW?!
HUH ?
WHAT TIME IS IT?
HM... IF IT'S NOT DONE YET...
YOU MUSTA HAD PLENTY O' LATENT POWER IN YA!
TMMM
I'M SICK OF THIS!

READ THIS WAY

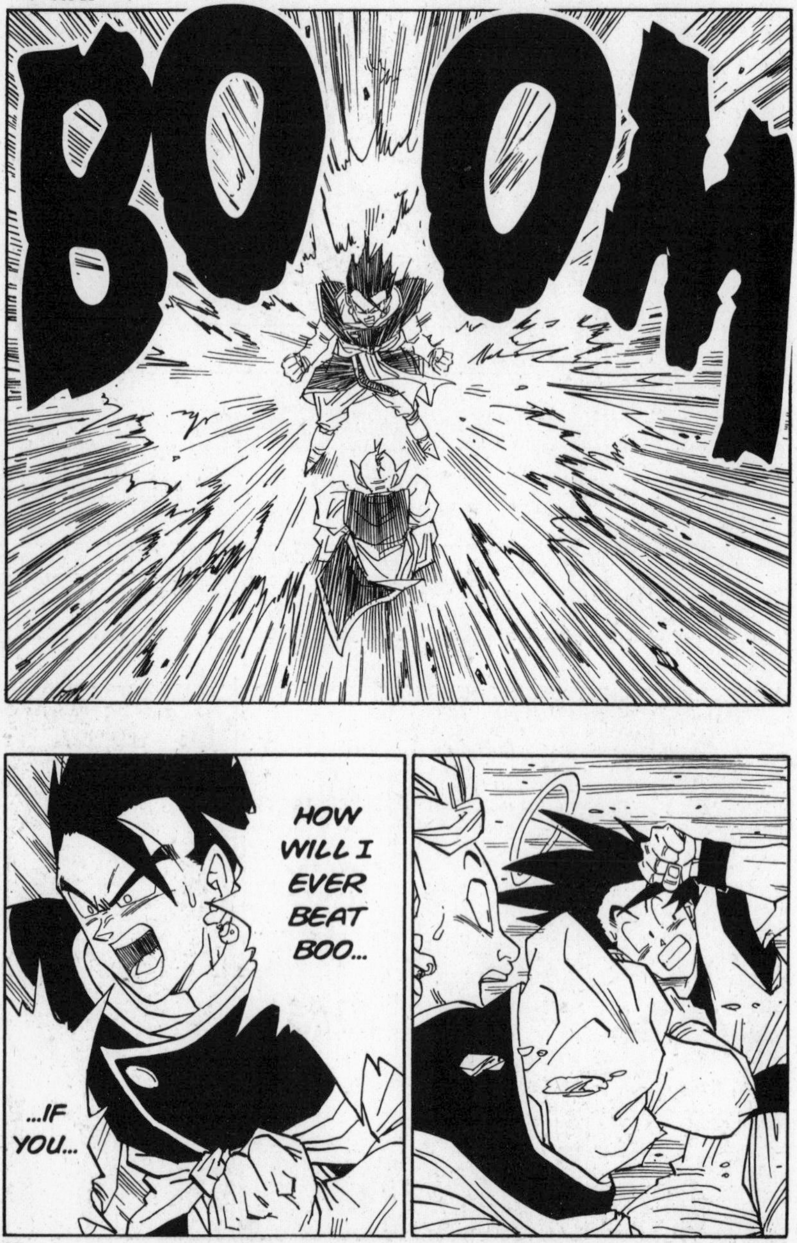
BOOM
HOW WILL I EVER BEAT BOO...
...IF YOU...

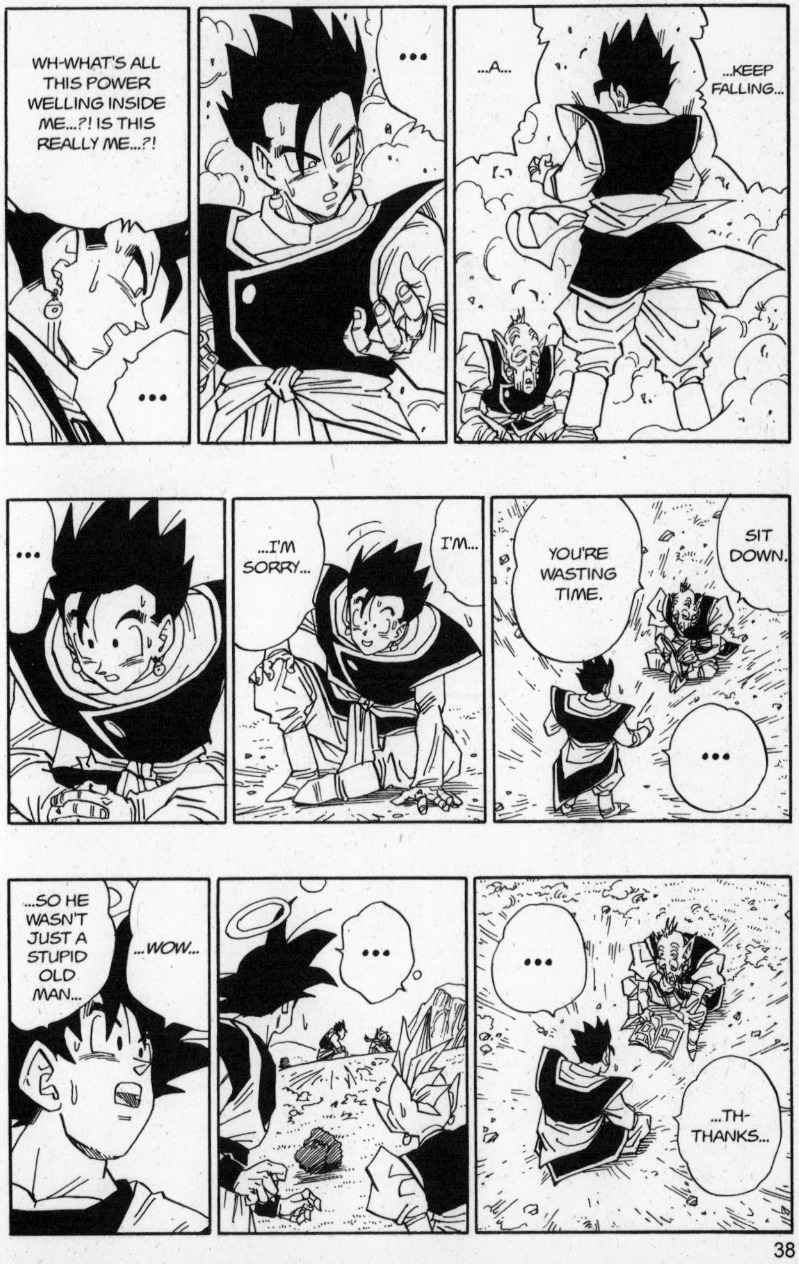
...KEEP FALLING...
...A...
...
WH-WHAT'S ALL THIS POWER WELLING INSIDE ME...?! IS THIS REALLY ME...?!
...
SIT DOWN.
YOU'RE WASTING TIME.
...
I'M...
...I'M SORRY...
...
...
...TH-THANKS...
...
...WOW...
...SO HE WASN'T JUST A STUPID OLD MAN...

READ THIS WAY

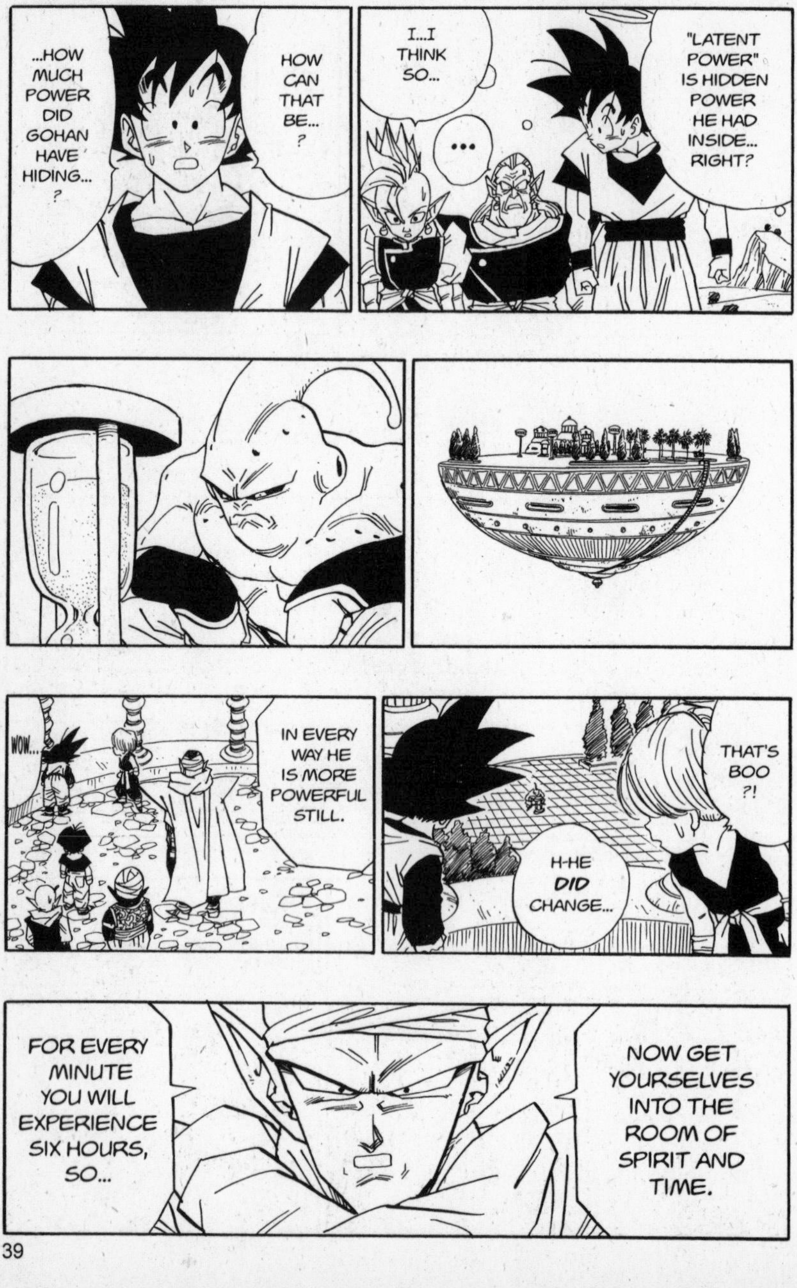

"LATENT POWER" IS HIDDEN POWER HE HAD INSIDE... RIGHT?
...
I...I THINK SO...
HOW CAN THAT BE...?
...HOW MUCH POWER DID GOHAN HAVE HIDING...?
THAT'S BOO?!
H-HE DID CHANGE...
IN EVERY WAY HE IS MORE POWERFUL STILL.
WOW...
NOW GET YOURSELVES INTO THE ROOM OF SPIRIT AND TIME.
FOR EVERY MINUTE YOU WILL EXPERIENCE SIX HOURS, SO...

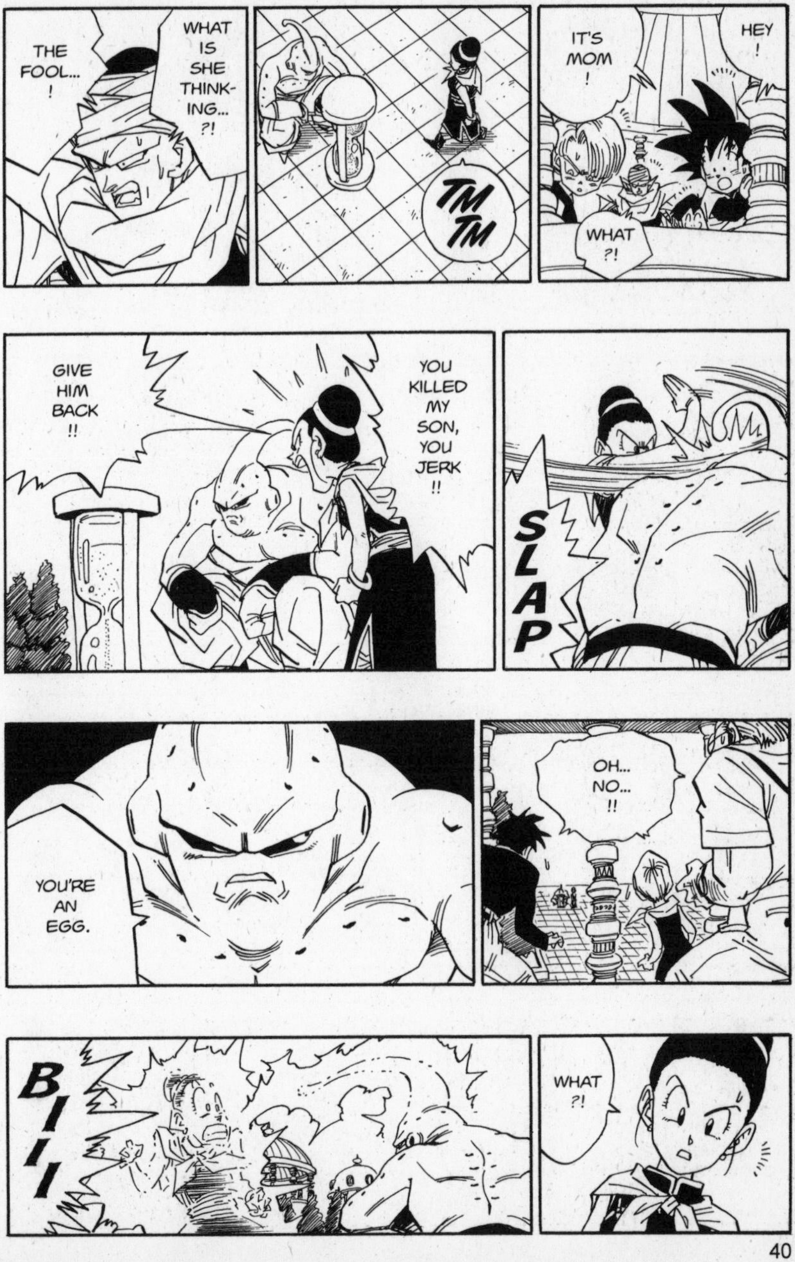
HEY!
IT'S MOM!
WHAT?!
TM TM
WHAT IS SHE THINKING...?!
THE FOOL...!
SLAP
YOU KILLED MY SON, YOU JERK!!
GIVE HIM BACK!!
OH... NO...!!
YOU'RE AN EGG.
WHAT?!
BIII

READ THIS WAY

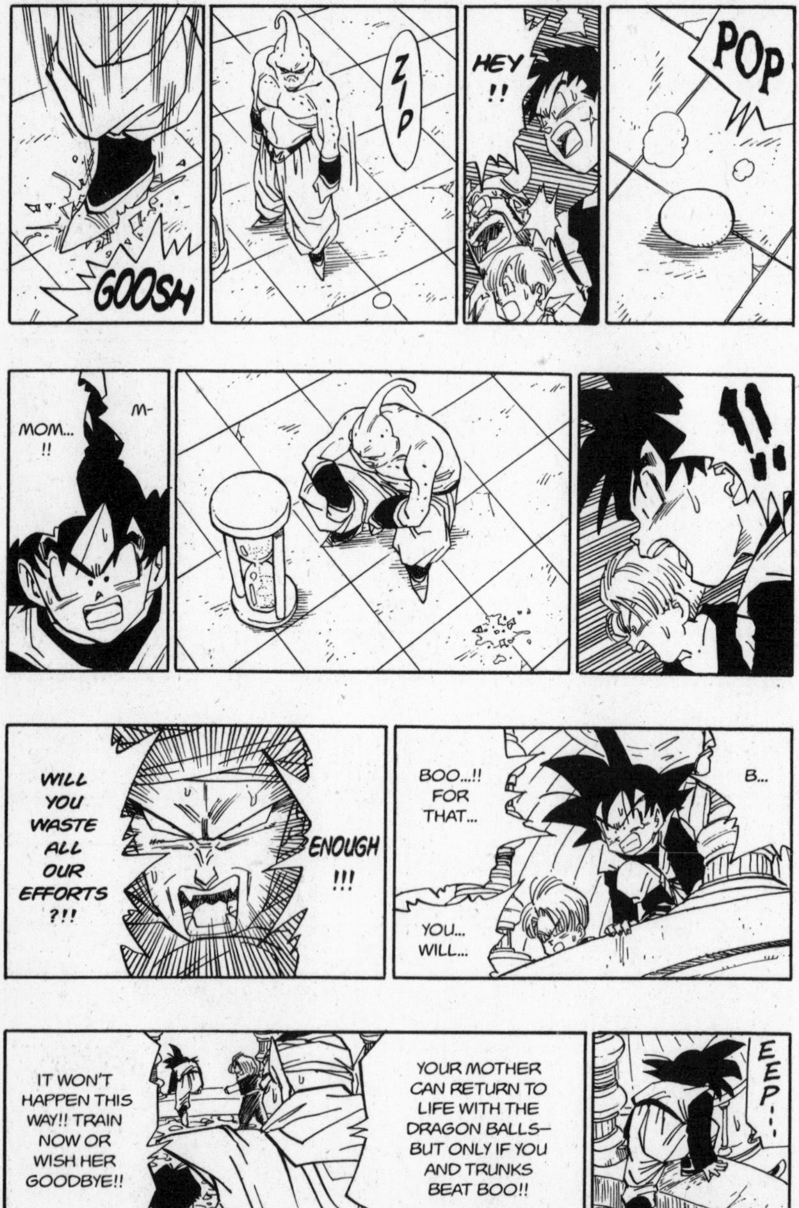
POP
HEY !!
ZIP
GOOSH
!!
M- MOM... !!
B...
BOO...!! FOR THAT...
YOU... WILL...
ENOUGH !!!
WILL YOU WASTE ALL OUR EFFORTS ?!!
EEP..
YOUR MOTHER CAN RETURN TO LIFE WITH THE DRAGON BALLS— BUT ONLY IF YOU AND TRUNKS BEAT BOO!!
IT WON'T HAPPEN THIS WAY!! TRAIN NOW OR WISH HER GOODBYE!!

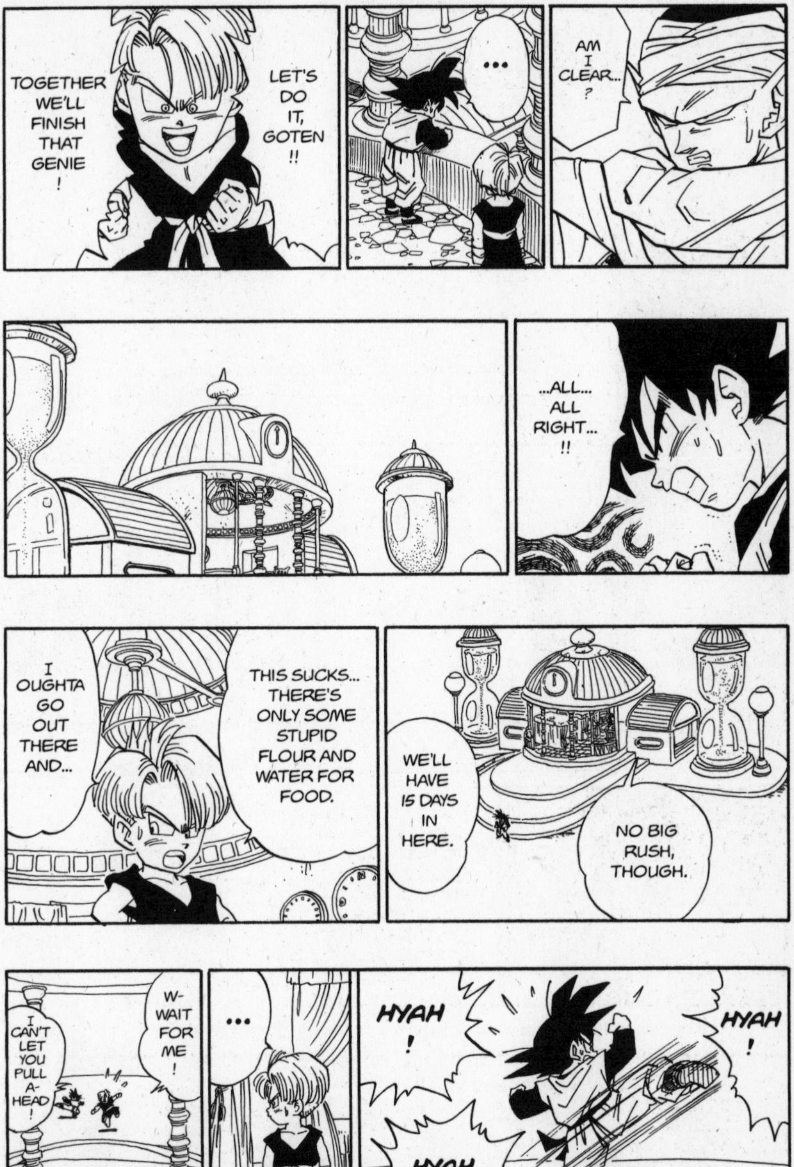
AM I CLEAR...?
...
LET'S DO IT, GOTEN!!
TOGETHER WE'LL FINISH THAT GENIE!
...ALL... ALL RIGHT...!!
WE'LL HAVE 15 DAYS IN HERE.
NO BIG RUSH, THOUGH.
THIS SUCKS... THERE'S ONLY SOME STUPID FLOUR AND WATER FOR FOOD.
I OUGHTA GO OUT THERE AND...
HYAH!
HYAH!
HYAH!
...
W-WAIT FOR ME!
I CAN'T LET YOU PULL A-HEAD!

READ THIS WAY

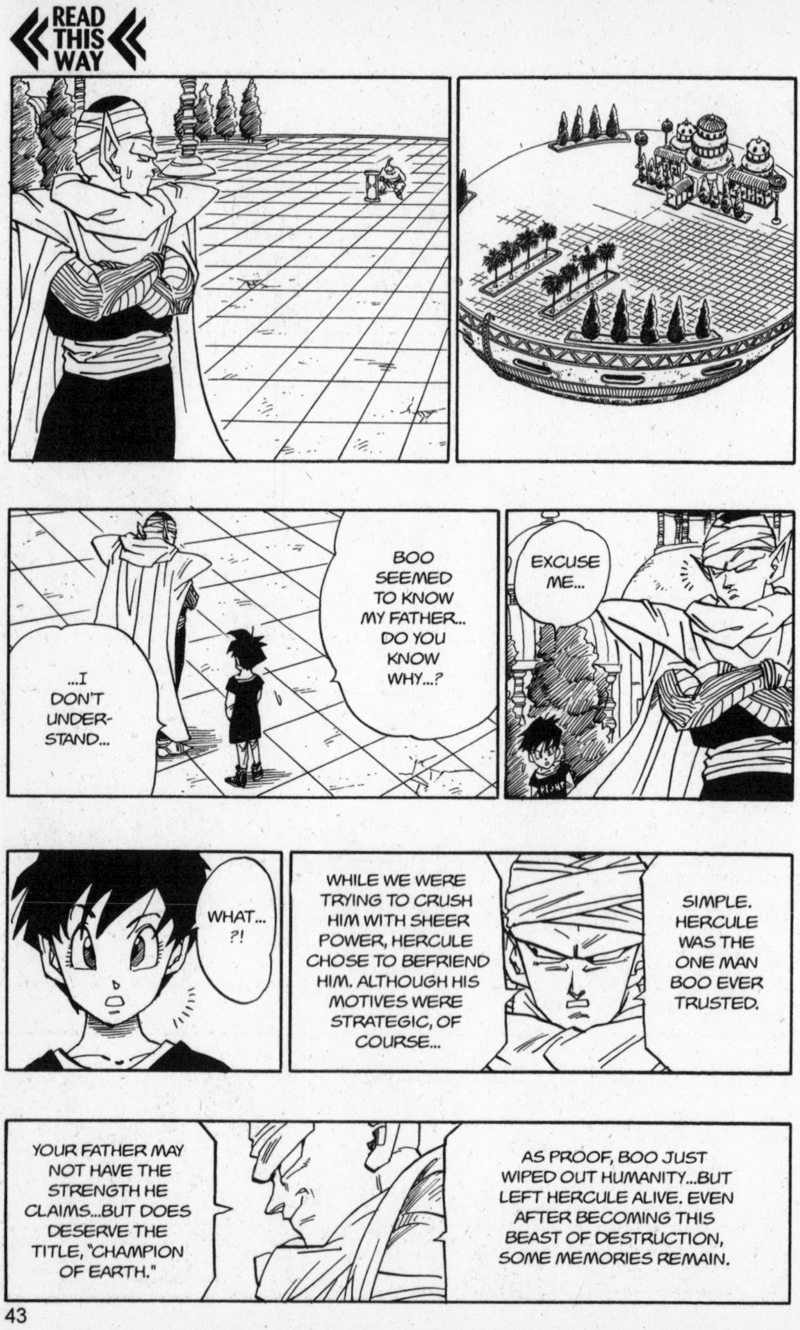

EXCUSE ME...
BOO SEEMED TO KNOW MY FATHER... DO YOU KNOW WHY...?
...I DON'T UNDER-STAND...
SIMPLE. HERCULE WAS THE ONE MAN BOO EVER TRUSTED.
WHILE WE WERE TRYING TO CRUSH HIM WITH SHEER POWER, HERCULE CHOSE TO BEFRIEND HIM. ALTHOUGH HIS MOTIVES WERE STRATEGIC, OF COURSE...
WHAT... ?!
AS PROOF, BOO JUST WIPED OUT HUMANITY...BUT LEFT HERCULE ALIVE. EVEN AFTER BECOMING THIS BEAST OF DESTRUCTION, SOME MEMORIES REMAIN.
YOUR FATHER MAY NOT HAVE THE STRENGTH HE CLAIMS...BUT DOES DESERVE THE TITLE, "CHAMPION OF EARTH."

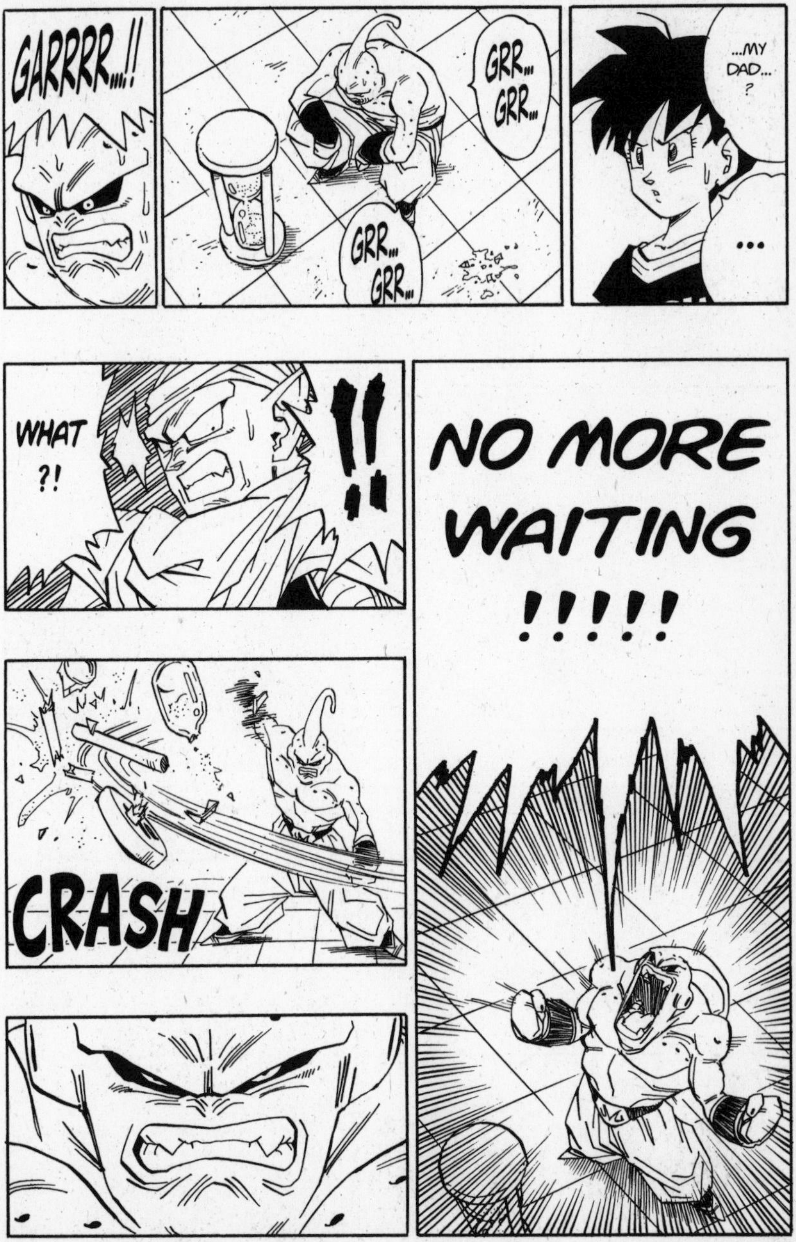
...MY DAD...?
...
GRR... GRR...
GRR... GRR...
GARRRR...!!
NO MORE WAITING !!!!!
WHAT?!
!!
CRASH

READ THIS WAY

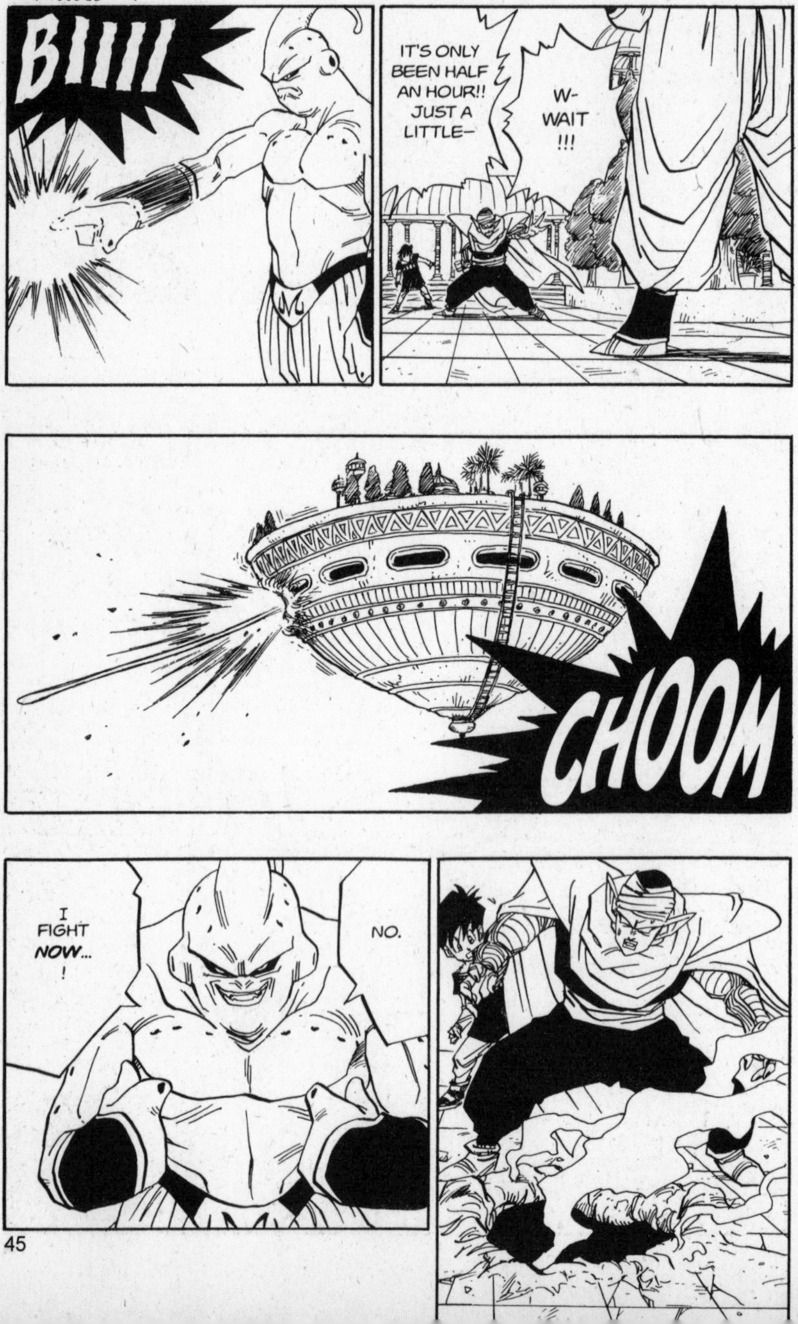
W-WAIT!!!
IT'S ONLY BEEN HALF AN HOUR!! JUST A LITTLE–
BIIII
CHOOM
NO.
I FIGHT *NOW*...!

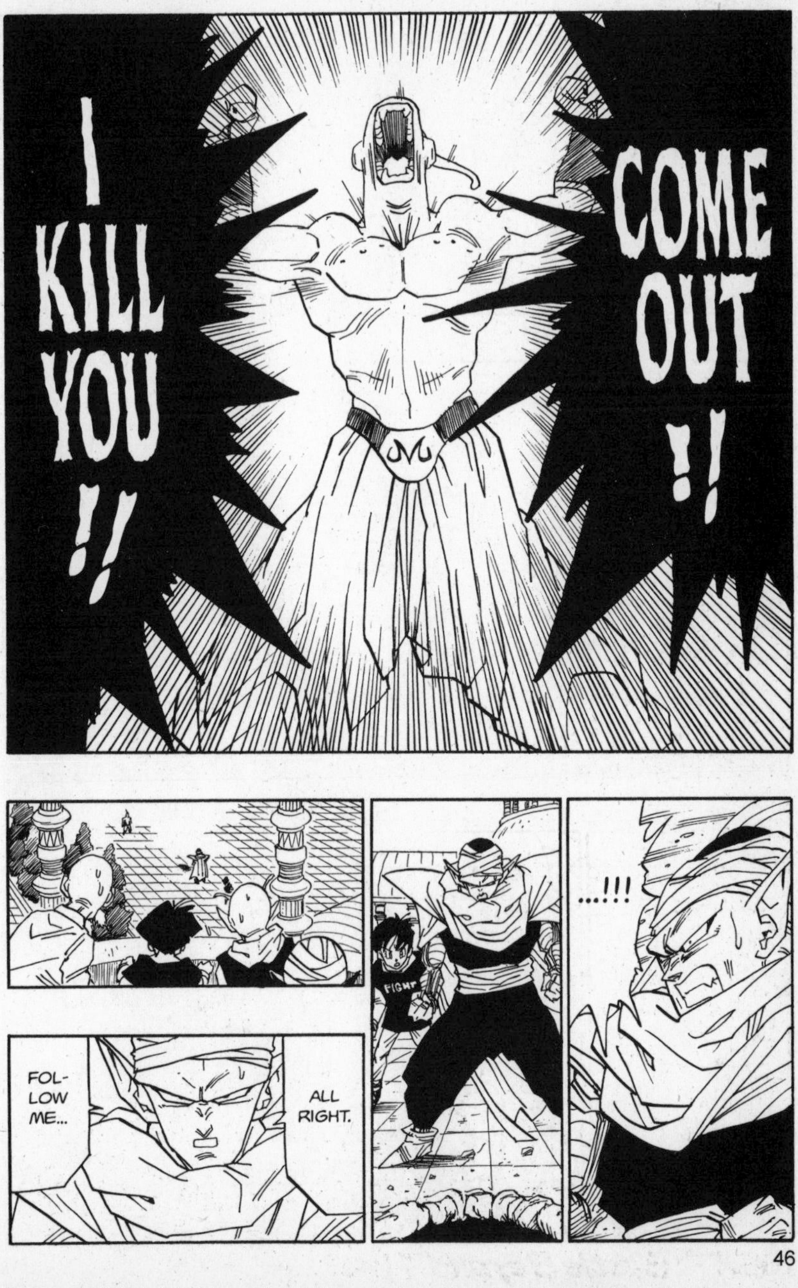
COME OUT!!
I KILL YOU!!
...!!!
ALL RIGHT.
FOL-LOW ME...

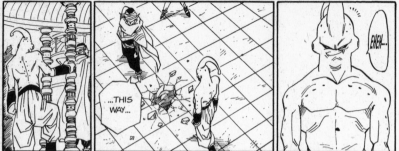

...THIS WAY...

EHEH...

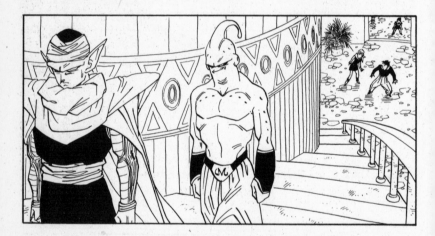

HEY... IS PICCOLO GONNA HAVE BOO FIGHT THEM *INSIDE* THE ROOM OF SPIRIT AN' TIME?

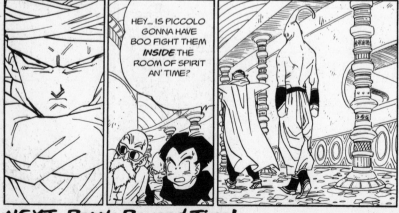

NEXT: Battle Beyond Time!

DBZ:295 • The Confidence of Gotenks!!

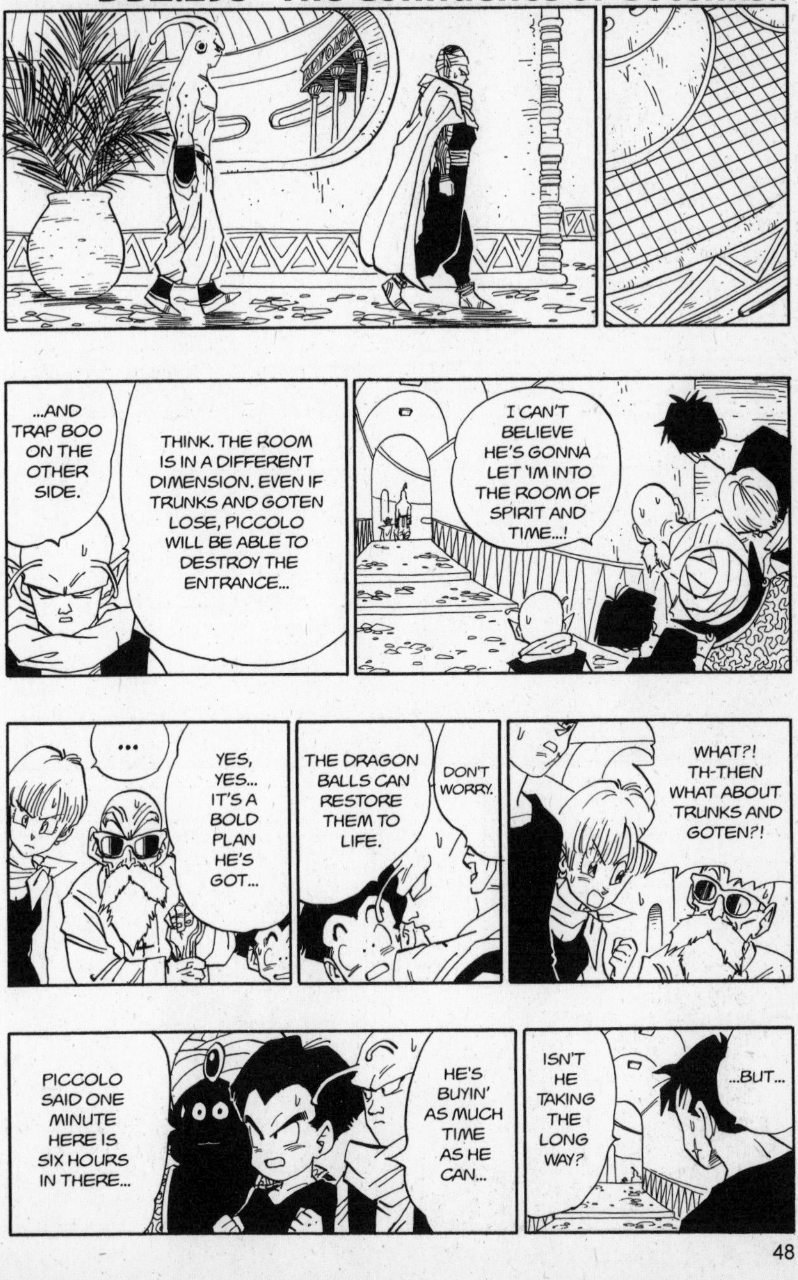
I CAN'T BELIEVE HE'S GONNA LET 'IM INTO THE ROOM OF SPIRIT AND TIME...!
THINK. THE ROOM IS IN A DIFFERENT DIMENSION. EVEN IF TRUNKS AND GOTEN LOSE, PICCOLO WILL BE ABLE TO DESTROY THE ENTRANCE...
...AND TRAP BOO ON THE OTHER SIDE.
WHAT?! TH-THEN WHAT ABOUT TRUNKS AND GOTEN?!
DON'T WORRY.
THE DRAGON BALLS CAN RESTORE THEM TO LIFE.
YES, YES... IT'S A BOLD PLAN HE'S GOT...
...
...BUT...
ISN'T HE TAKING THE LONG WAY?
HE'S BUYIN' AS MUCH TIME AS HE CAN...
PICCOLO SAID ONE MINUTE HERE IS SIX HOURS IN THERE...

READ THIS WAY

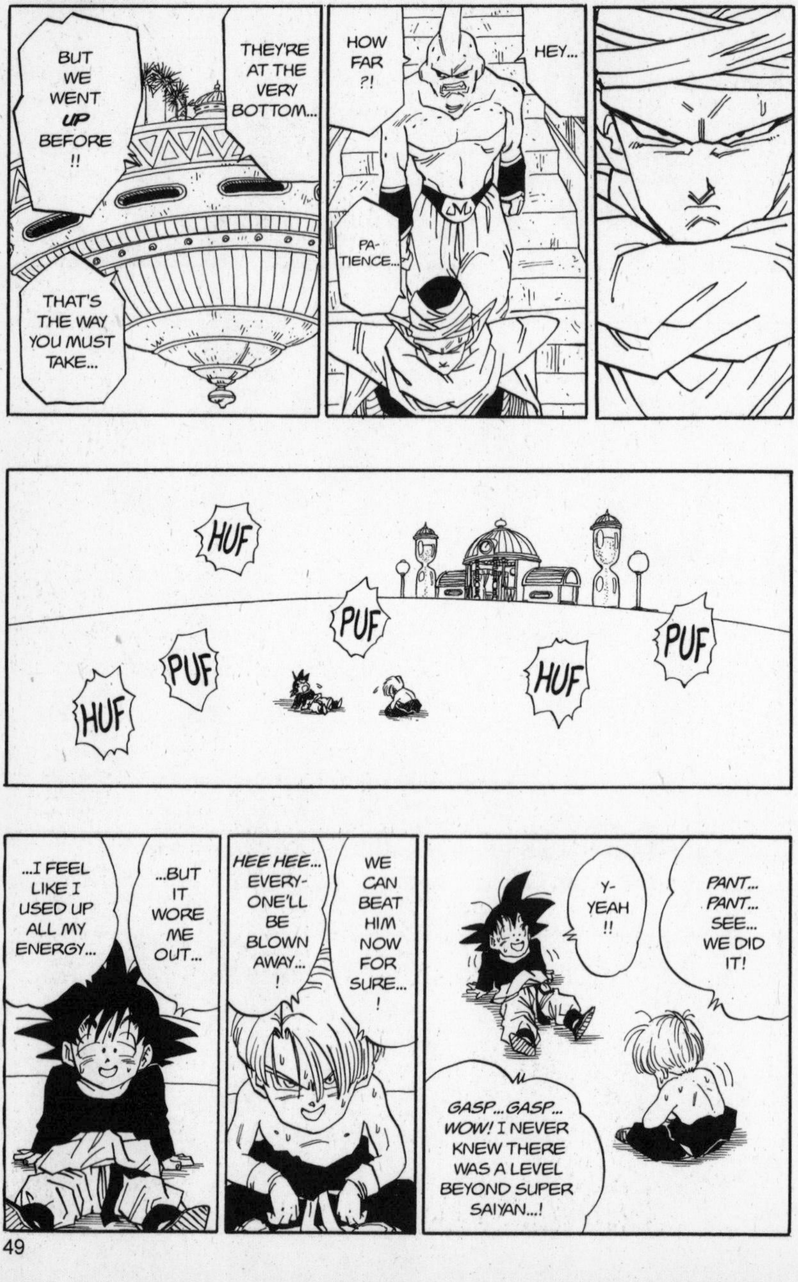
HEY...
HOW FAR ?!
PA-TIENCE...
THEY'RE AT THE VERY BOTTOM...
BUT WE WENT *UP* BEFORE !!
THAT'S THE WAY YOU MUST TAKE...
PUF
HUF
PUF
PUF
HUF
HUF
PANT... PANT... SEE... WE DID IT!
Y-YEAH !!
GASP...GASP... WOW! I NEVER KNEW THERE WAS A LEVEL BEYOND SUPER SAIYAN...!
WE CAN BEAT HIM NOW FOR SURE...!
HEE HEE... EVERYONE'LL BE BLOWN AWAY...!
...BUT IT WORE ME OUT...
...I FEEL LIKE I USED UP ALL MY ENERGY...

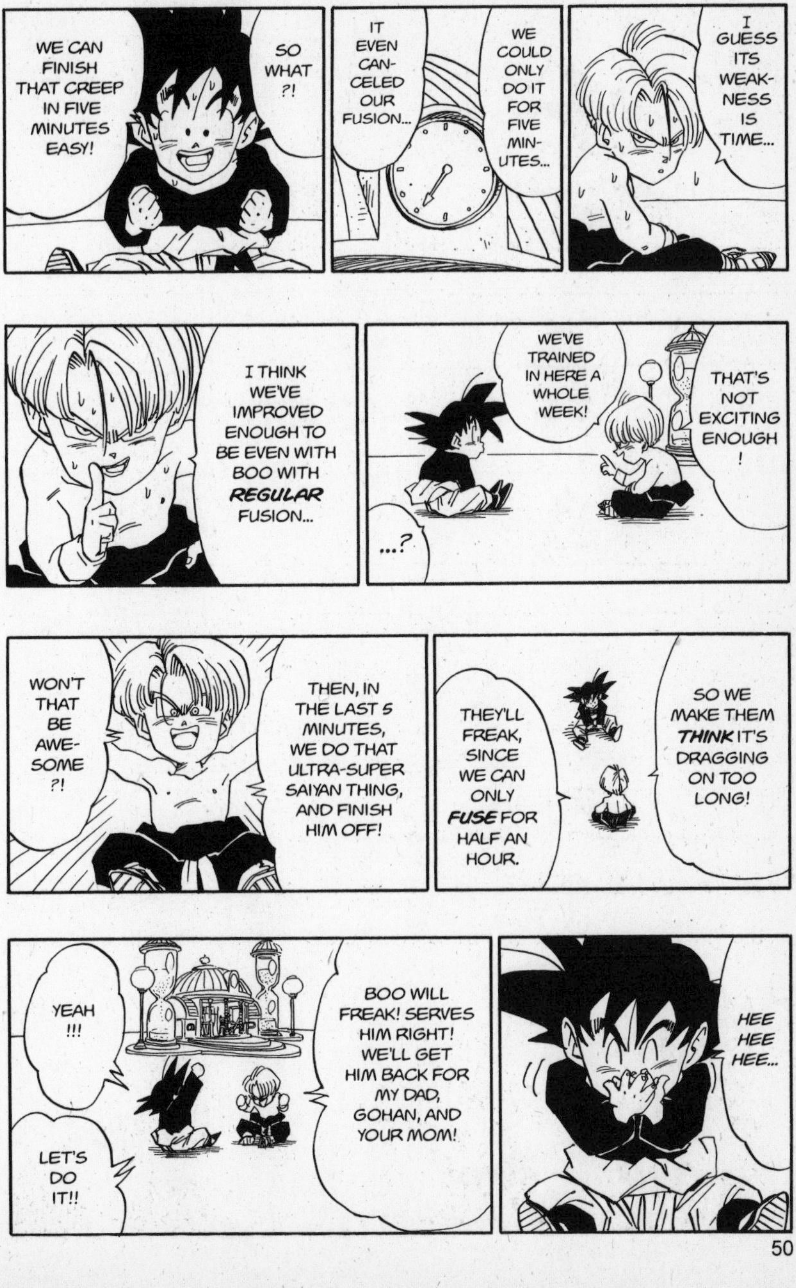
I GUESS ITS WEAKNESS IS TIME...
WE COULD ONLY DO IT FOR FIVE MINUTES...
IT EVEN CANCELED OUR FUSION...
SO WHAT ?!
WE CAN FINISH THAT CREEP IN FIVE MINUTES EASY!
THAT'S NOT EXCITING ENOUGH!
WE'VE TRAINED IN HERE A WHOLE WEEK!
...?
I THINK WE'VE IMPROVED ENOUGH TO BE EVEN WITH BOO WITH ***REGULAR*** FUSION...
SO WE MAKE THEM ***THINK*** IT'S DRAGGING ON TOO LONG!
THEY'LL FREAK, SINCE WE CAN ONLY ***FUSE*** FOR HALF AN HOUR.
THEN, IN THE LAST 5 MINUTES, WE DO THAT ULTRA-SUPER SAIYAN THING, AND FINISH HIM OFF!
WON'T THAT BE AWESOME ?!
HEE HEE HEE...
BOO WILL FREAK! SERVES HIM RIGHT! WE'LL GET HIM BACK FOR MY DAD, GOHAN, AND YOUR MOM!
YEAH !!!
LET'S DO IT!!

READ THIS WAY

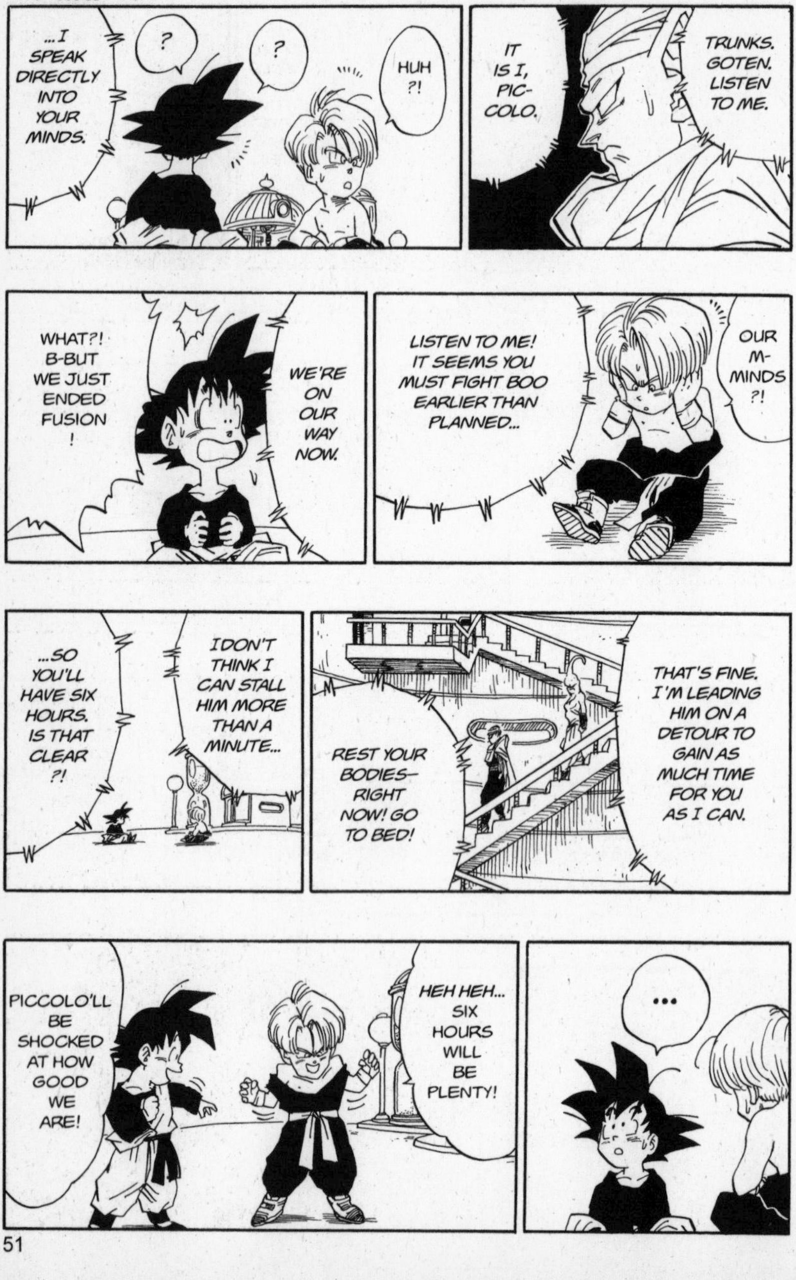
TRUNKS. GOTEN. LISTEN TO ME.
IT IS I, PICCOLO.
HUH ?!
?
?
...I SPEAK DIRECTLY INTO YOUR MINDS.
OUR M-MINDS ?!
LISTEN TO ME! IT SEEMS YOU MUST FIGHT BOO EARLIER THAN PLANNED...
WE'RE ON OUR WAY NOW.
WHAT?! B-BUT WE JUST ENDED FUSION !
THAT'S FINE. I'M LEADING HIM ON A DETOUR TO GAIN AS MUCH TIME FOR YOU AS I CAN.
REST YOUR BODIES— RIGHT NOW! GO TO BED!
I DON'T THINK I CAN STALL HIM MORE THAN A MINUTE...
...SO YOU'LL HAVE SIX HOURS. IS THAT CLEAR ?!
...
HEH HEH... SIX HOURS WILL BE PLENTY!
PICCOLO'LL BE SHOCKED AT HOW GOOD WE ARE!

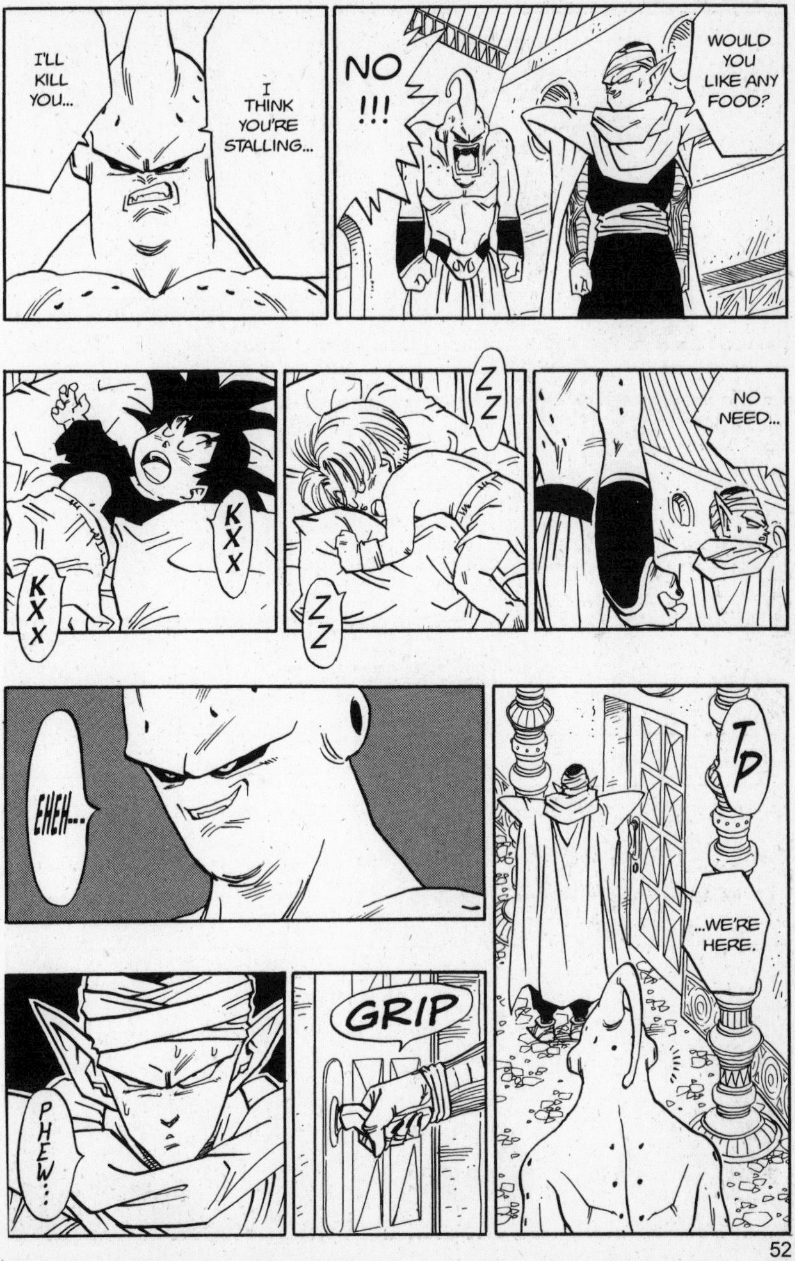
WOULD YOU LIKE ANY FOOD?
NO !!!
I THINK YOU'RE STALLING...
I'LL KILL YOU...
NO NEED...
ZZ
ZZ
KXX
KXX
TP
...WE'RE HERE.
EHEH...
GRIP
PHEW...

READ THIS WAY

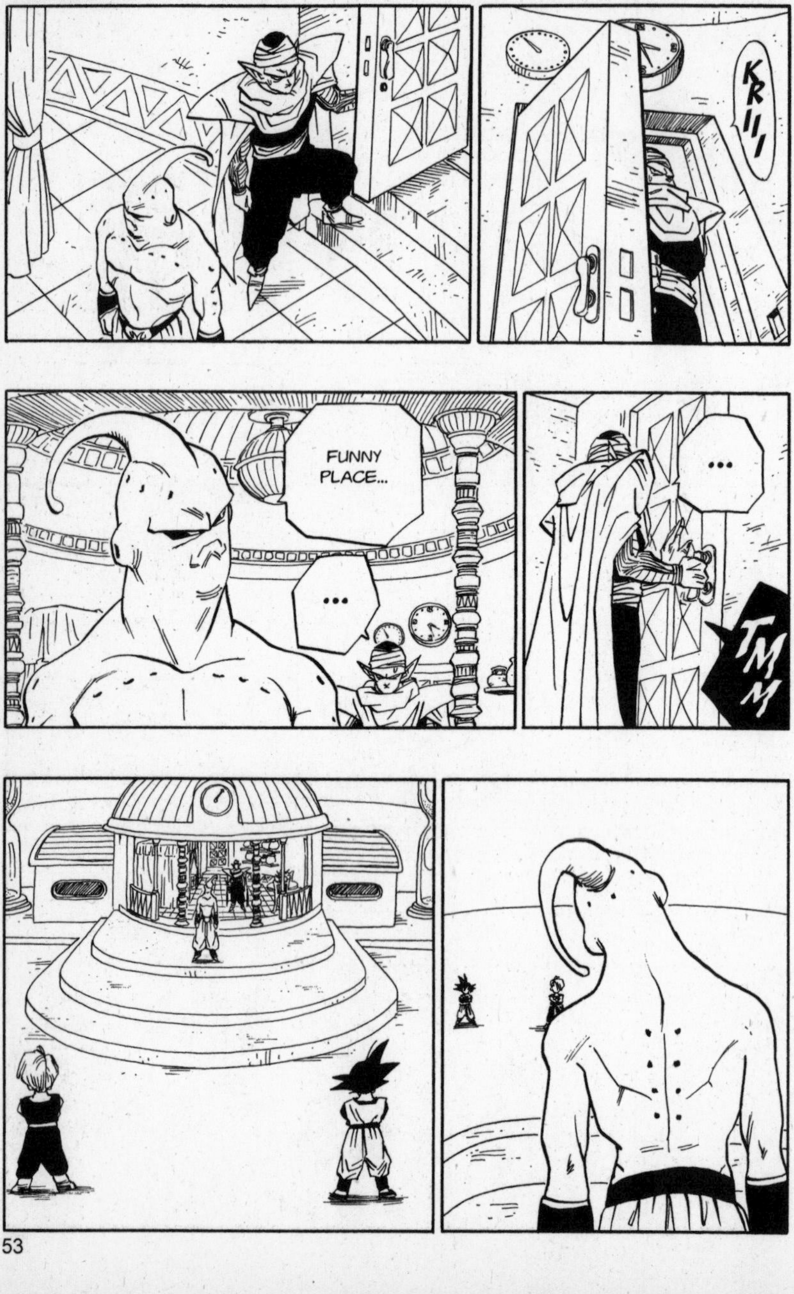
KRIII
...
TMM
FUNNY PLACE...
...

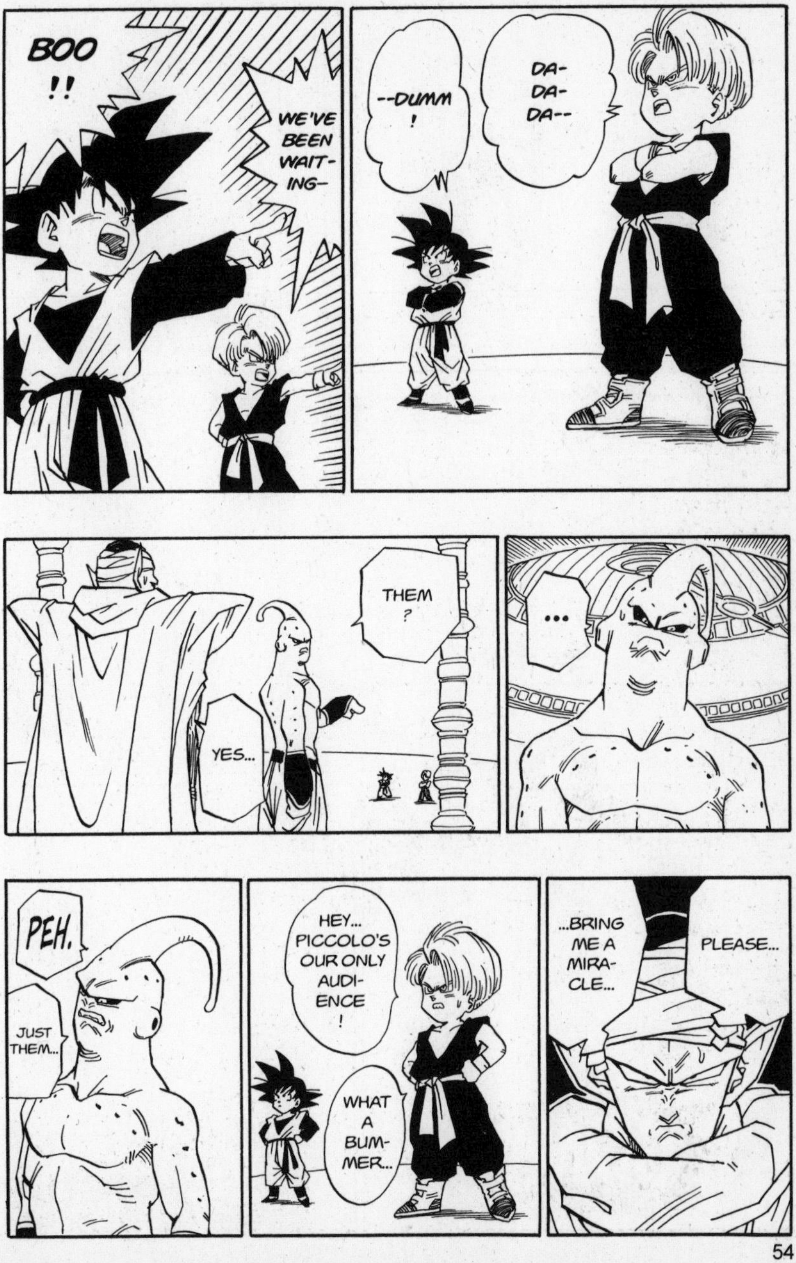
DA-DA-DA--
--DUMM!
BOO!!
WE'VE BEEN WAITING-
...
THEM?
YES...
PLEASE...
...BRING ME A MIRACLE...
HEY... PICCOLO'S OUR ONLY AUDIENCE!
WHAT A BUMMER...
PEH.
JUST THEM...

READ THIS WAY

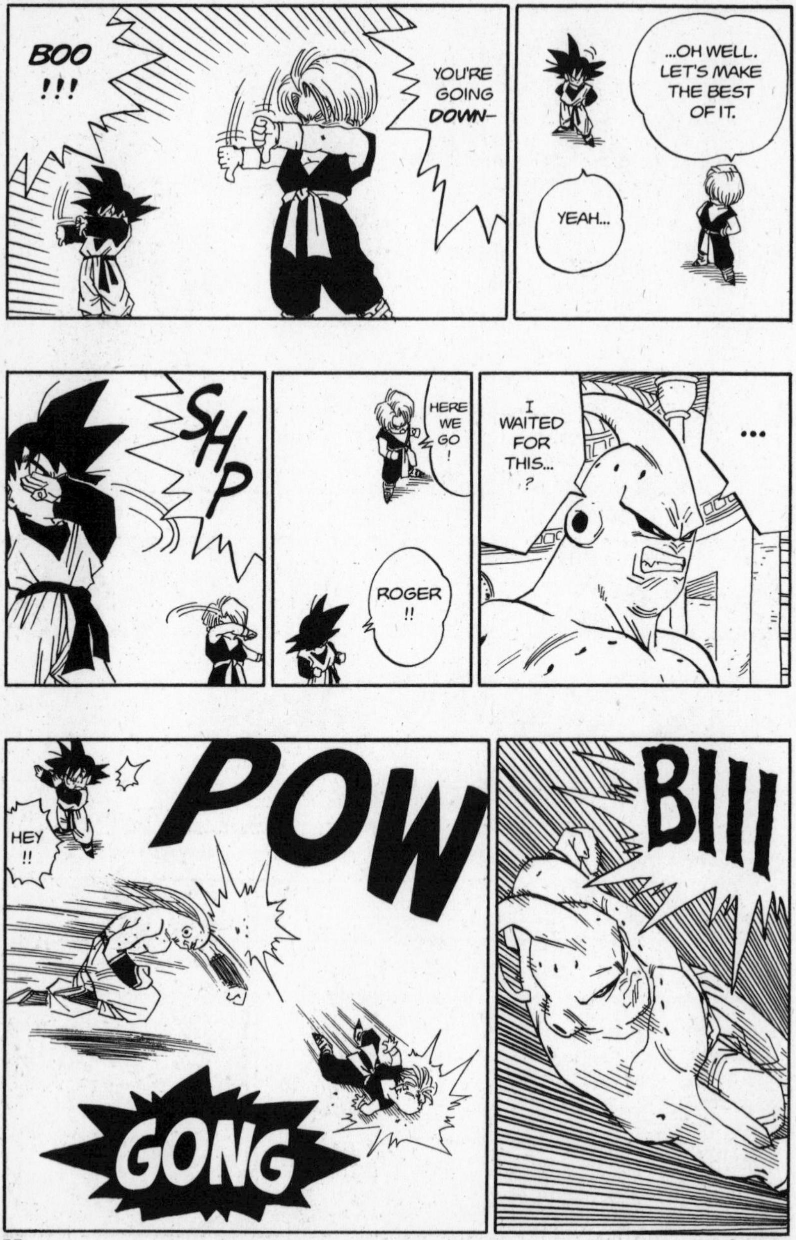

...OH WELL. LET'S MAKE THE BEST OF IT.
YEAH...
YOU'RE GOING DOWN-
BOO !!!
...
I WAITED FOR THIS... ?
HERE WE GO !
ROGER !!
SHP
BIII
POW
HEY !!
GONG

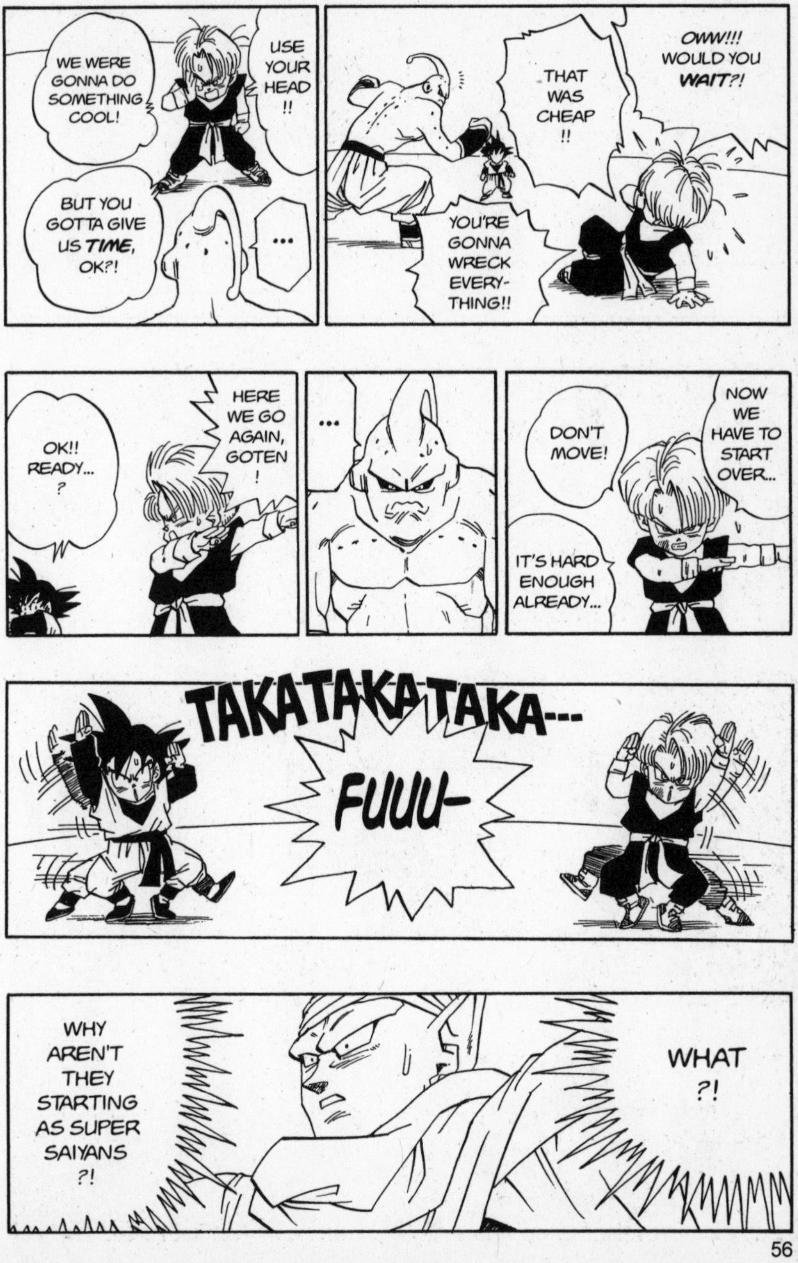
OWW!!! WOULD YOU WAIT?!
THAT WAS CHEAP!!
YOU'RE GONNA WRECK EVERYTHING!!
USE YOUR HEAD!!
WE WERE GONNA DO SOMETHING COOL!
...
BUT YOU GOTTA GIVE US TIME, OK?!
NOW WE HAVE TO START OVER...
DON'T MOVE!
IT'S HARD ENOUGH ALREADY...
...
HERE WE GO AGAIN, GOTEN!
OK!! READY...?
TAKATAKATAKA---
FUUU-
WHAT?!
WHY AREN'T THEY STARTING AS SUPER SAIYANS?!

READ THIS WAY

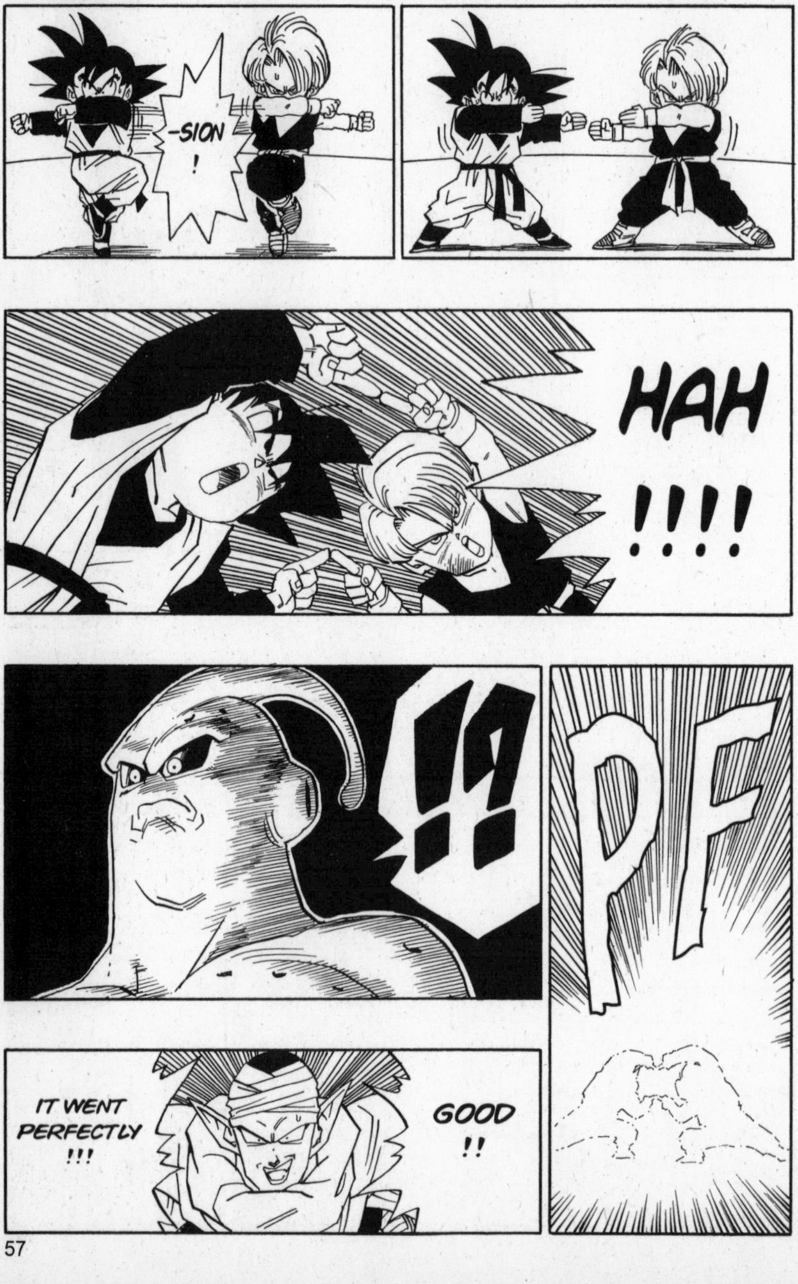
-SION !
HAH !!!!
PF
!?
GOOD !!
IT WENT PERFECTLY !!!

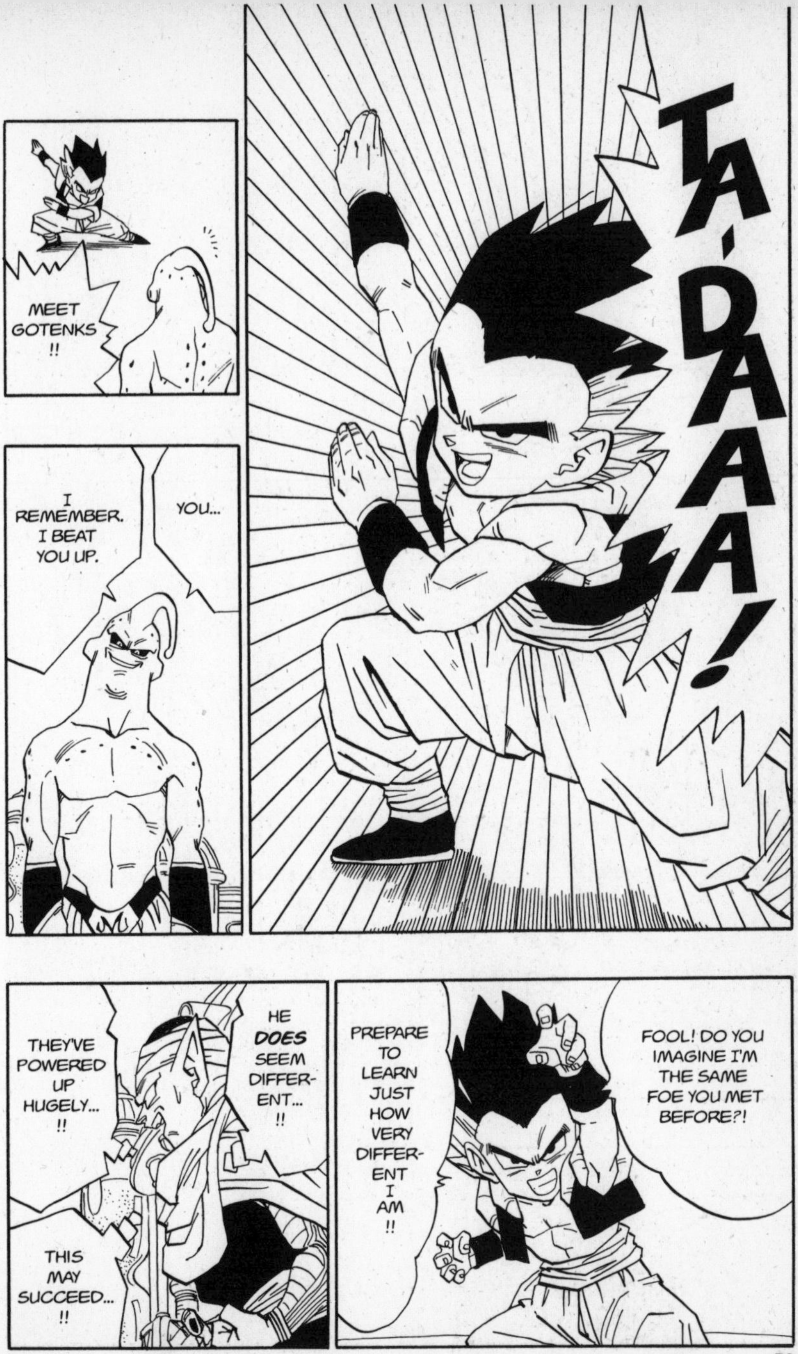
TA-DAAA!
MEET GOTENKS !!
YOU...
I REMEMBER. I BEAT YOU UP.
FOOL! DO YOU IMAGINE I'M THE SAME FOE YOU MET BEFORE?!
PREPARE TO LEARN JUST HOW VERY DIFFERENT I AM !!
HE **DOES** SEEM DIFFERENT... !!
THEY'VE POWERED UP HUGELY... !!
THIS MAY SUCCEED... !!

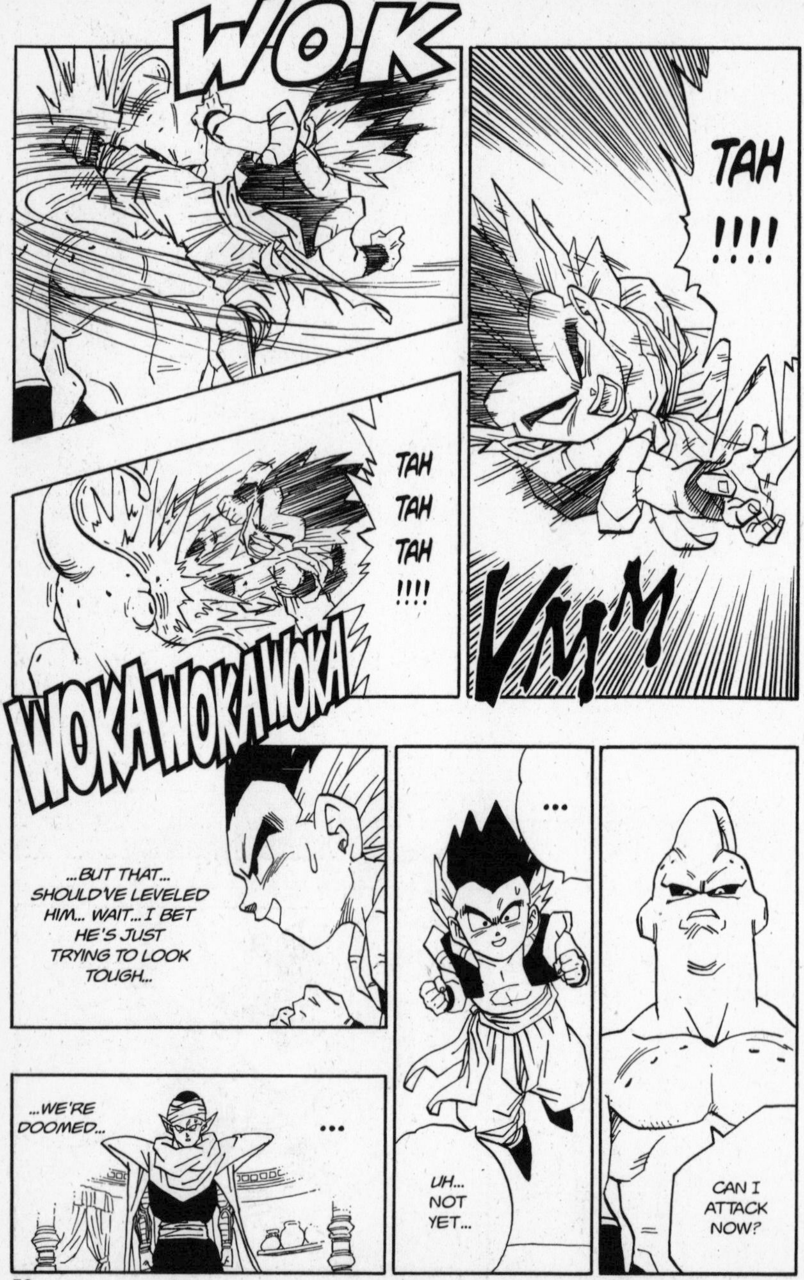
TAH
!!!!
VMM
WOK
TAH
TAH
TAH
!!!!
WOKAWOKAWOKA
CAN I ATTACK NOW?
...
UH... NOT YET...
...BUT THAT... SHOULD'VE LEVELED HIM... WAIT... I BET HE'S JUST TRYING TO LOOK TOUGH...
...WE'RE DOOMED...
...

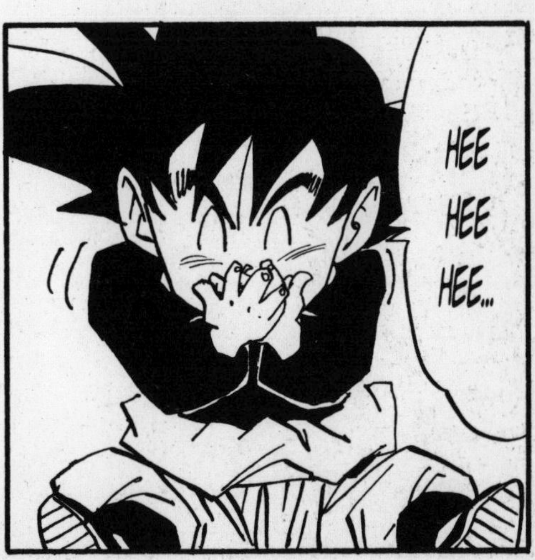
HEE
HEE
HEE...

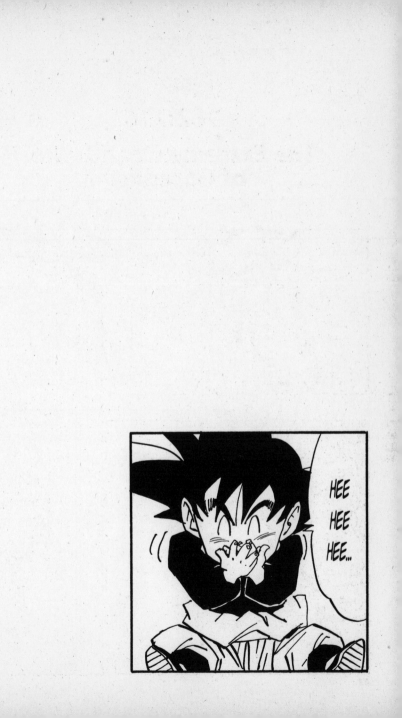

DBZ:296

The *Extreme* Confidence of Gotenks!!

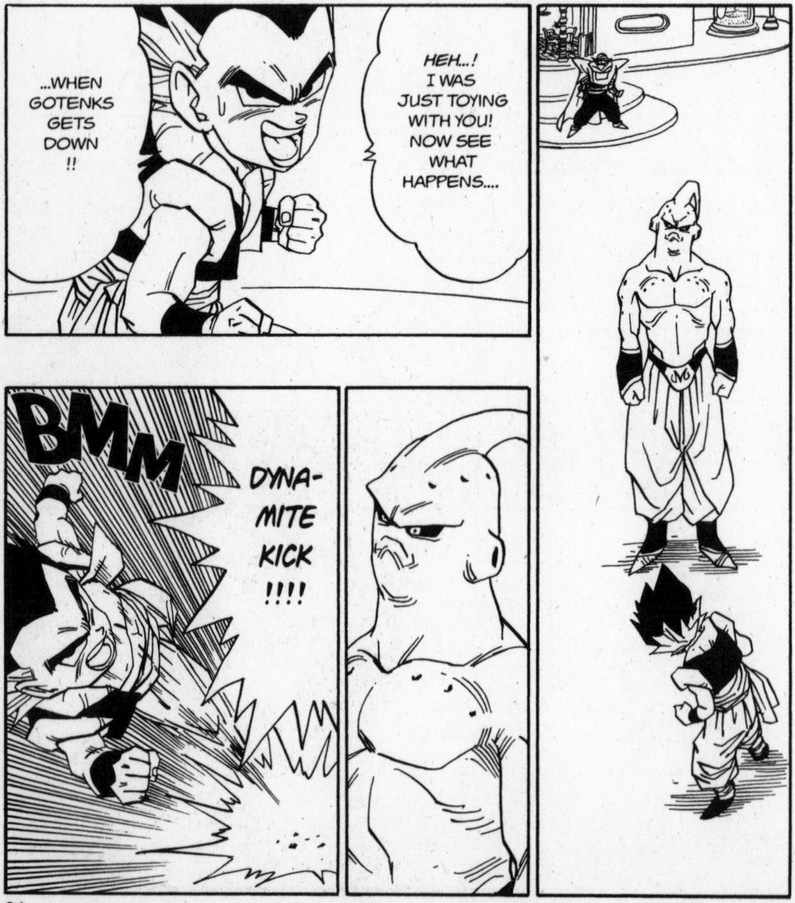
HEH...! I WAS JUST TOYING WITH YOU! NOW SEE WHAT HAPPENS....
...WHEN GOTENKS GETS DOWN !!
DYNA-MITE KICK !!!!
BMM

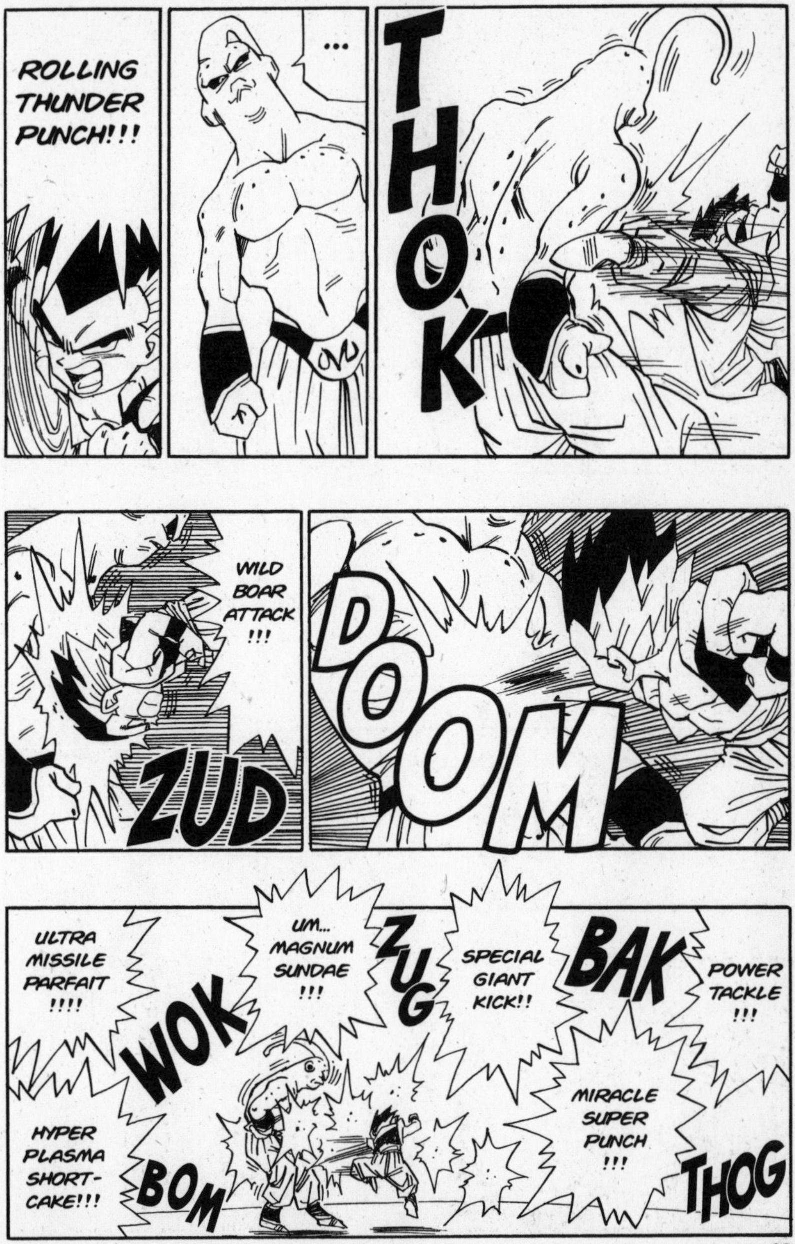
THOK
...
ROLLING THUNDER PUNCH!!!
DOOOM
WILD BOAR ATTACK !!!
ZUD
POWER TACKLE !!!
BAK
SPECIAL GIANT KICK!!
ZUG
UM... MAGNUM SUNDAE !!!
WOK
ULTRA MISSILE PARFAIT !!!!
THOG
MIRACLE SUPER PUNCH !!!
BOM
HYPER PLASMA SHORT-CAKE!!!

READ THIS WAY

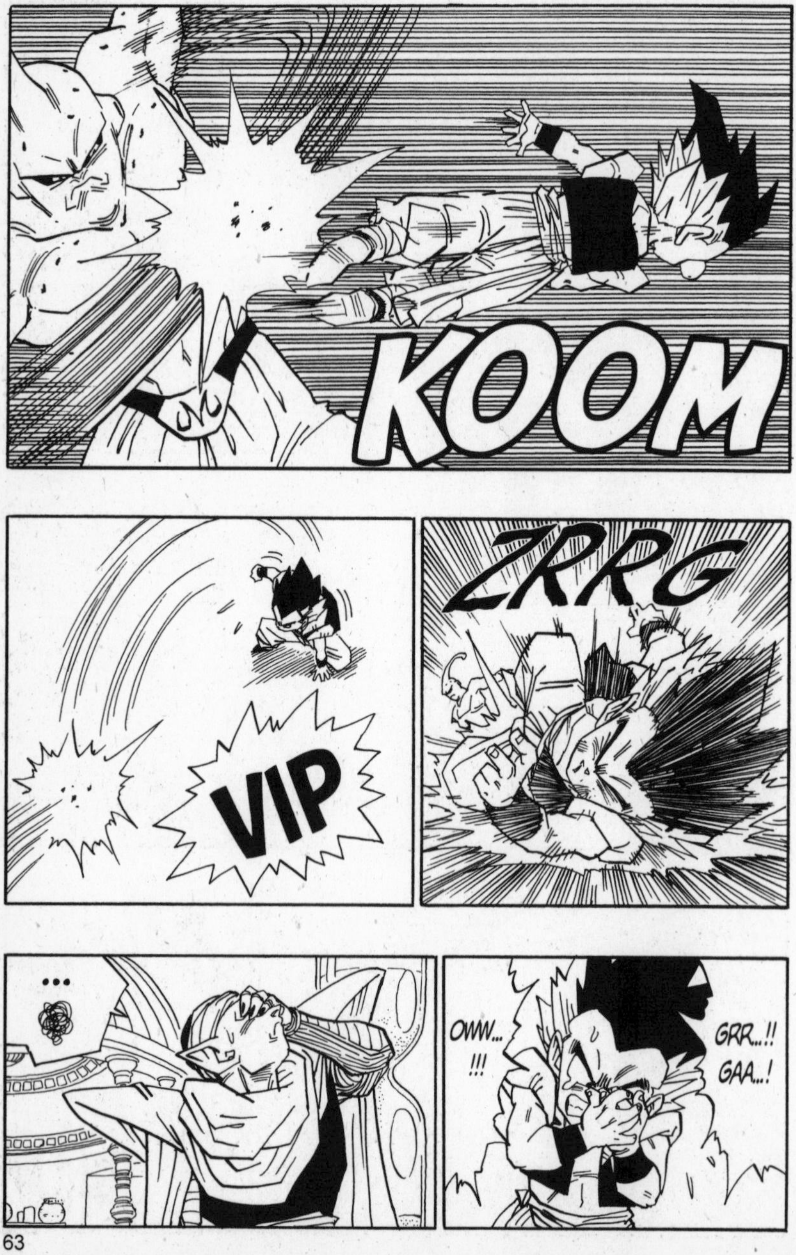
KOOM
ZRRG
VIP
GRR...!! GAA...!
OWW... !!!
...

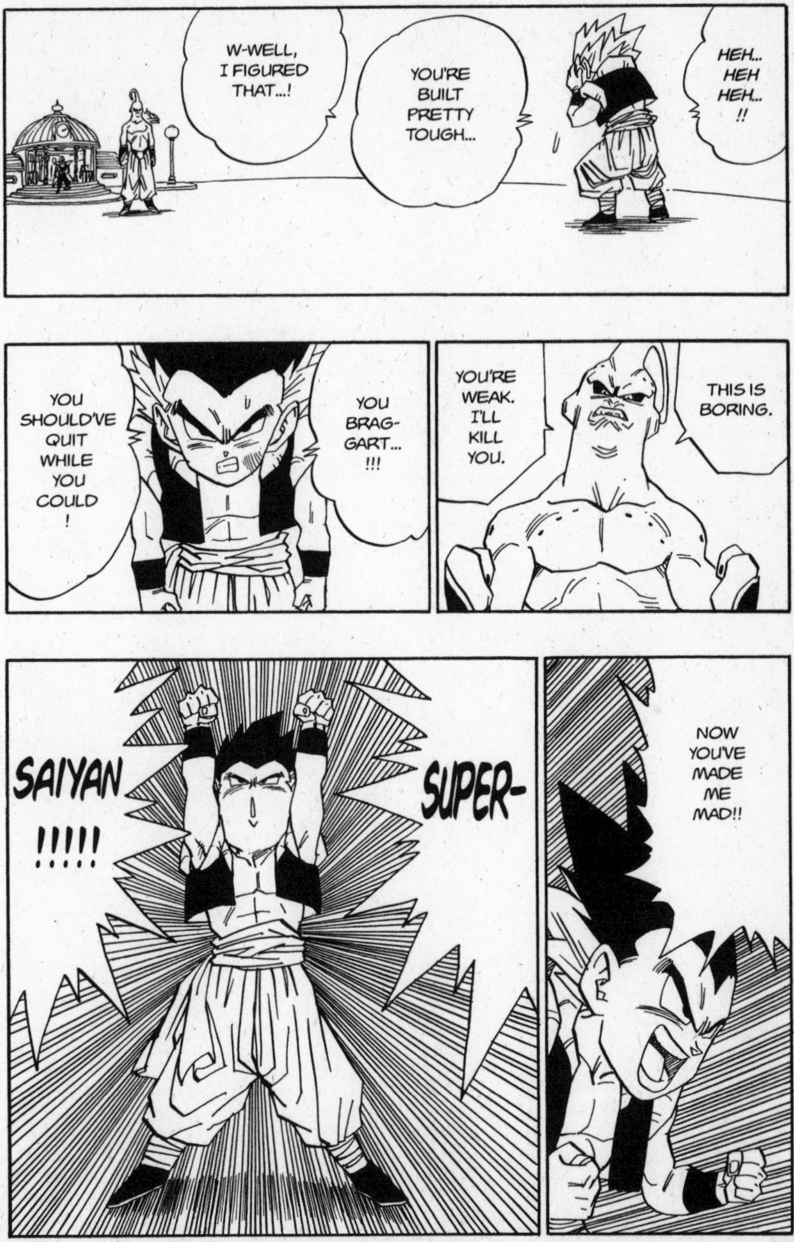
HEH... HEH HEH... !!
YOU'RE BUILT PRETTY TOUGH...
W-WELL, I FIGURED THAT...!
THIS IS BORING.
YOU'RE WEAK. I'LL KILL YOU.
YOU BRAG-GART... !!!
YOU SHOULD'VE QUIT WHILE YOU COULD !
NOW YOU'VE MADE ME MAD!!
SUPER-
SAIYAN !!!!!

READ THIS WAY

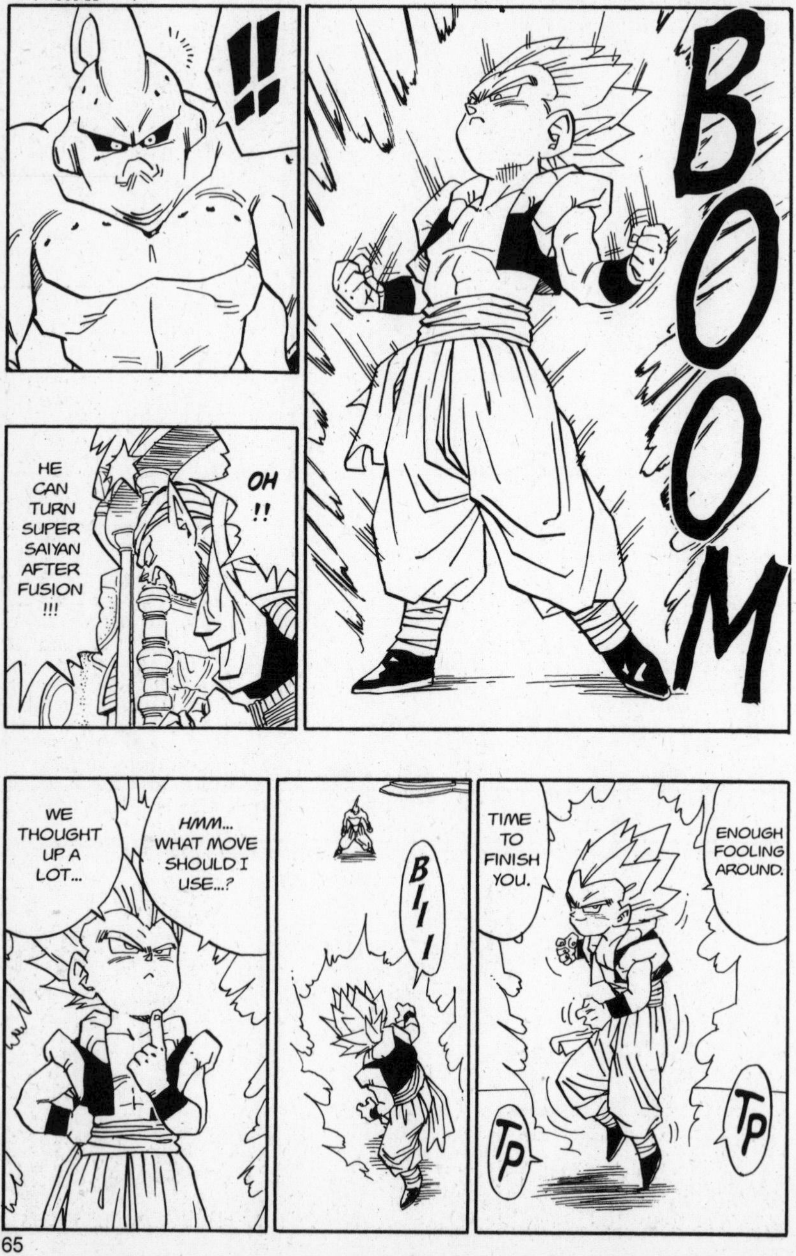
BOOM
!!
OH !!
HE CAN TURN SUPER SAIYAN AFTER FUSION !!!
ENOUGH FOOLING AROUND.
TIME TO FINISH YOU.
TP
TP
BIII
HMM... WHAT MOVE SHOULD I USE...?
WE THOUGHT UP A LOT...

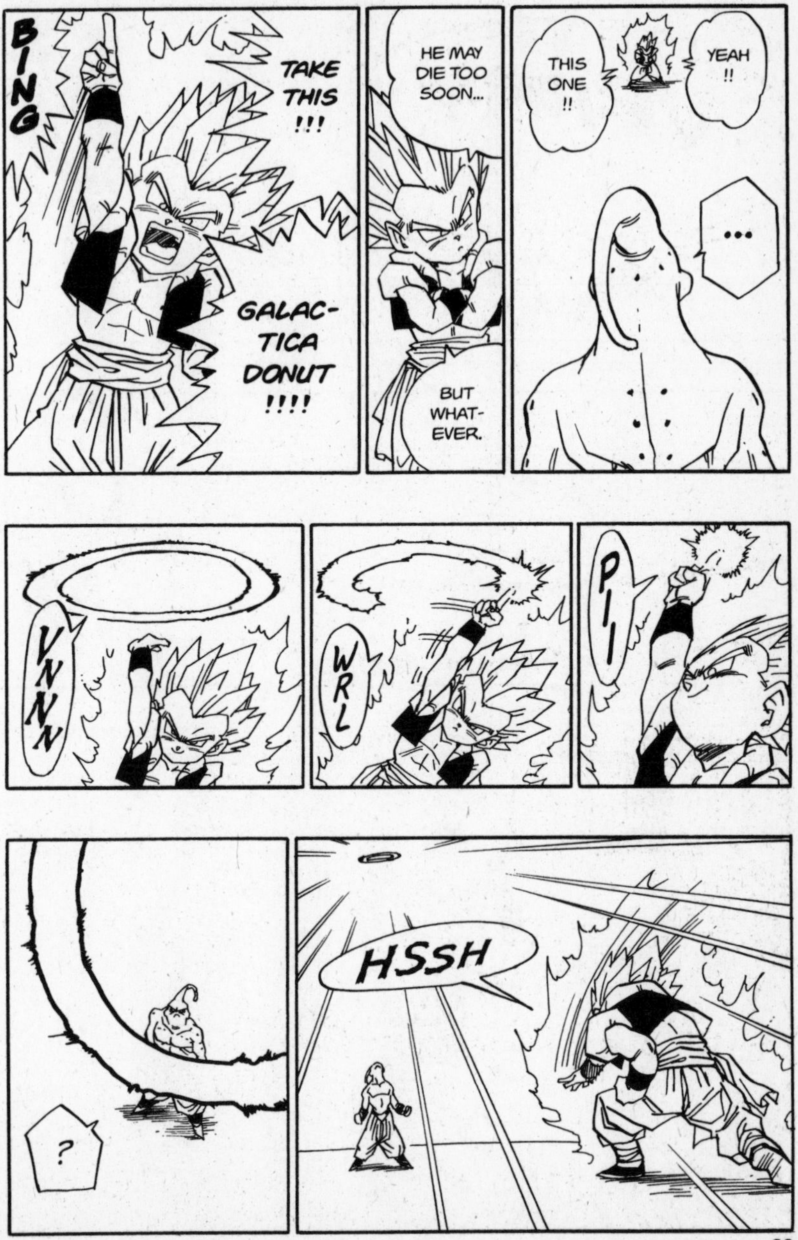
YEAH !!
THIS ONE !!
...
HE MAY DIE TOO SOON...
BUT WHAT-EVER.
TAKE THIS !!!
BING
GALAC-TICA DONUT !!!!
PI
WRL
VNNN
HSSH
?

READ THIS WAY

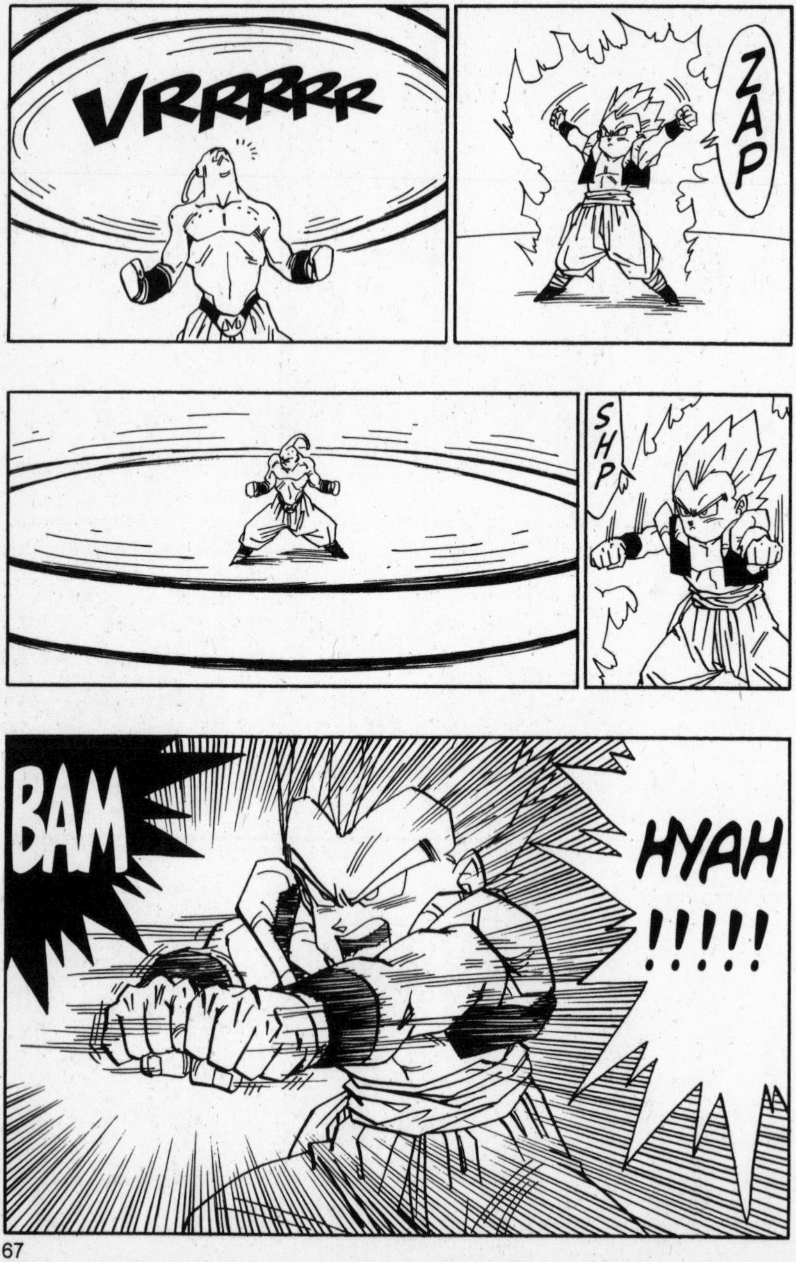
ZAP
VRRRRR
SHP
HYAH!!!!!
BAM

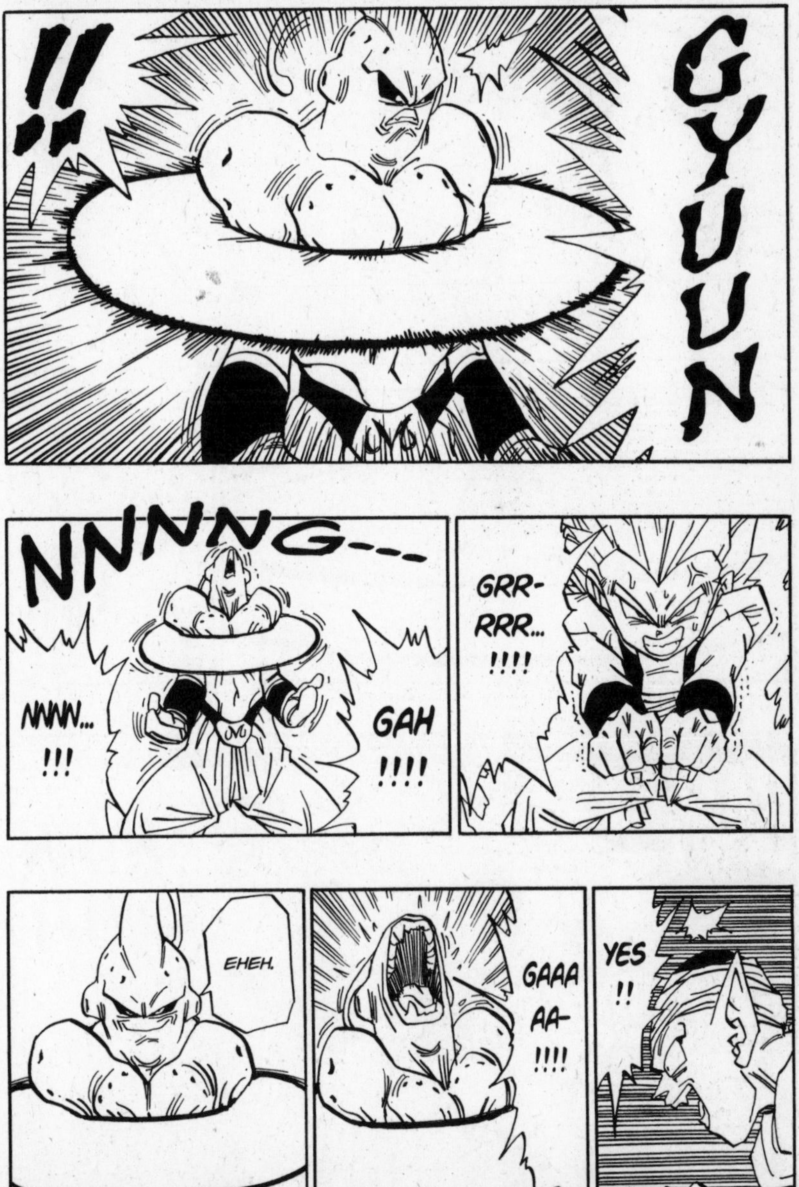
GYUN
!!
NNNNG---
GAH !!!!
NNNN... !!!
GRR-RRR... !!!!
YES !!
GAAAAA- !!!!
EHEH.

READ THIS WAY

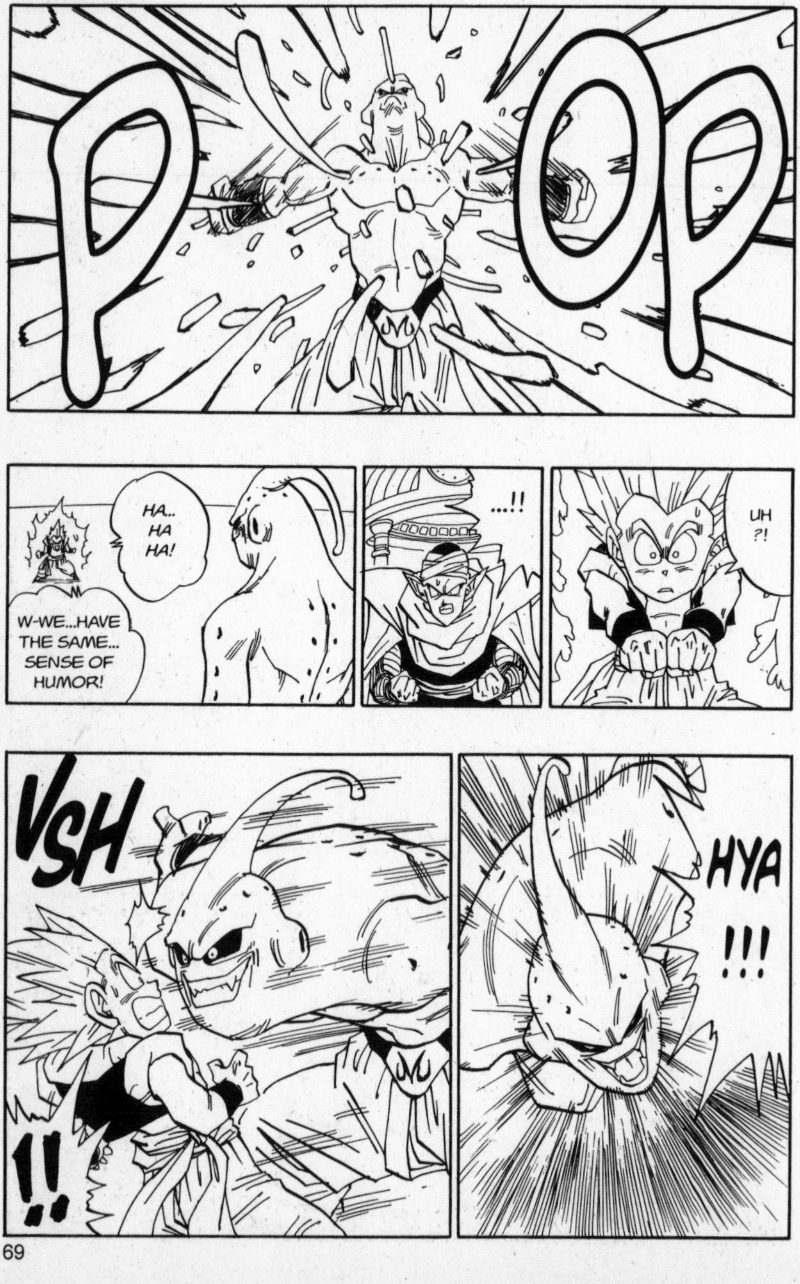
POP
UH ?!
...!!
HA... HA HA!
W-WE...HAVE THE SAME... SENSE OF HUMOR!
HYA !!!
VSH
!!

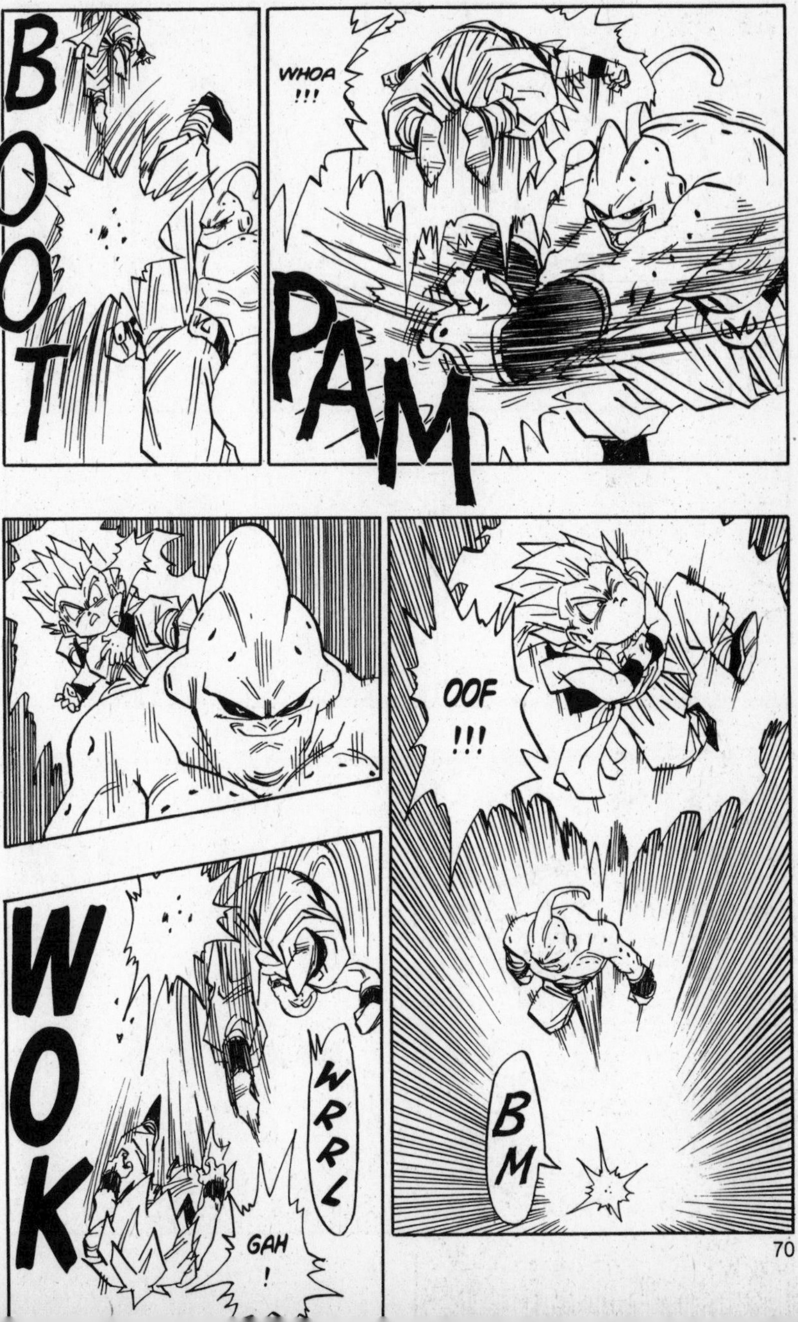
WHOA !!!
PAM
BOOT
OOF !!!
BM
WOK
WRRL
GAH !

READ THIS WAY

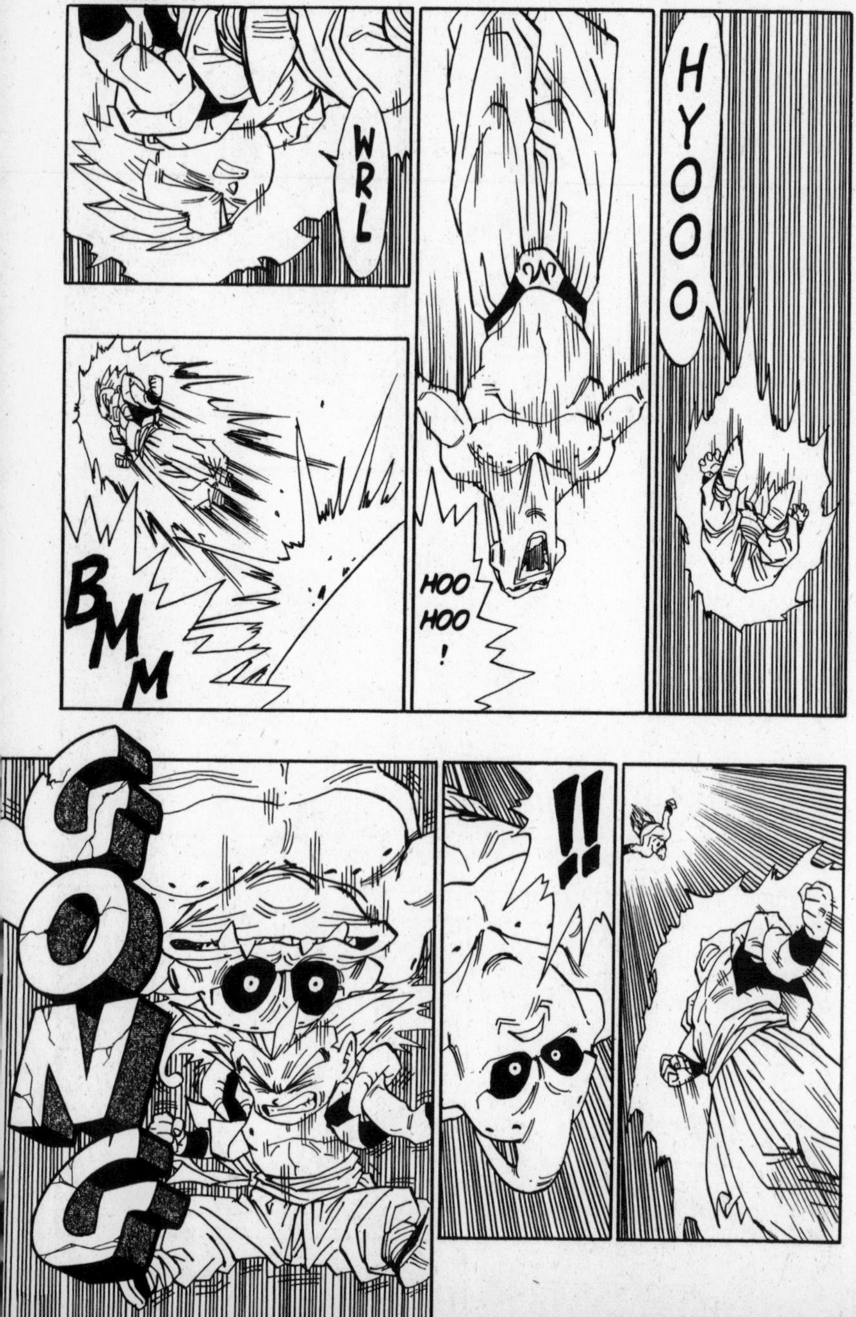
HYOOO
HOO HOO!
WRL
BMM
!!
GONG

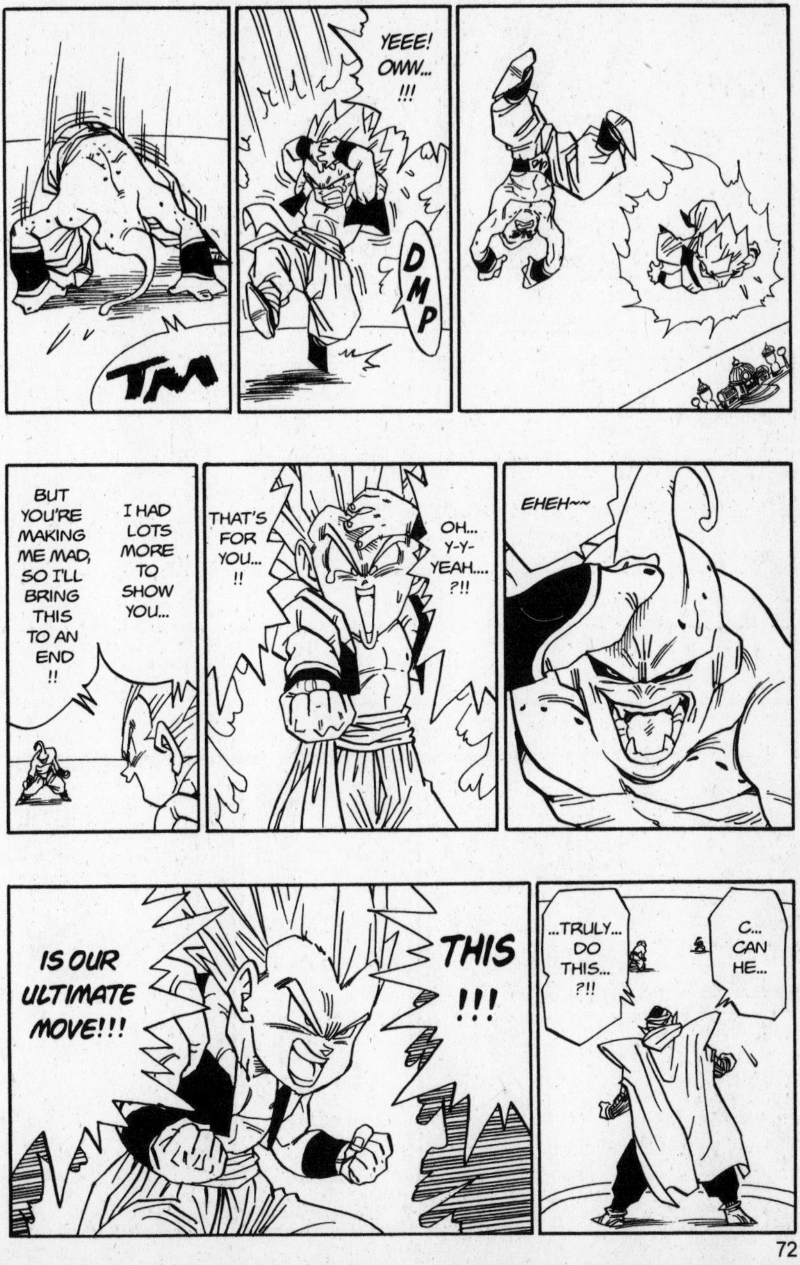
YEEE! OWW... !!!
DMP
TM
EHEH~~
OH... Y-Y-YEAH.... ?!!
THAT'S FOR YOU... !!
I HAD LOTS MORE TO SHOW YOU...
BUT YOU'RE MAKING ME MAD, SO I'LL BRING THIS TO AN END !!
C... CAN HE...
...TRULY... DO THIS... ?!!
THIS !!!
IS OUR ULTIMATE MOVE!!!

READ THIS WAY

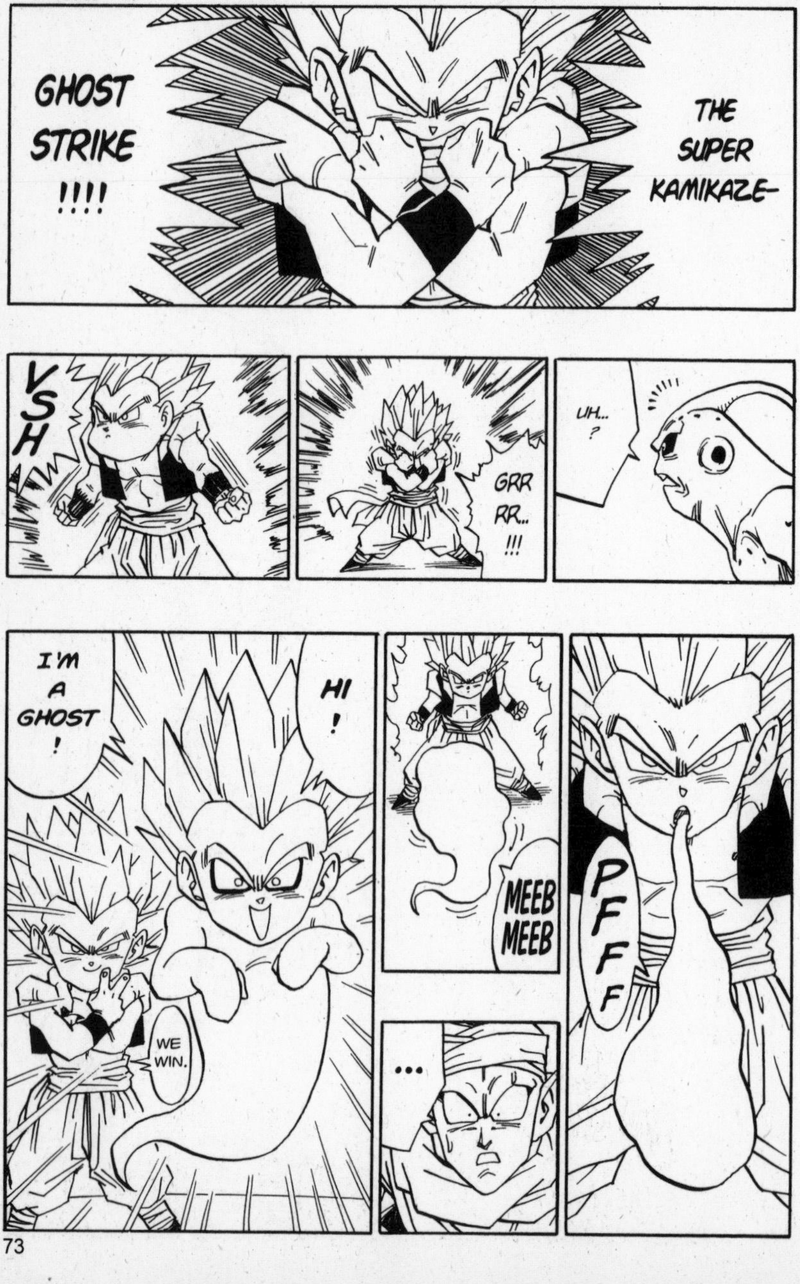

THE SUPER KAMIKAZE-
GHOST STRIKE !!!!
UH... ?
GRR RR... !!!
VSH
PFFF
MEEB MEEB
...
HI !
I'M A GHOST !
WE WIN.

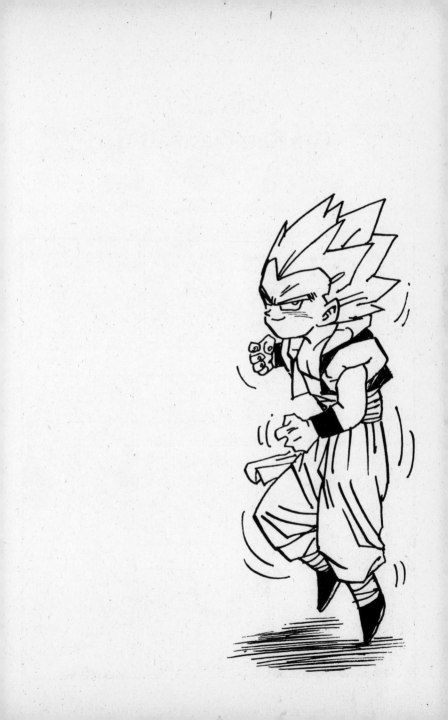

DBZ:297
The Kamikaze Ghost!

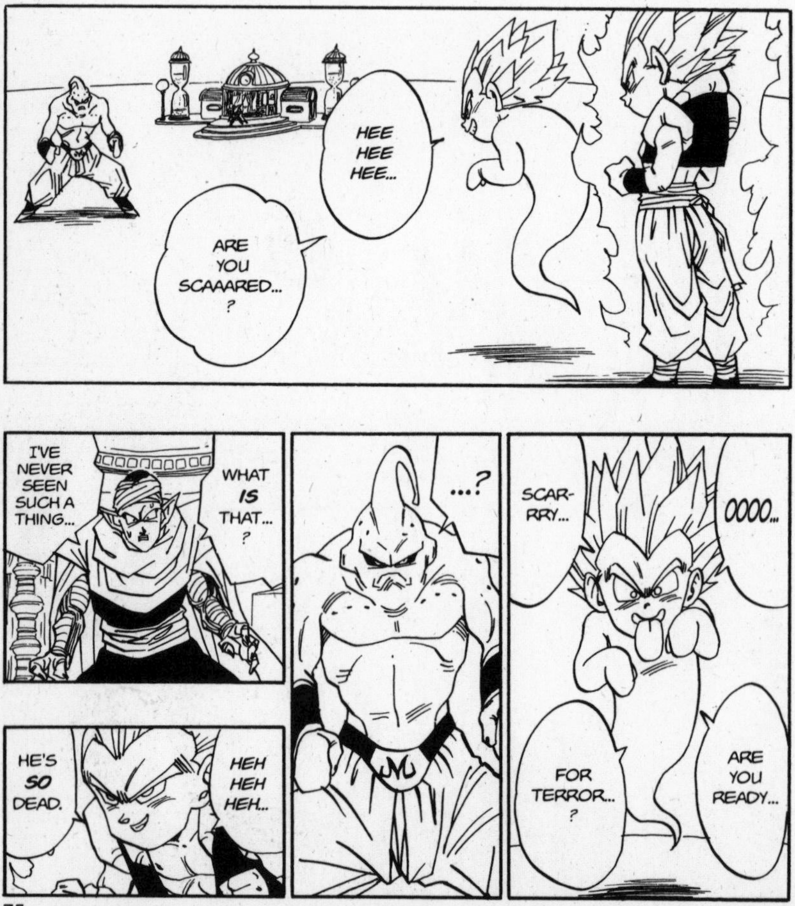
HEE HEE HEE...
ARE YOU SCAAARED...?
OOOO...
SCAR-RRY...
ARE YOU READY...
FOR TERROR...?
...?
WHAT *IS* THAT...?
I'VE NEVER SEEN SUCH A THING...
HEH HEH HEH...
HE'S *SO* DEAD.

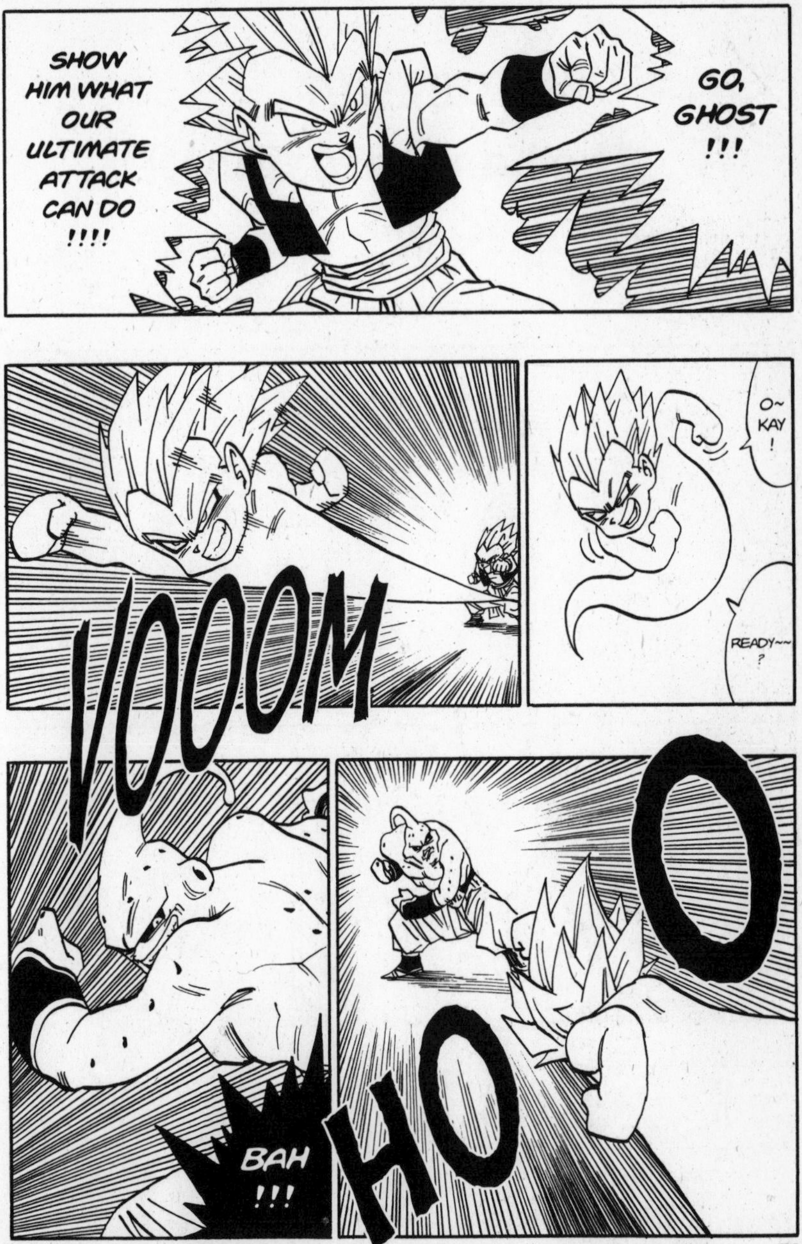
GO, GHOST!!!
SHOW HIM WHAT OUR ULTIMATE ATTACK CAN DO!!!!
O~KAY!
READY~~?
VOOOM
HOOO
BAH!!!

READ THIS WAY

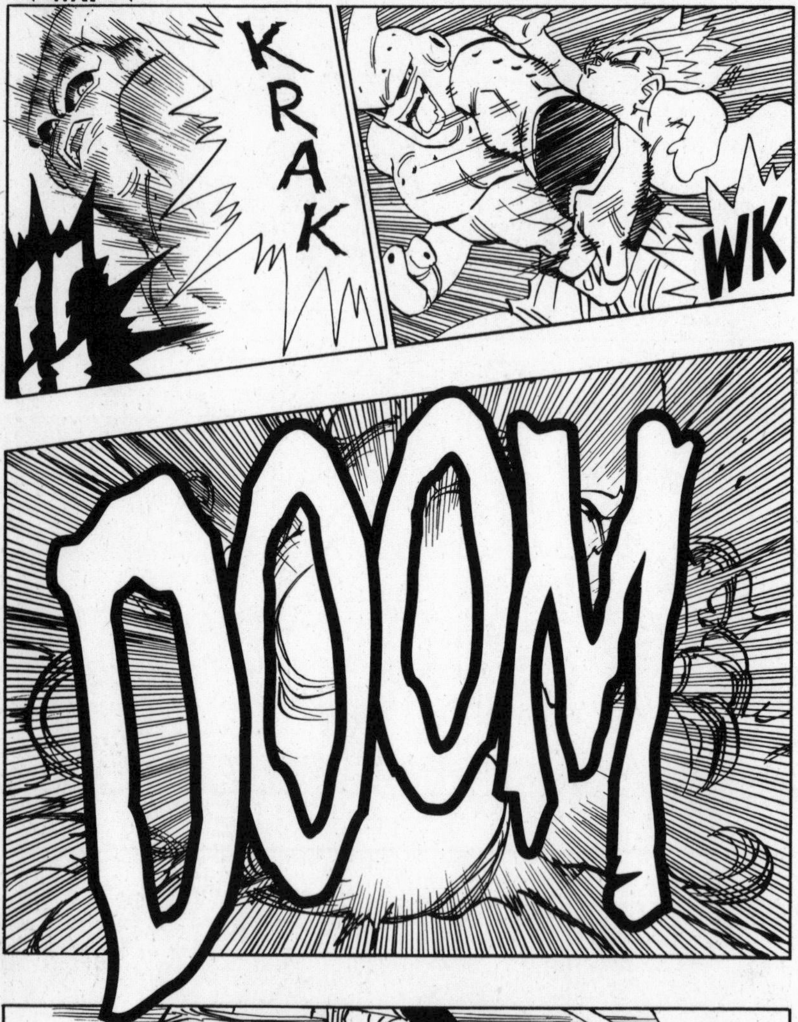
WK
KRAK
DOOM
AGH !!!!!

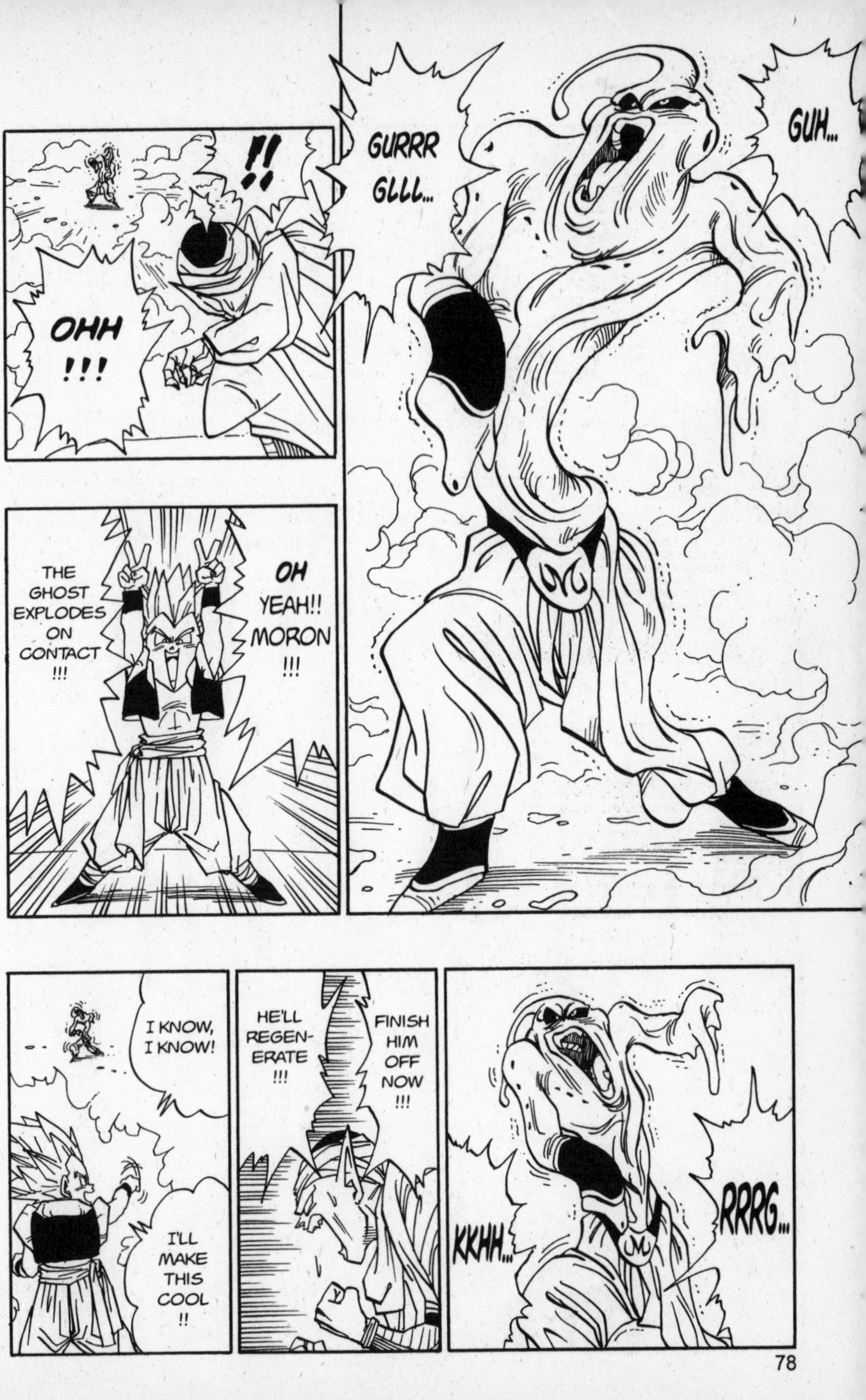
GUH...
GURRR GLLL...
!!
OHH !!!
OH YEAH!! MORON !!!
THE GHOST EXPLODES ON CONTACT !!!
RRRG...
KKHH...
FINISH HIM OFF NOW !!!
HE'LL REGEN-ERATE !!!
I KNOW, I KNOW!
I'LL MAKE THIS COOL !!

READ THIS WAY

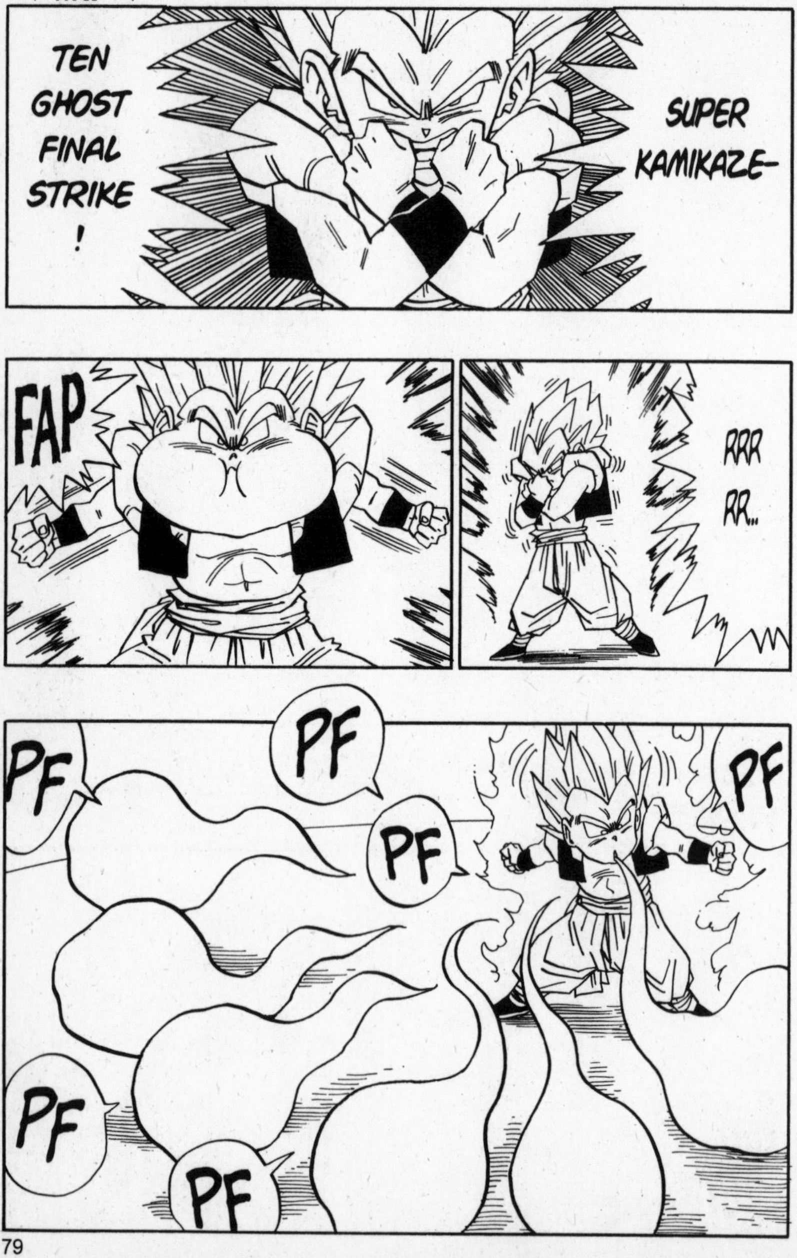

SUPER KAMIKAZE-
TEN GHOST FINAL STRIKE !
RRR RR...
FAP
PF
PF
PF
PF
PF
PF

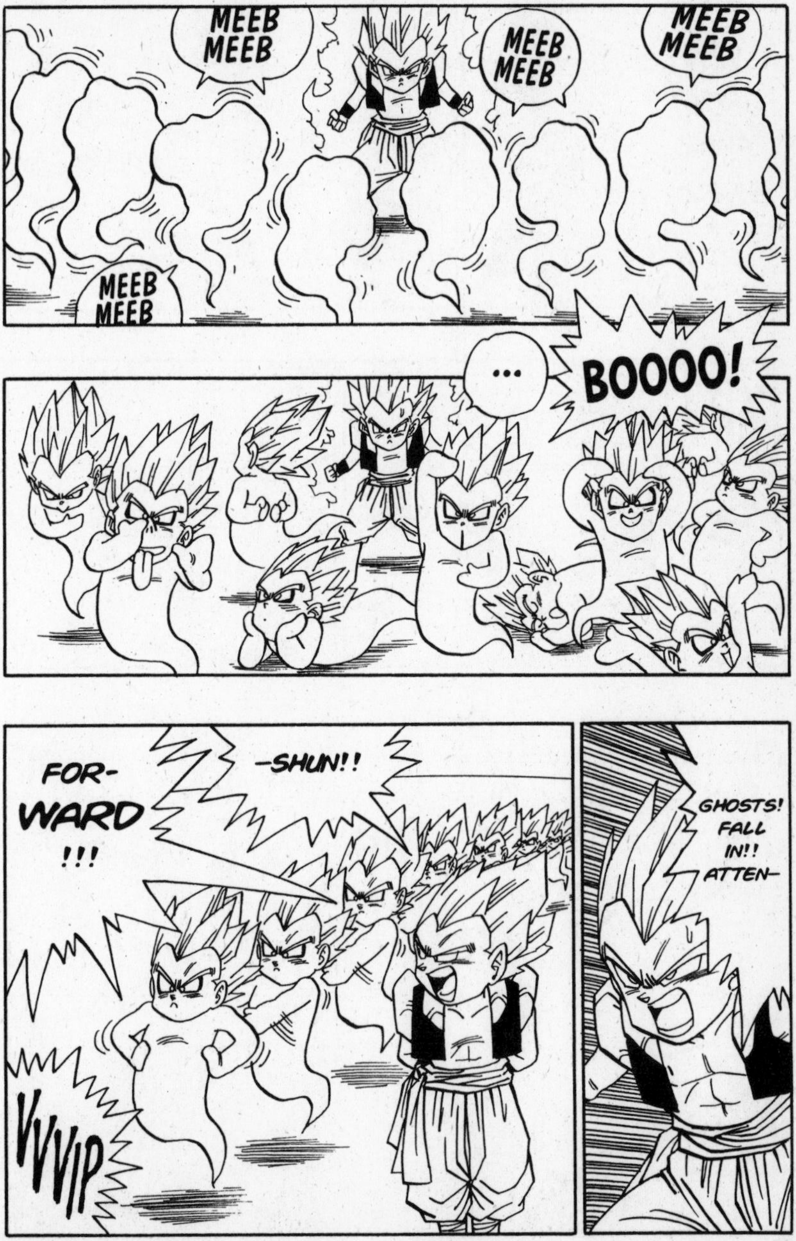
MEEB MEEB
MEEB MEEB
MEEB MEEB
MEEB MEEB
BOOOO!
...
GHOSTS! FALL IN!! ATTEN-
-SHUN!!
FOR-WARD!!!
VVVIP

READ THIS WAY

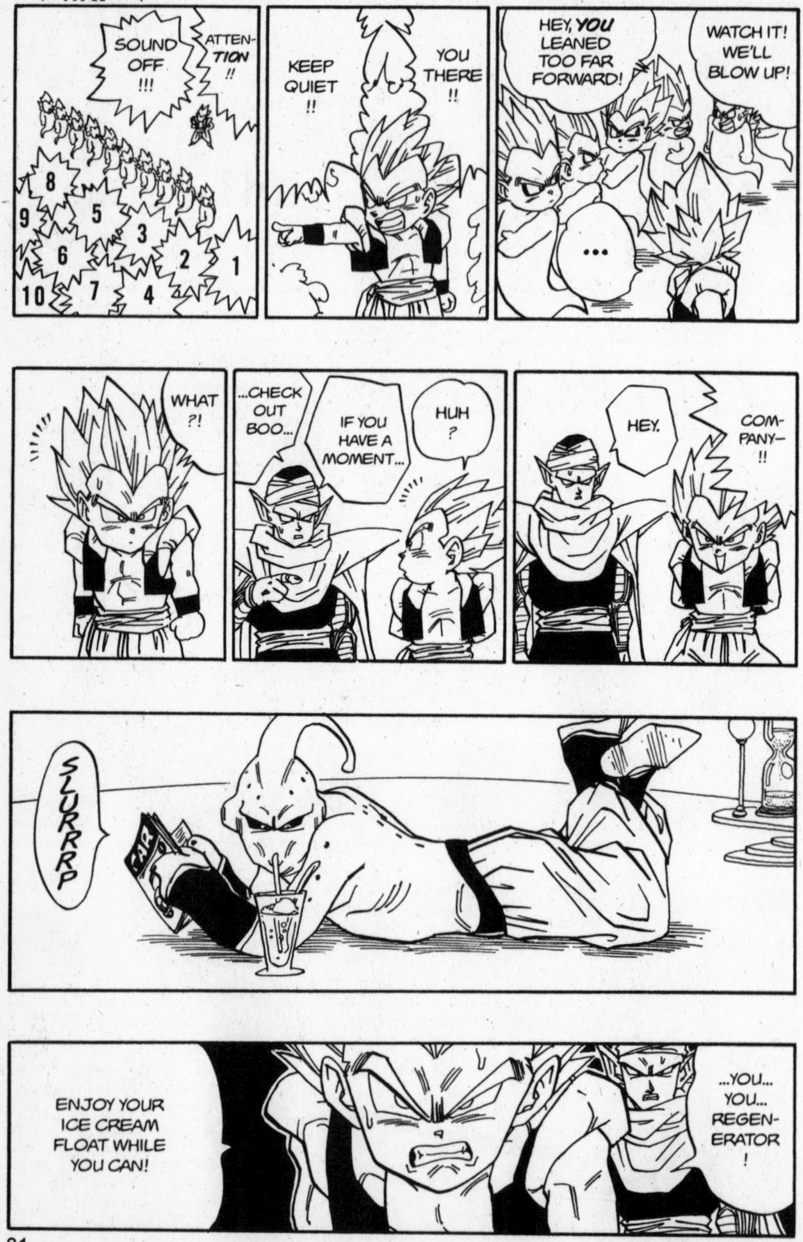
WATCH IT! WE'LL BLOW UP!
HEY, YOU LEANED TOO FAR FORWARD!
...
YOU THERE!!
KEEP QUIET!!
ATTEN-TION!!
SOUND OFF!!!
1
2
3
4
5
6
7
8
9
10
COM-PANY—!!
HEY.
HUH?
IF YOU HAVE A MOMENT...
...CHECK OUT BOO...
WHAT?!
SLURRRP
...YOU... YOU... REGEN-ERATOR!
ENJOY YOUR ICE CREAM FLOAT WHILE YOU CAN!

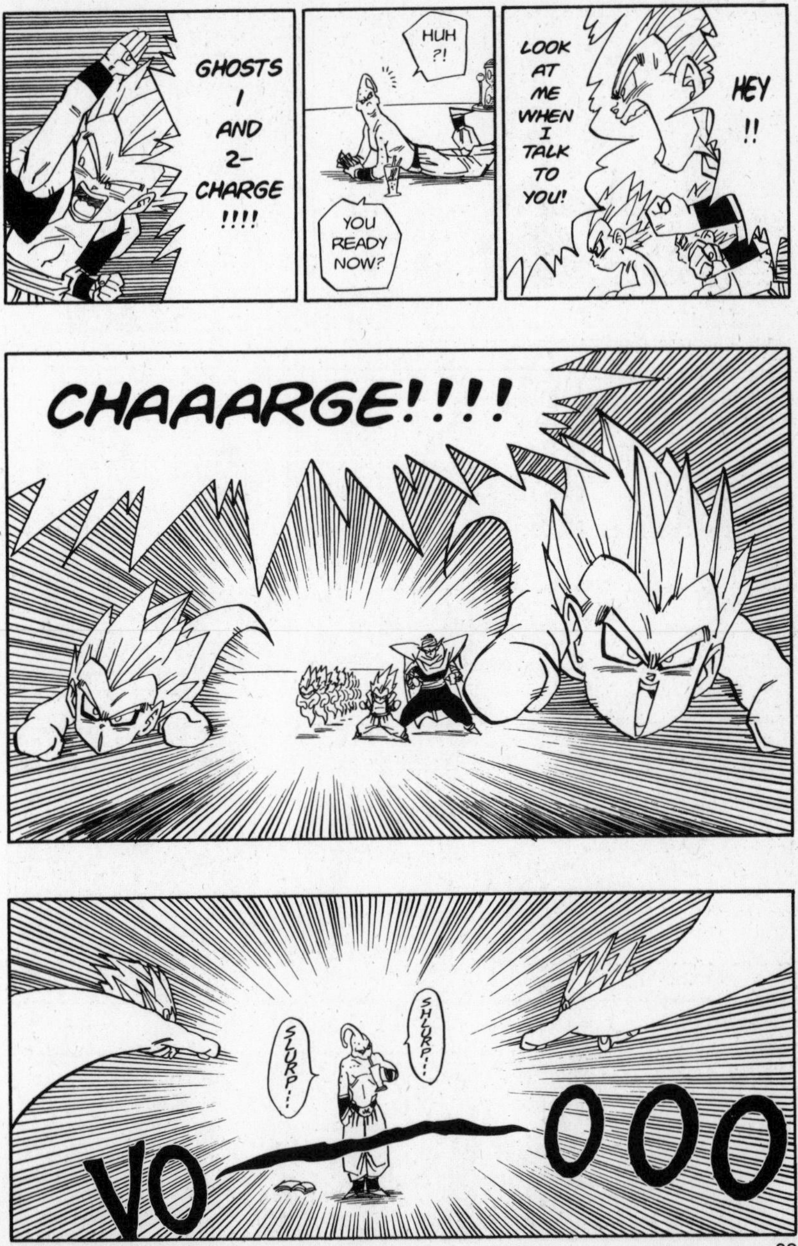
HEY!!
LOOK AT ME WHEN I TALK TO YOU!
HUH?!
YOU READY NOW?
GHOSTS 1 AND 2—CHARGE!!!!
CHAAARGE!!!!
SHLURP!!
SLURP!!
VOOOOO

READ THIS WAY

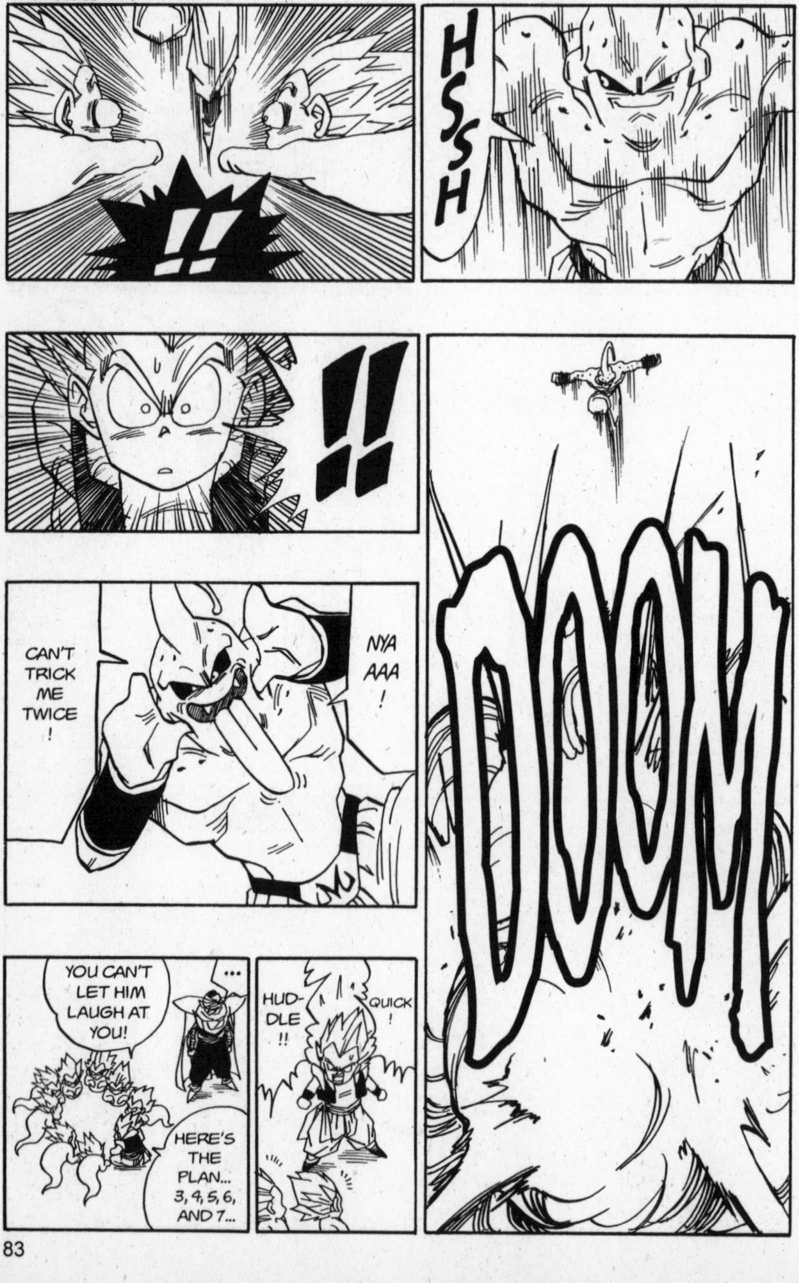
HSSH
!!
DOOM
!!
NYA AAA!
CAN'T TRICK ME TWICE!
QUICK!
HUD-DLE!!
...
YOU CAN'T LET HIM LAUGH AT YOU!
HERE'S THE PLAN... 3, 4, 5, 6, AND 7...

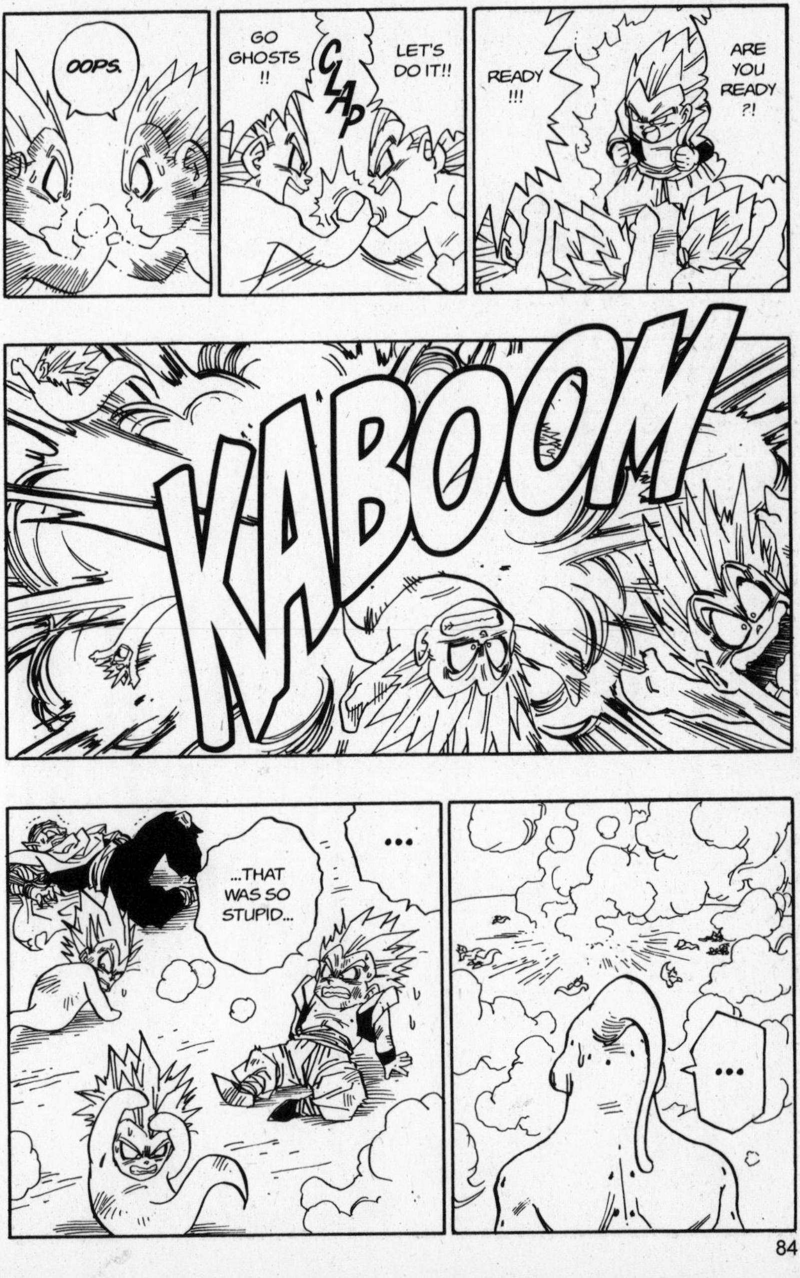
ARE YOU READY ?!
READY !!!
LET'S DO IT!!
CLAP
GO GHOSTS !!
OOPS.
KABOOM
...
...
...THAT WAS SO STUPID...

READ THIS WAY

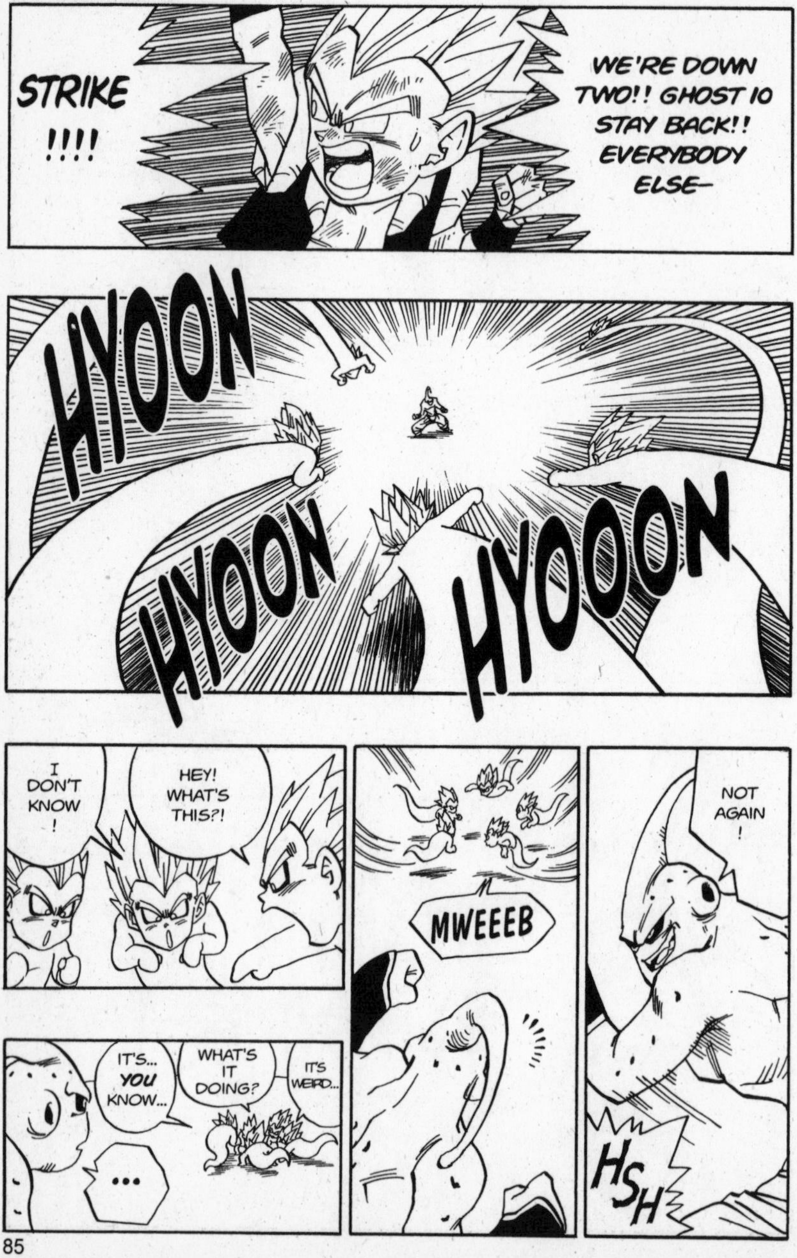

WE'RE DOWN TWO!! GHOST 10 STAY BACK!! EVERYBODY ELSE—
STRIKE !!!!
HYOOON
HYOON
HYOON
NOT AGAIN !
HSH
MWEEEB
HEY! WHAT'S THIS?!
I DON'T KNOW !
IT'S WEIRD...
WHAT'S IT DOING?
IT'S... YOU KNOW...
...

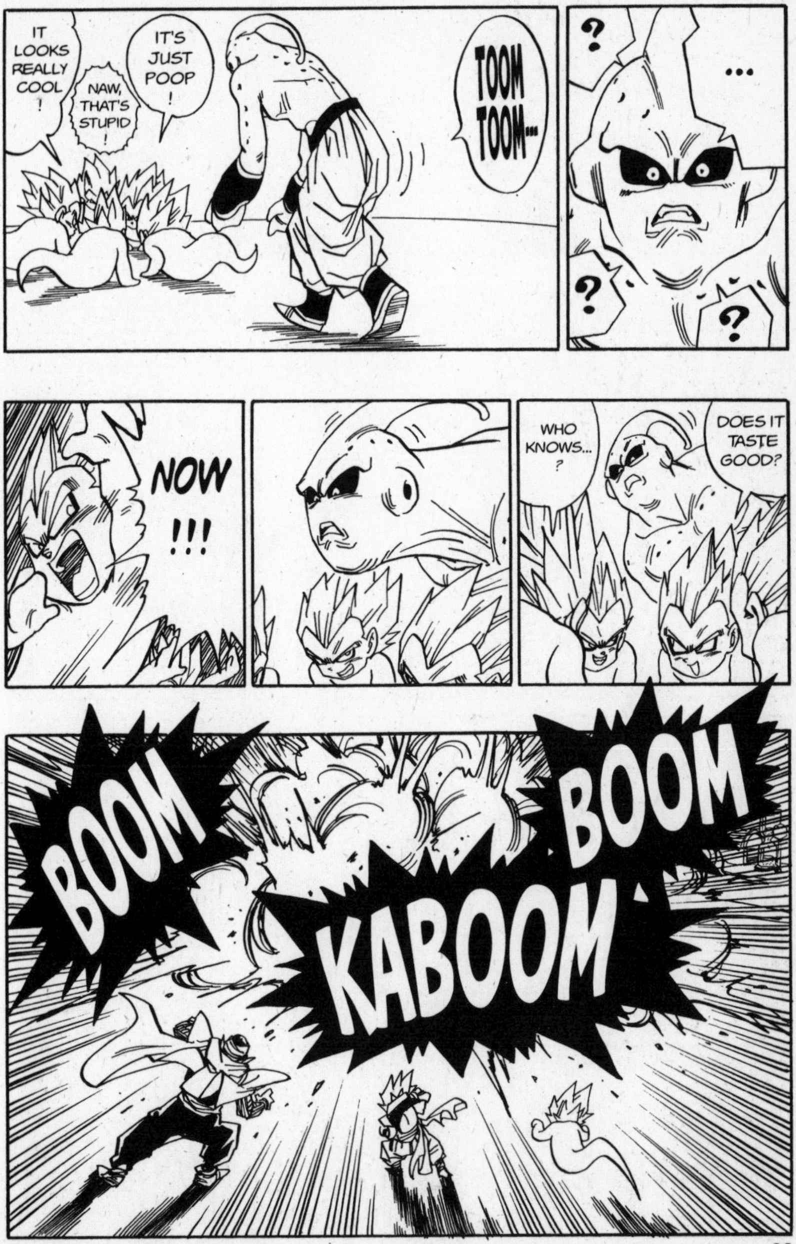

?
...
?
?
TOOM TOOM...
IT'S JUST POOP!
IT LOOKS REALLY COOL!
NAW, THAT'S STUPID!
DOES IT TASTE GOOD?
WHO KNOWS...?
NOW!!!
BOOM
KABOOM
BOOM

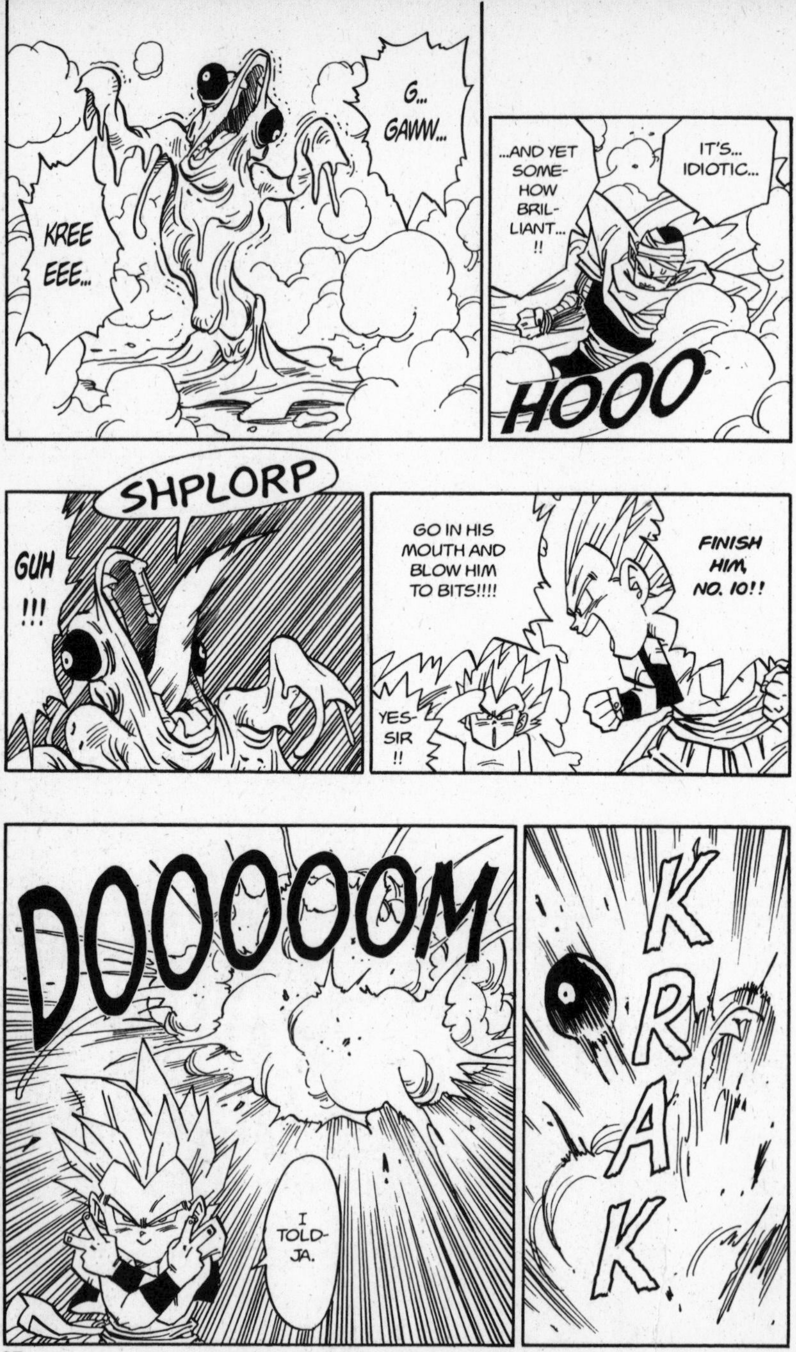
IT'S... IDIOTIC...
...AND YET SOME-HOW BRIL-LIANT... !!
HOOO
G... GAWW...
KREE EEE...
FINISH HIM, NO. 10!!
GO IN HIS MOUTH AND BLOW HIM TO BITS!!!!
YES-SIR !!
SHPLORP
GUH !!!
KRAK
DOOOOOOM
I TOLD-JA.

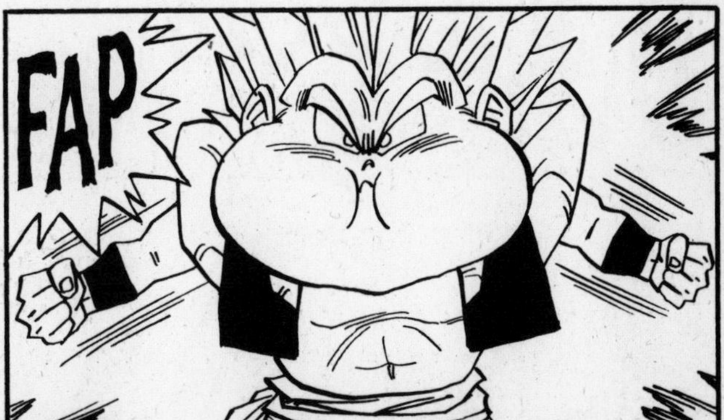
FAP

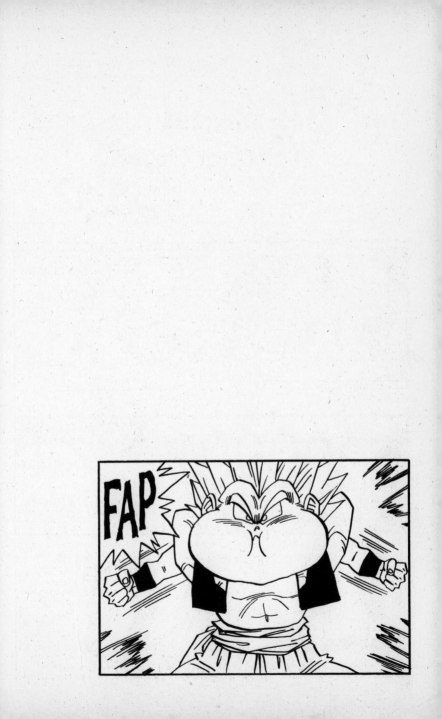

DBZ:298
The Door Closes

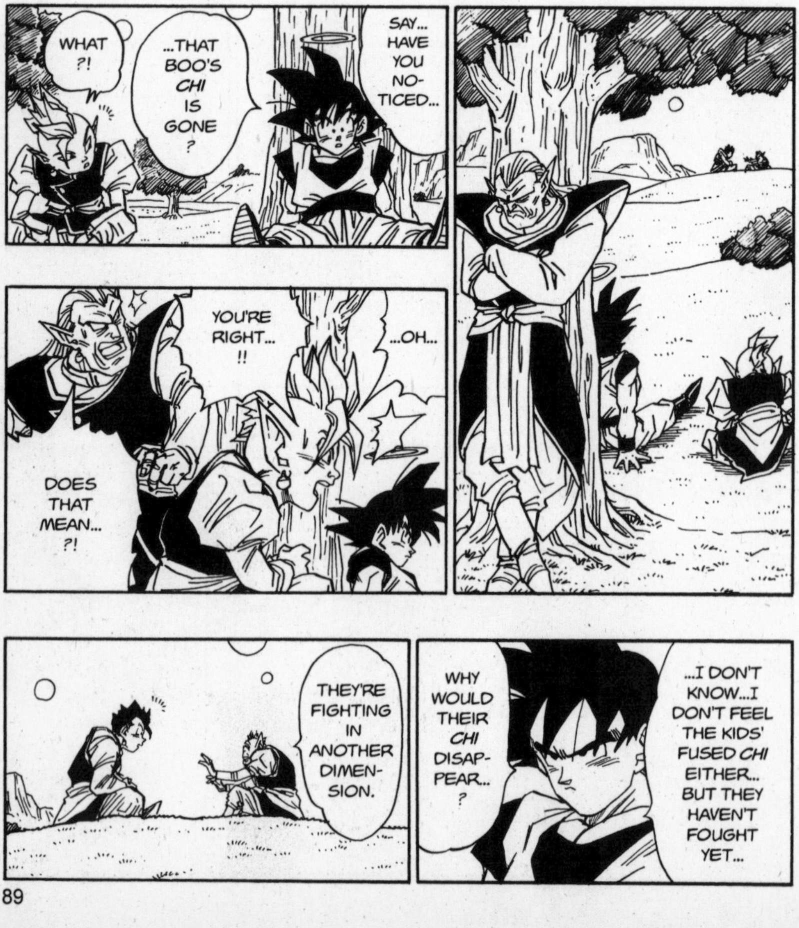

SAY... HAVE YOU NO-TICED...
...THAT BOO'S *CHI* IS GONE?
WHAT?!
...OH...
YOU'RE RIGHT...!!
DOES THAT MEAN...?!
...I DON'T KNOW...I DON'T FEEL THE KIDS' FUSED *CHI* EITHER... BUT THEY HAVEN'T FOUGHT YET...
WHY WOULD THEIR *CHI* DISAP-PEAR...?
THEY'RE FIGHTING IN ANOTHER DIMEN-SION.

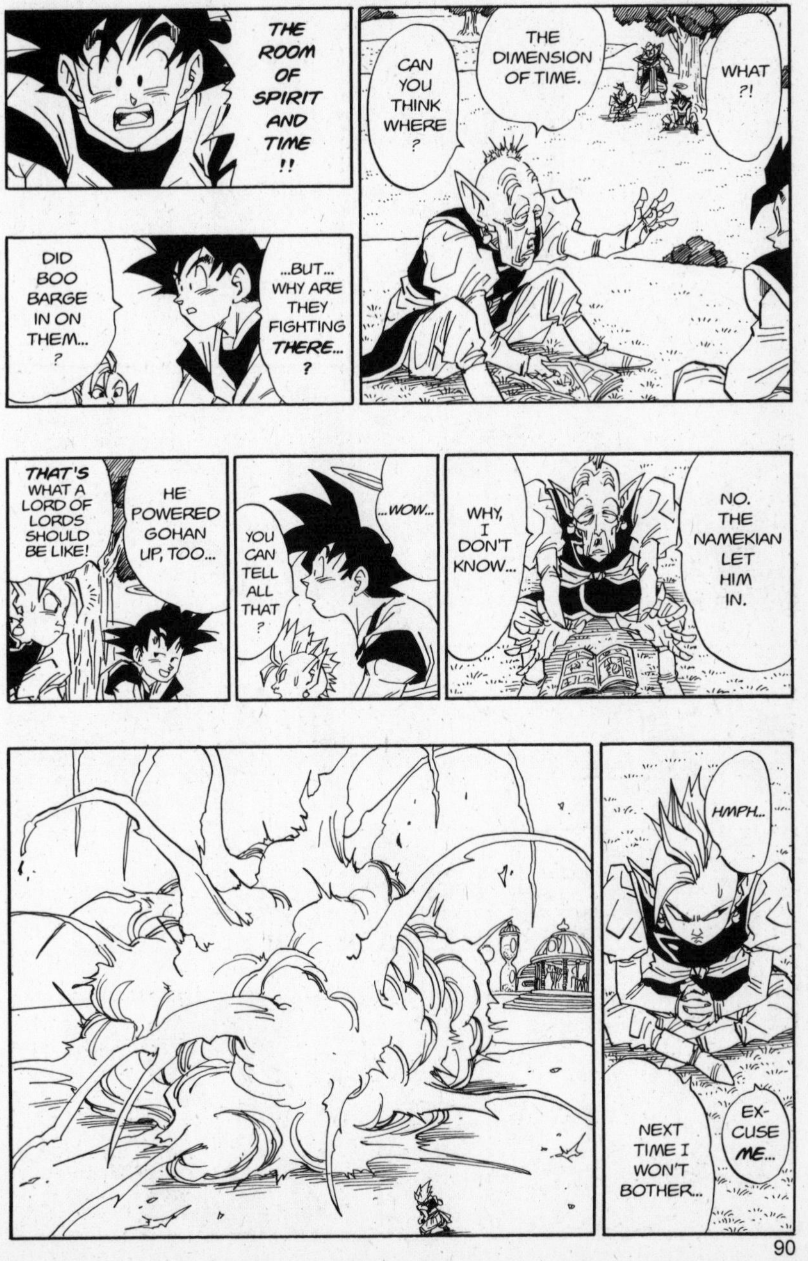
WHAT ?!
THE DIMENSION OF TIME.
CAN YOU THINK WHERE ?
THE ROOM OF SPIRIT AND TIME !!
...BUT... WHY ARE THEY FIGHTING THERE... ?
DID BOO BARGE IN ON THEM... ?
NO. THE NAMEKIAN LET HIM IN.
WHY, I DON'T KNOW...
...WOW...
YOU CAN TELL ALL THAT ?
HE POWERED GOHAN UP, TOO...
THAT'S WHAT A LORD OF LORDS SHOULD BE LIKE!
HMPH...
EX-CUSE ME...
NEXT TIME I WON'T BOTHER...

READ THIS WAY

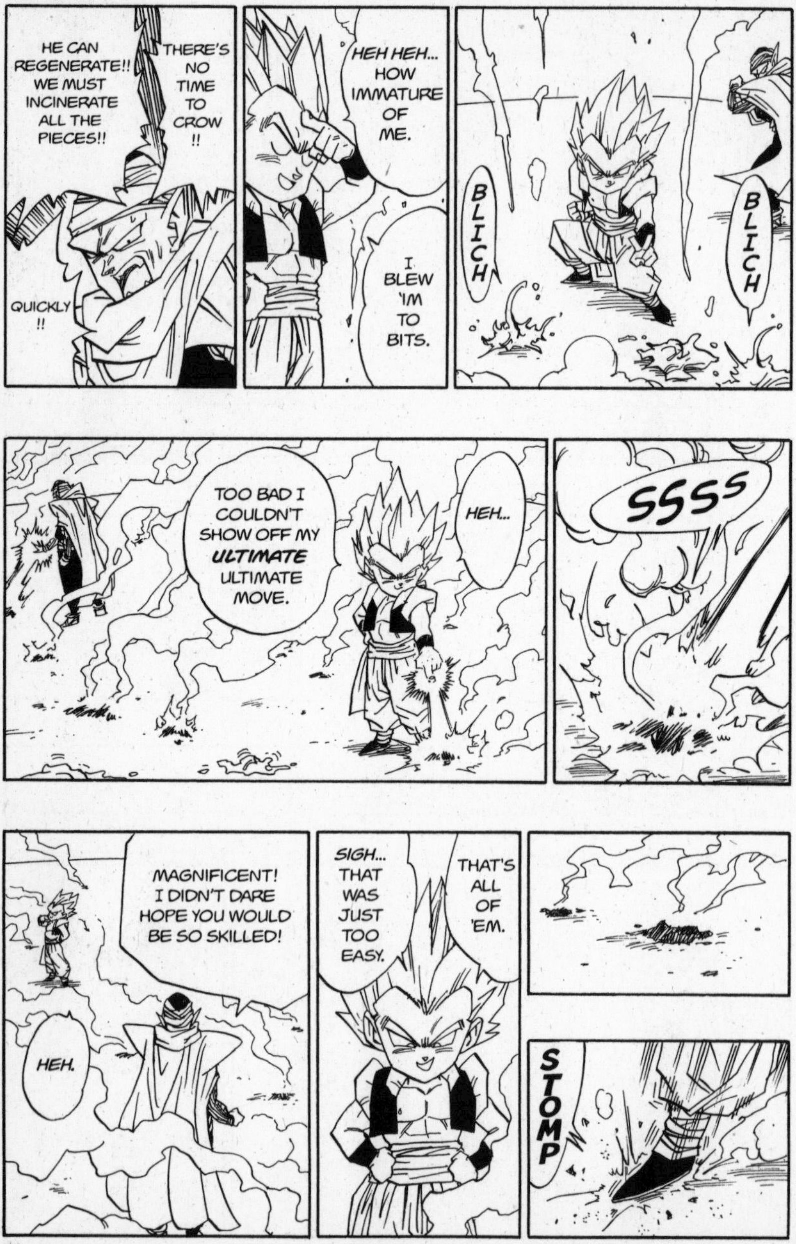

BLICH
BLICH
HEH HEH... HOW IMMATURE OF ME.
I BLEW 'IM TO BITS.
THERE'S NO TIME TO CROW!!
HE CAN REGENERATE!! WE MUST INCINERATE ALL THE PIECES!!
QUICKLY!!
SSSS
HEH...
TOO BAD I COULDN'T SHOW OFF MY ULTIMATE ULTIMATE MOVE.
STOMP
THAT'S ALL OF 'EM.
SIGH... THAT WAS JUST TOO EASY.
MAGNIFICENT! I DIDN'T DARE HOPE YOU WOULD BE SO SKILLED!
HEH.

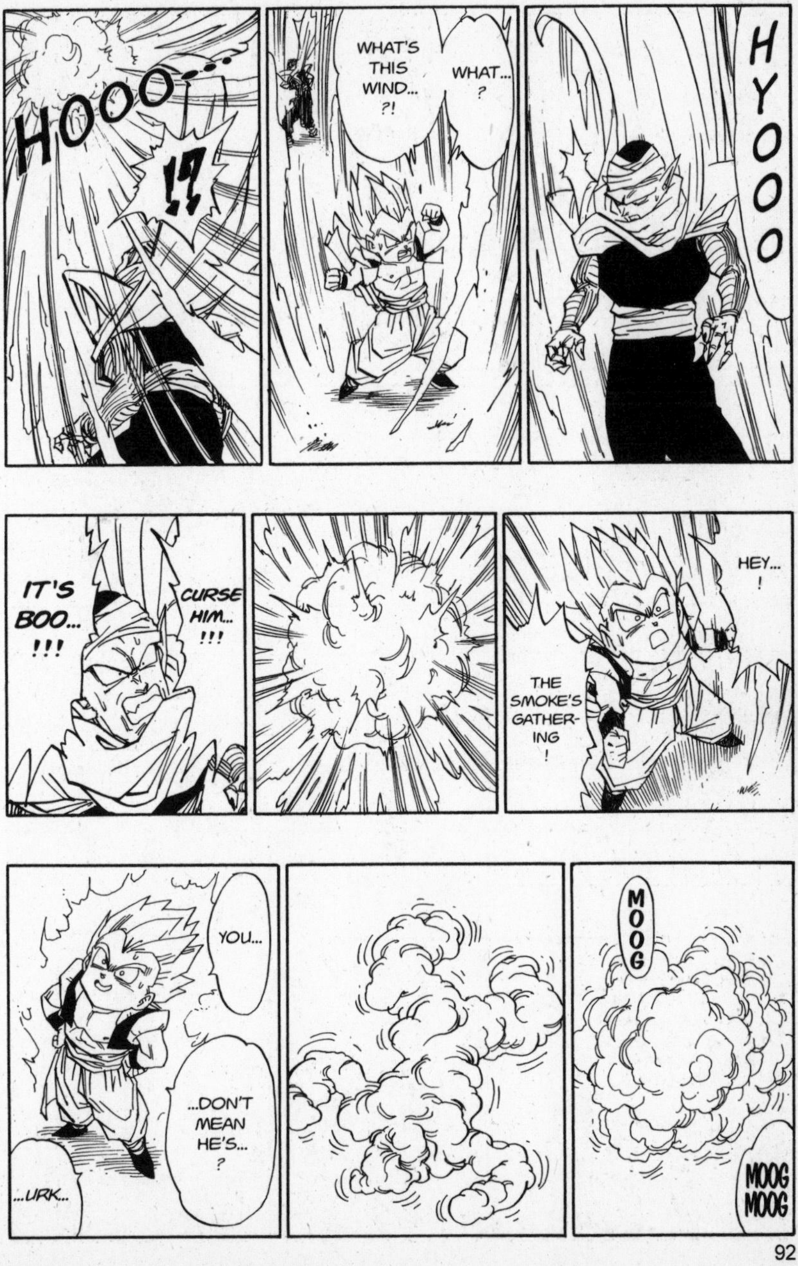
HYOOO
WHAT...?
WHAT'S THIS WIND...?!
HOOO...
!?
HEY...!
THE SMOKE'S GATHERING!
CURSE HIM...!!!
IT'S BOO...!!!
MOOG
MOOG MOOG
YOU...
...DON'T MEAN HE'S...?
...URK...

READ THIS WAY

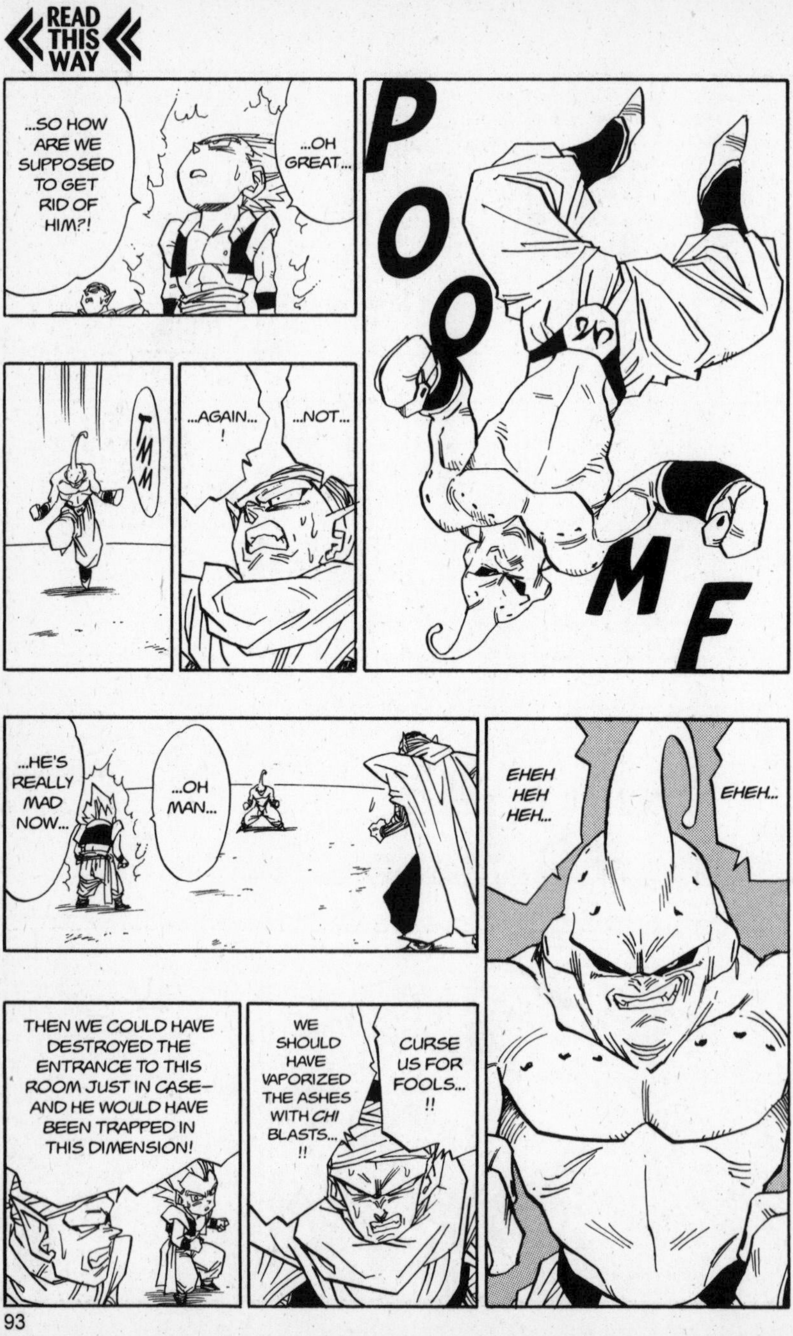

POOMF
...OH GREAT...
...SO HOW ARE WE SUPPOSED TO GET RID OF HIM?!
...NOT...
...AGAIN... !
TMM
EHEH...
EHEH HEH HEH...
...OH MAN...
...HE'S REALLY MAD NOW...
CURSE US FOR FOOLS... !!
WE SHOULD HAVE VAPORIZED THE ASHES WITH *CHI* BLASTS... !!
THEN WE COULD HAVE DESTROYED THE ENTRANCE TO THIS ROOM JUST IN CASE— AND HE WOULD HAVE BEEN TRAPPED IN THIS DIMENSION!

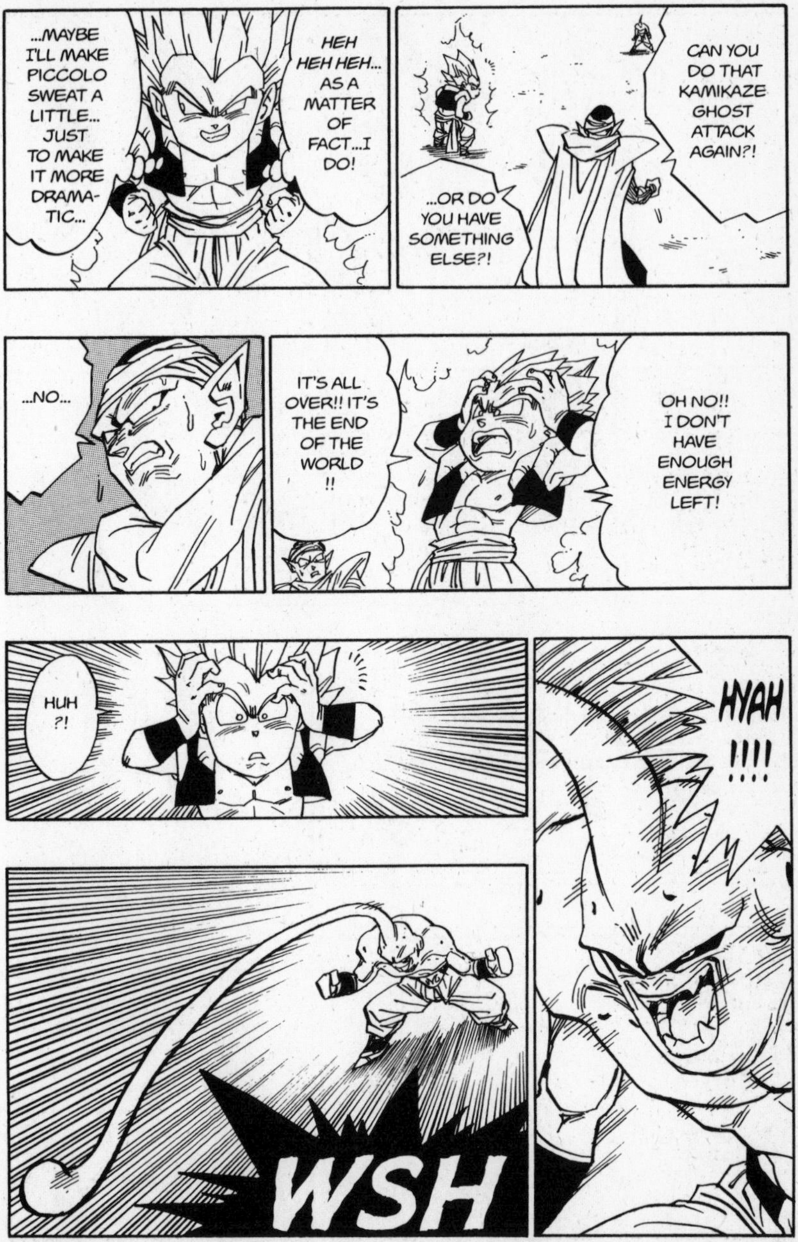
CAN YOU DO THAT KAMIKAZE GHOST ATTACK AGAIN?!
...OR DO YOU HAVE SOMETHING ELSE?!
HEH HEH HEH... AS A MATTER OF FACT...I DO!
...MAYBE I'LL MAKE PICCOLO SWEAT A LITTLE... JUST TO MAKE IT MORE DRAMA-TIC...
OH NO!! I DON'T HAVE ENOUGH ENERGY LEFT!
IT'S ALL OVER!! IT'S THE END OF THE WORLD !!
...NO...
HYAH !!!!
HUH ?!
WSH

READ THIS WAY

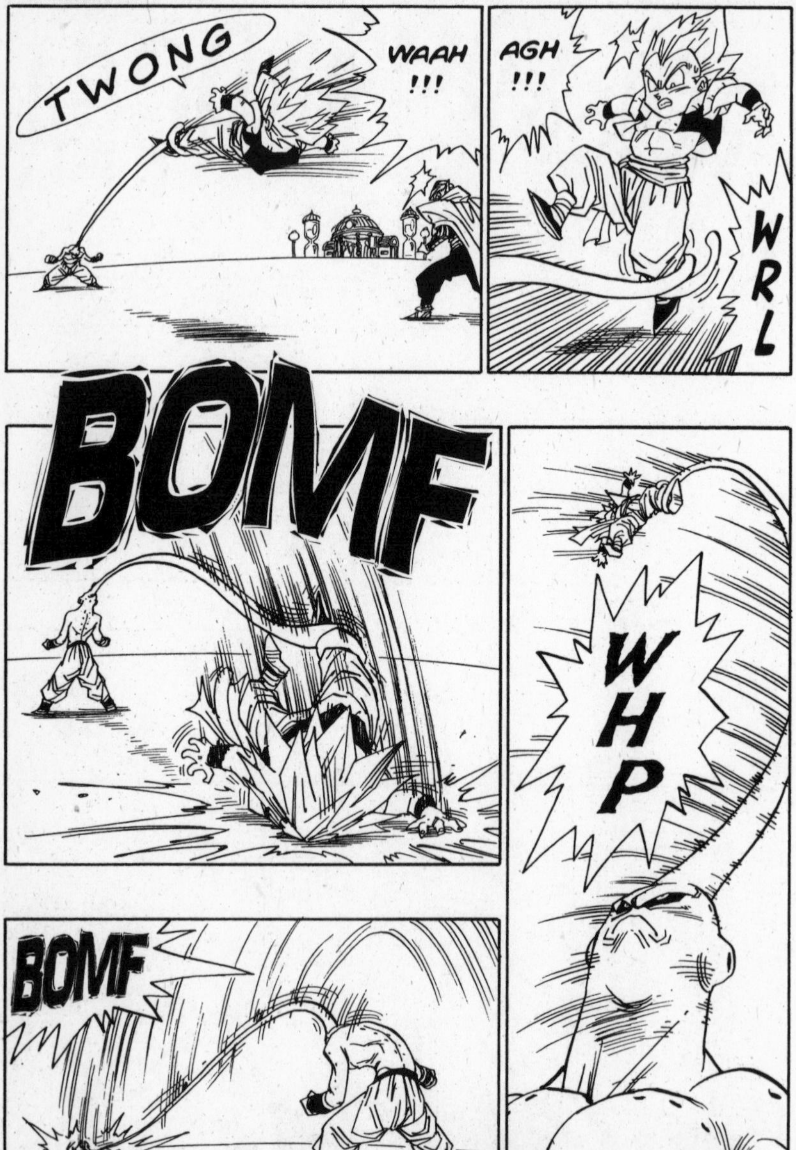
AGH !!!
WRL
TWONG
WAAH !!!
WHP
BOMF
BOMF

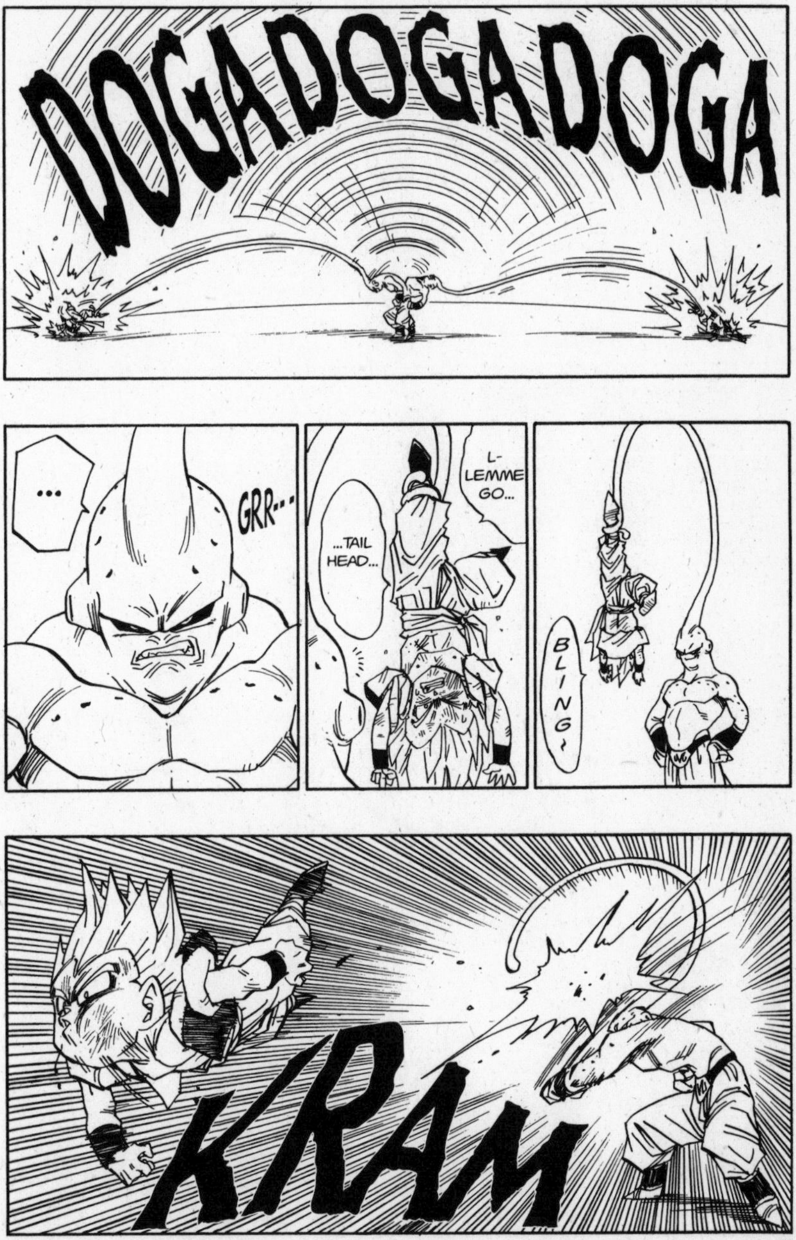
DOGADOGADOGA
BLING
L-LEMME GO...
...TAIL HEAD...
GRR...
...
KRAM

READ THIS WAY

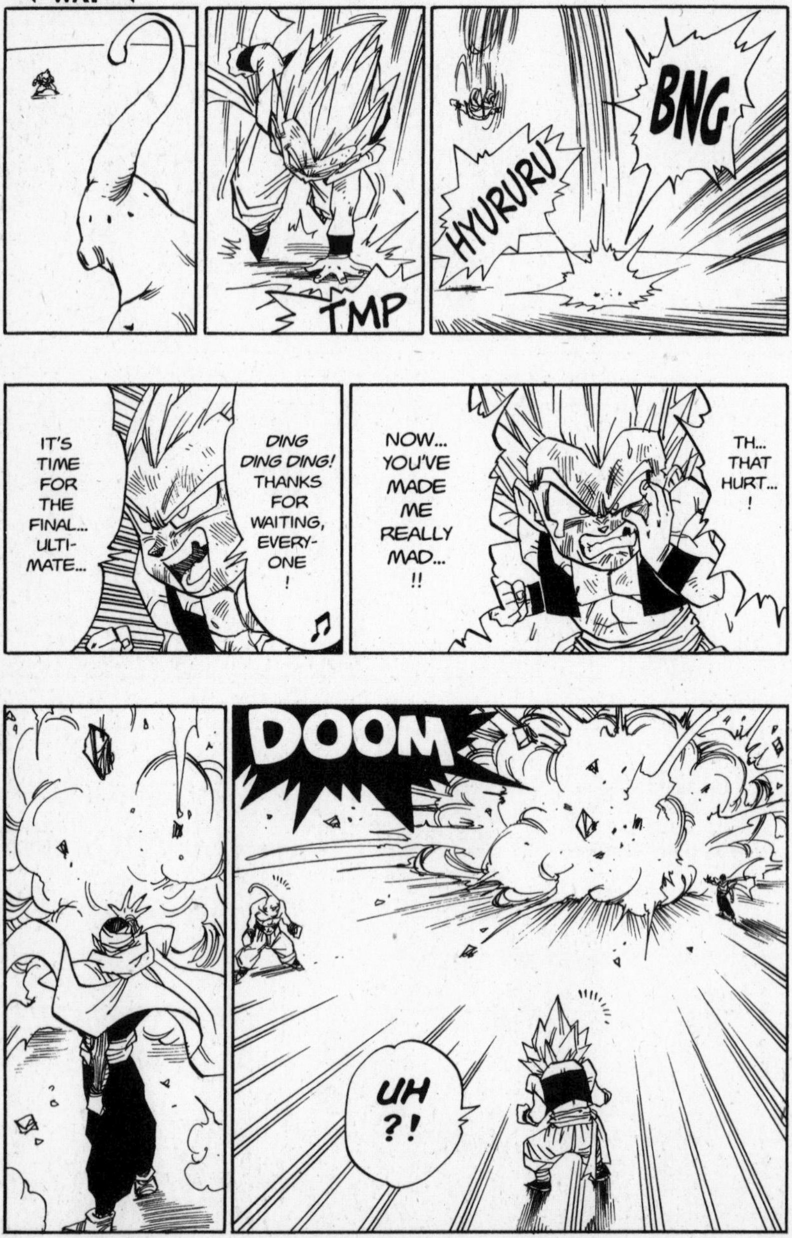
BNG
HYURURU
TMP
TH... THAT HURT...!
NOW... YOU'VE MADE ME REALLY MAD...!!
DING DING DING! THANKS FOR WAITING, EVERYONE! ♪
IT'S TIME FOR THE FINAL... ULTIMATE...
DOOM
UH?!

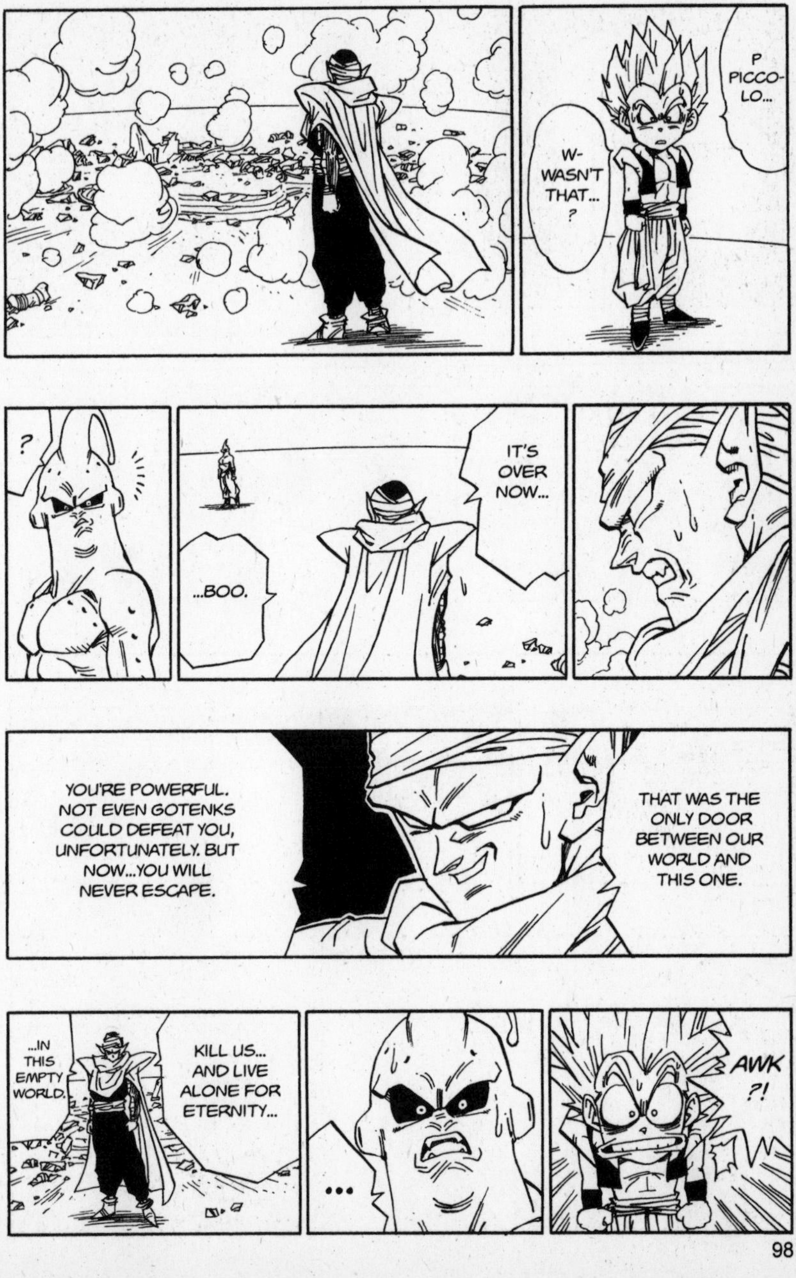
P PICCOLO...
W- WASN'T THAT... ?
IT'S OVER NOW...
...BOO.
?
THAT WAS THE ONLY DOOR BETWEEN OUR WORLD AND THIS ONE.
YOU'RE POWERFUL. NOT EVEN GOTENKS COULD DEFEAT YOU, UNFORTUNATELY. BUT NOW...YOU WILL NEVER ESCAPE.
AWK ?!
...
KILL US... AND LIVE ALONE FOR ETERNITY...
...IN THIS EMPTY WORLD.

READ THIS WAY

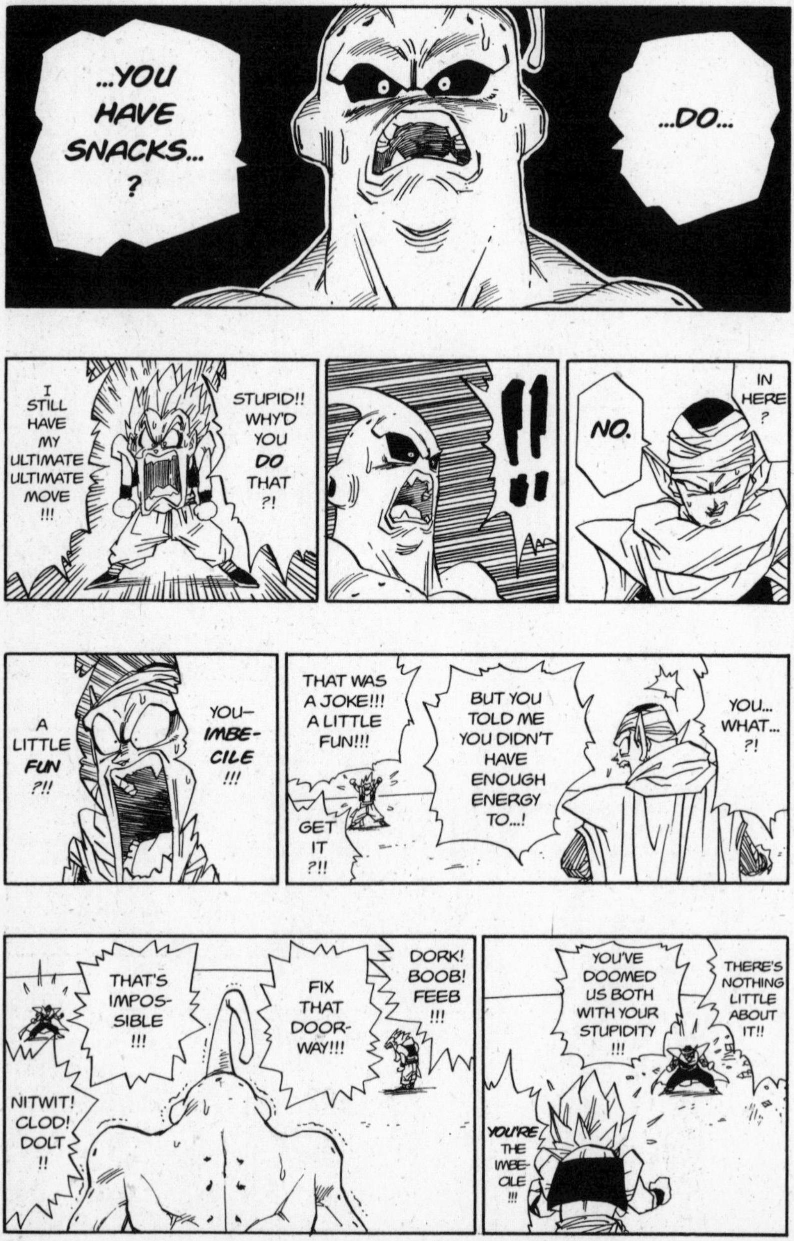

...DO...
...YOU HAVE SNACKS...?
IN HERE?
NO.
!!
STUPID!! WHY'D YOU DO THAT?!
I STILL HAVE MY ULTIMATE ULTIMATE MOVE!!!
YOU... WHAT...?!
BUT YOU TOLD ME YOU DIDN'T HAVE ENOUGH ENERGY TO...!
THAT WAS A JOKE!!! A LITTLE FUN!!!
GET IT?!!
YOU— IMBECILE!!!
A LITTLE FUN?!!
THERE'S NOTHING LITTLE ABOUT IT!!
YOU'VE DOOMED US BOTH WITH YOUR STUPIDITY!!!
YOU'RE THE IMBECILE!!!
DORK! BOOB! FEEB!!!
FIX THAT DOORWAY!!!
THAT'S IMPOSSIBLE!!!
NITWIT! CLOD! DOLT!!

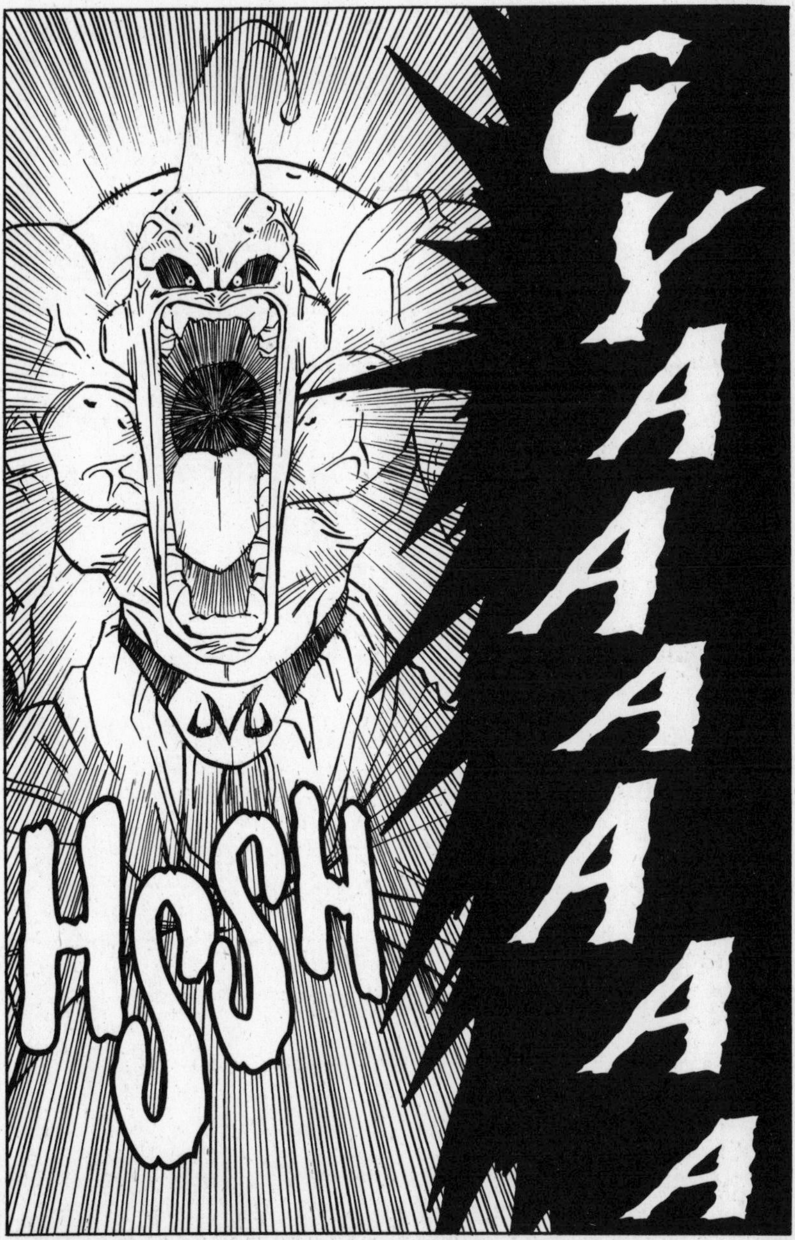
GYAAAAAAAA
HSSH

READ THIS WAY

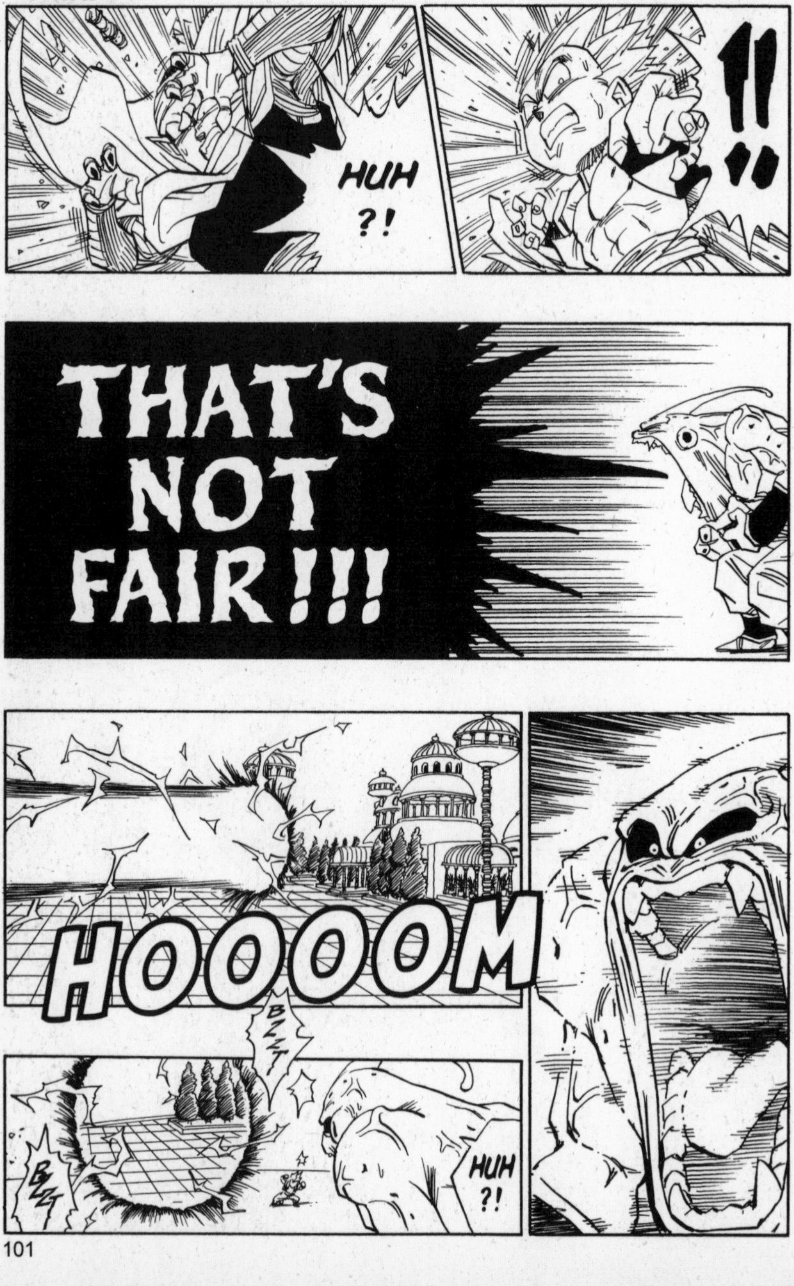

!!
HUH ?!
THAT'S NOT FAIR!!!
HOOOOM
BZZZT
BZZT
HUH ?!

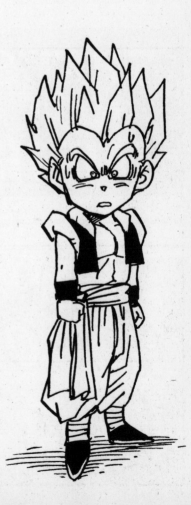

DBZ:299

Escape from the Time Dimension

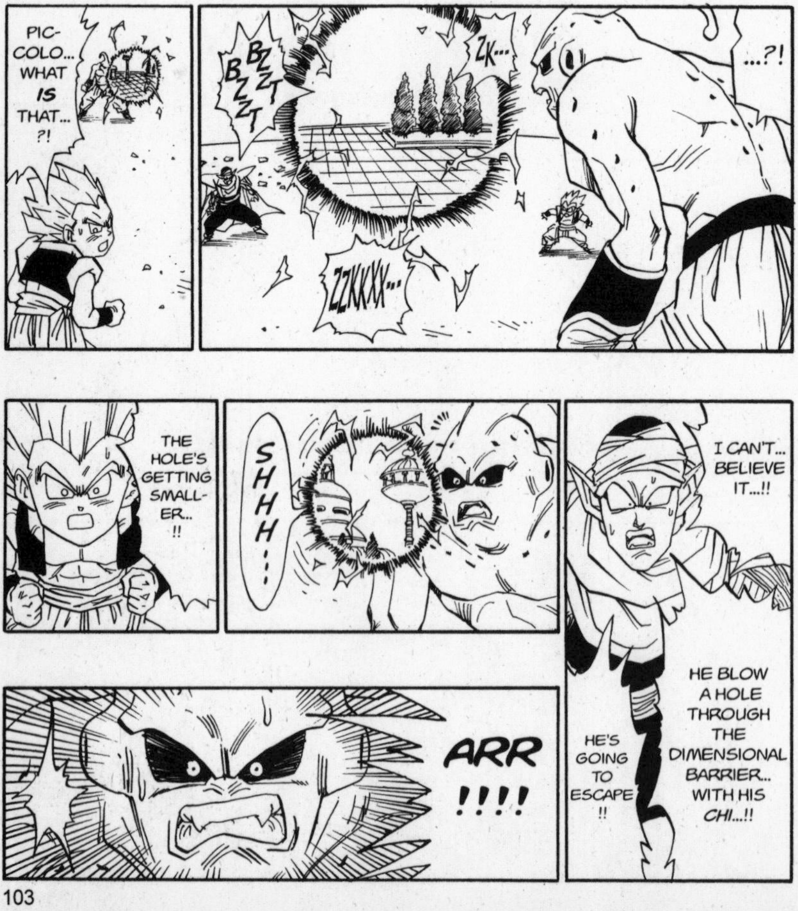
ZK...
...?!
BZZT BZZT
ZZKKXX...
PIC-COLO... WHAT *IS* THAT...?!
I CAN'T... BELIEVE IT...!!
HE BLOW A HOLE THROUGH THE DIMENSIONAL BARRIER... WITH HIS *CHI*...!!
HE'S GOING TO ESCAPE!!
SHHH...
THE HOLE'S GETTING SMALLER...!!
ARR!!!!

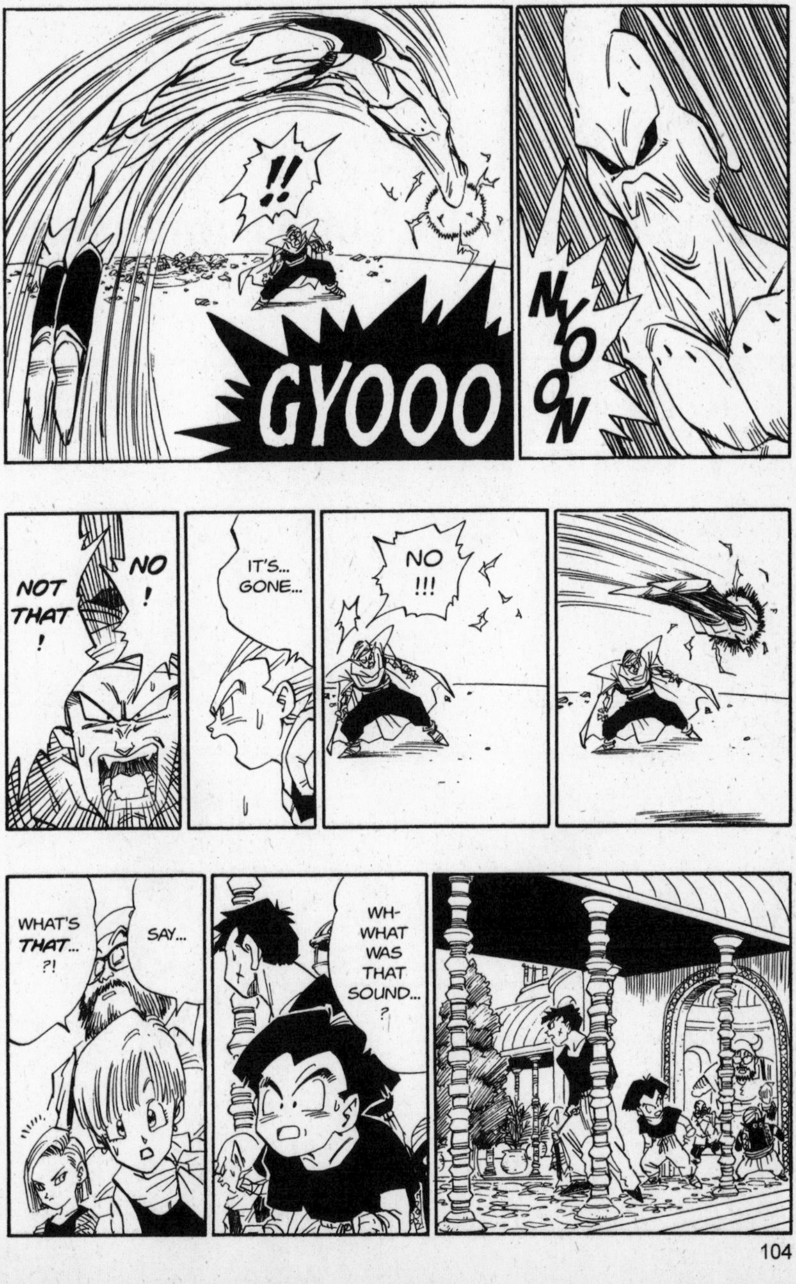
NYOON
!!
GYOOO
NO !!!
IT'S... GONE...
NO !
NOT THAT !
WH- WHAT WAS THAT SOUND... ?
SAY...
WHAT'S THAT... ?!

READ THIS WAY

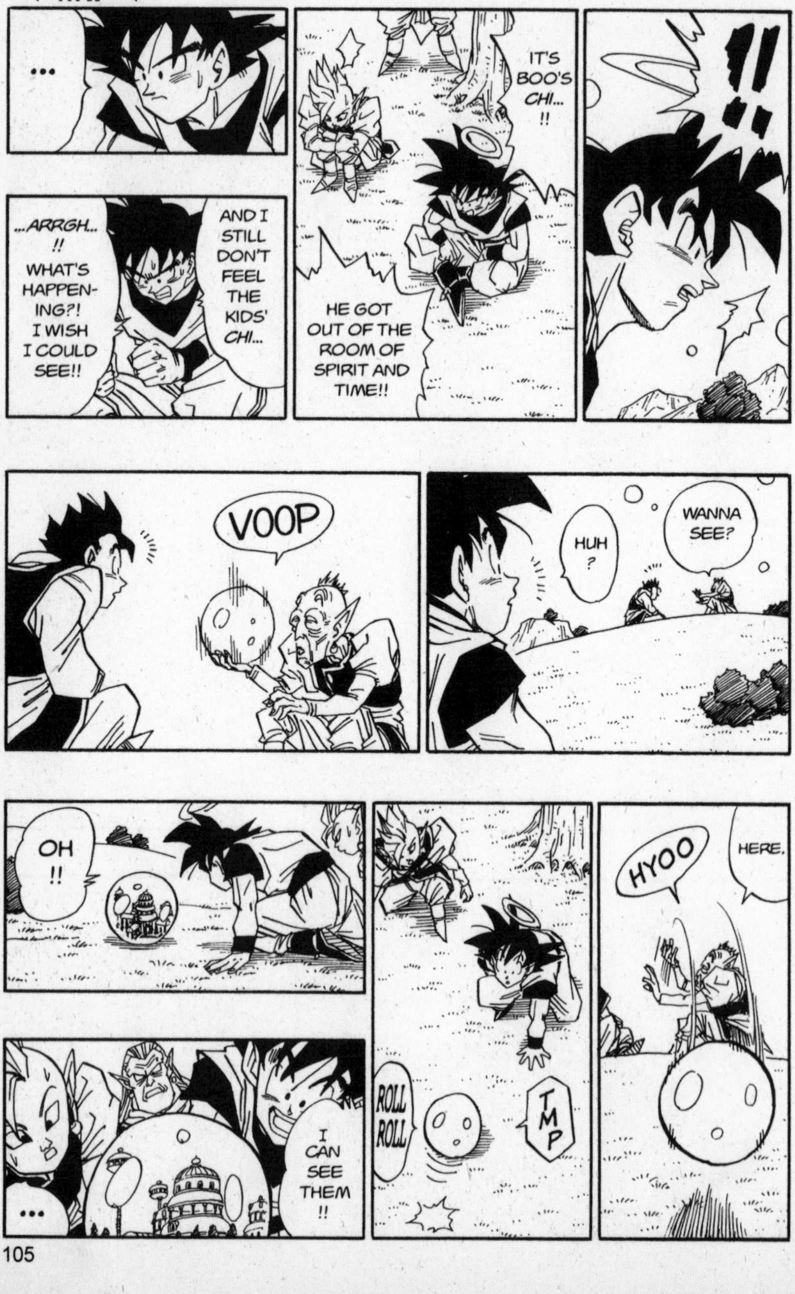
!!
IT'S BOO'S CHI... !!
HE GOT OUT OF THE ROOM OF SPIRIT AND TIME!!
...
AND I STILL DON'T FEEL THE KIDS' CHI...
...ARRGH... !! WHAT'S HAPPENING?! I WISH I COULD SEE!!
WANNA SEE?
HUH?
VOOP
HERE.
HYOO
TMP
ROLL ROLL
OH !!
I CAN SEE THEM !!
...

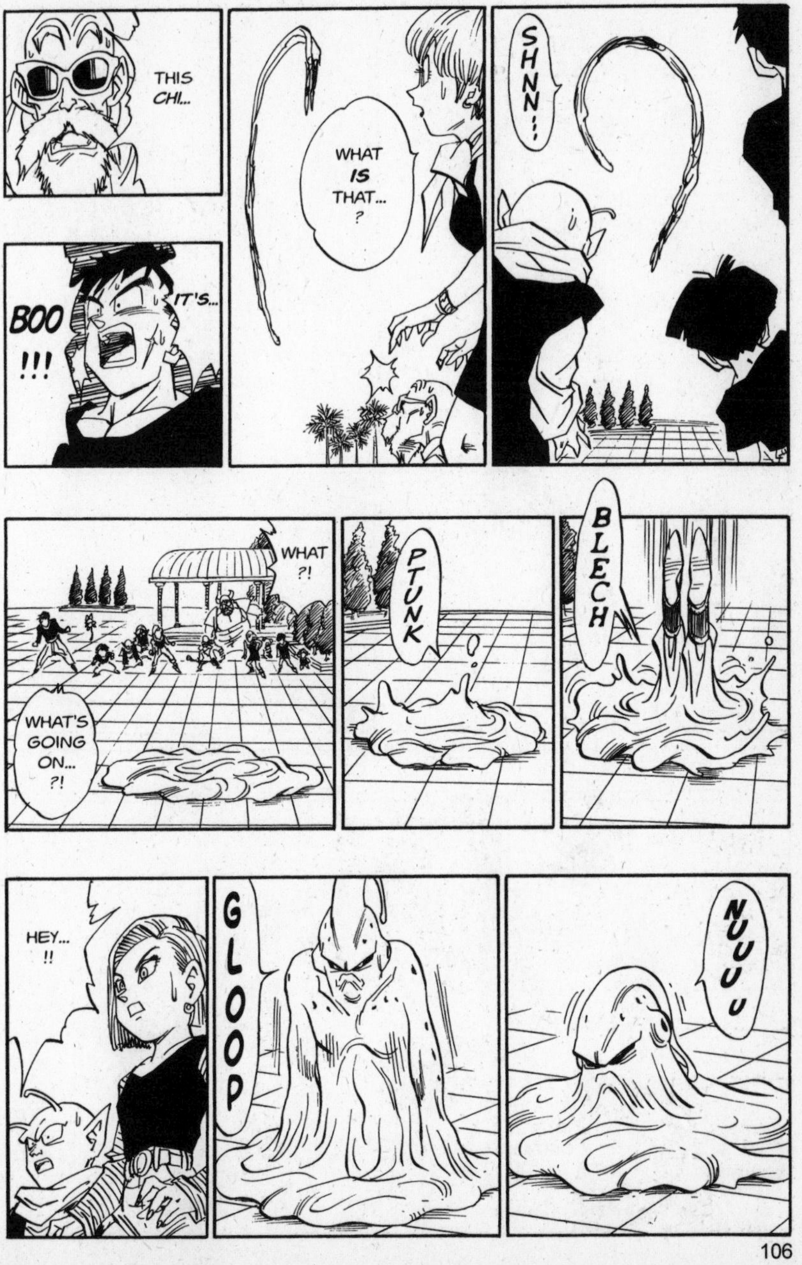
SHNN...
WHAT IS THAT...?
THIS CHI...
IT'S...
BOO!!!
BLECH
PTUNK
WHAT?!
WHAT'S GOING ON...?!
NUUUU
GLOOP
HEY...!!

READ THIS WAY

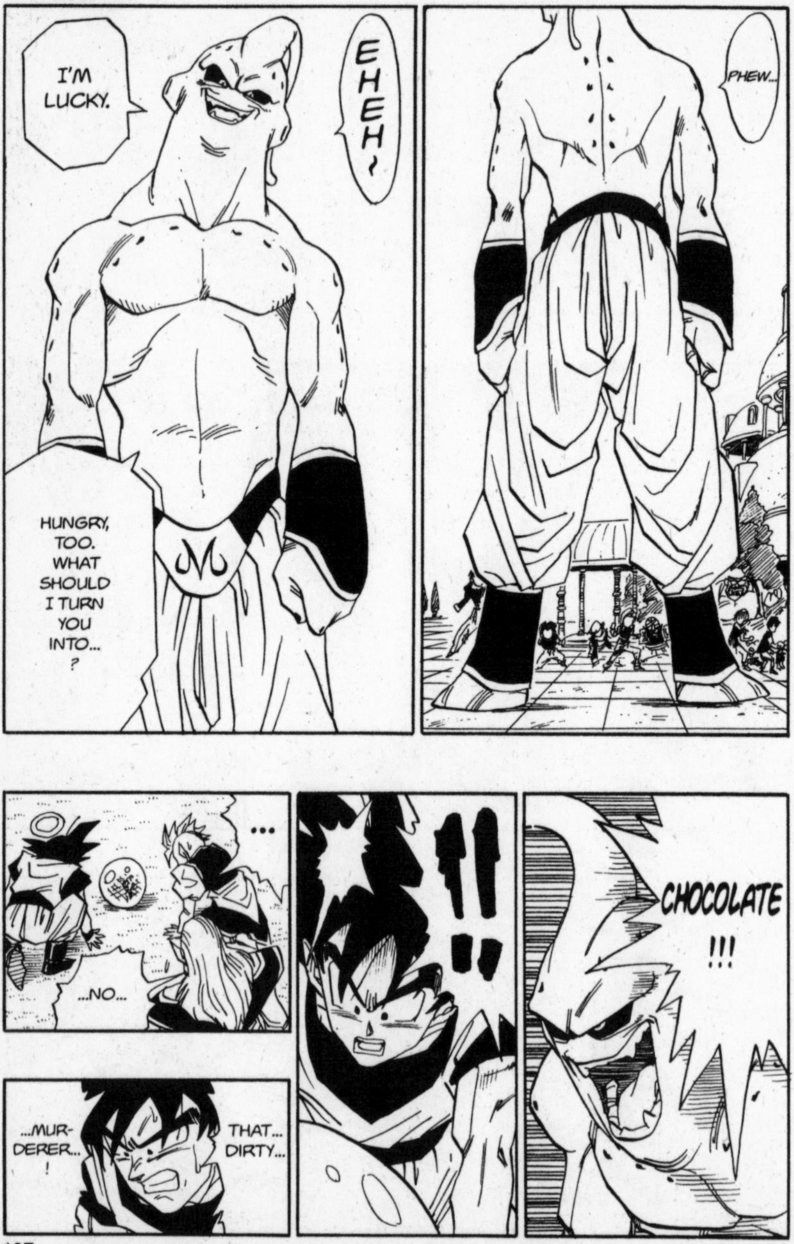
PHEW...
EHEH~
I'M LUCKY.
HUNGRY, TOO. WHAT SHOULD I TURN YOU INTO...?
CHOCOLATE!!!
!!
!!
...
...NO...
THAT... DIRTY...
...MURDERER...!

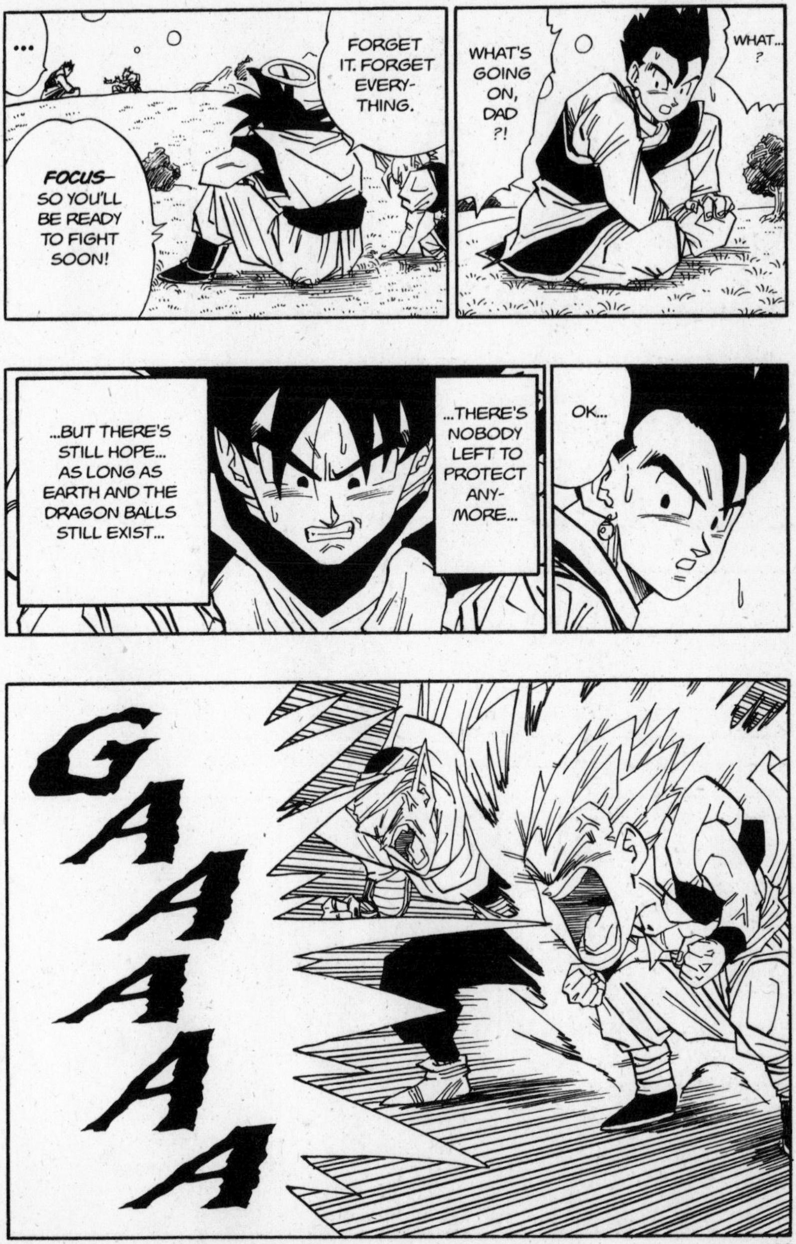
WHAT... ?
WHAT'S GOING ON, DAD ?!
FORGET IT. FORGET EVERY-THING.
...
FOCUS— SO YOU'LL BE READY TO FIGHT SOON!
OK...
...THERE'S NOBODY LEFT TO PROTECT ANY-MORE...
...BUT THERE'S STILL HOPE... AS LONG AS EARTH AND THE DRAGON BALLS STILL EXIST...
GAAAAA

READ THIS WAY

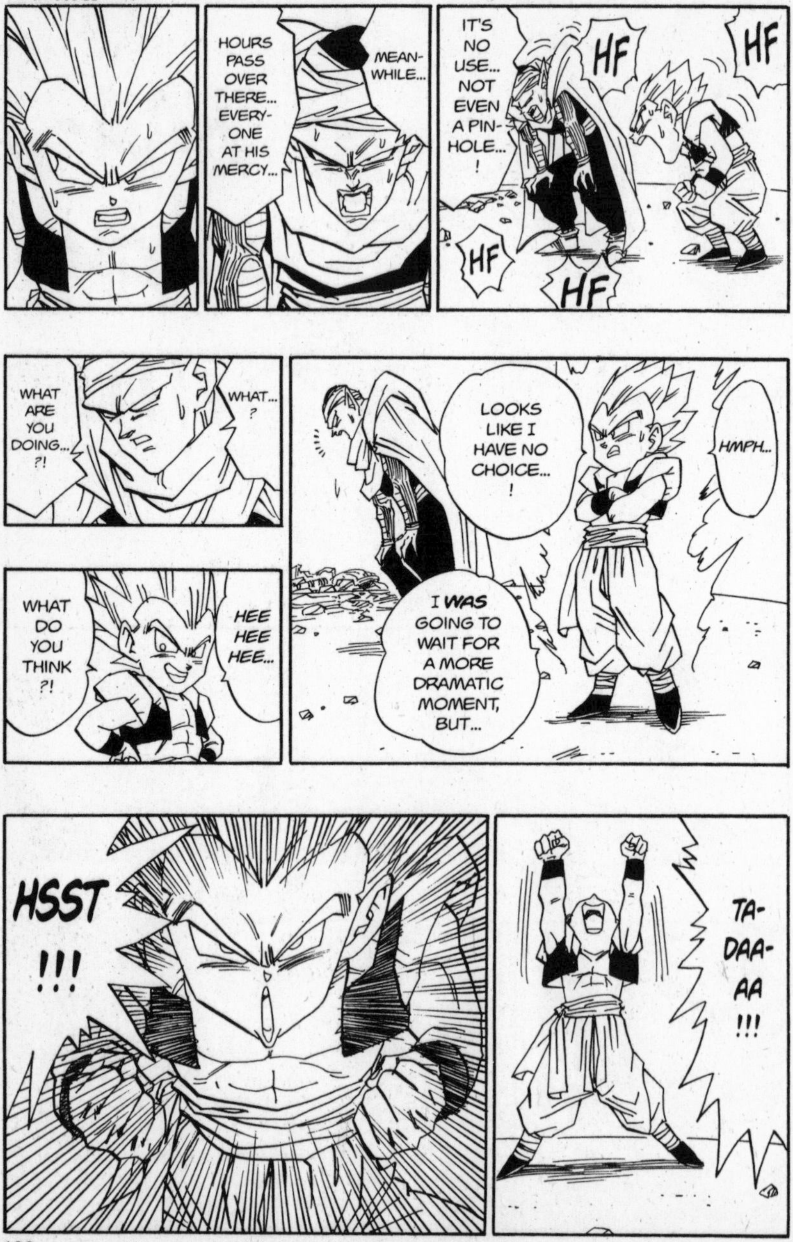
HF
HF
IT'S NO USE... NOT EVEN A PIN-HOLE...!
HF
HF
MEAN-WHILE...
HOURS PASS OVER THERE... EVERY-ONE AT HIS MERCY...
HMPH...
LOOKS LIKE I HAVE NO CHOICE...!
I *WAS* GOING TO WAIT FOR A MORE DRAMATIC MOMENT, BUT...
WHAT...?
WHAT ARE YOU DOING...?!
HEE HEE HEE...
WHAT DO YOU THINK?!
TA-DAAAA!!!
HSST!!!

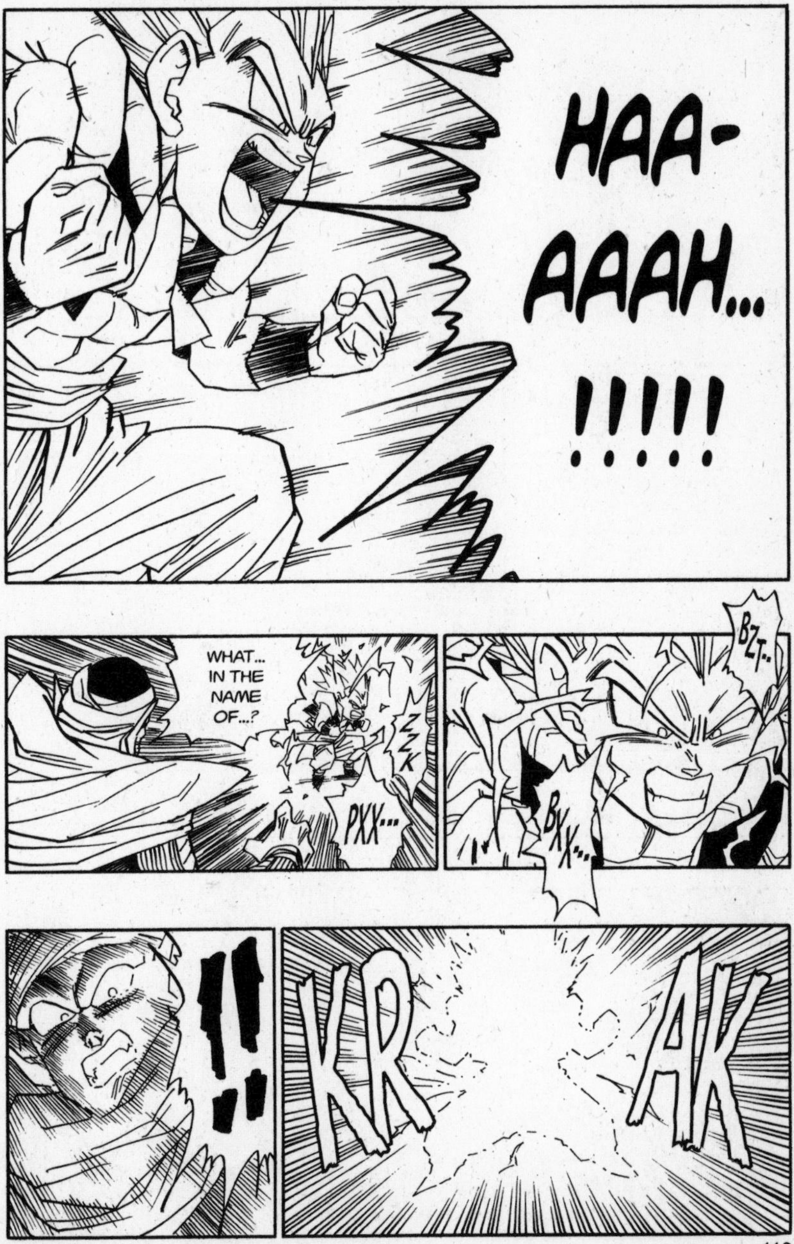
HAA-AAAH...!!!!!!
BZT..
BXX...
WHAT... IN THE NAME OF...?
ZZK
PXX...
KR AK
!!

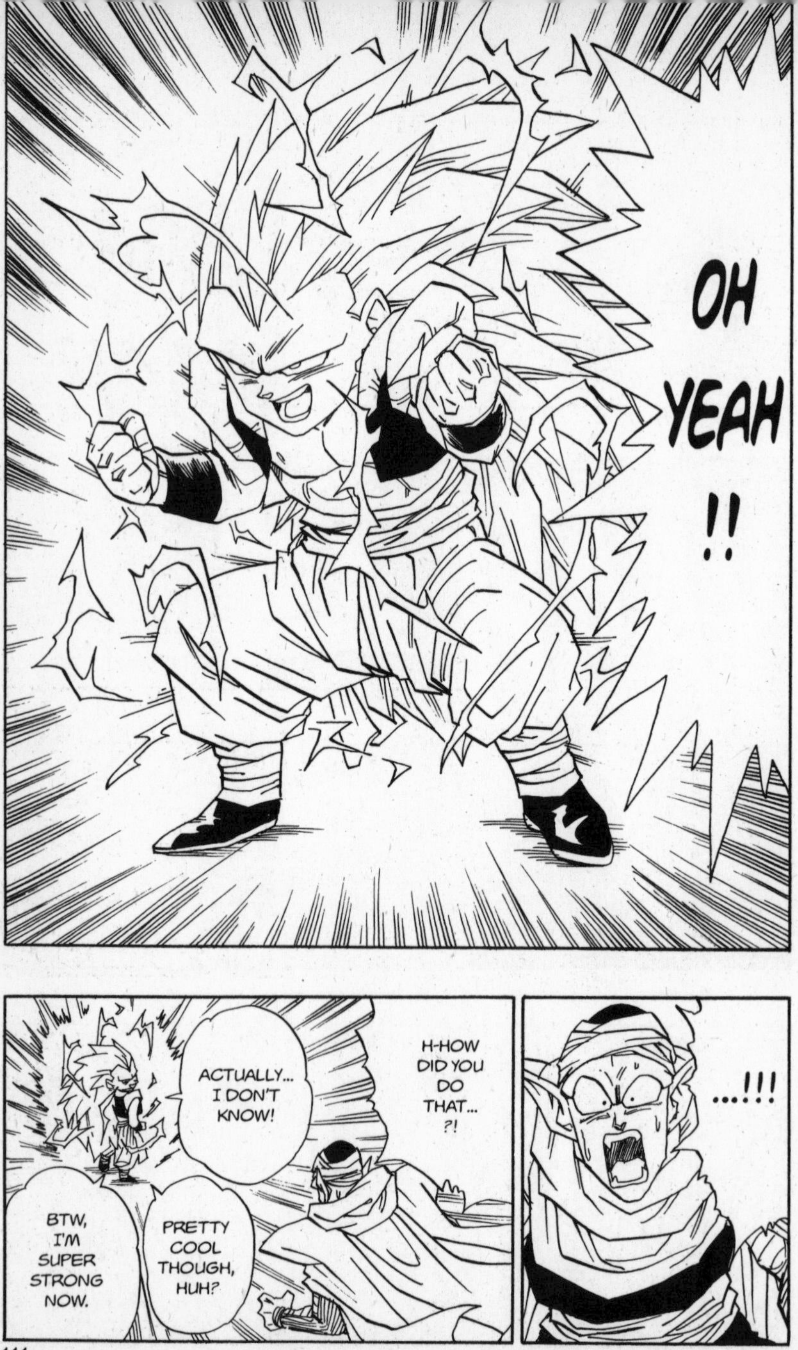
OH YEAH !!
...!!!
H-HOW DID YOU DO THAT... ?!
ACTUALLY... I DON'T KNOW!
PRETTY COOL THOUGH, HUH?
BTW, I'M SUPER STRONG NOW.

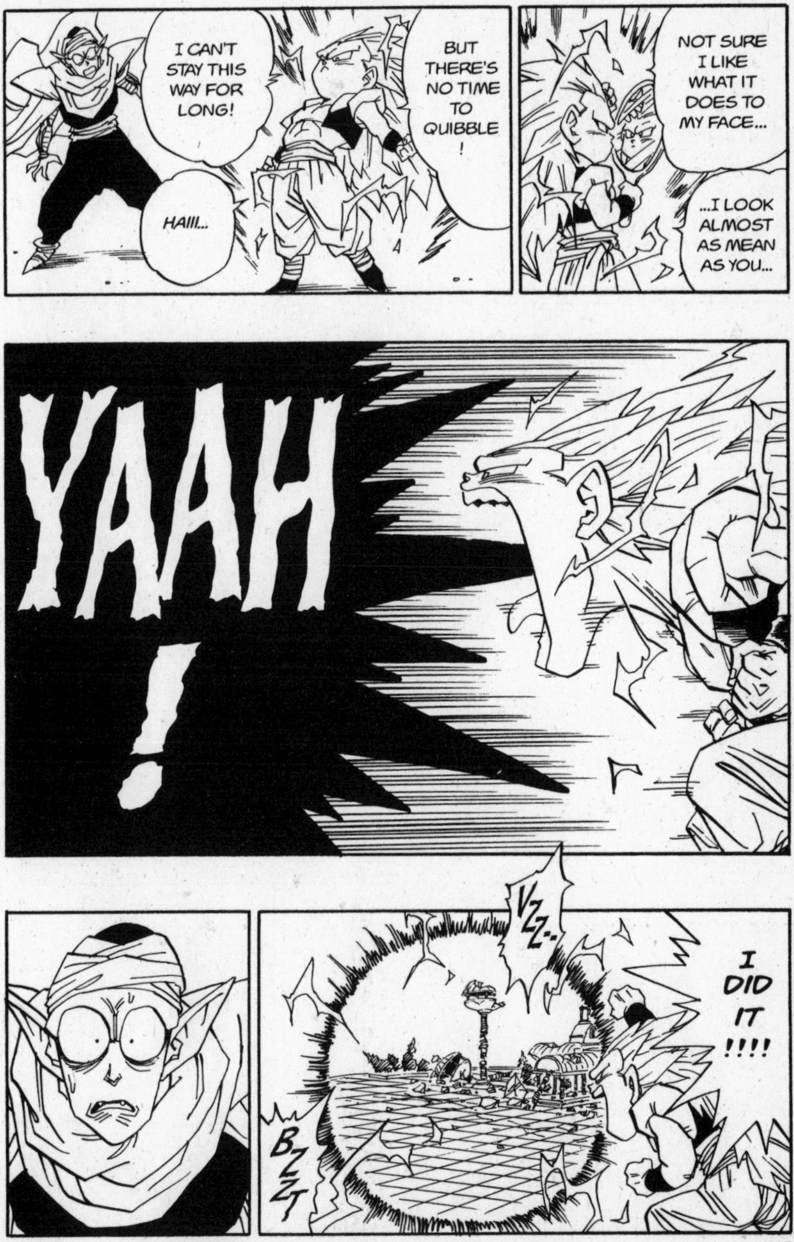
NOT SURE I LIKE WHAT IT DOES TO MY FACE...
...I LOOK ALMOST AS MEAN AS YOU...
BUT THERE'S NO TIME TO QUIBBLE!
I CAN'T STAY THIS WAY FOR LONG!
HAIII...
YAAH!
VZZ..
I DID IT!!!!
BZZT

READ THIS WAY

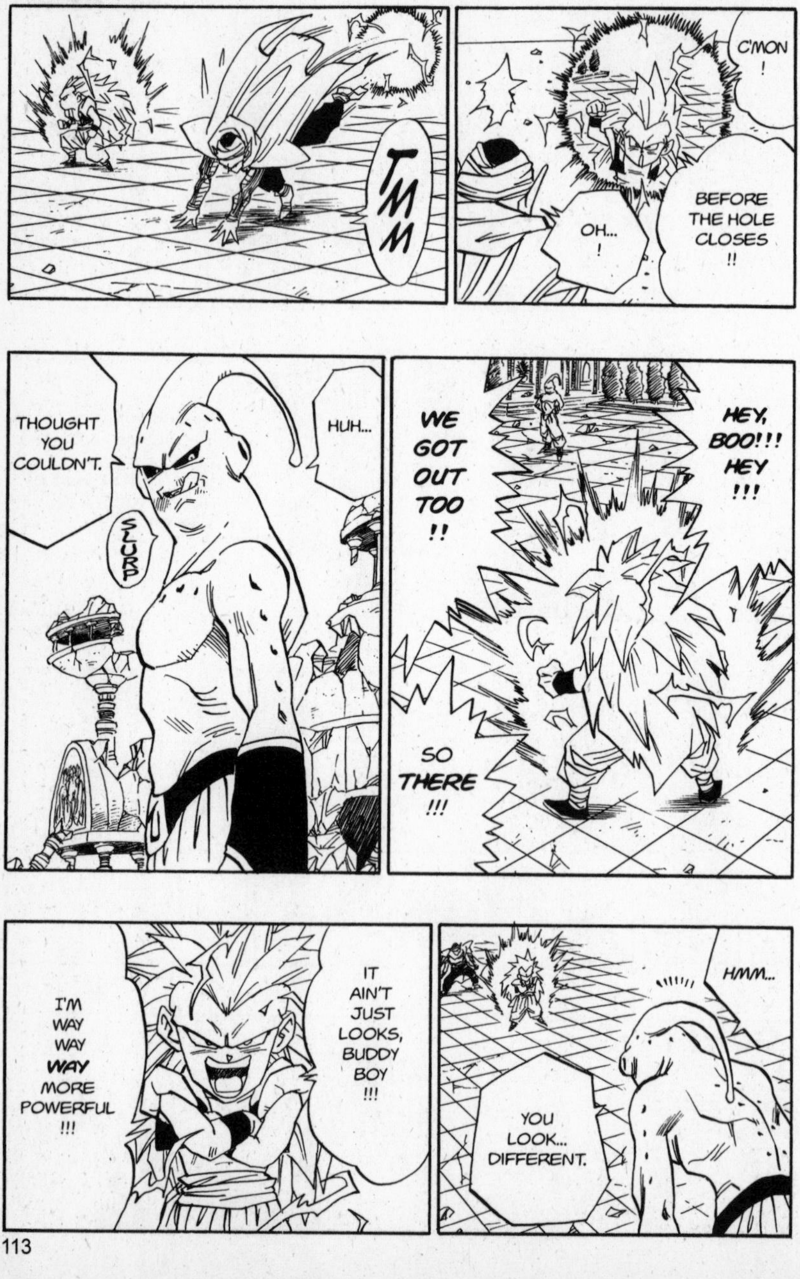

C'MON!
BEFORE THE HOLE CLOSES!!
OH...!
TMM
HEY, BOO!!! HEY!!!
WE GOT OUT TOO!!
SO THERE!!!
HUH...
THOUGHT YOU COULDN'T.
SLURP
HMM...
YOU LOOK... DIFFERENT.
IT AIN'T JUST LOOKS, BUDDY BOY!!!
I'M WAY WAY WAY MORE POWERFUL!!!

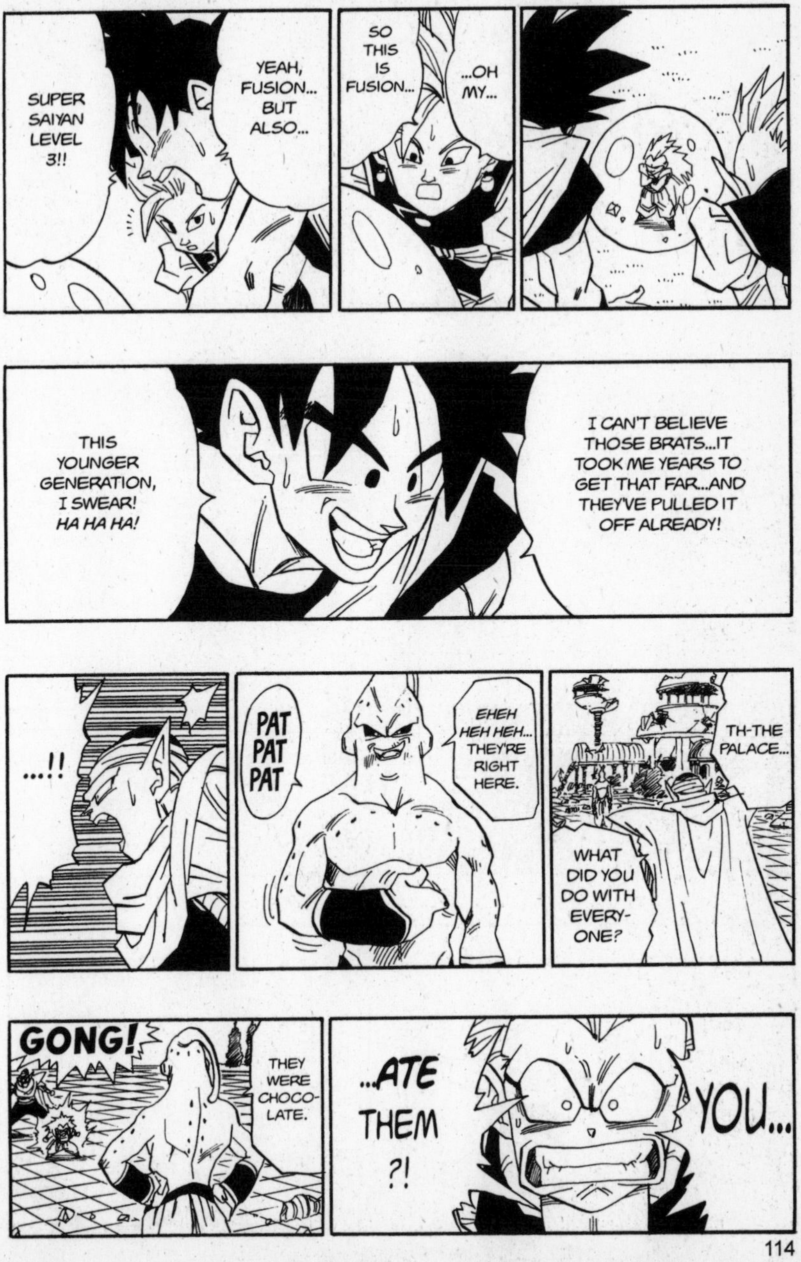
...OH MY...
SO THIS IS FUSION...
YEAH, FUSION... BUT ALSO...
SUPER SAIYAN LEVEL 3!!
I CAN'T BELIEVE THOSE BRATS...IT TOOK ME YEARS TO GET THAT FAR...AND THEY'VE PULLED IT OFF ALREADY!
THIS YOUNGER GENERATION, I SWEAR! *HA HA HA!*
TH-THE PALACE...
WHAT DID YOU DO WITH EVERY-ONE?
EHEH HEH HEH... THEY'RE RIGHT HERE.
PAT PAT PAT
...!!
YOU...
...ATE THEM ?!
THEY WERE CHOCO-LATE.
GONG!

READ THIS WAY

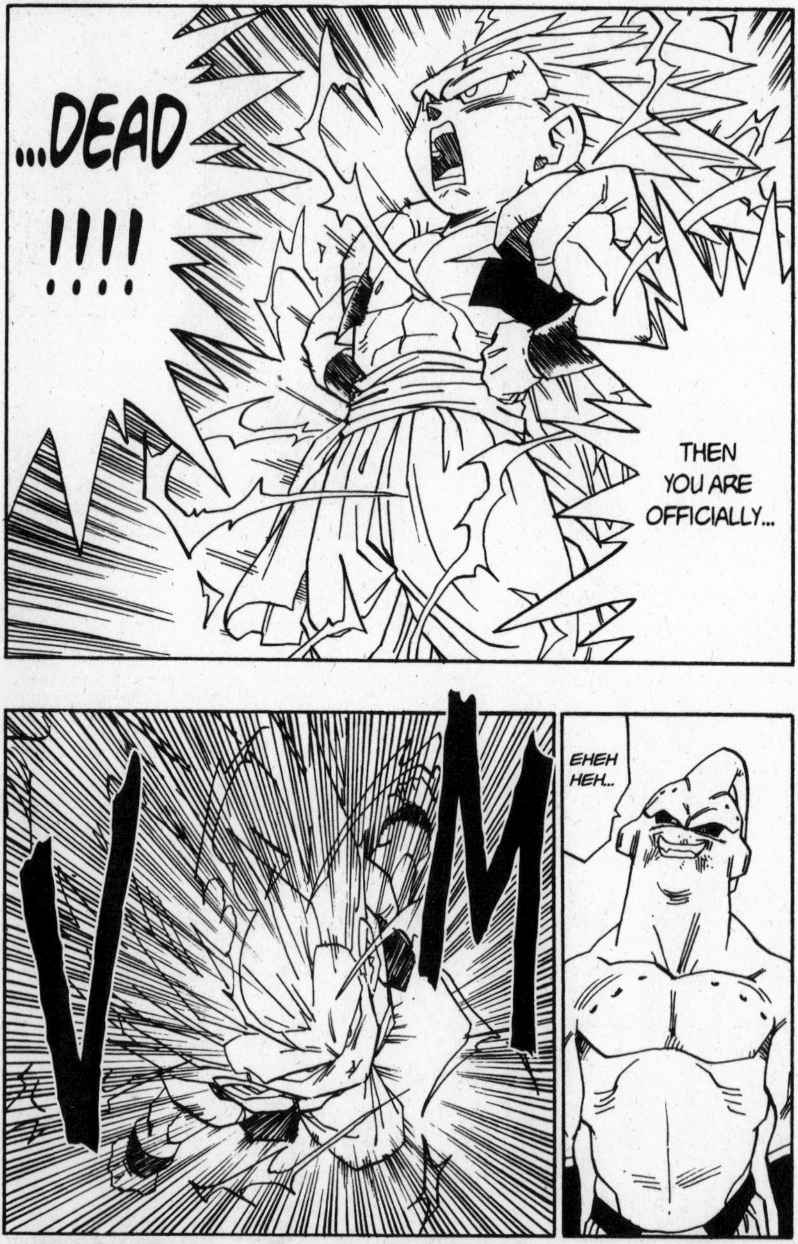

THEN YOU ARE OFFICIALLY...
...DEAD !!!!
EHEH HEH...
VM

NEXT: Boo vs. Super Gotenks!

DBZ:300 · Super Gotenks!

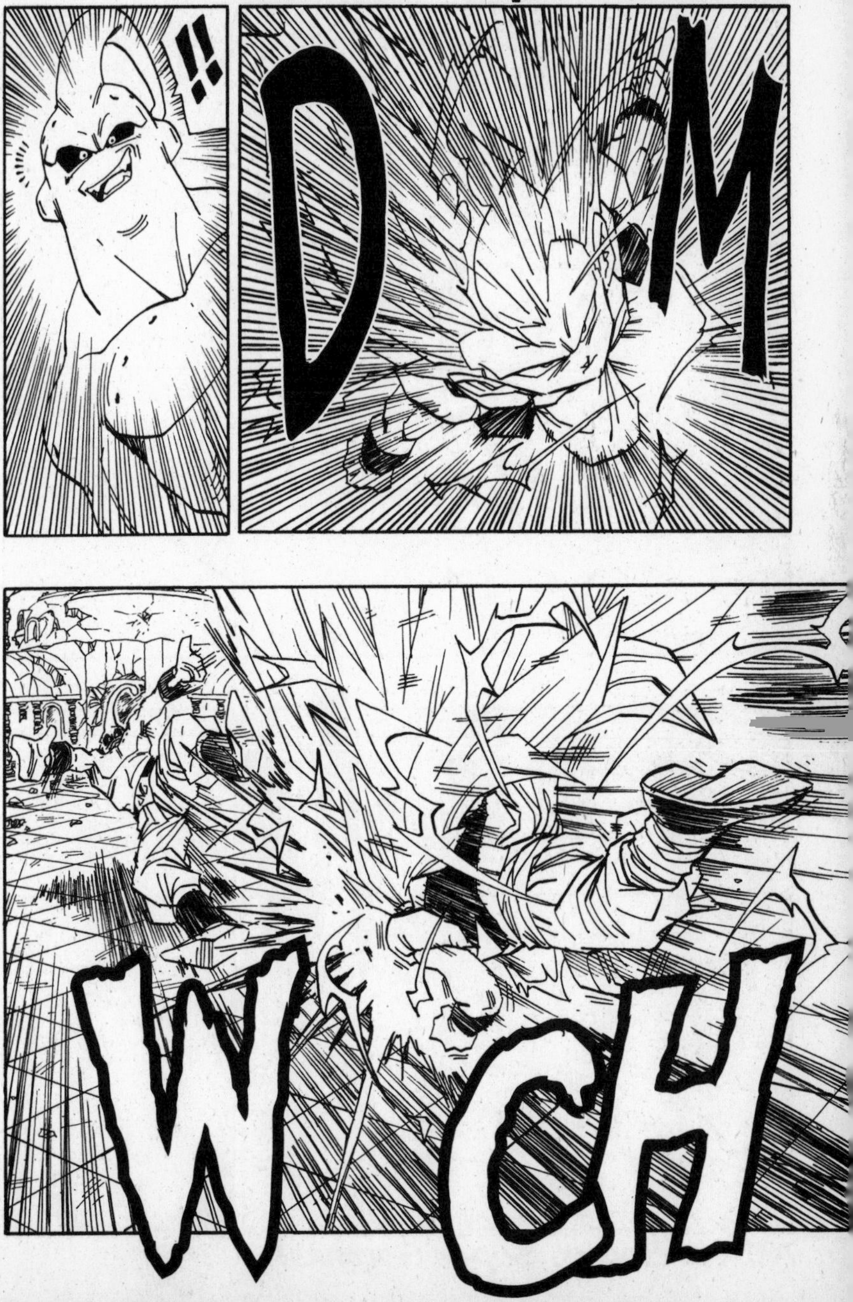
DM
!!
WCH

READ THIS WAY

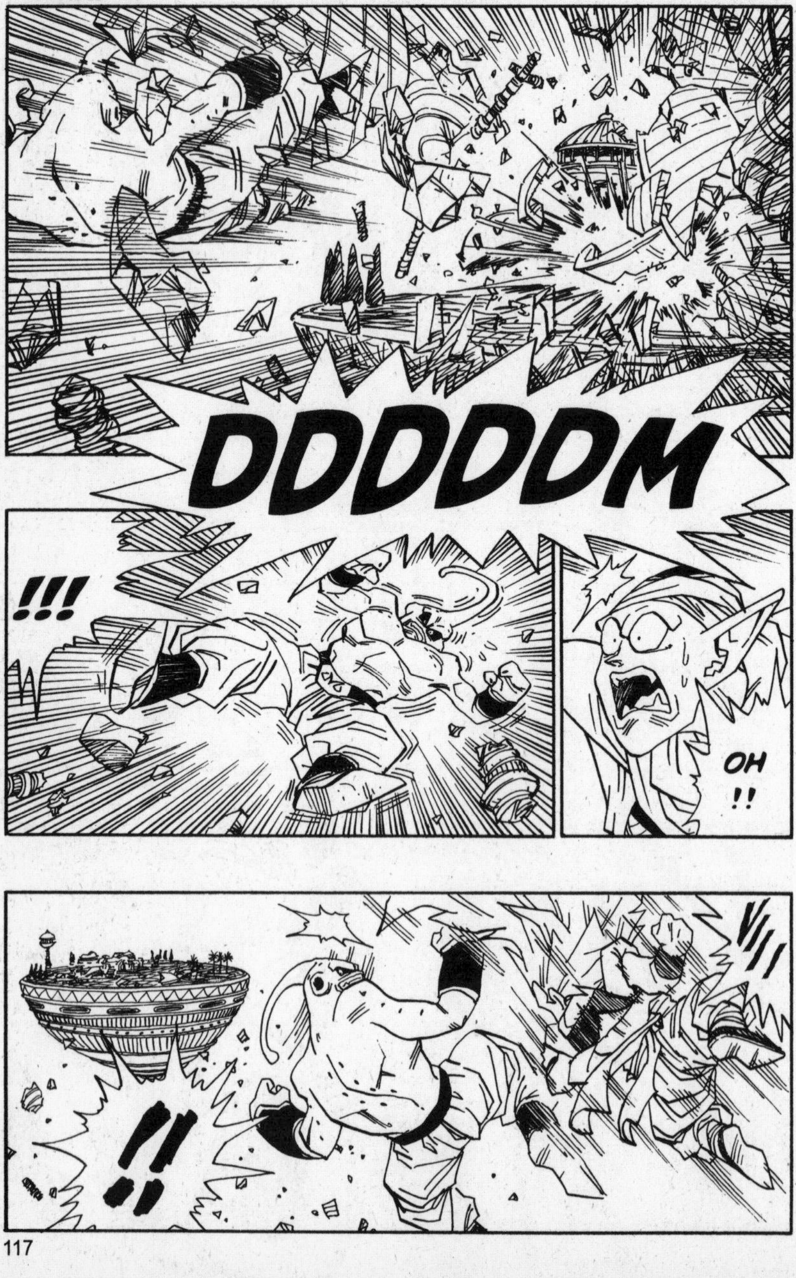
DDDDDM
OH !!
!!!
!!

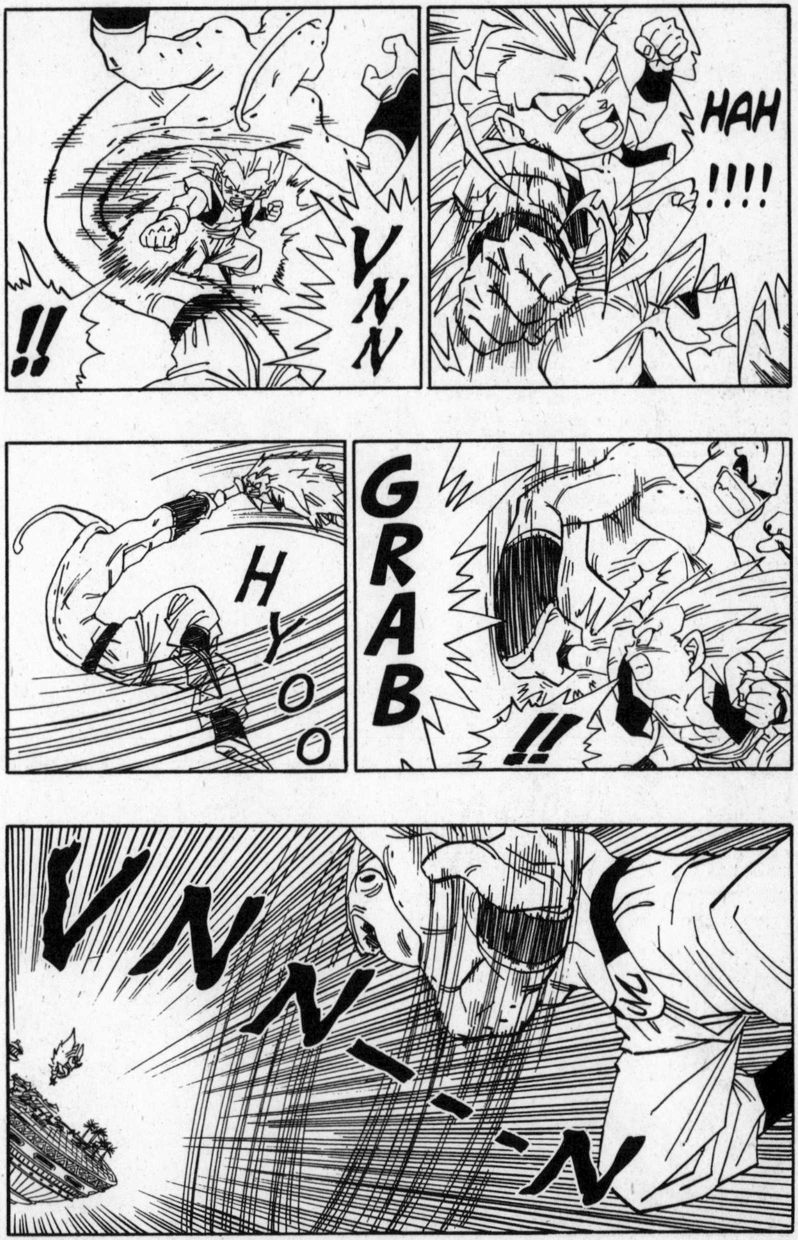
HAH !!!!
VNN
!!
GRAB
!!
HYOO
VNN--N

READ THIS WAY

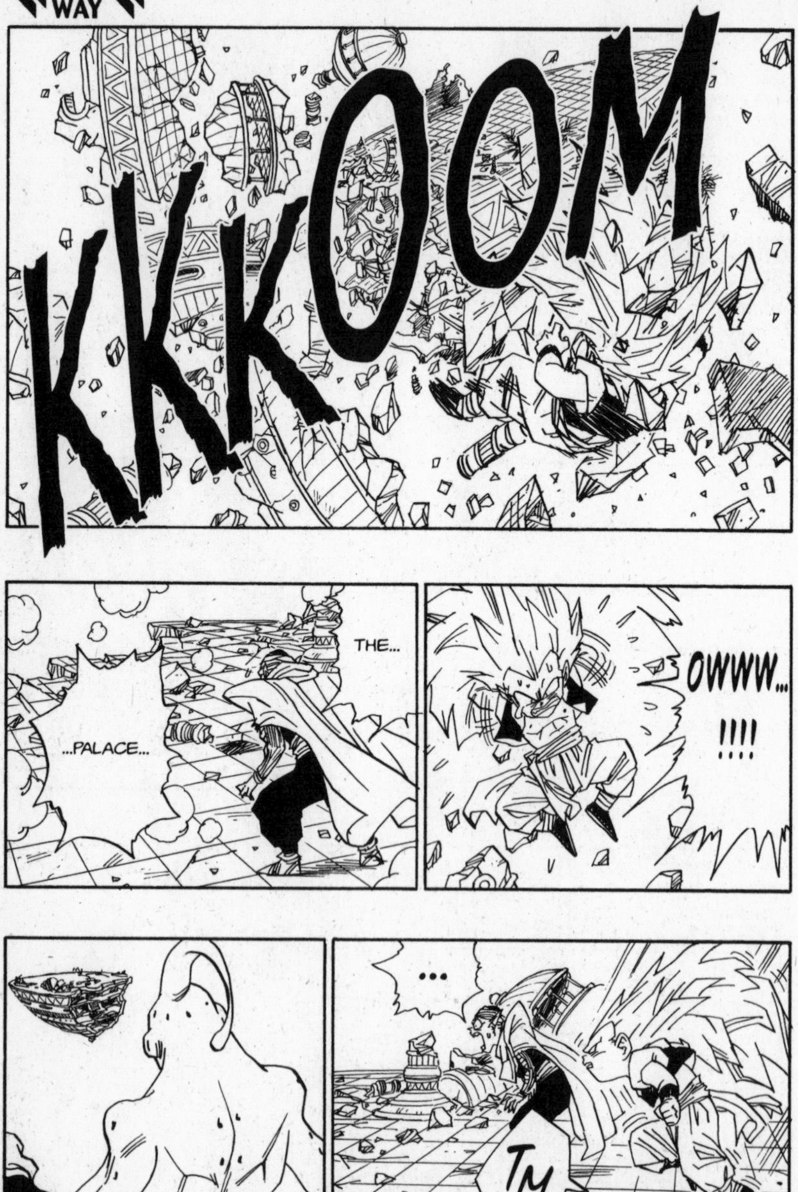
KKOOM
OWWW... !!!!
THE...
...PALACE...
...
TM

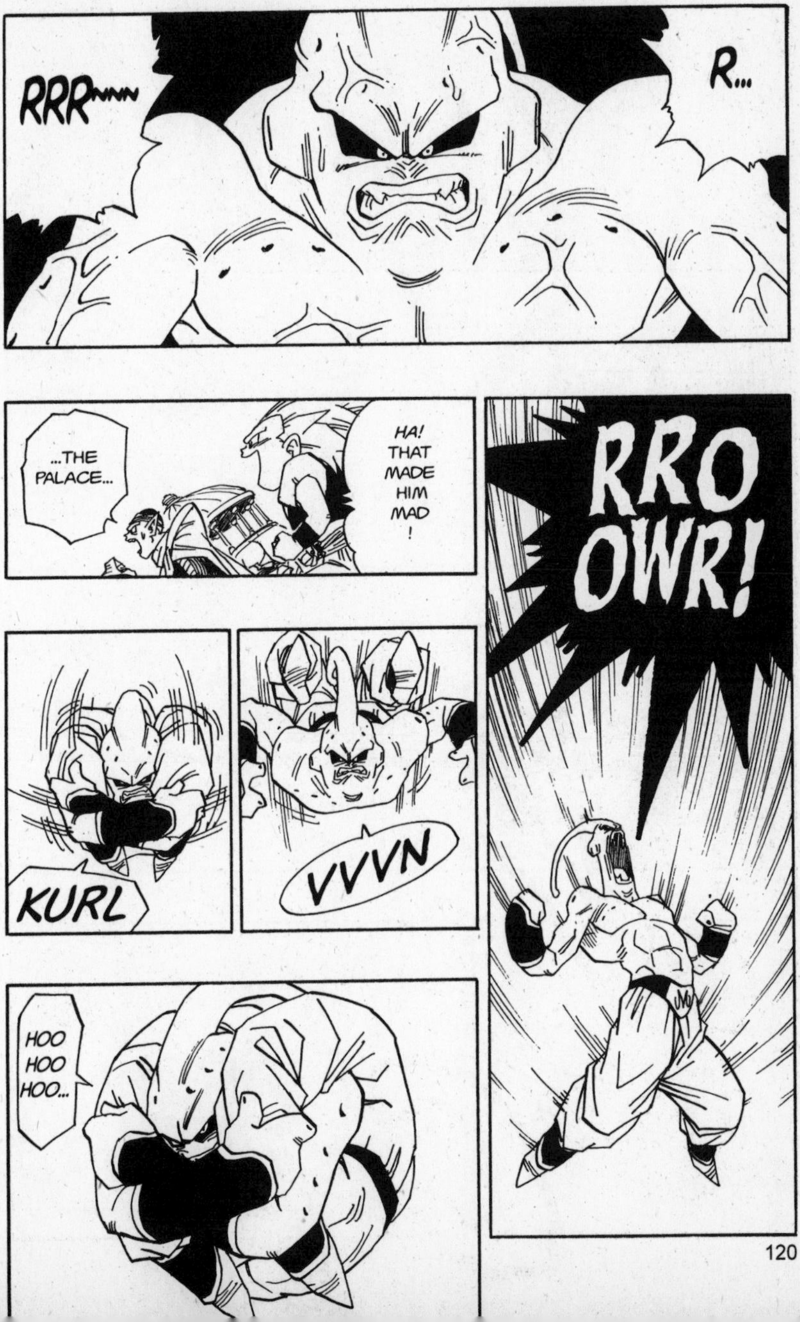
RRRNNN
R...
...THE PALACE...
HA! THAT MADE HIM MAD!
KURL
VVVN
HOO HOO HOO...
RRO OWR!

READ THIS WAY

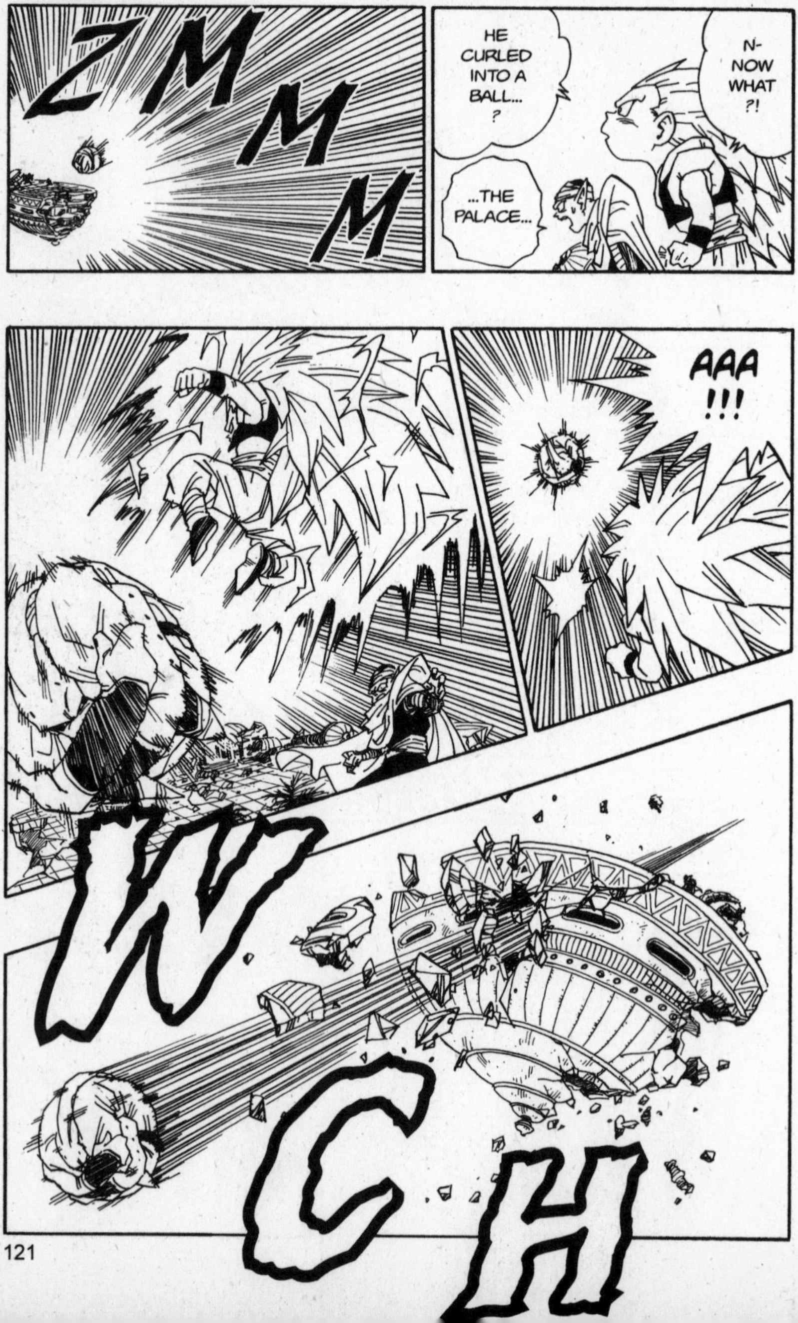
N- NOW WHAT ?!
HE CURLED INTO A BALL... ?
...THE PALACE...
ZMMM
AAA !!!
WNCH

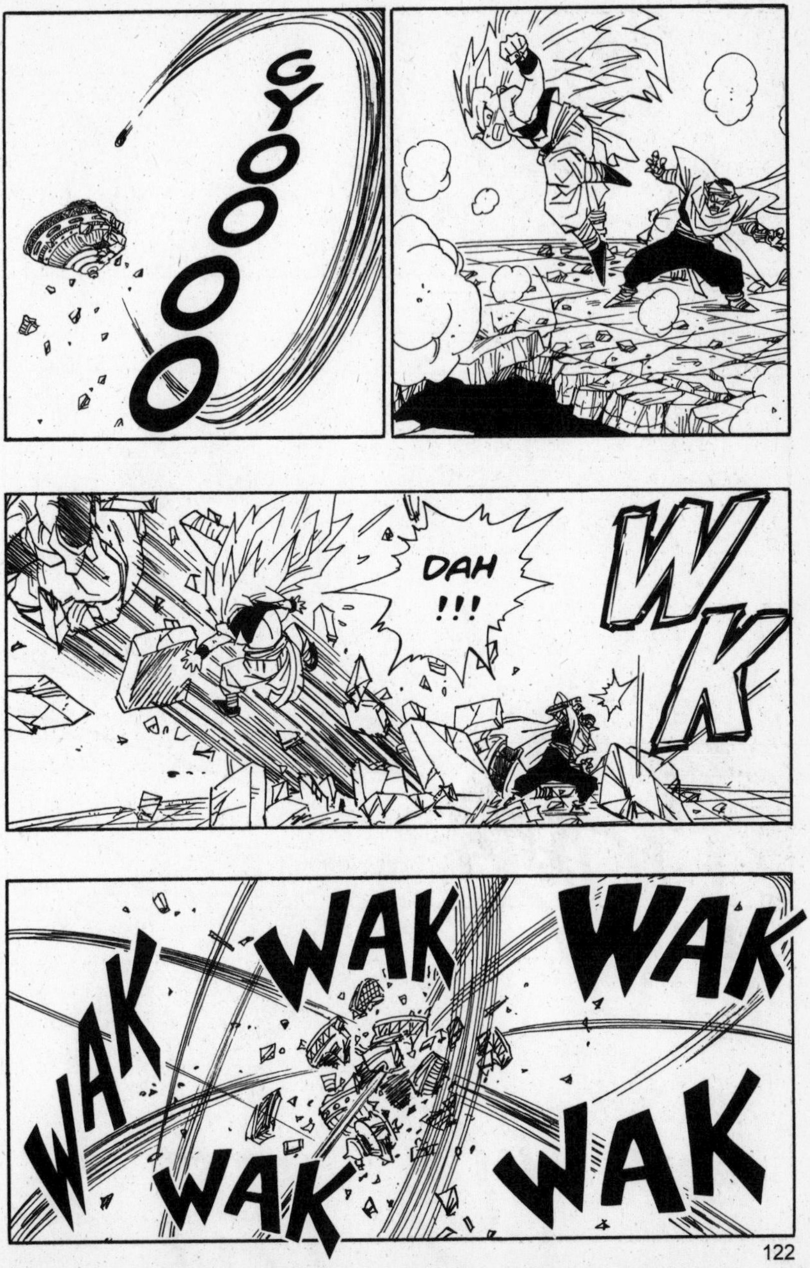
GYOOOOOO
WK
DAH !!!
WAK
WAK
WAK
WAK
WAK

READ THIS WAY

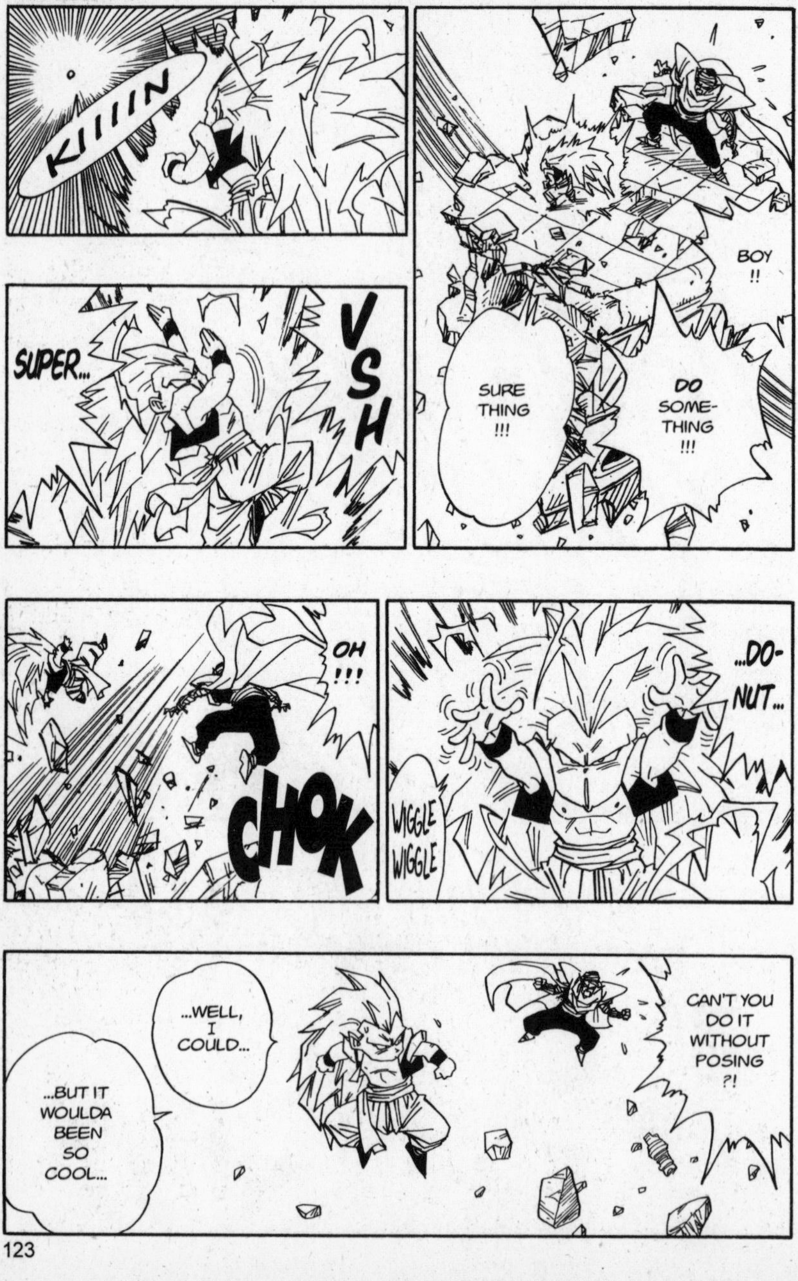

BOY!!
DO SOMETHING!!!
SURE THING!!!
KIIIIN
VSH
SUPER...
...DO-NUT...
WIGGLE WIGGLE
OH!!!
CHOK
CAN'T YOU DO IT WITHOUT POSING?!
...WELL, I COULD...
...BUT IT WOULDA BEEN SO COOL...

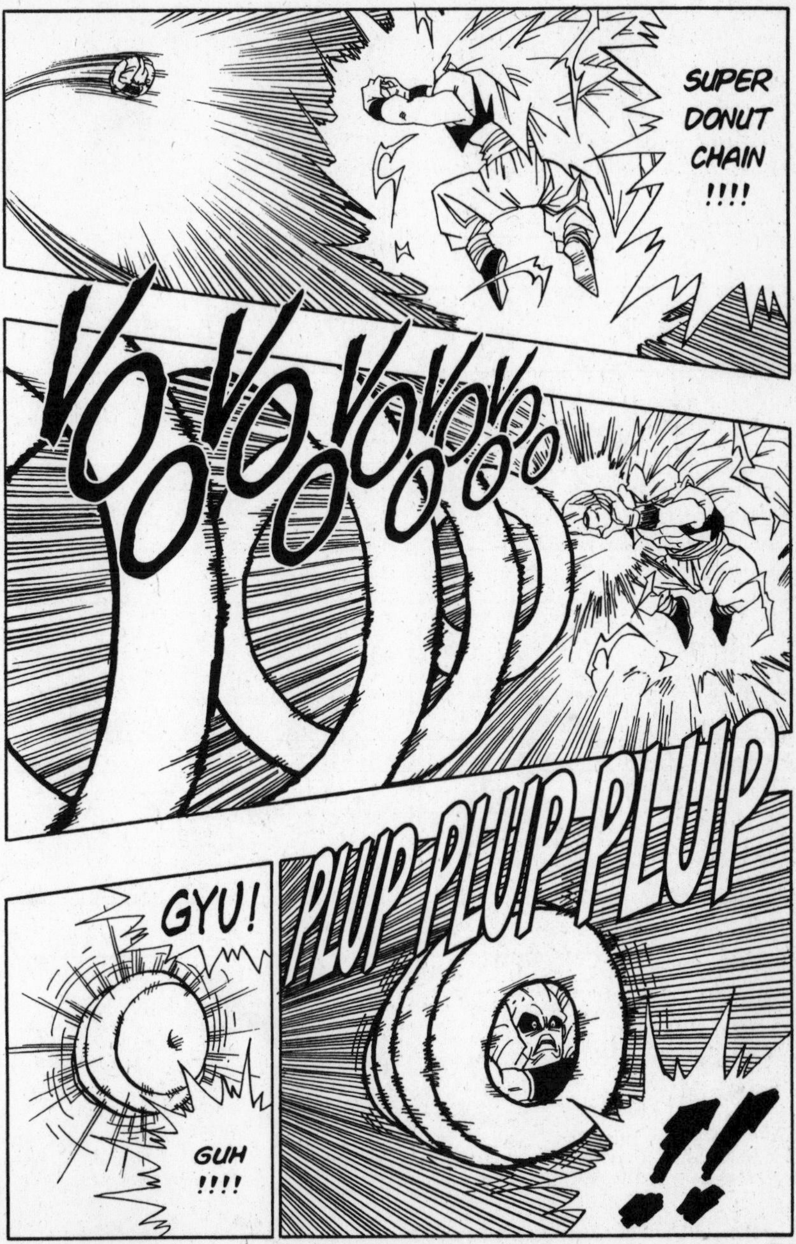
SUPER DONUT CHAIN !!!!
VOOVOOVOOVOOVOO
PLUP PLUP PLUP
!!
GYU!
GUH !!!!

READ THIS WAY

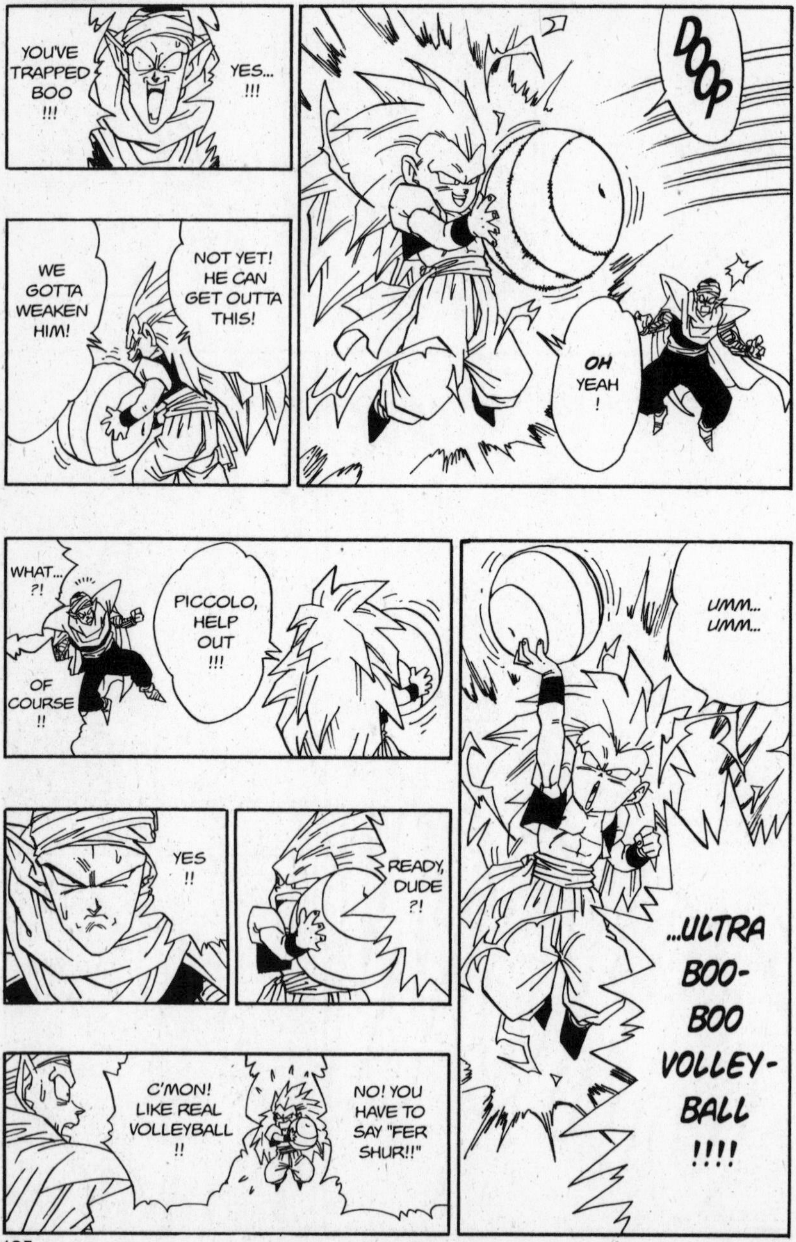
DOOP
OH YEAH!
YES...!!!
YOU'VE TRAPPED BOO!!!
NOT YET! HE CAN GET OUTTA THIS!
WE GOTTA WEAKEN HIM!
UMM... UMM...
...ULTRA BOO-BOO VOLLEY-BALL!!!!
PICCOLO, HELP OUT!!!
WHAT...?!
OF COURSE!!
READY, DUDE?!
YES!!
NO! YOU HAVE TO SAY "FER SHUR!!"
C'MON! LIKE REAL VOLLEYBALL!!

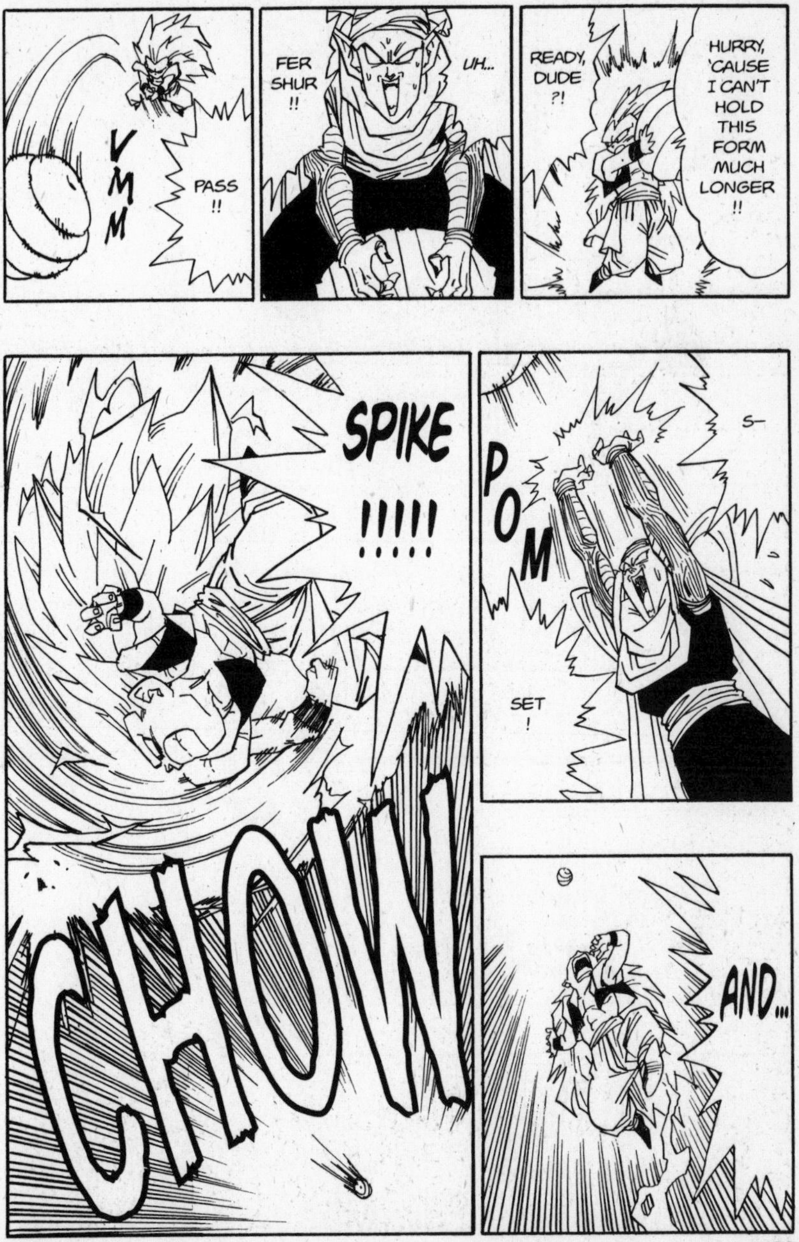
HURRY, 'CAUSE I CAN'T HOLD THIS FORM MUCH LONGER!!
READY, DUDE?!
UH...
FER SHUR!!
VMM
PASS!!
S—
POM
SET!
AND...
SPIKE!!!!!
CHOW

READ THIS WAY

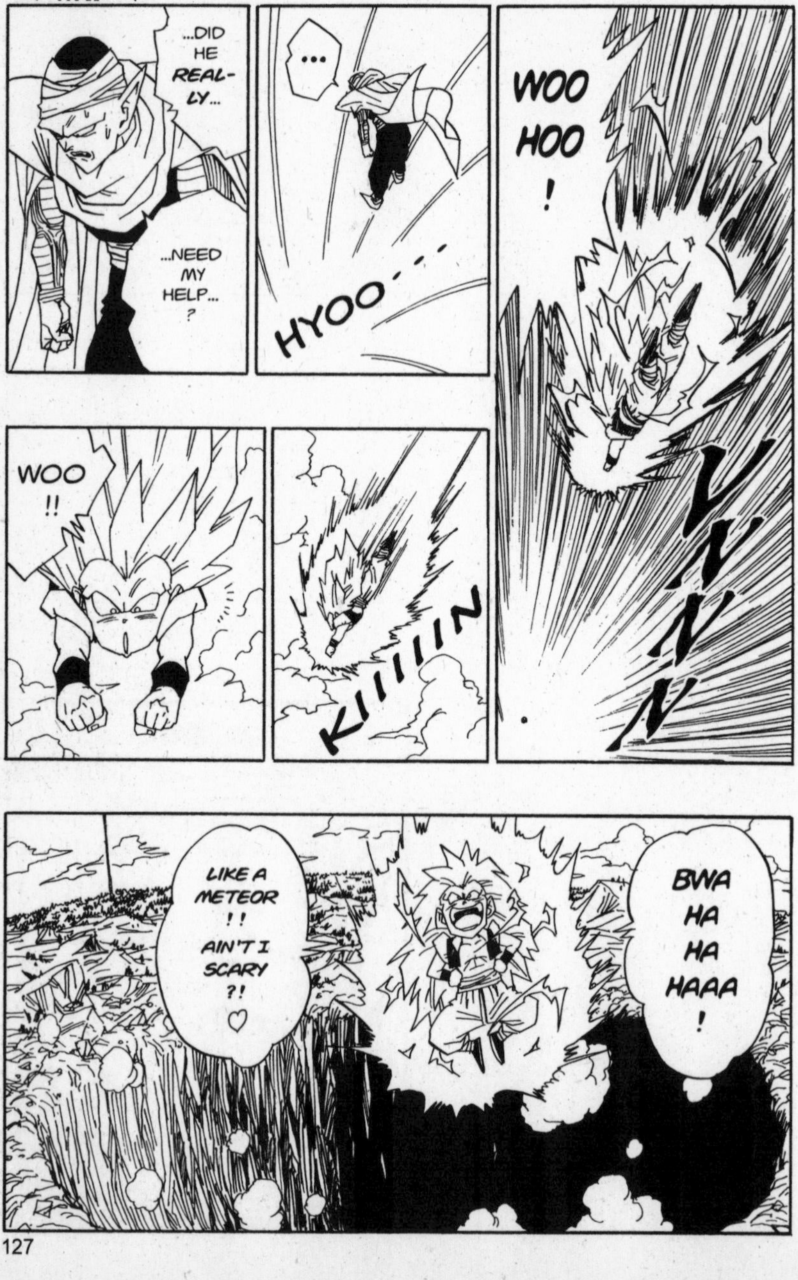
WOO HOO !
VNNNN
...
HYOO . . .
...DID HE REAL-LY...
...NEED MY HELP... ?
KIIIIIN
WOO !!
BWA HA HA HAAA !
LIKE A METEOR ! ! AIN'T I SCARY ?! ♡

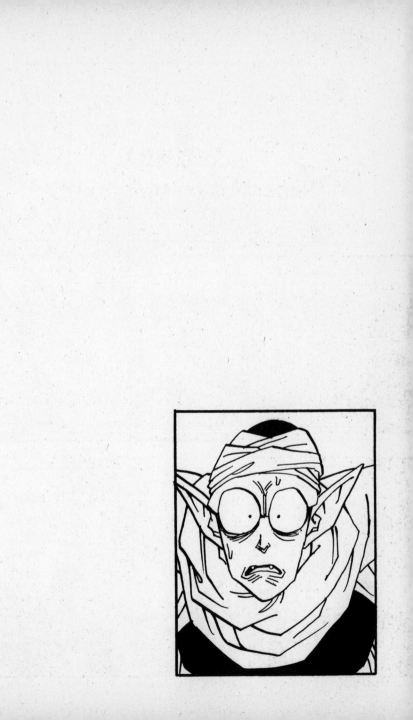

DBZ:301
Super Fusion Unleashed!!

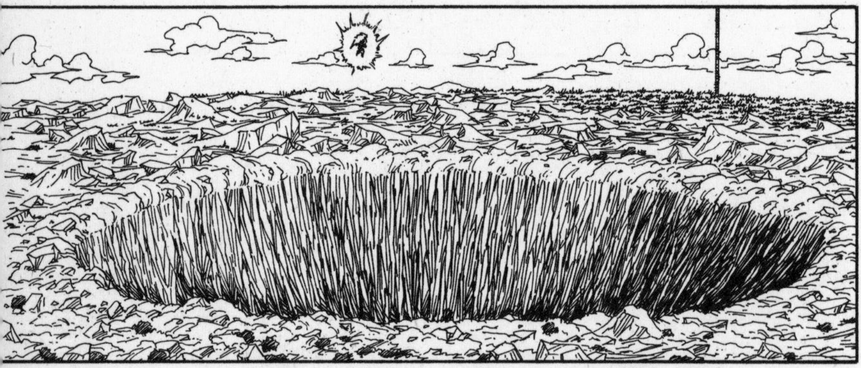

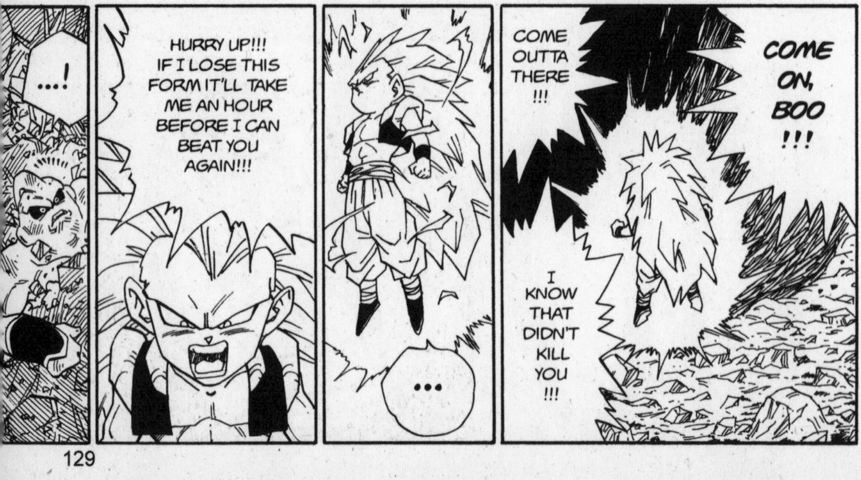
COME ON, BOO!!!
COME OUTTA THERE!!!
I KNOW THAT DIDN'T KILL YOU!!!
...
HURRY UP!!! IF I LOSE THIS FORM IT'LL TAKE ME AN HOUR BEFORE I CAN BEAT YOU AGAIN!!!
...!

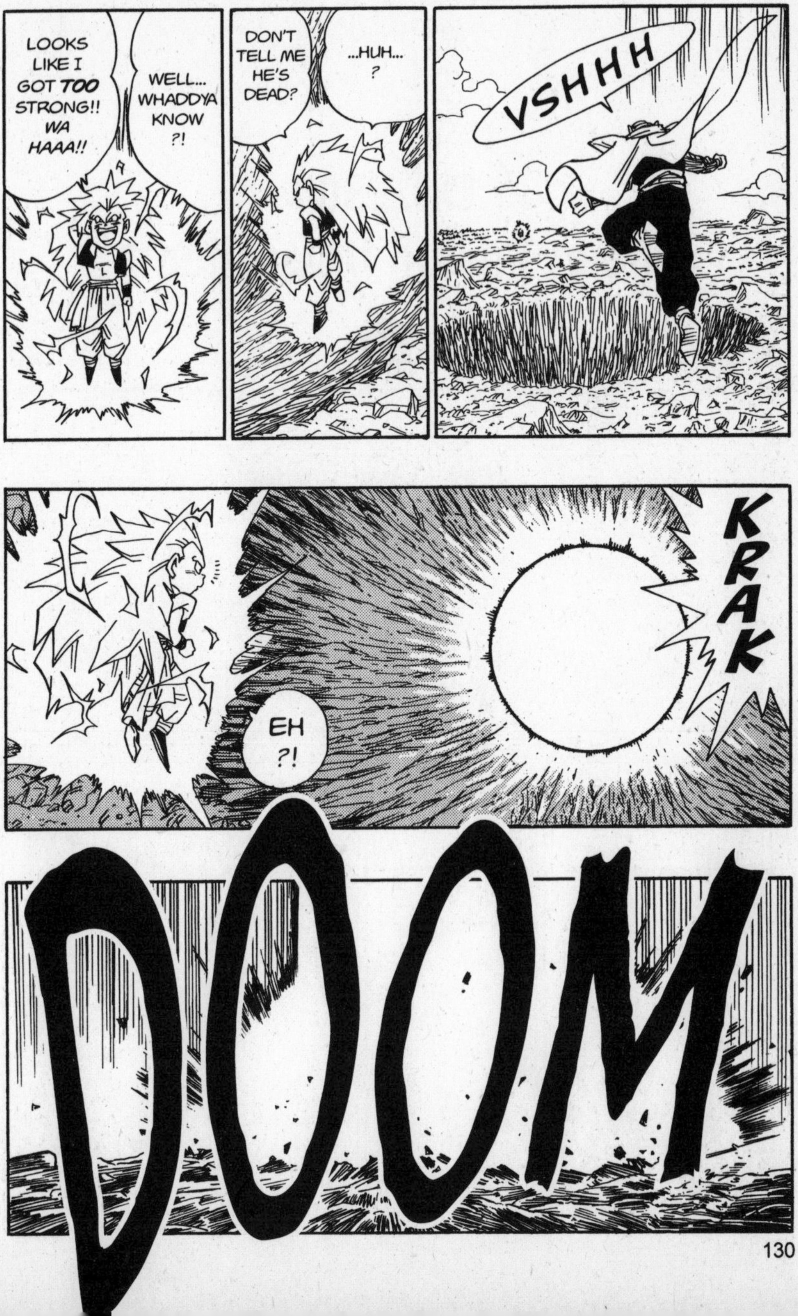
VSHHH
...HUH... ?
DON'T TELL ME HE'S DEAD?
WELL... WHADDYA KNOW ?!
LOOKS LIKE I GOT **TOO** STRONG!! *WA HAAA!!*
KRAK
EH ?!
DOOM

READ THIS WAY

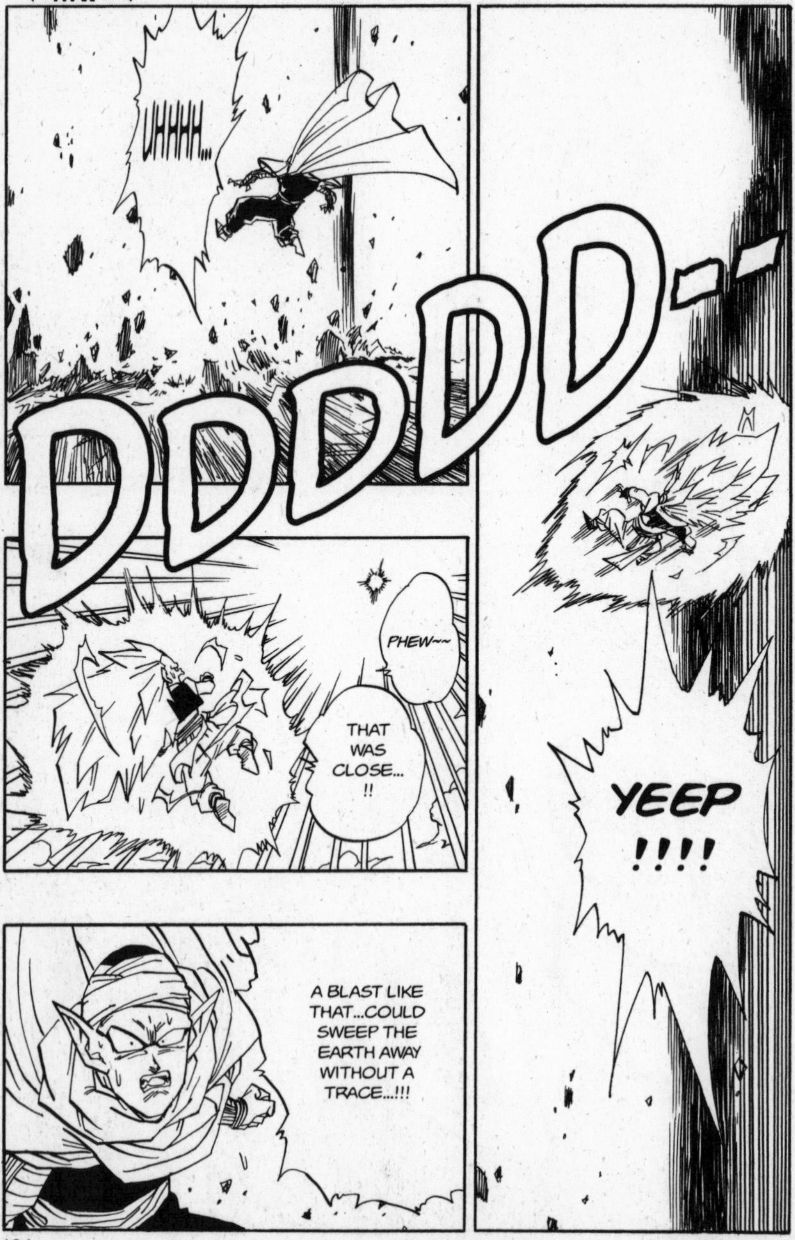
DDDDDD--
YEEP !!!!
UHHHH...
PHEW~~
THAT WAS CLOSE... !!
A BLAST LIKE THAT...COULD SWEEP THE EARTH AWAY WITHOUT A TRACE...!!!

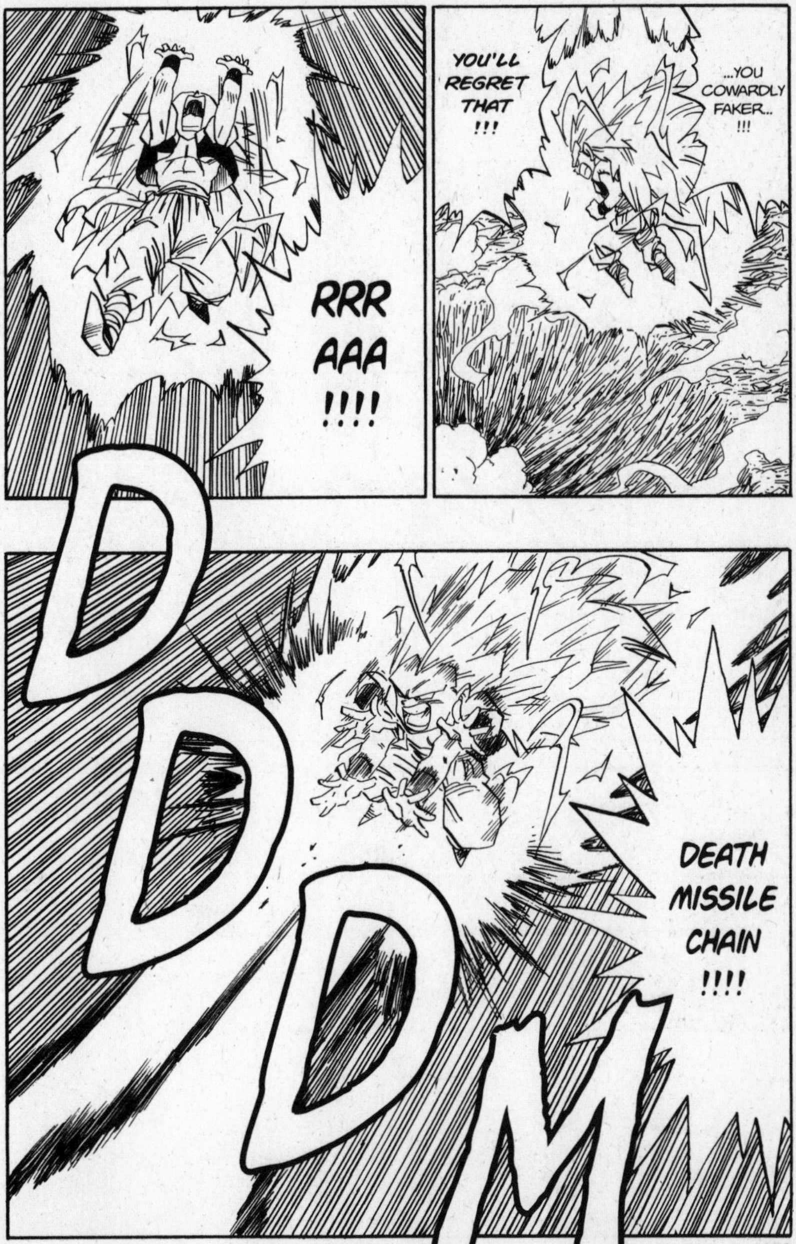
...YOU COWARDLY FAKER.. !!!
YOU'LL REGRET THAT !!!
RRR AAA !!!!
DEATH MISSILE CHAIN !!!!
DDDM

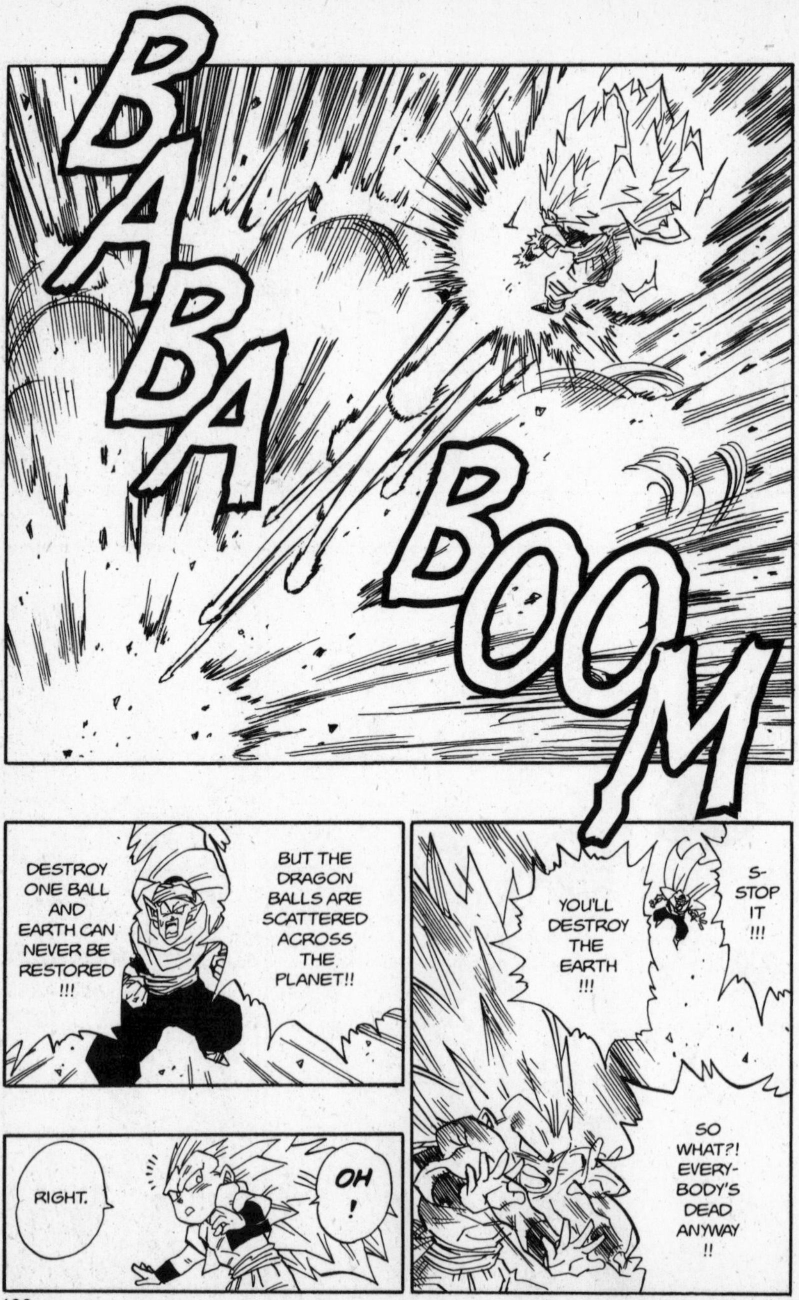
BABABOOM
S-STOP IT!!!
YOU'LL DESTROY THE EARTH!!!
SO WHAT?! EVERYBODY'S DEAD ANYWAY!!
BUT THE DRAGON BALLS ARE SCATTERED ACROSS THE PLANET!!
DESTROY ONE BALL AND EARTH CAN NEVER BE RESTORED!!!
OH!
RIGHT.

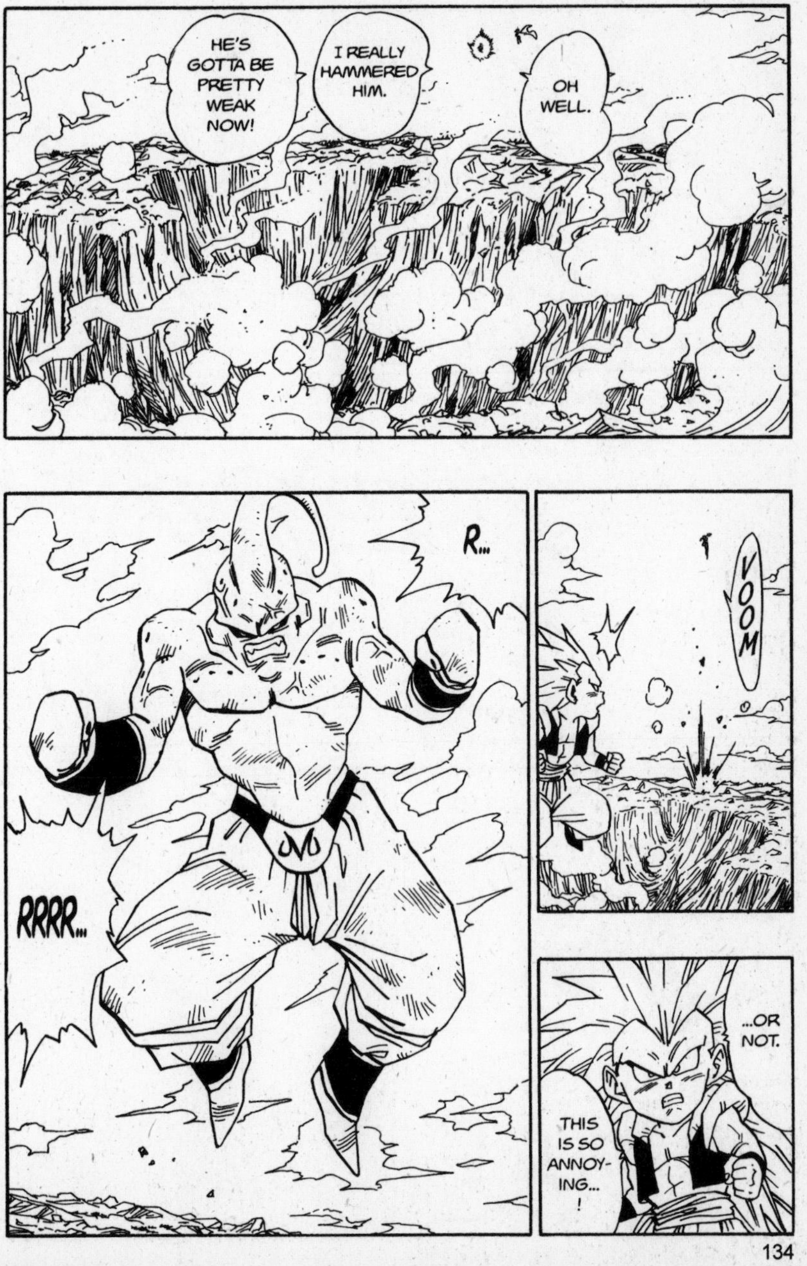
OH WELL.
I REALLY HAMMERED HIM.
HE'S GOTTA BE PRETTY WEAK NOW!
VOOM
...OR NOT.
THIS IS SO ANNOY-ING...!
R...
RRRR...

READ THIS WAY

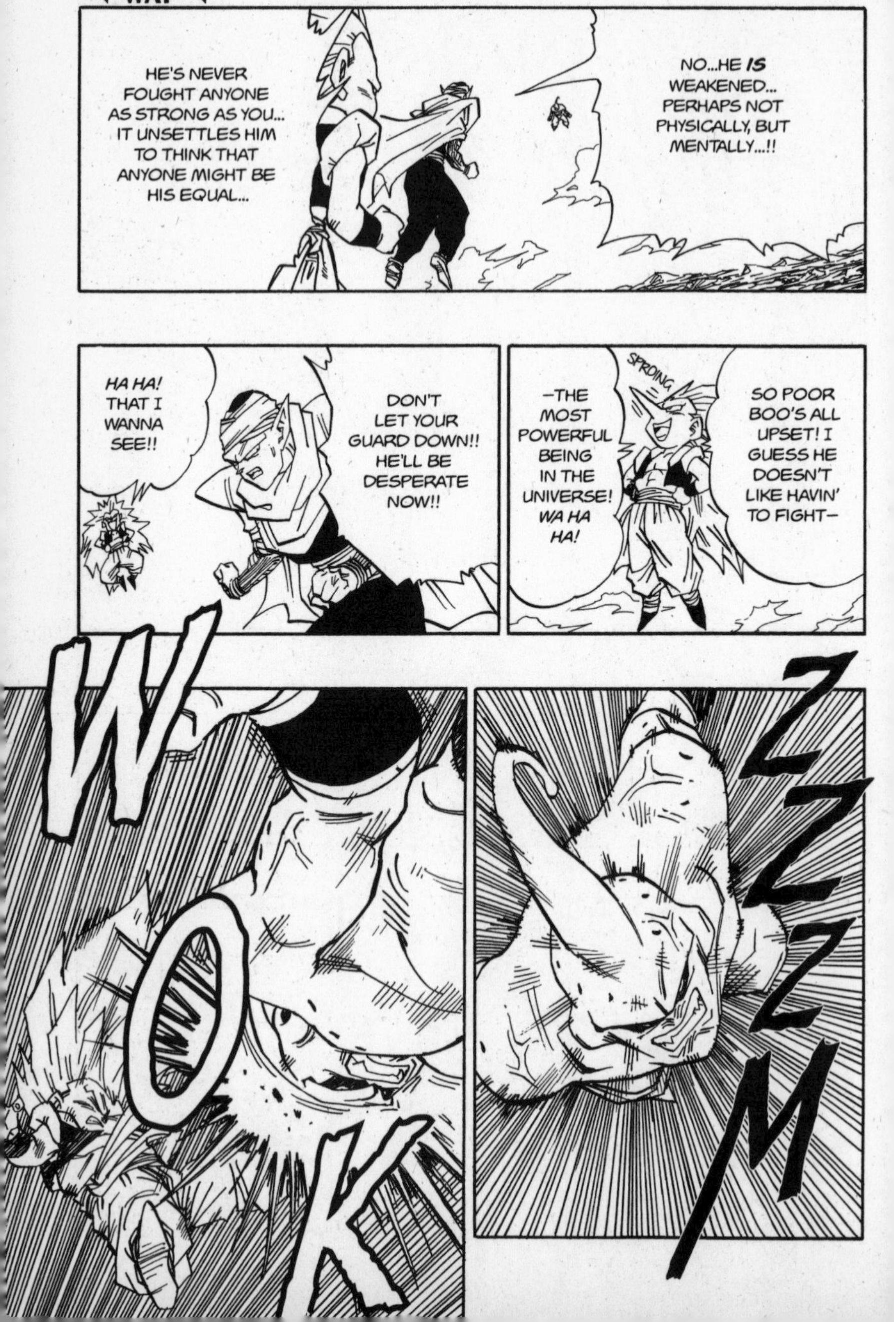
NO...HE *IS* WEAKENED... PERHAPS NOT PHYSICALLY, BUT MENTALLY...!!
HE'S NEVER FOUGHT ANYONE AS STRONG AS YOU... IT UNSETTLES HIM TO THINK THAT ANYONE MIGHT BE HIS EQUAL...
SO POOR BOO'S ALL UPSET! I GUESS HE DOESN'T LIKE HAVIN' TO FIGHT—
SPROING
—THE MOST POWERFUL BEING IN THE UNIVERSE! *WA HA HA!*
DON'T LET YOUR GUARD DOWN!! HE'LL BE DESPERATE NOW!!
HA HA! THAT I WANNA SEE!!
ZZZZM
WOK

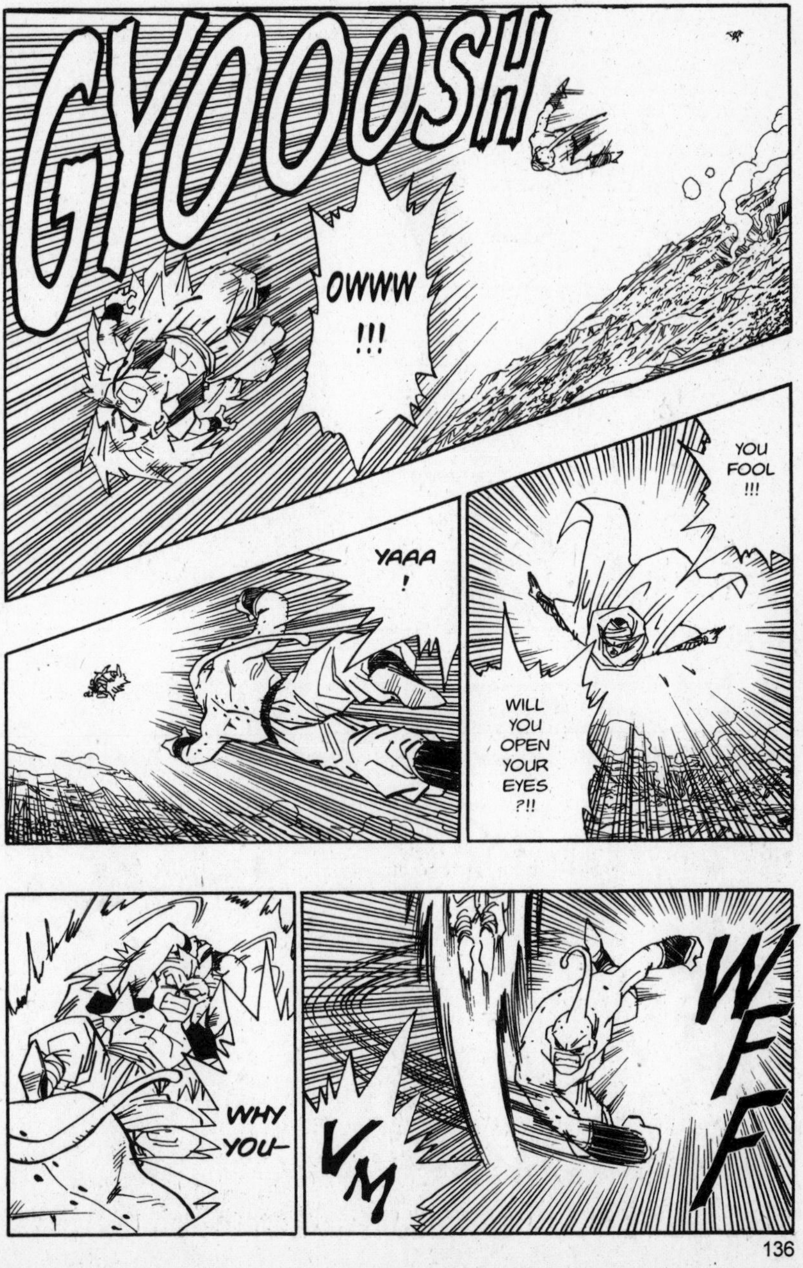
GYOOOSH
OWWW!!!
YOU FOOL!!!
WILL YOU OPEN YOUR EYES?!!
YAAA!
WFF
VM
WHY YOU-

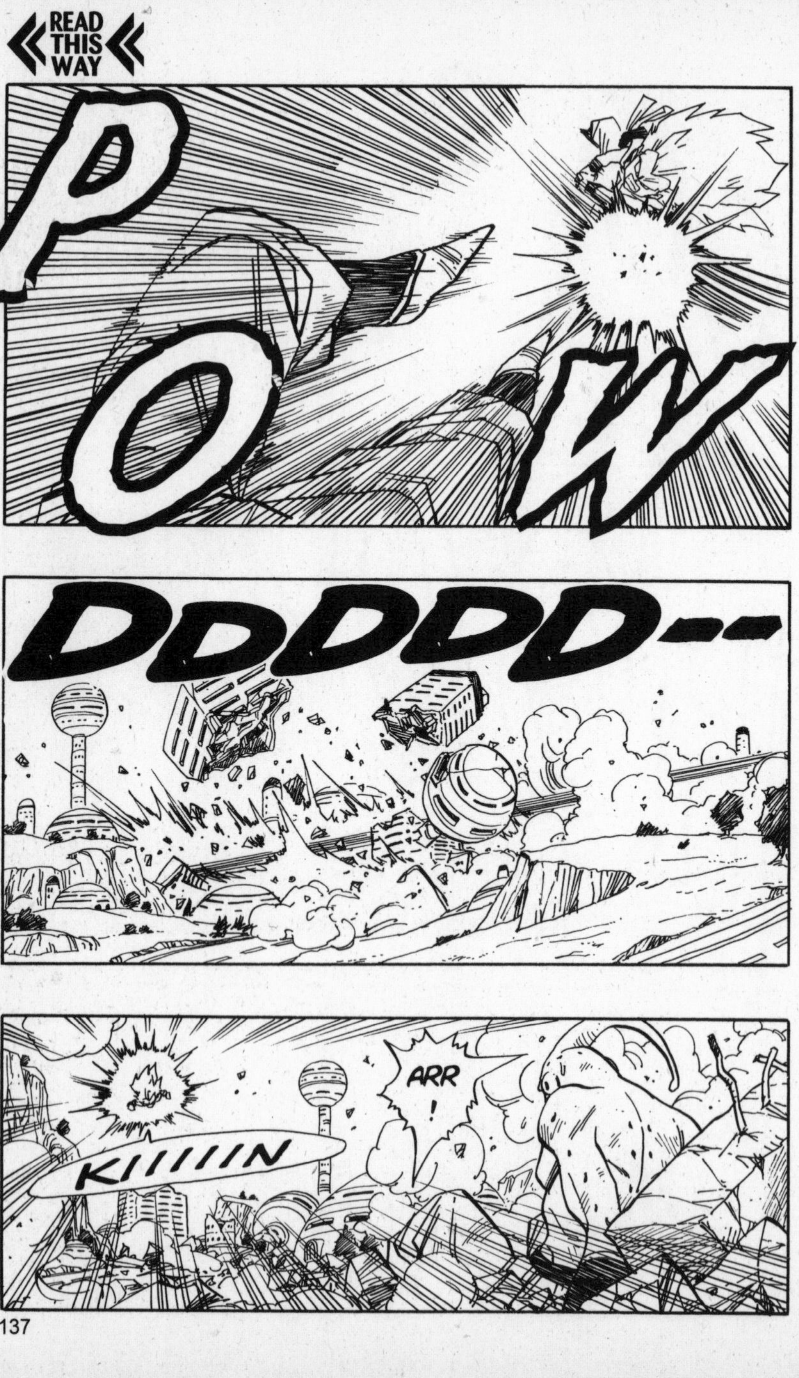
READ THIS WAY
POW
DDDDD--
ARR!
KIIIIIN

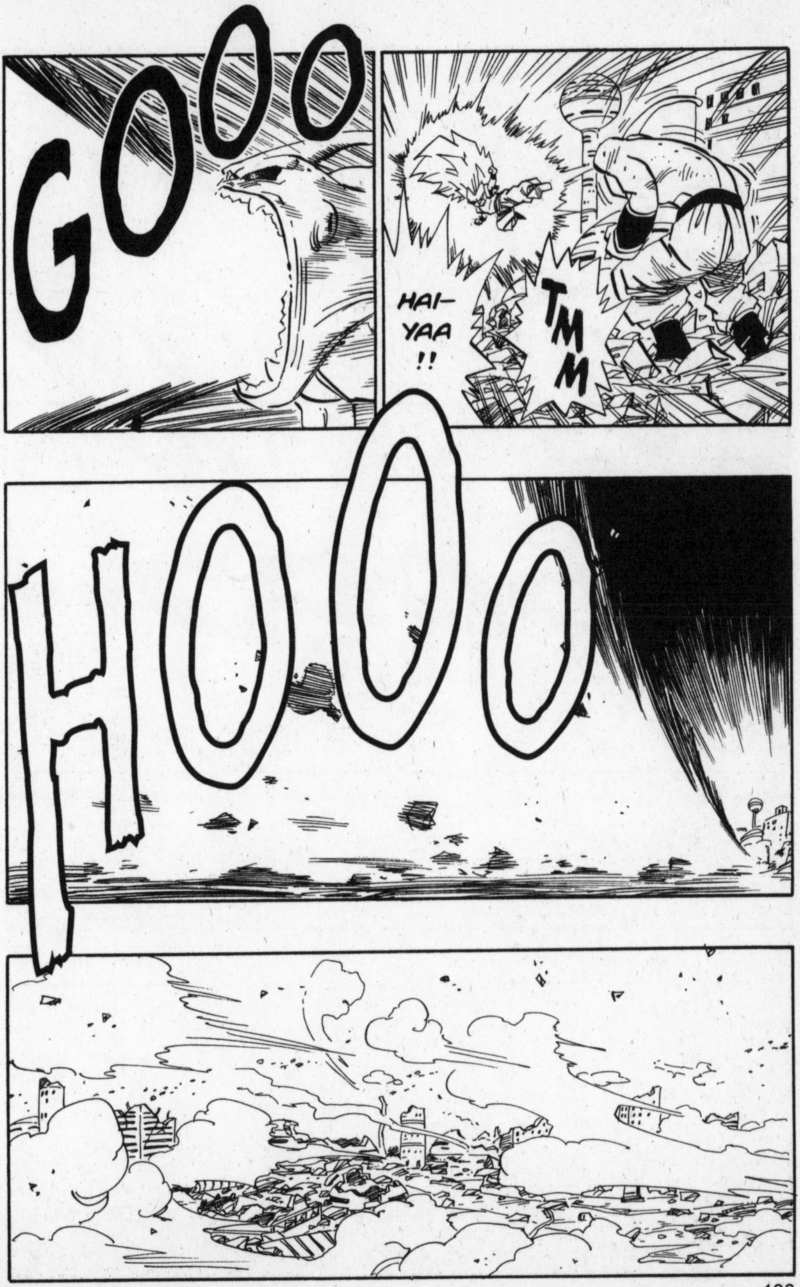
HAI-YAA!!
TMM
GOOOO
HOOOO

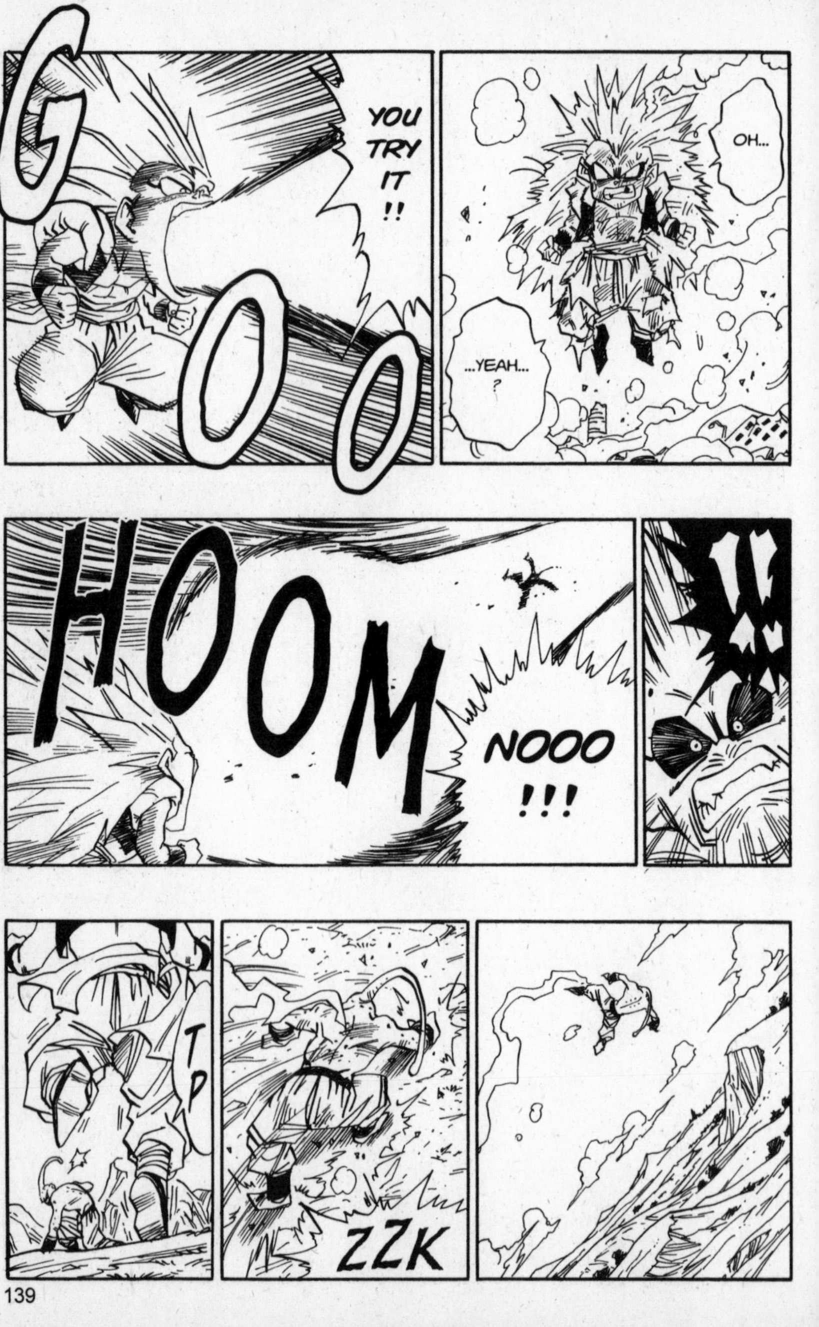
OH...
...YEAH...?
YOU TRY IT!!
GOO
!!
HOOM
NOOO!!!
ZZK
TP

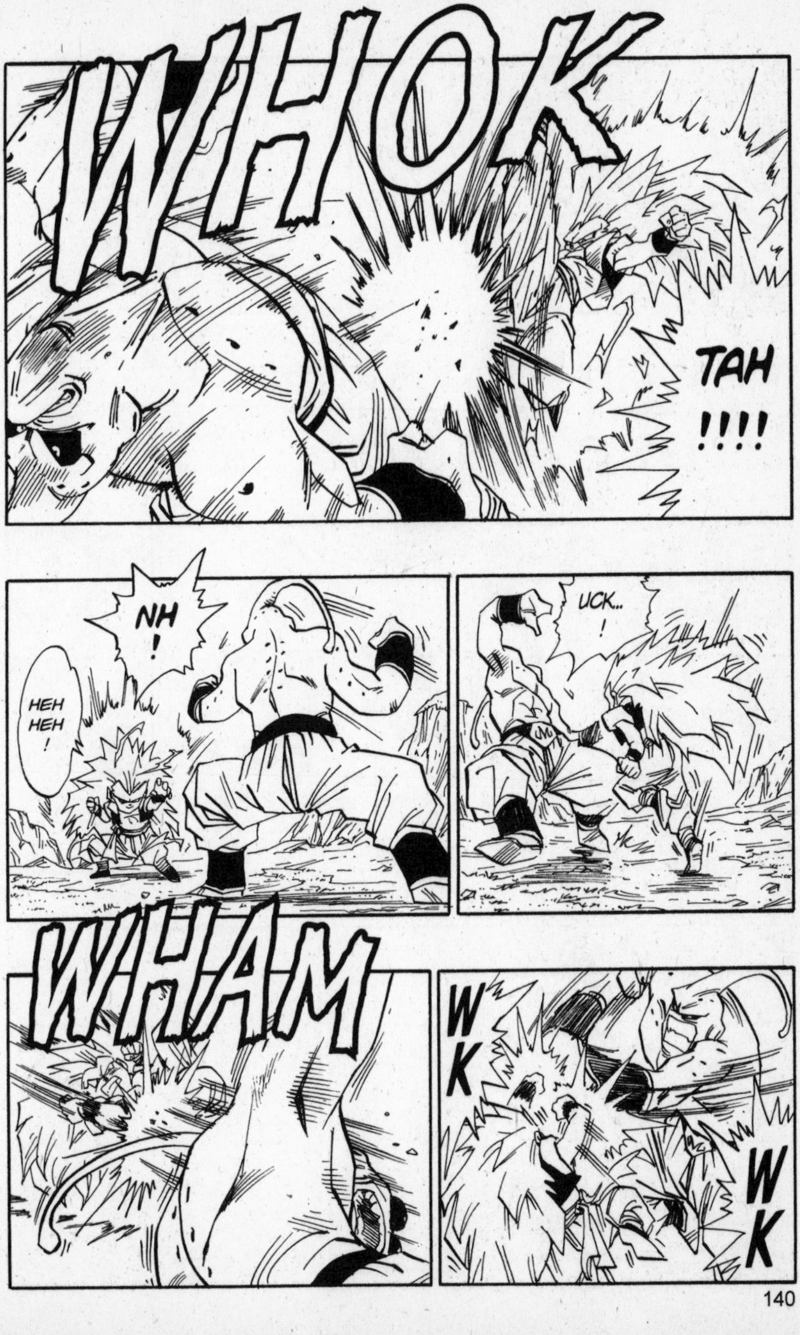
WHOK
TAH!!!!
UCK...!
NH!
HEH HEH!
WK
WK
WHAM

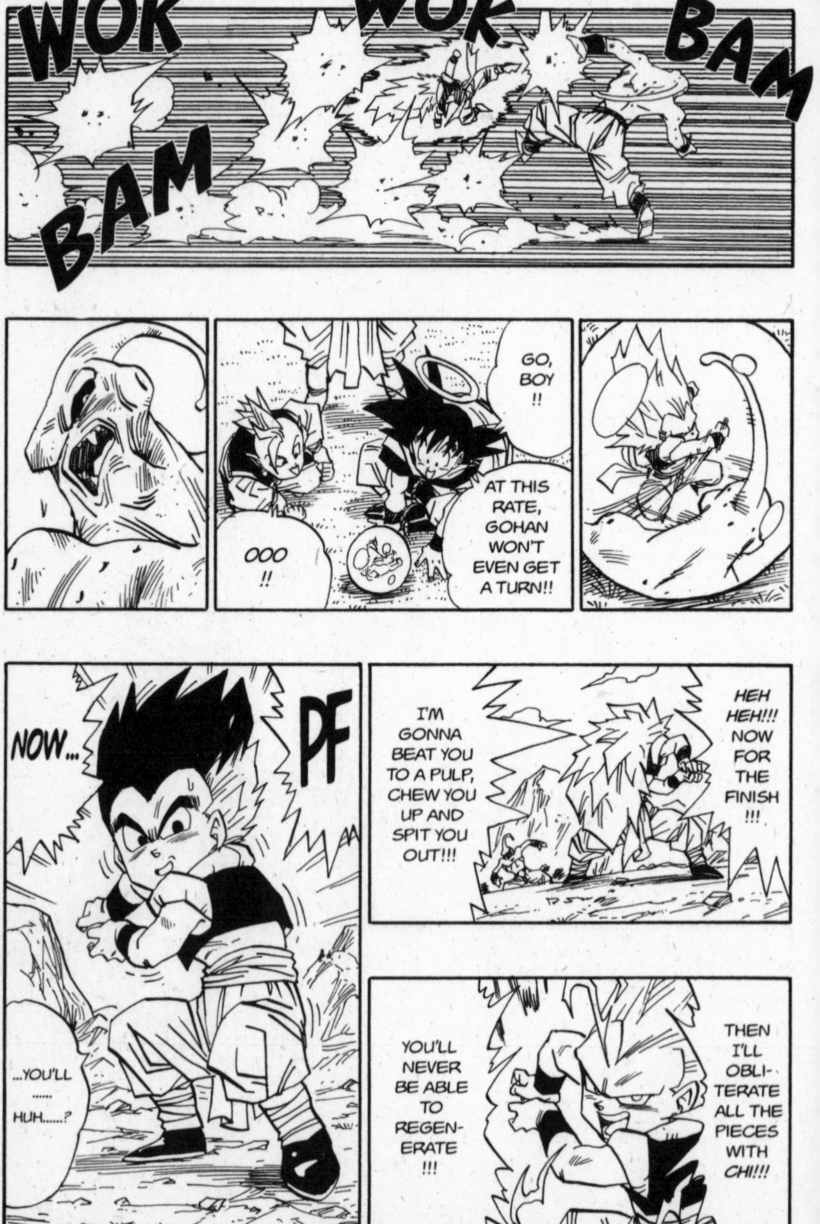
BAM
WOK
WOK
BAM
GO, BOY!!
AT THIS RATE, GOHAN WON'T EVEN GET A TURN!!
OOO!!
HEH HEH!!! NOW FOR THE FINISH!!!
I'M GONNA BEAT YOU TO A PULP, CHEW YOU UP AND SPIT YOU OUT!!!
THEN I'LL OBLITERATE ALL THE PIECES WITH CHI!!!
YOU'LL NEVER BE ABLE TO REGENERATE!!!
PF
NOW...
...YOU'LL ...... HUH......?

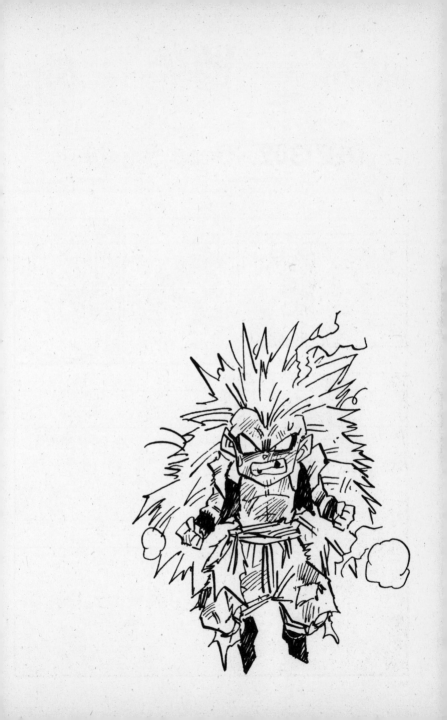

DBZ:302 · Deep Trouble!!

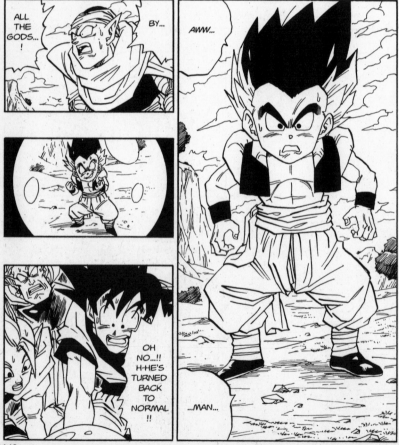

ALL THE GODS...!

BY...

AWW...

OH NO...!! H-HE'S TURNED BACK TO NORMAL!!

...MAN...

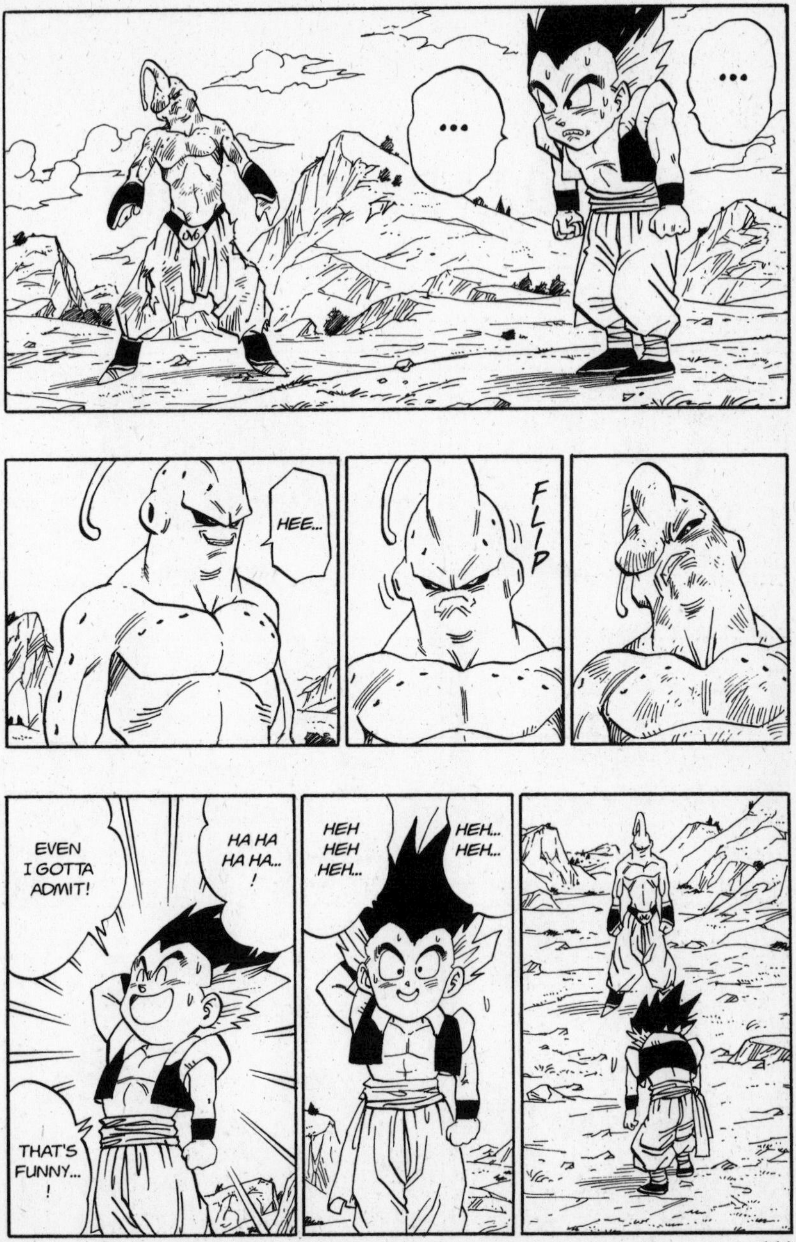
...
...
FLIP
HEE...
HEH... HEH...
HEH HEH HEH...
HA HA HA HA...!
EVEN I GOTTA ADMIT!
THAT'S FUNNY...!

READ THIS WAY

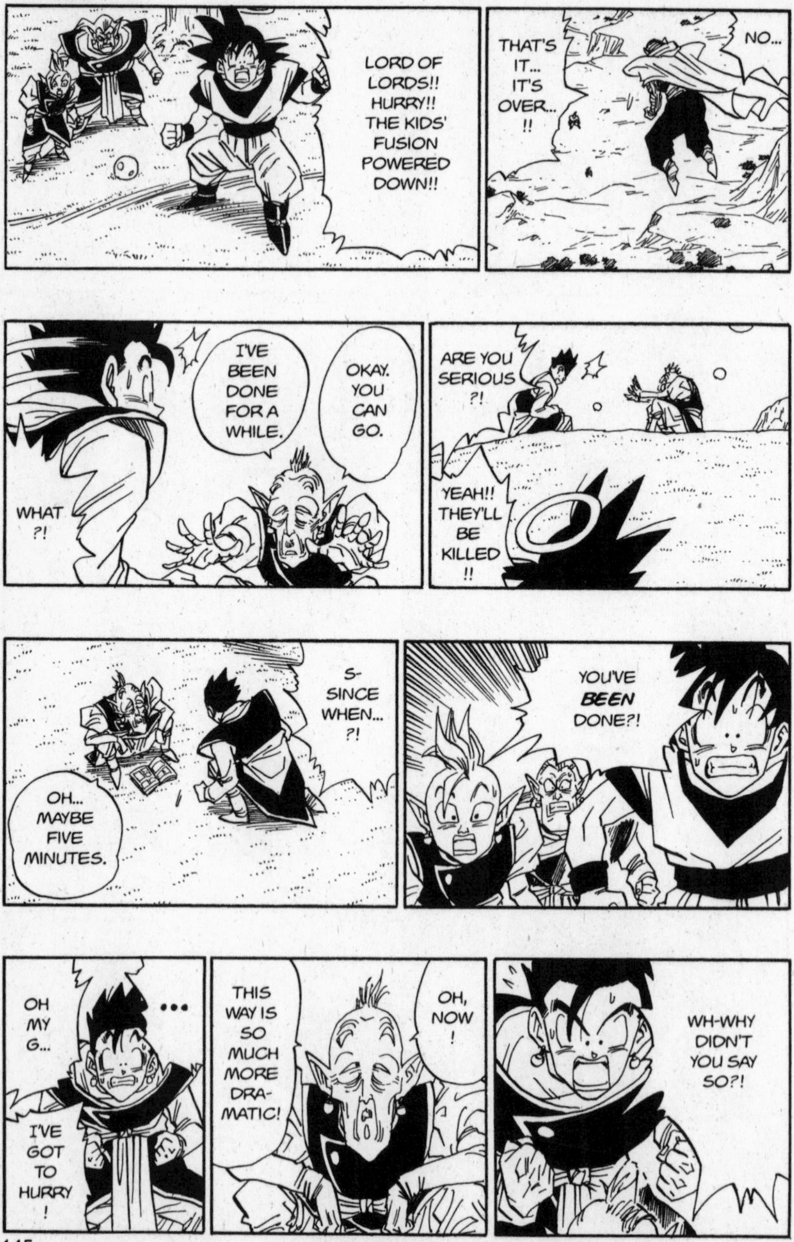
NO...
THAT'S IT... IT'S OVER... !!
LORD OF LORDS!! HURRY!! THE KIDS' FUSION POWERED DOWN!!
ARE YOU SERIOUS ?!
YEAH!! THEY'LL BE KILLED !!
OKAY. YOU CAN GO.
I'VE BEEN DONE FOR A WHILE.
WHAT ?!
YOU'VE BEEN DONE?!
S- SINCE WHEN... ?!
OH... MAYBE FIVE MINUTES.
WH-WHY DIDN'T YOU SAY SO?!
OH, NOW !
THIS WAY IS SO MUCH MORE DRAMATIC!
...
OH MY G...
I'VE GOT TO HURRY !

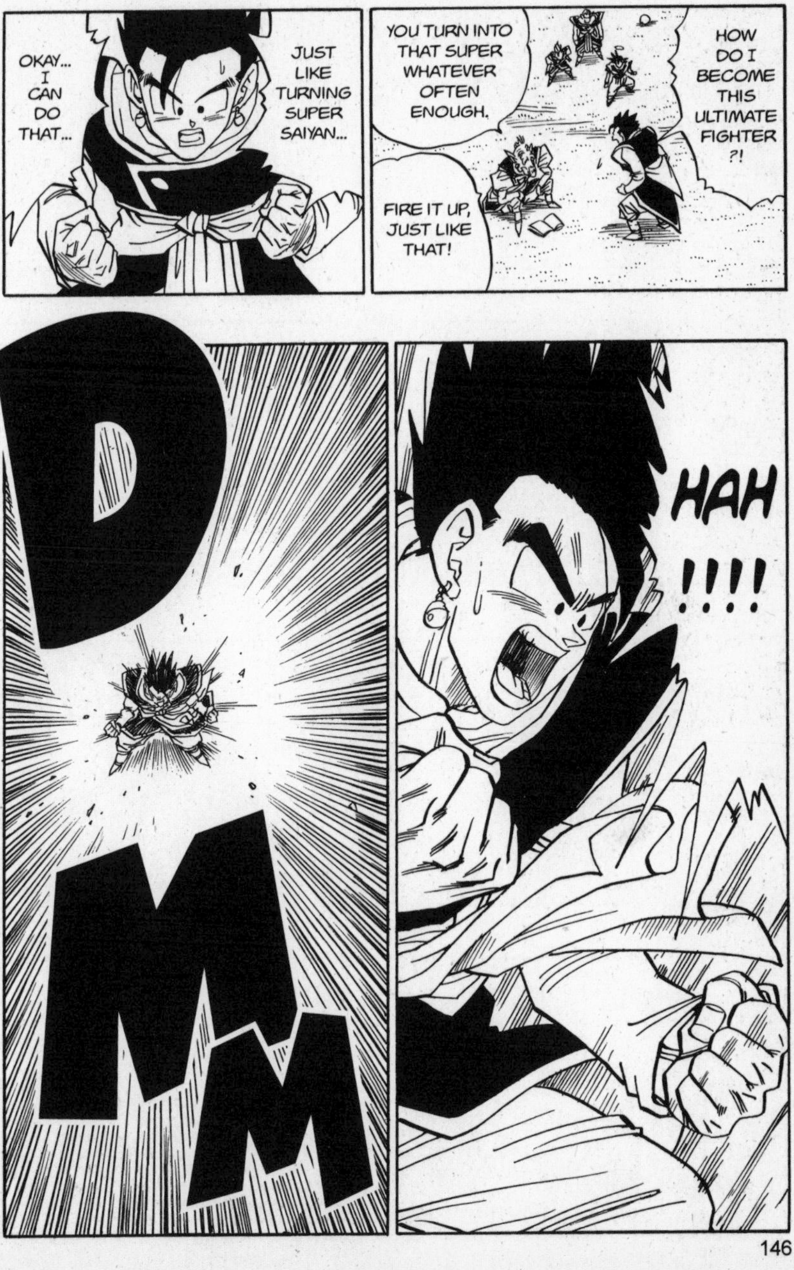
HOW DO I BECOME THIS ULTIMATE FIGHTER?!
YOU TURN INTO THAT SUPER WHATEVER OFTEN ENOUGH.
FIRE IT UP, JUST LIKE THAT!
JUST LIKE TURNING SUPER SAIYAN...
OKAY... I CAN DO THAT...
HAH!!!!
DMM

READ THIS WAY

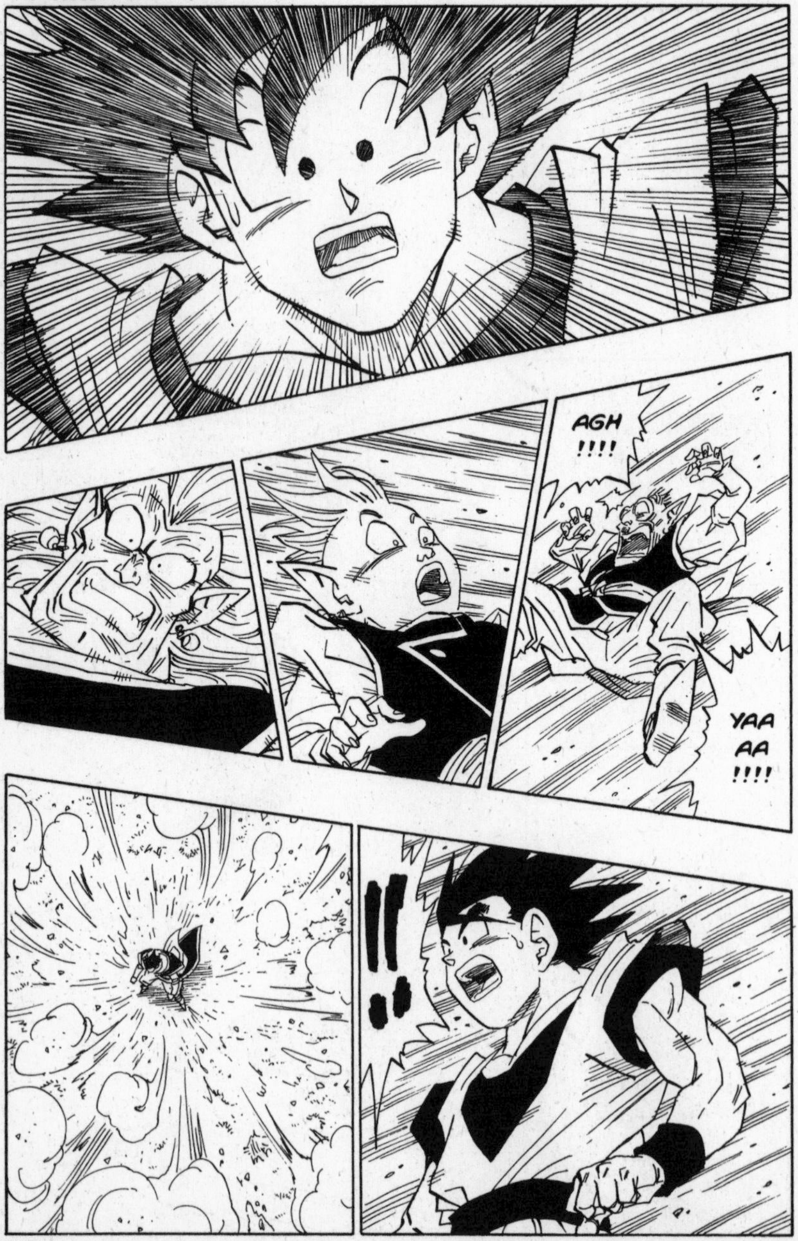
AGH !!!!
YAAAA !!!!
!!

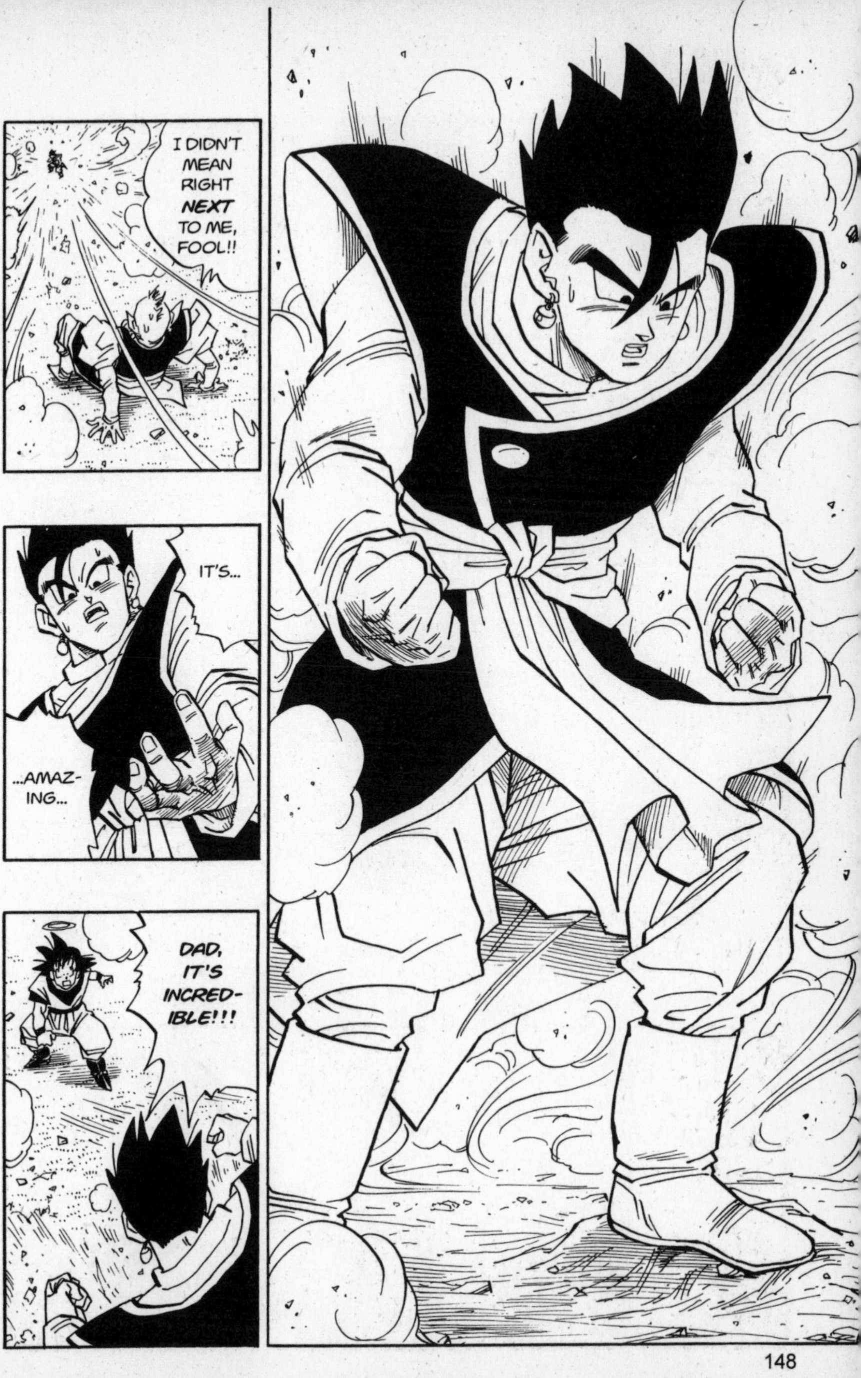
I DIDN'T MEAN RIGHT NEXT TO ME, FOOL!!
IT'S...
...AMAZ-ING...
DAD, IT'S INCRED-IBLE!!!

READ THIS WAY

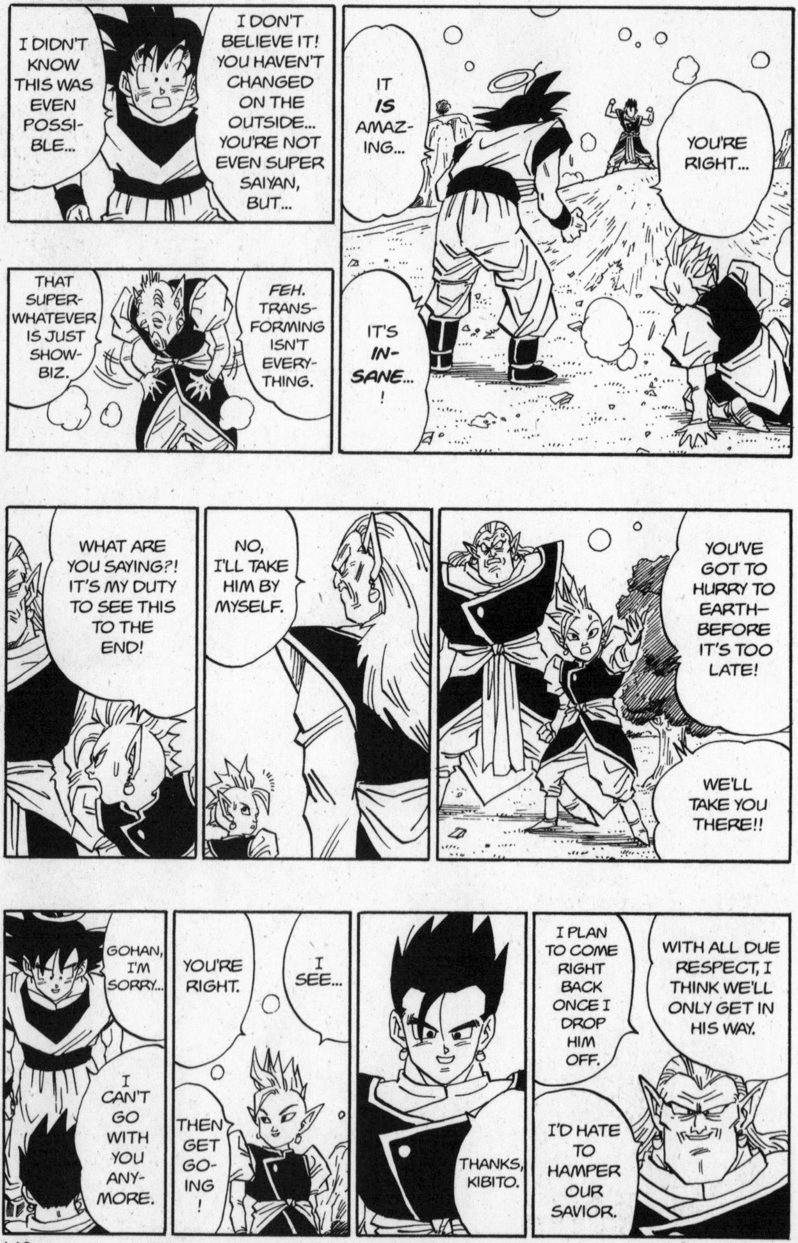

YOU'RE RIGHT...
IT IS AMAZING...
IT'S INSANE...!
I DON'T BELIEVE IT! YOU HAVEN'T CHANGED ON THE OUTSIDE... YOU'RE NOT EVEN SUPER SAIYAN, BUT...
I DIDN'T KNOW THIS WAS EVEN POSSIBLE...
FEH. TRANSFORMING ISN'T EVERYTHING.
THAT SUPER-WHATEVER IS JUST SHOW-BIZ.
YOU'VE GOT TO HURRY TO EARTH—BEFORE IT'S TOO LATE!
WE'LL TAKE YOU THERE!!
NO, I'LL TAKE HIM BY MYSELF.
WHAT ARE YOU SAYING?! IT'S MY DUTY TO SEE THIS TO THE END!
WITH ALL DUE RESPECT, I THINK WE'LL ONLY GET IN HIS WAY.
I PLAN TO COME RIGHT BACK ONCE I DROP HIM OFF.
I'D HATE TO HAMPER OUR SAVIOR.
THANKS, KIBITO.
I SEE...
YOU'RE RIGHT.
THEN GET GOING!
GOHAN, I'M SORRY...
I CAN'T GO WITH YOU ANYMORE.

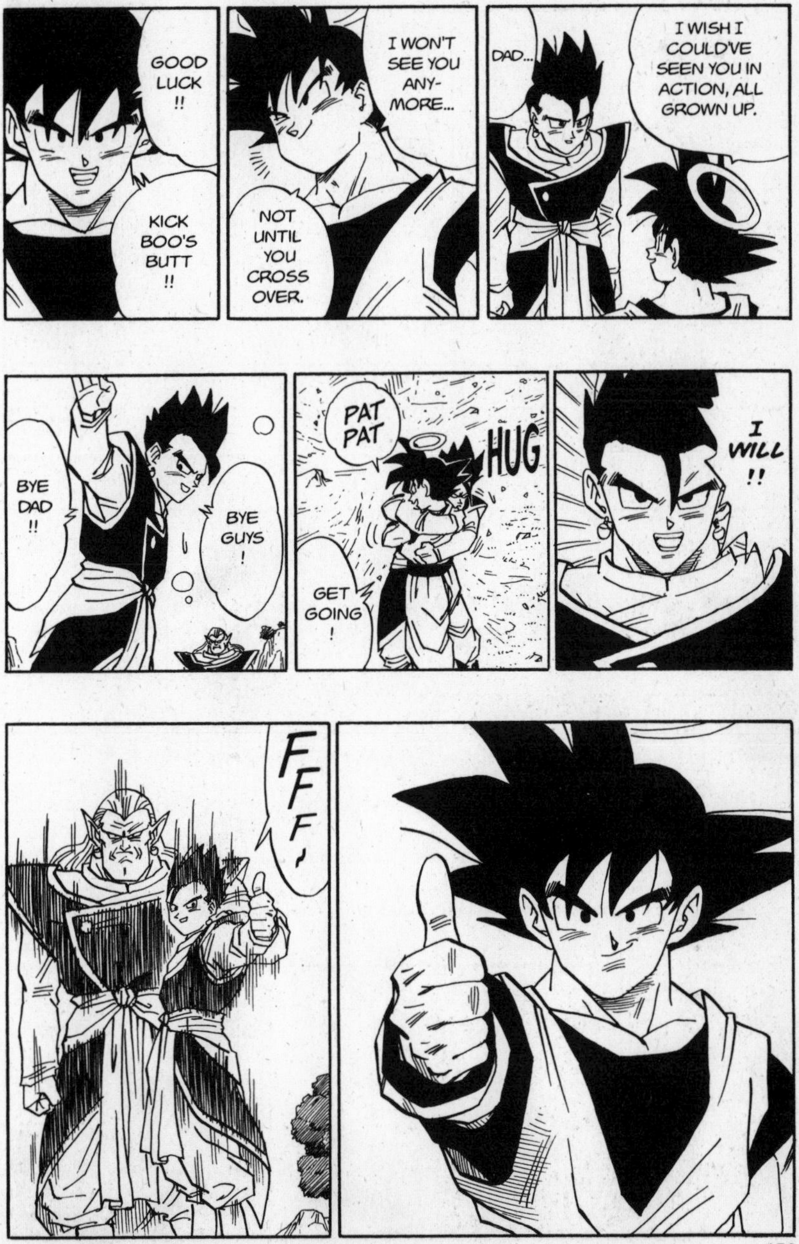
I WISH I COULD'VE SEEN YOU IN ACTION, ALL GROWN UP.
DAD...
I WON'T SEE YOU ANYMORE...
NOT UNTIL YOU CROSS OVER.
GOOD LUCK !!
KICK BOO'S BUTT !!
I WILL !!
HUG
PAT PAT
GET GOING !
BYE GUYS !
BYE DAD !!
FFF

READ THIS WAY

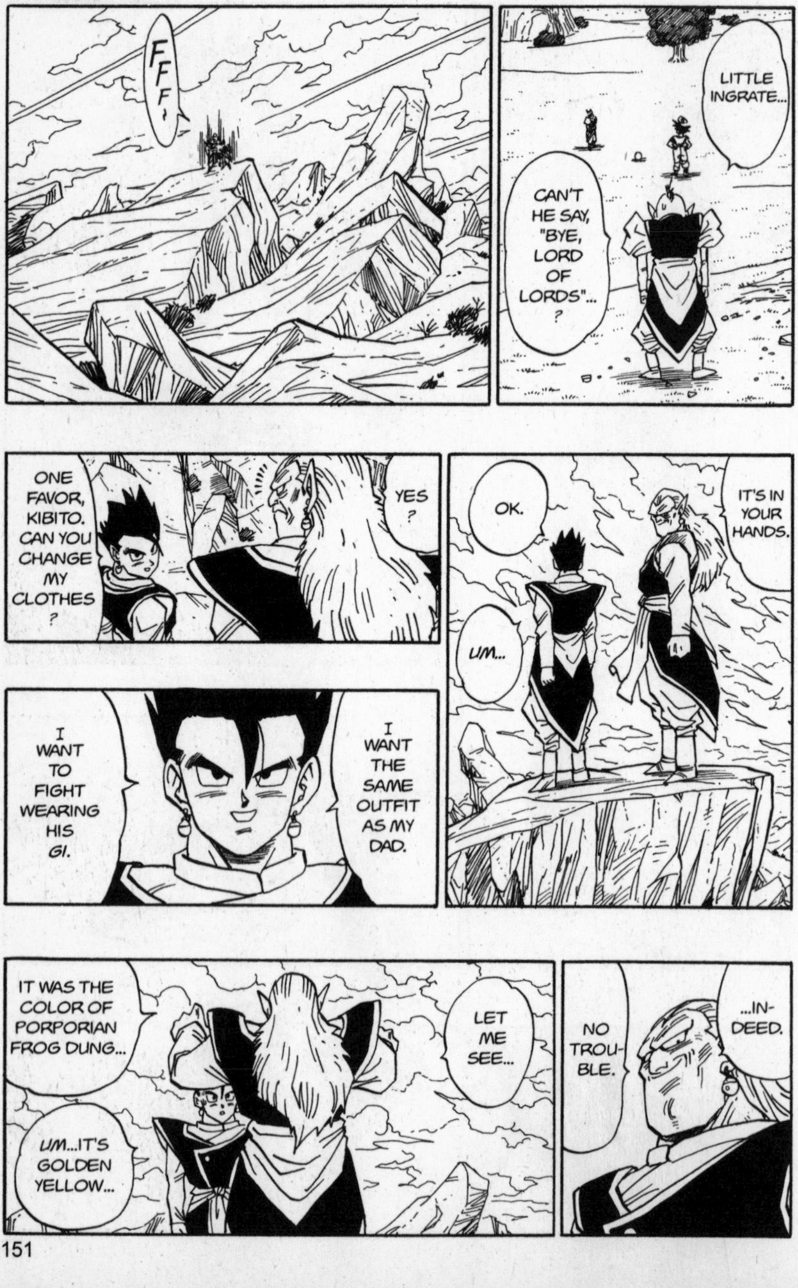
LITTLE INGRATE...
CAN'T HE SAY, "BYE, LORD OF LORDS"...?
FFF
IT'S IN YOUR HANDS.
OK.
UM...
YES?
ONE FAVOR, KIBITO. CAN YOU CHANGE MY CLOTHES?
I WANT THE SAME OUTFIT AS MY DAD.
I WANT TO FIGHT WEARING HIS *GI*.
...INDEED.
NO TROUBLE.
LET ME SEE...
IT WAS THE COLOR OF PORPORIAN FROG DUNG...
UM...IT'S GOLDEN YELLOW...

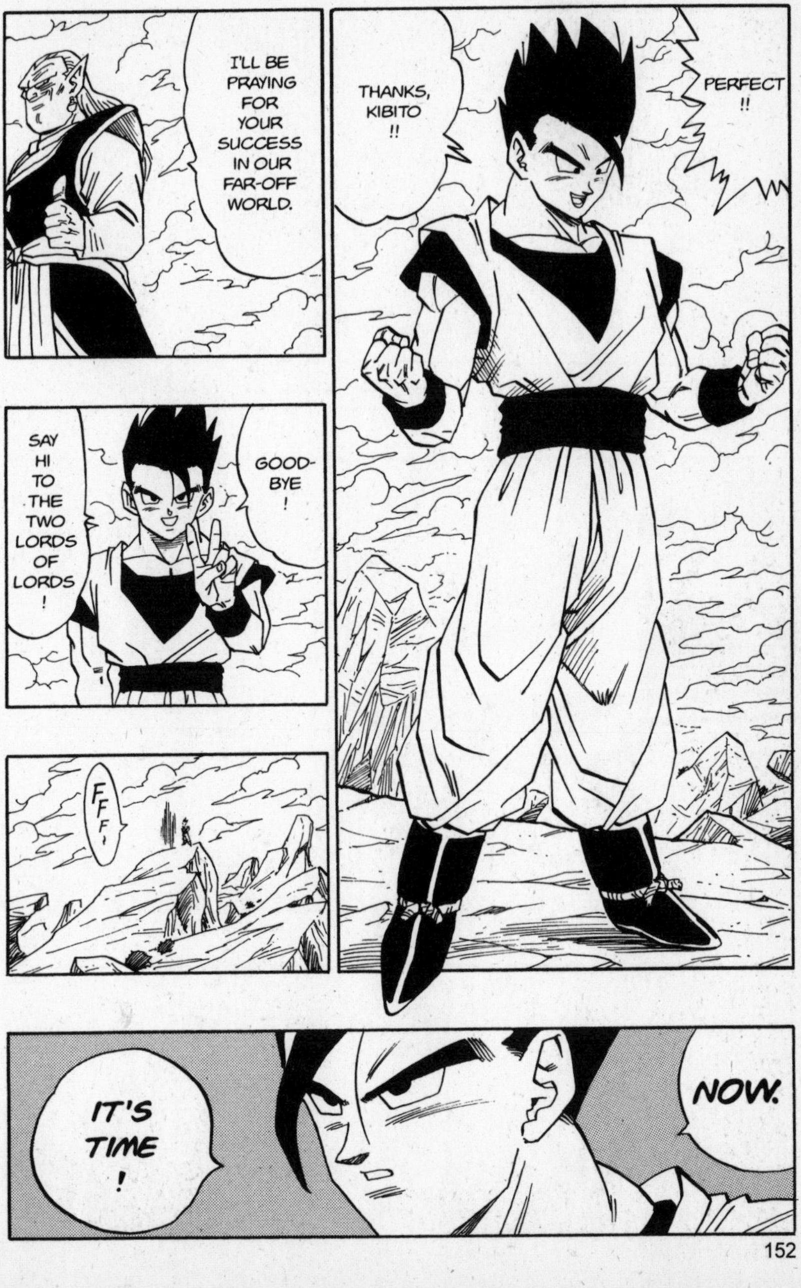
PERFECT !!
THANKS, KIBITO !!
I'LL BE PRAYING FOR YOUR SUCCESS IN OUR FAR-OFF WORLD.
GOOD-BYE !
SAY HI TO THE TWO LORDS OF LORDS !
FFF
NOW.
IT'S TIME !

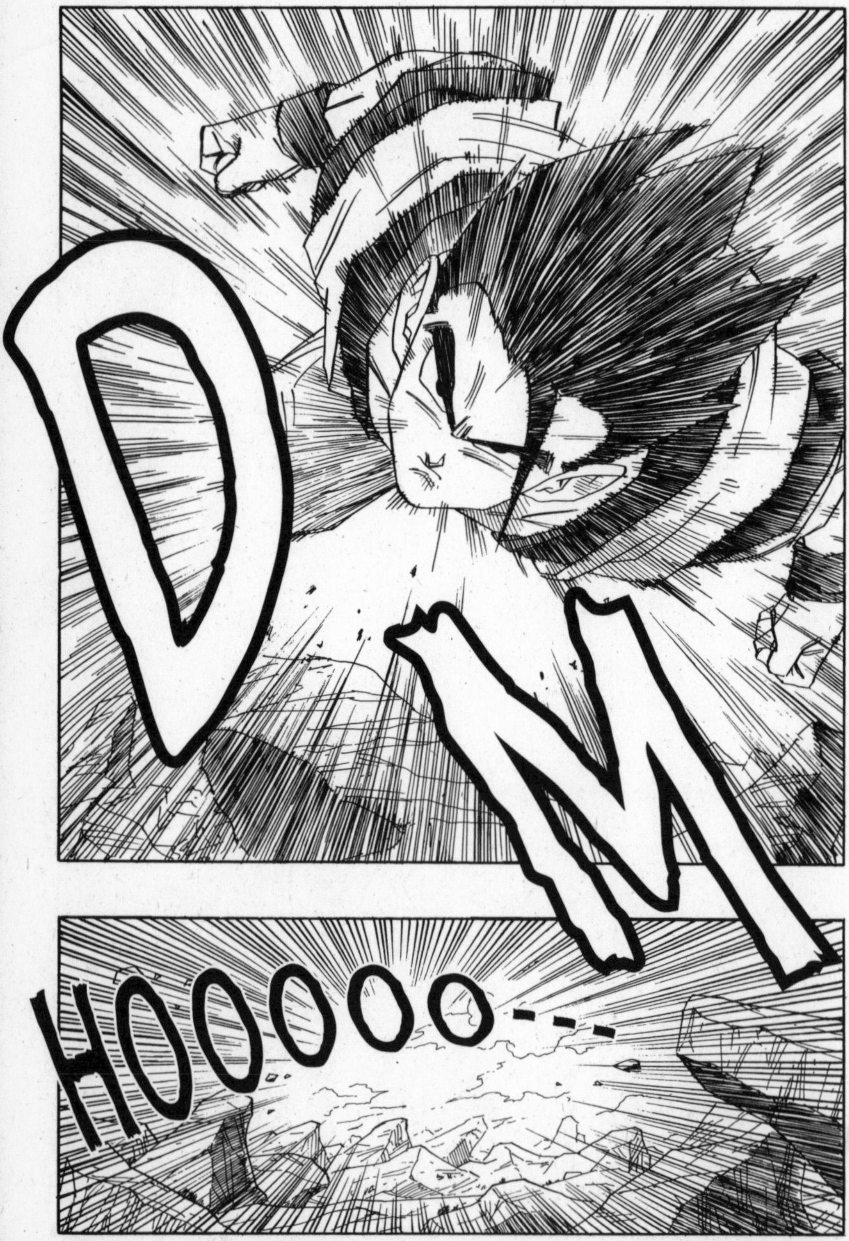
DOM
HOOOOO...

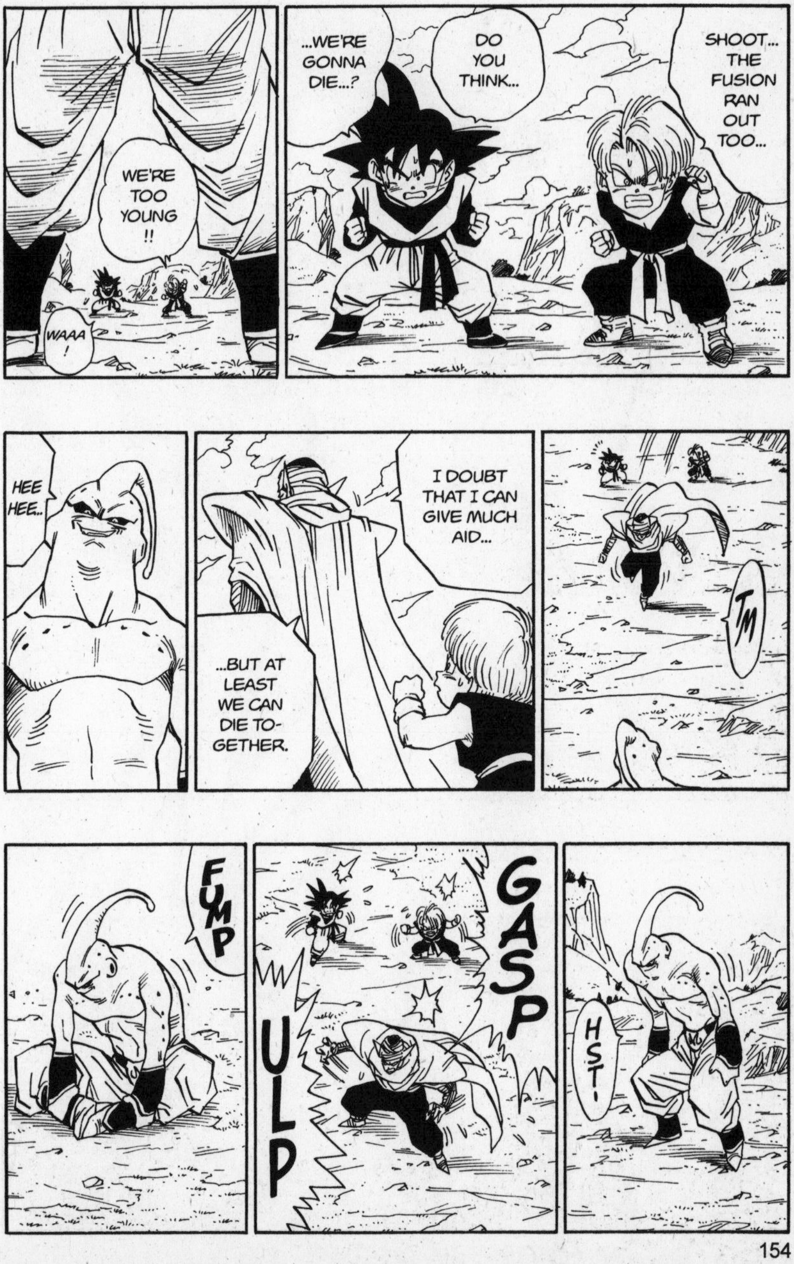
SHOOT... THE FUSION RAN OUT TOO...
DO YOU THINK...
...WE'RE GONNA DIE...?
WE'RE TOO YOUNG !!
WAAA !
TM
I DOUBT THAT I CAN GIVE MUCH AID...
...BUT AT LEAST WE CAN DIE TO-GETHER.
HEE HEE..
HST!
GASP
ULP
FUMP

READ THIS WAY

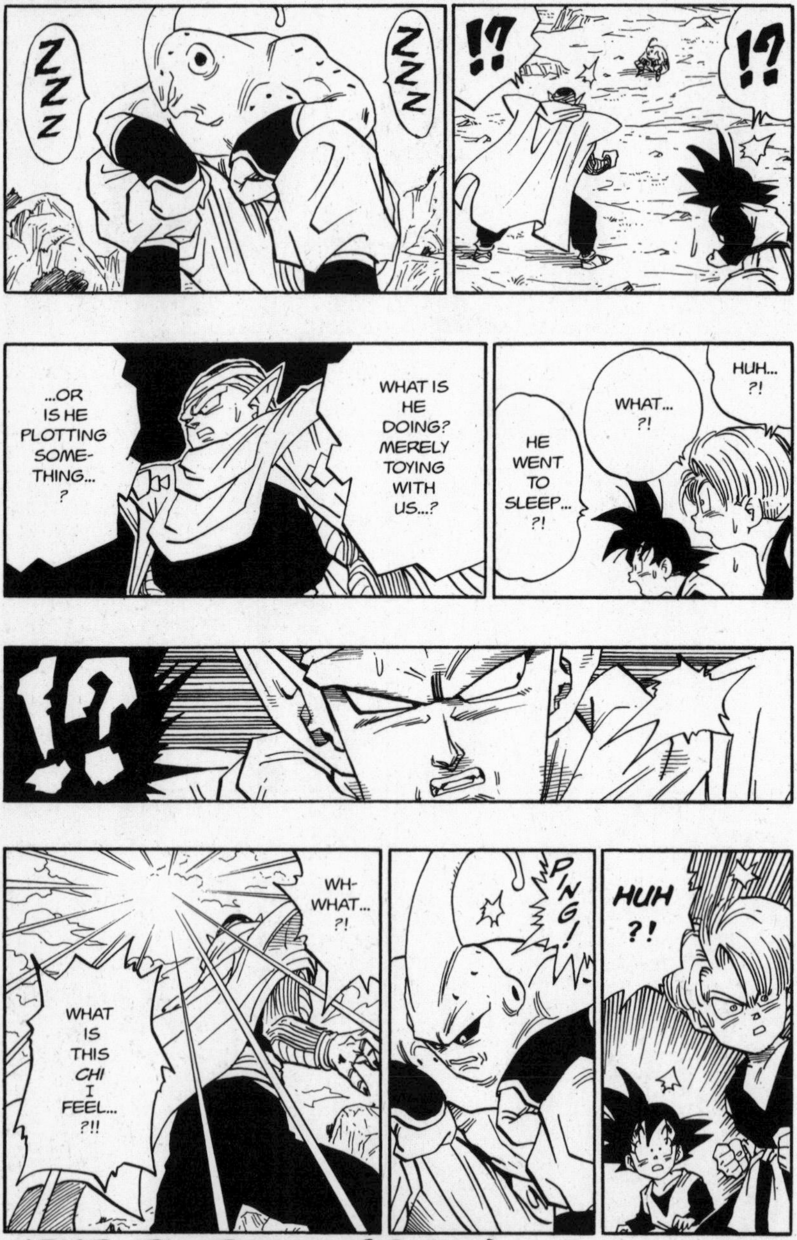
!?
!?
ZZZ
ZZZ
HUH... ?!
WHAT... ?!
HE WENT TO SLEEP... ?!
WHAT IS HE DOING? MERELY TOYING WITH US...?
...OR IS HE PLOTTING SOMETHING... ?
!?
HUH ?!
PING!
WH-WHAT... ?!
WHAT IS THIS *CHI* I FEEL... ?!!

NEXT: The Return of Gohan!

DBZ:303 · Gohan's Counterattack!

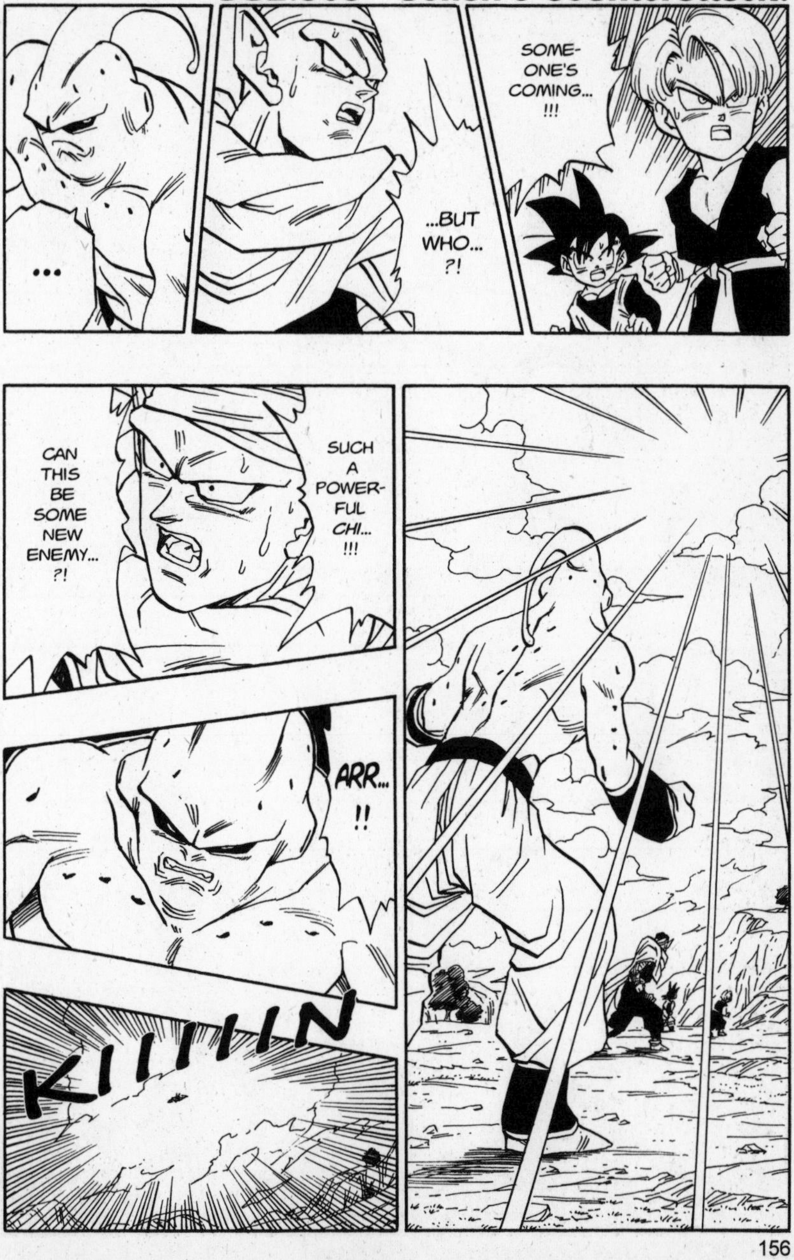

SOME-ONE'S COMING... !!!
...BUT WHO... ?!
...
SUCH A POWER-FUL CHI... !!!
CAN THIS BE SOME NEW ENEMY... ?!
ARR... !!
KIIIIIN

READ THIS WAY

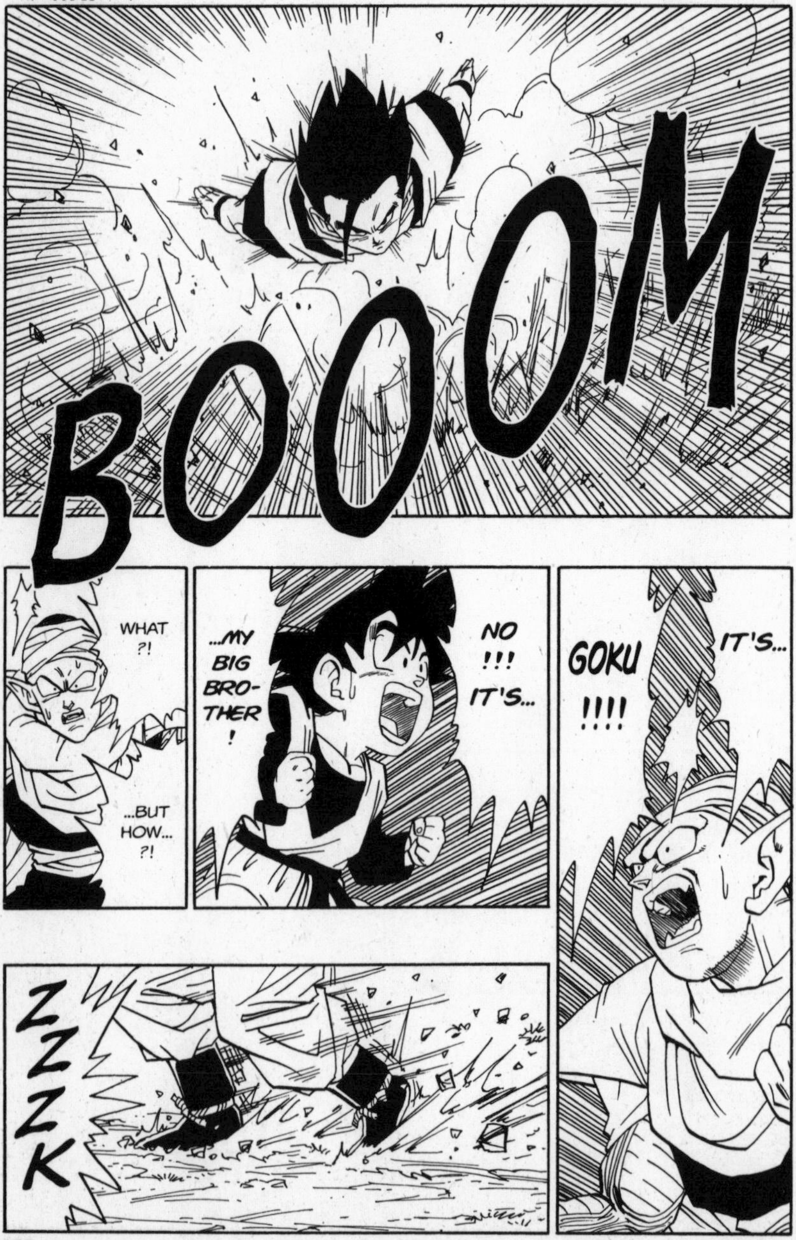
BOOOM
IT'S...
GOKU !!!!
NO !!! IT'S...
...MY BIG BROTHER !
WHAT ?!
...BUT HOW... ?!
ZZZK

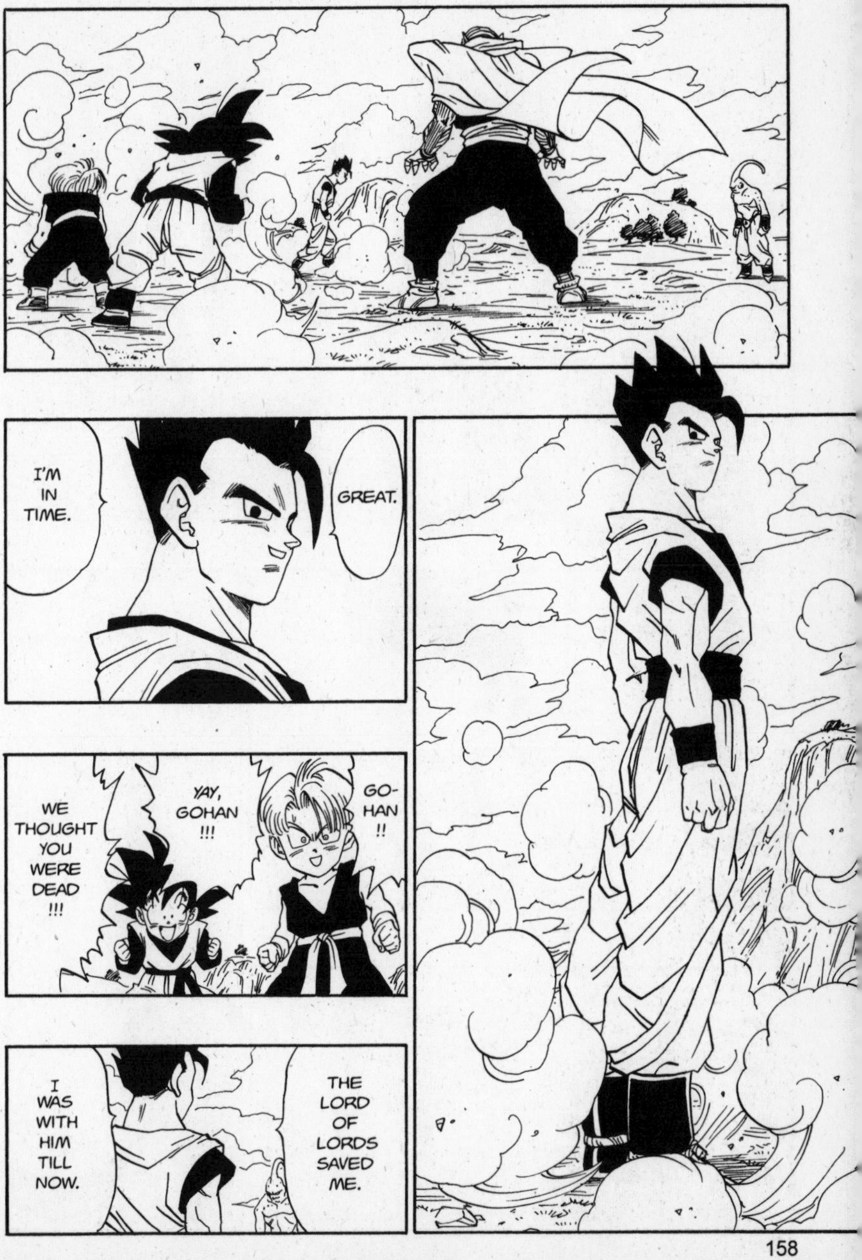
GREAT.
I'M IN TIME.
GO-HAN!!
YAY, GOHAN!!!
WE THOUGHT YOU WERE DEAD!!!
THE LORD OF LORDS SAVED ME.
I WAS WITH HIM TILL NOW.

READ THIS WAY

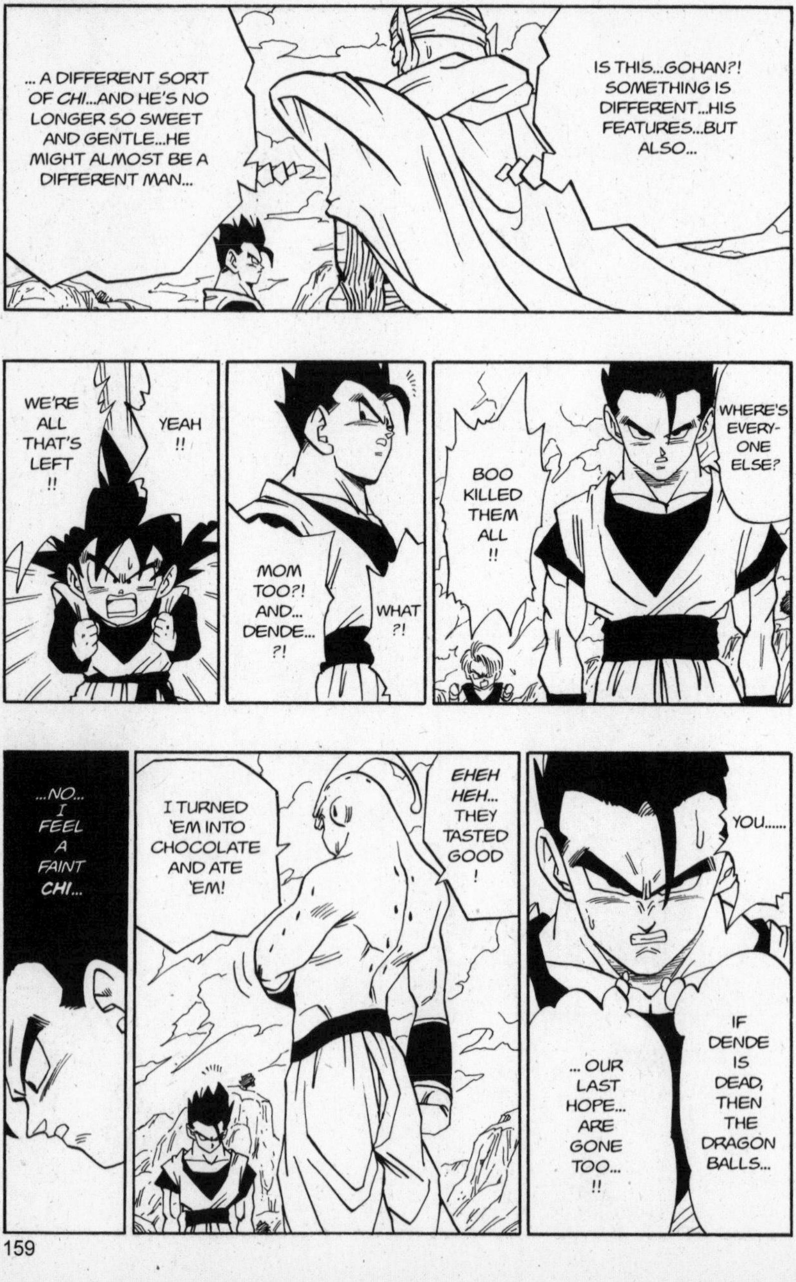
IS THIS...GOHAN?! SOMETHING IS DIFFERENT...HIS FEATURES...BUT ALSO...
... A DIFFERENT SORT OF *CHI*...AND HE'S NO LONGER SO SWEET AND GENTLE...HE MIGHT ALMOST BE A DIFFERENT MAN...
WHERE'S EVERY-ONE ELSE?
BOO KILLED THEM ALL !!
WHAT ?!
MOM TOO?! AND... DENDE... ?!
YEAH !!
WE'RE ALL THAT'S LEFT !!
YOU......
IF DENDE IS DEAD, THEN THE DRAGON BALLS...
... OUR LAST HOPE... ARE GONE TOO... !!
EHEH HEH... THEY TASTED GOOD !
I TURNED 'EM INTO CHOCOLATE AND ATE 'EM!
...NO... I FEEL A FAINT *CHI*...

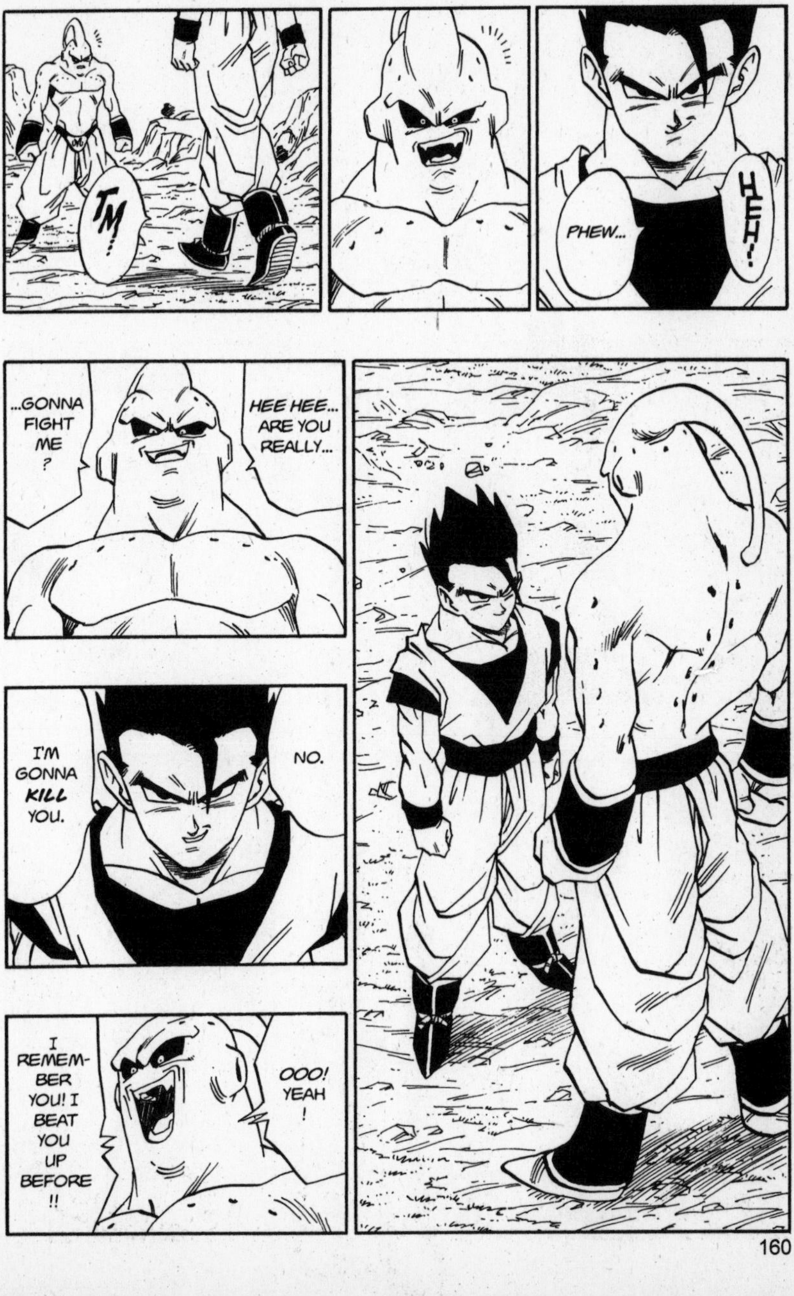
HEH!
PHEW...
TM!
HEE HEE... ARE YOU REALLY...
...GONNA FIGHT ME?
NO.
I'M GONNA **KILL** YOU.
OOO! YEAH!
I REMEMBER YOU! I BEAT YOU UP BEFORE!!

READ THIS WAY

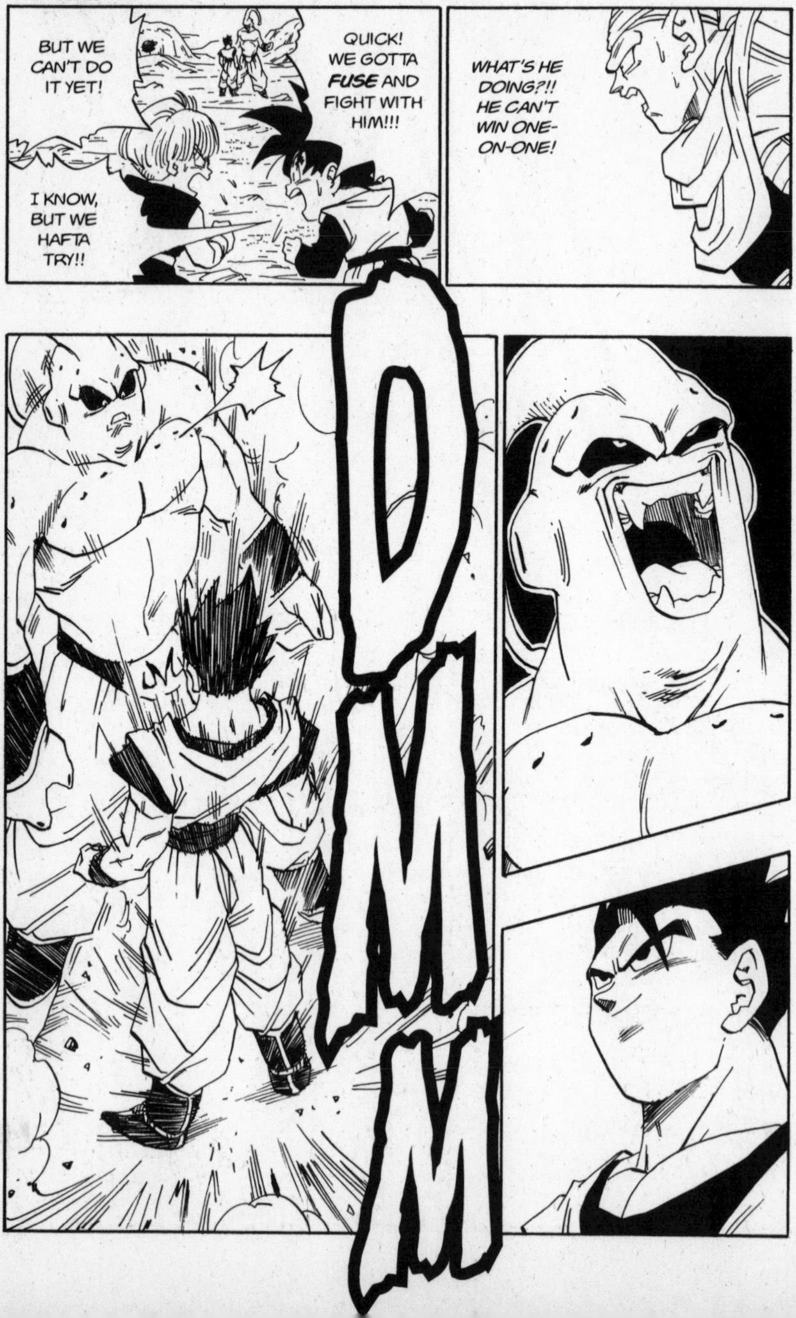

WHAT'S HE DOING?!! HE CAN'T WIN ONE-ON-ONE!
QUICK! WE GOTTA **FUSE** AND FIGHT WITH HIM!!!
BUT WE CAN'T DO IT YET!
I KNOW, BUT WE HAFTA TRY!!
DMM

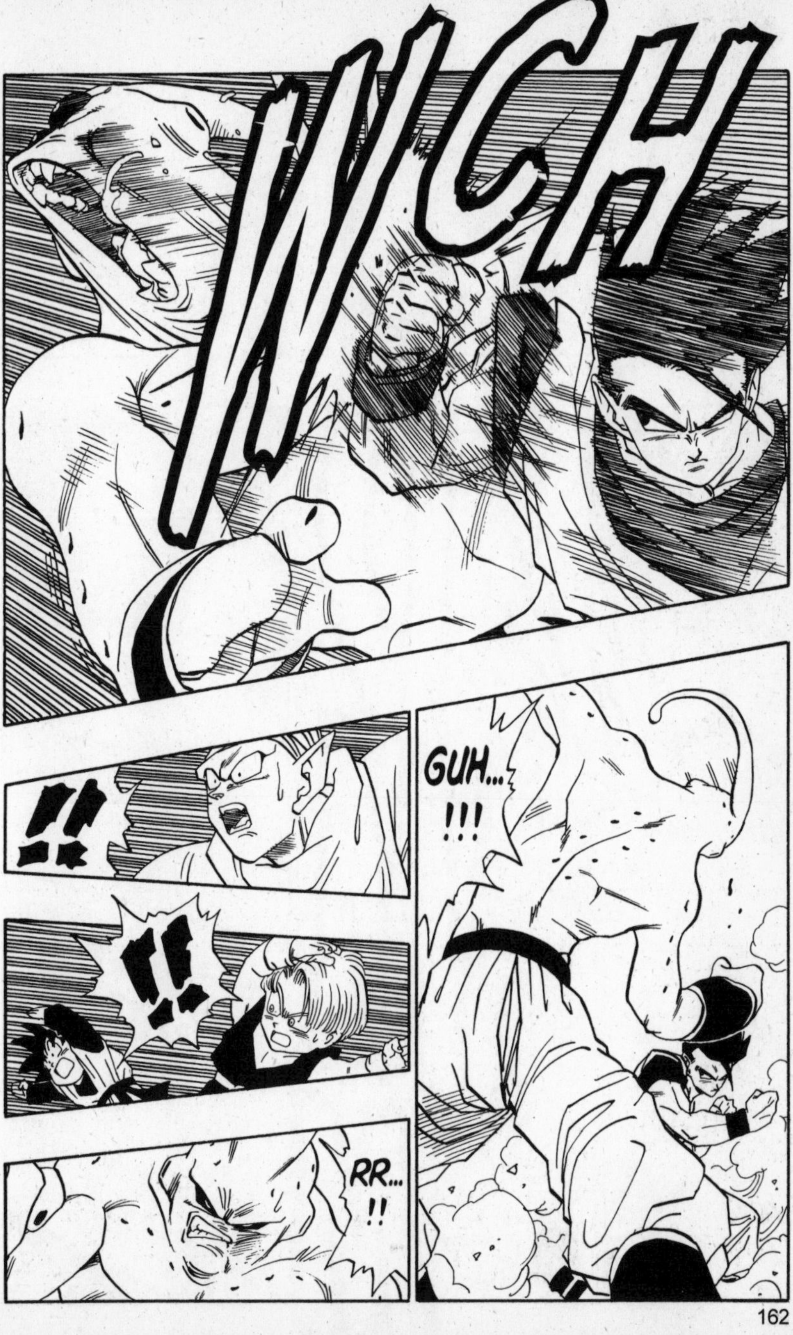
WCH
GUH... !!!
!!
!!
RR... !!

READ THIS WAY

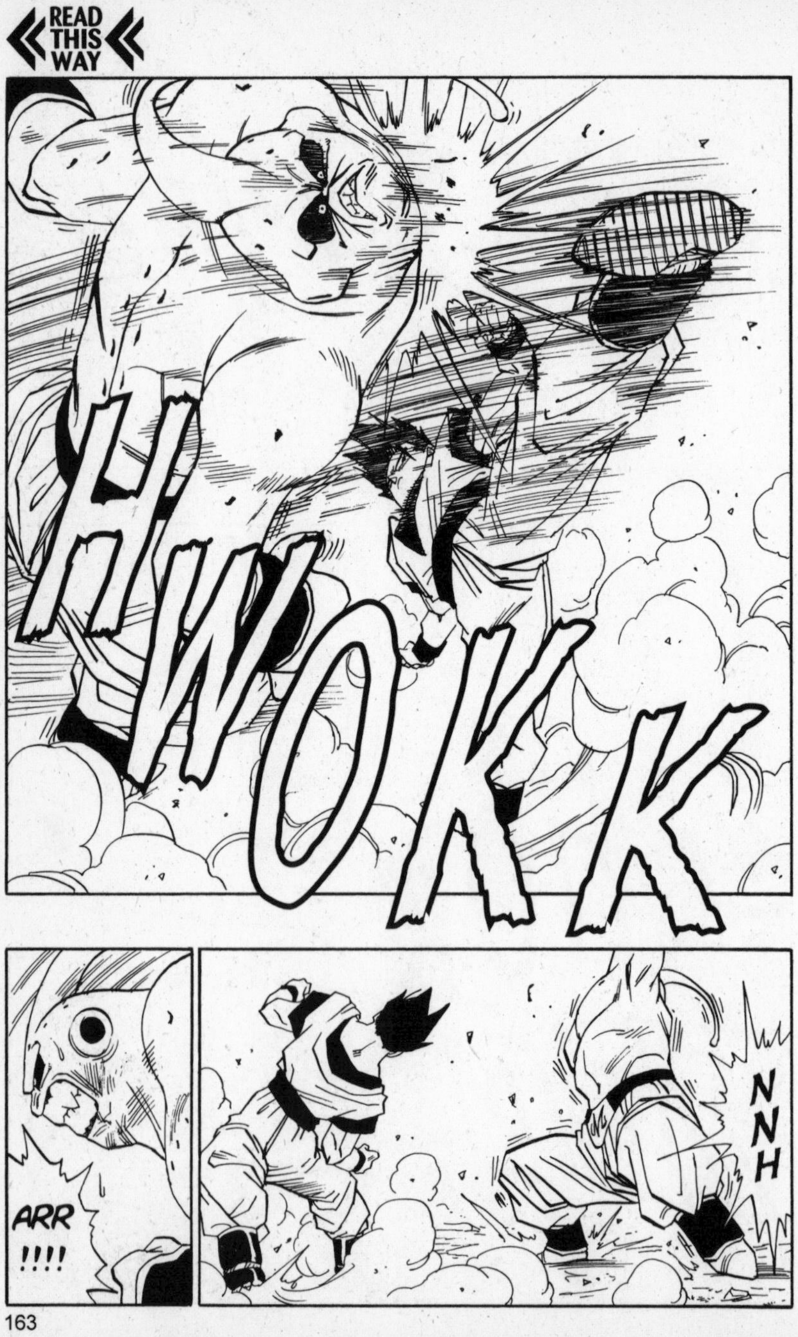
HWOKK
NNH
ARR !!!!

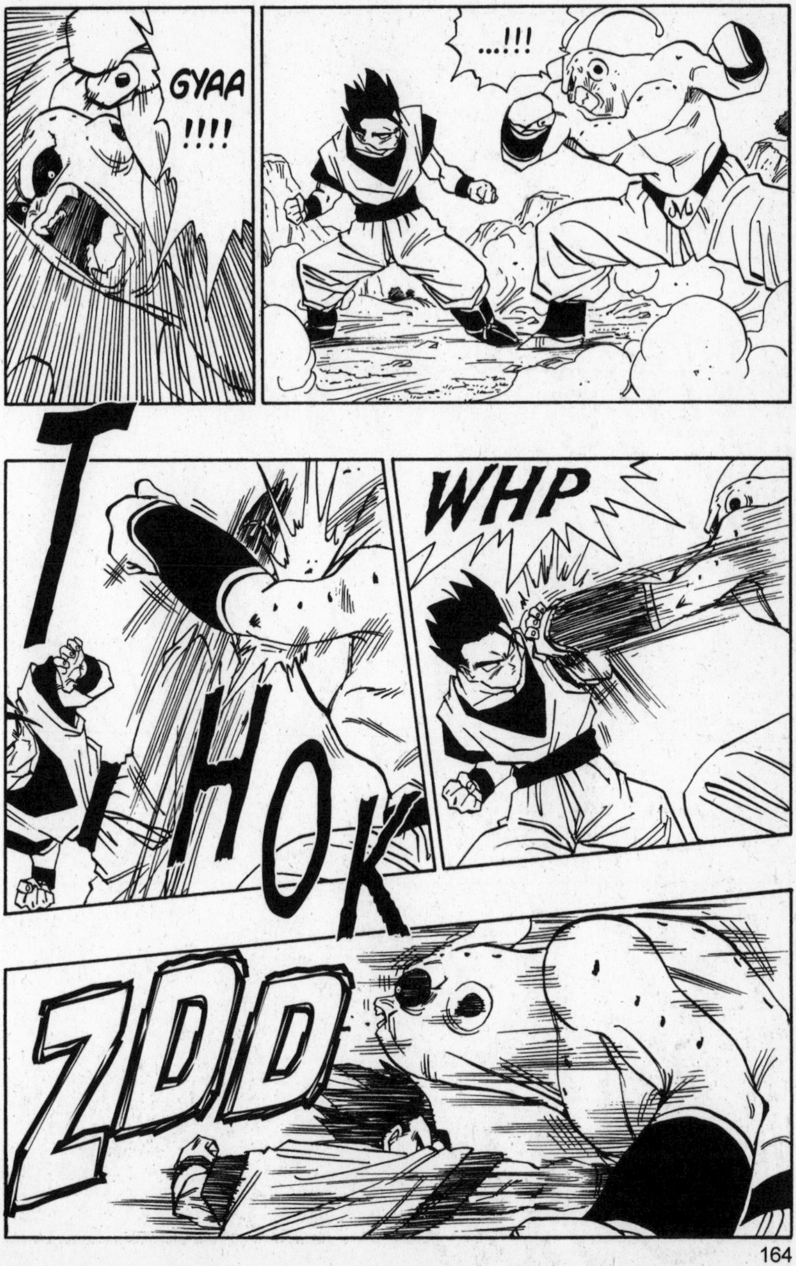
...!!!
GYAA !!!!
WHP
THOK
ZDD

READ THIS WAY

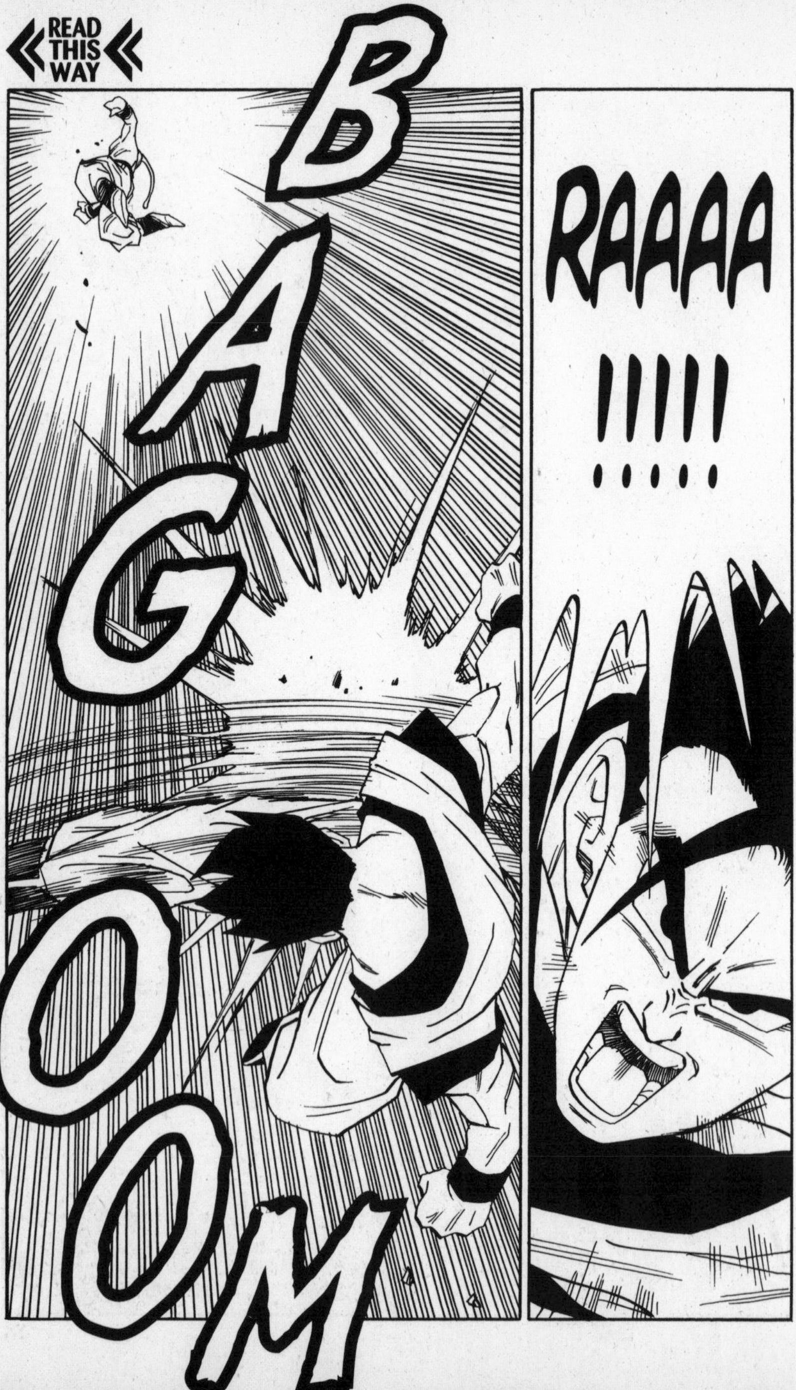
RAAAA!!!!!
BAGOOOM

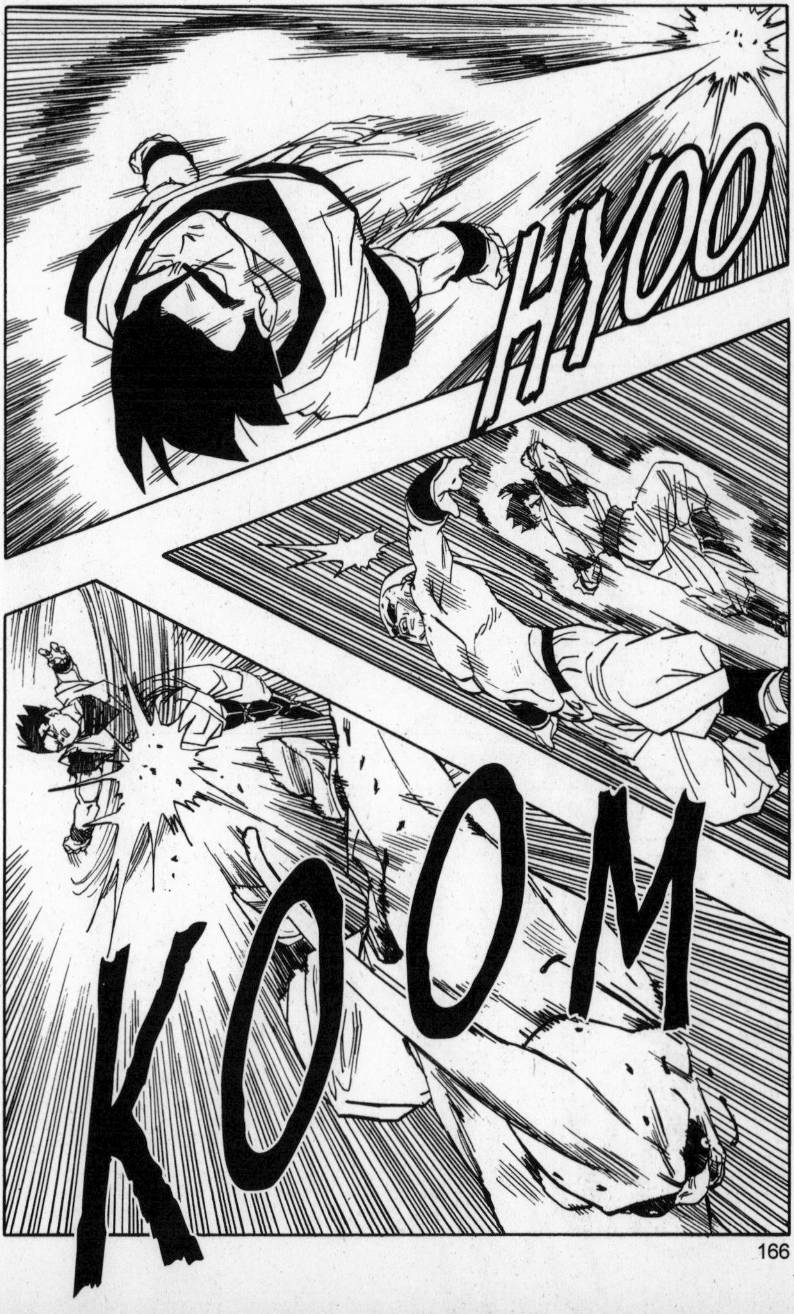
HYOO
KOOM

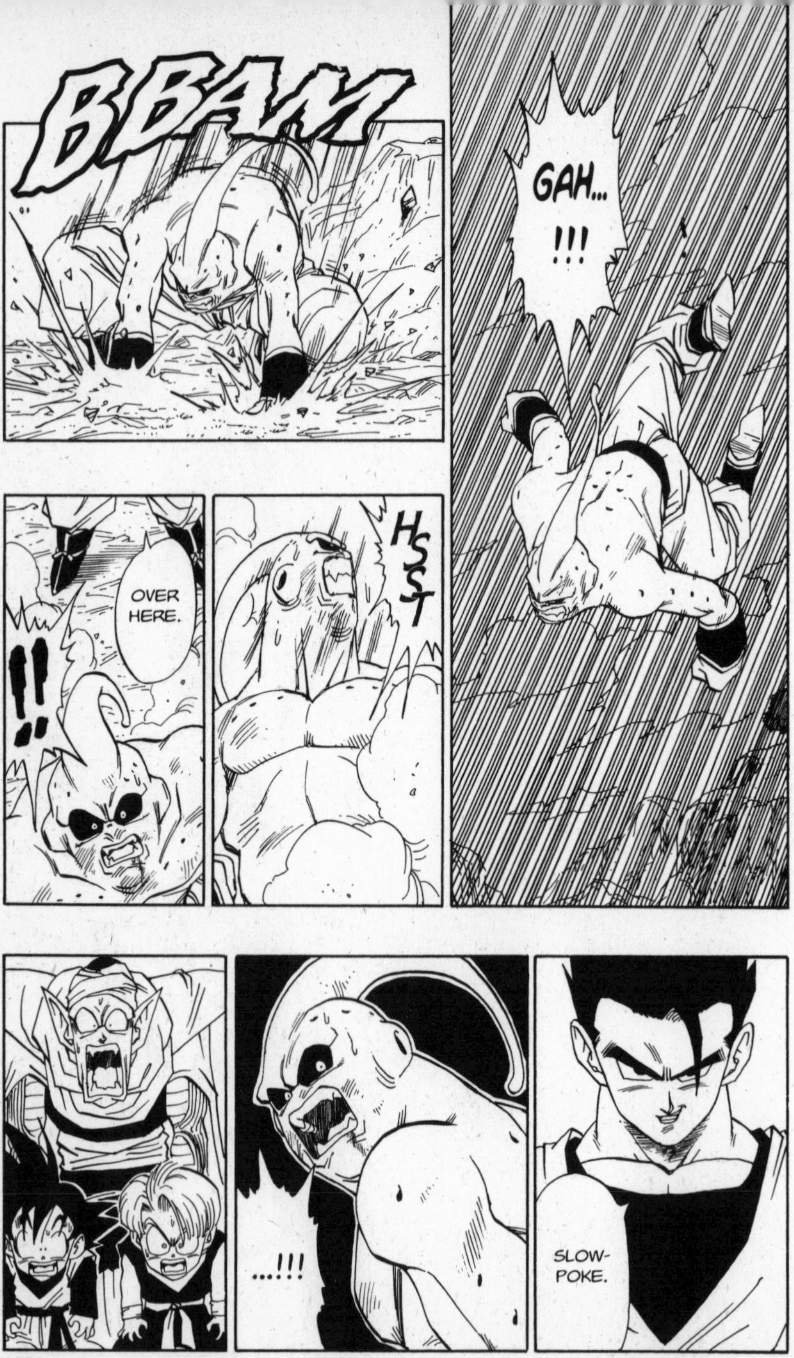
GAH...
!!!
BBAM
HSST
OVER HERE.
!!
SLOW-POKE.
...!!!

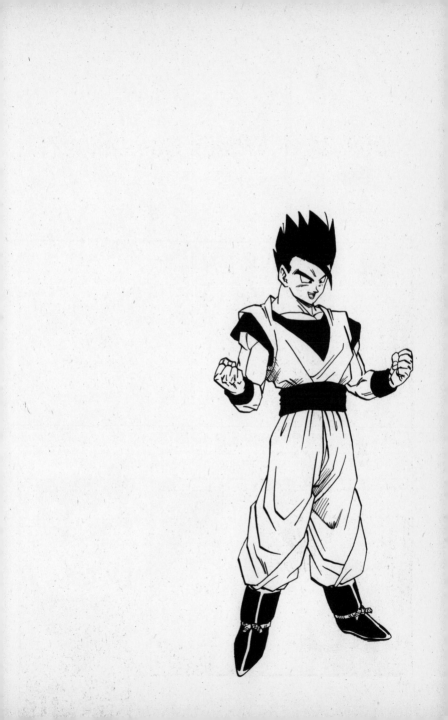

DBZ:304 • What's Boo Doing?!

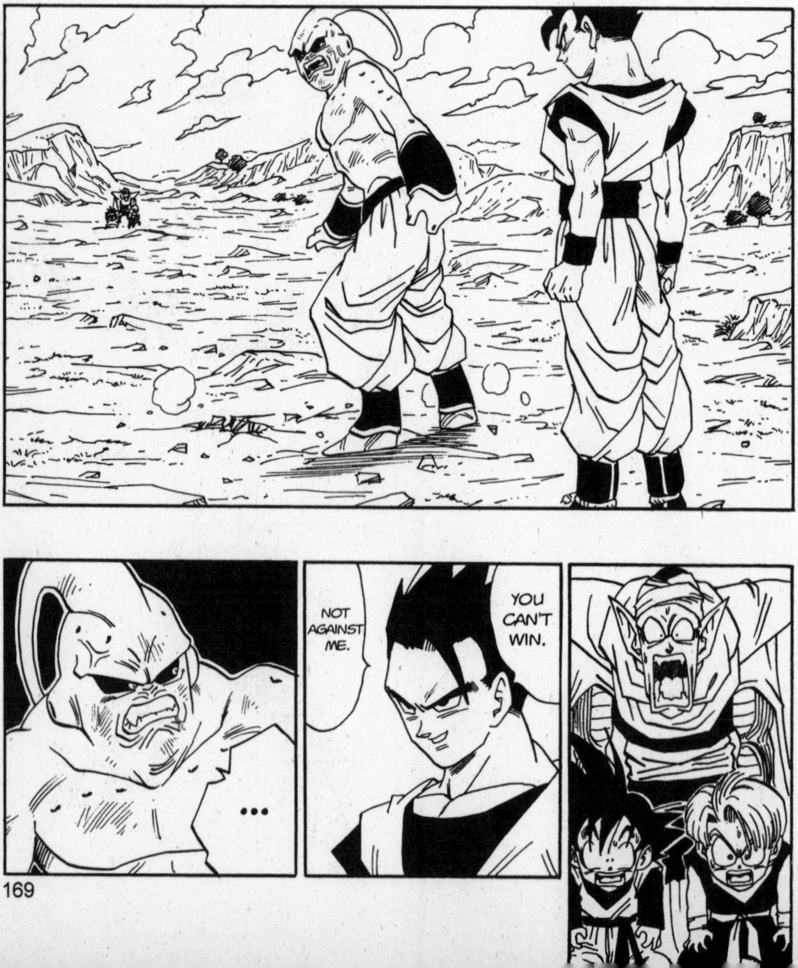
YOU CAN'T WIN.
NOT AGAINST ME.
...

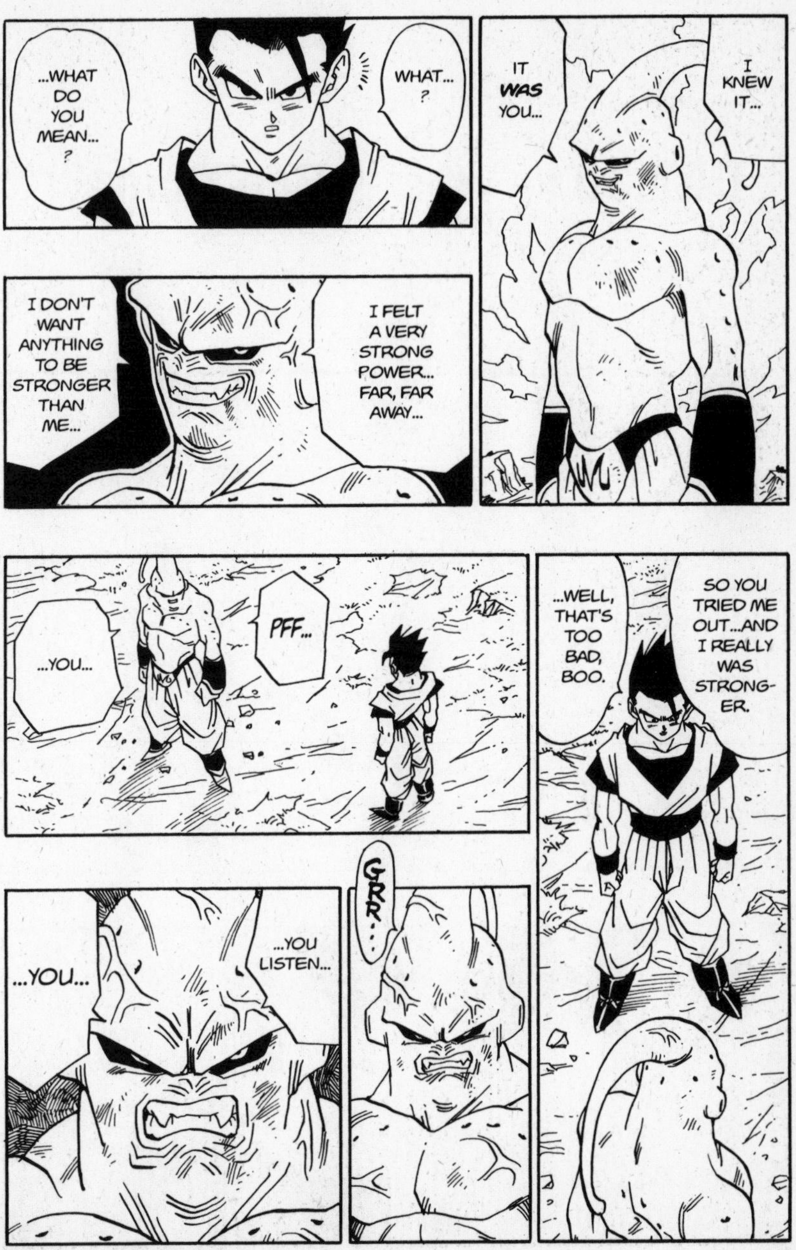
I KNEW IT...
IT WAS YOU...
WHAT...?
...WHAT DO YOU MEAN...?
I FELT A VERY STRONG POWER... FAR, FAR AWAY...
I DON'T WANT ANYTHING TO BE STRONGER THAN ME...
SO YOU TRIED ME OUT...AND I REALLY WAS STRONGER.
...WELL, THAT'S TOO BAD, BOO.
PFF...
...YOU...
GRR...
...YOU LISTEN...
...YOU...

READ THIS WAY

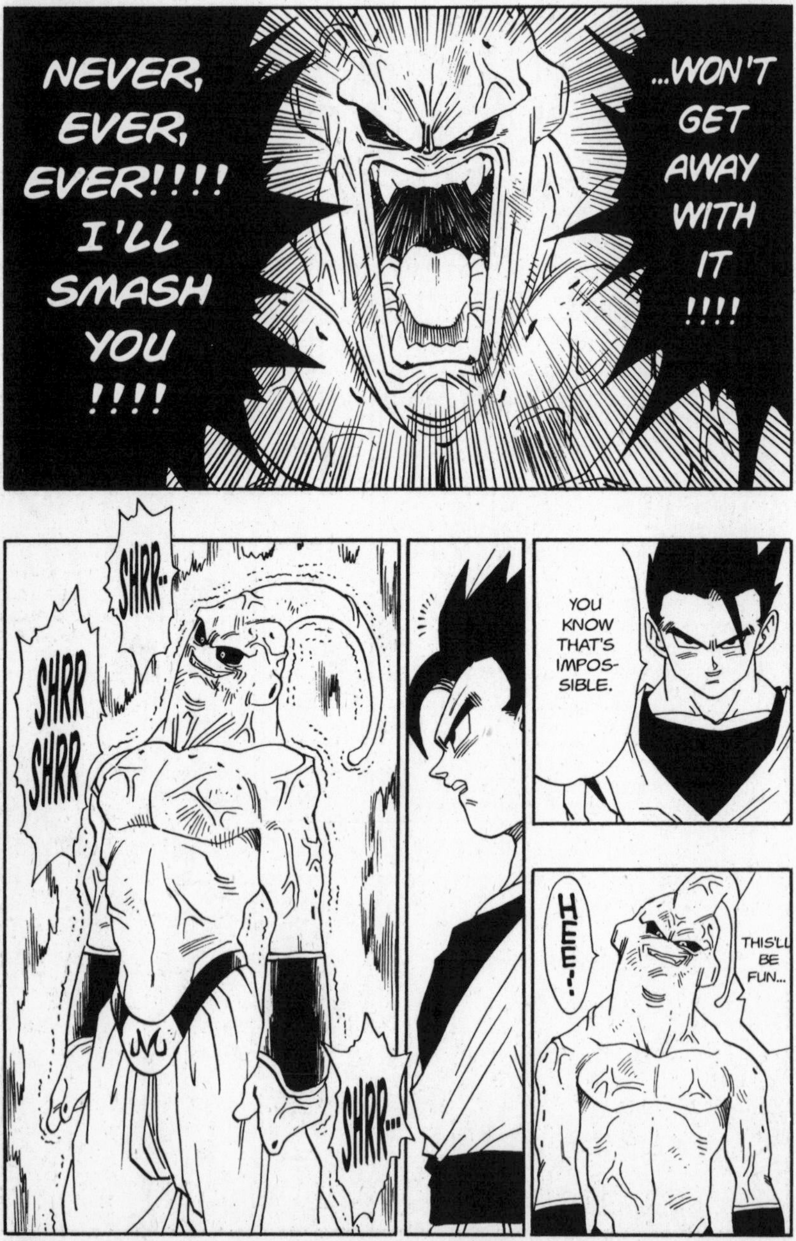
...WON'T GET AWAY WITH IT !!!!
NEVER, EVER, EVER!!!! I'LL SMASH YOU !!!!
YOU KNOW THAT'S IMPOS-SIBLE.
HEE!
THIS'LL BE FUN...
SHRR..
SHRR SHRR
SHRR...

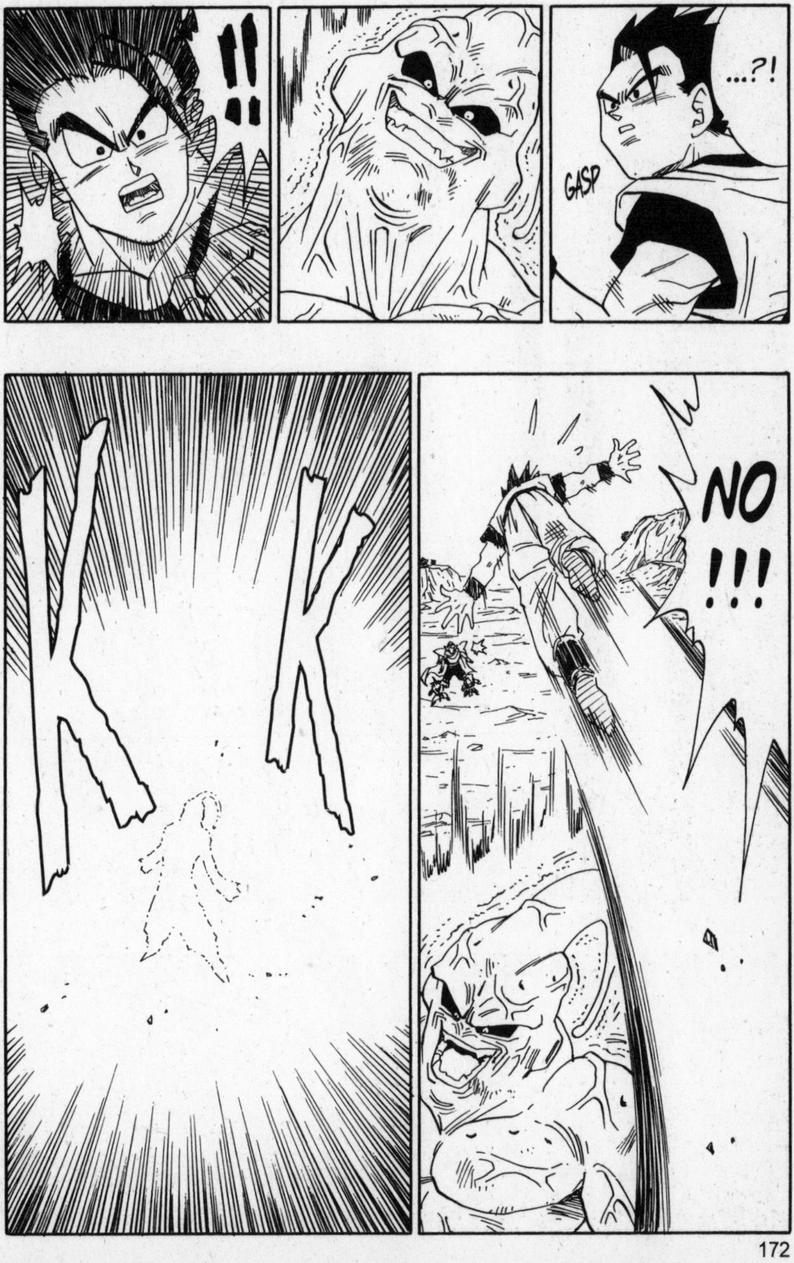
...?!
GASP
!!
NO !!!
KK

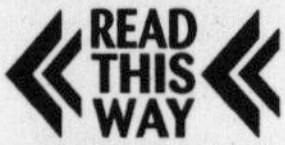
READ THIS WAY

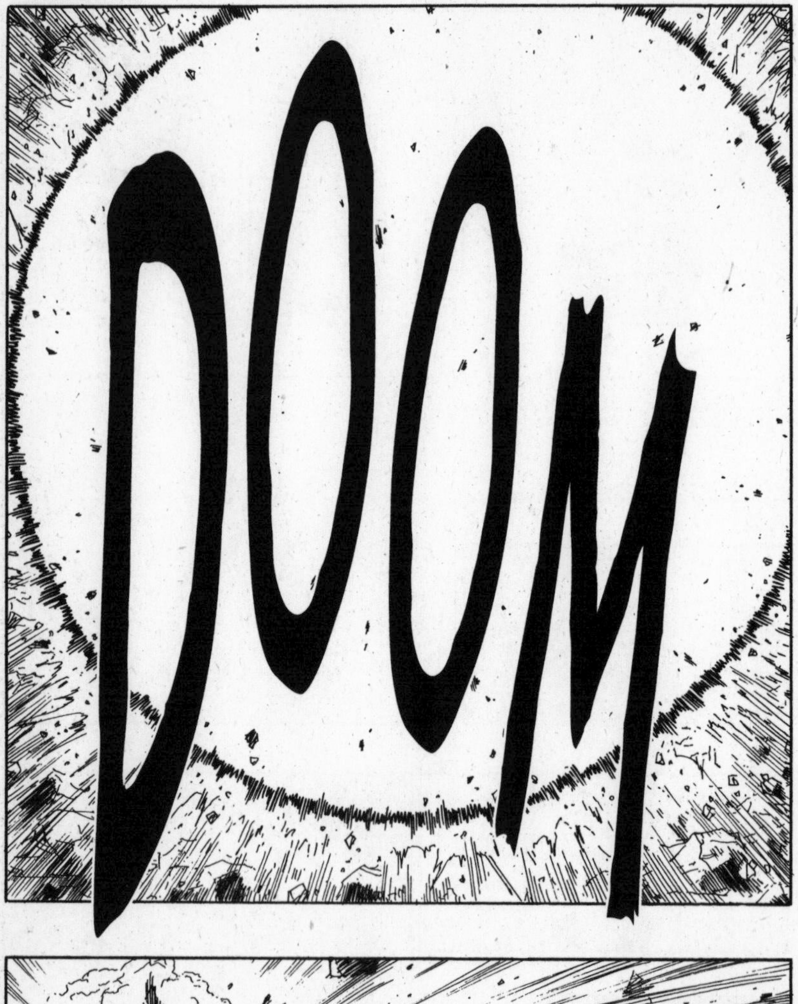
DOOM

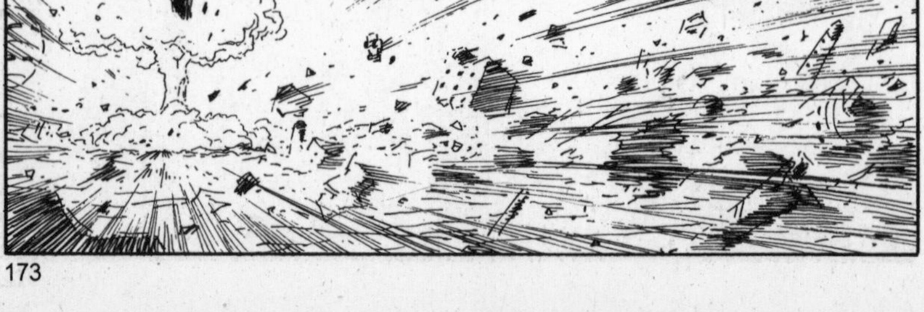

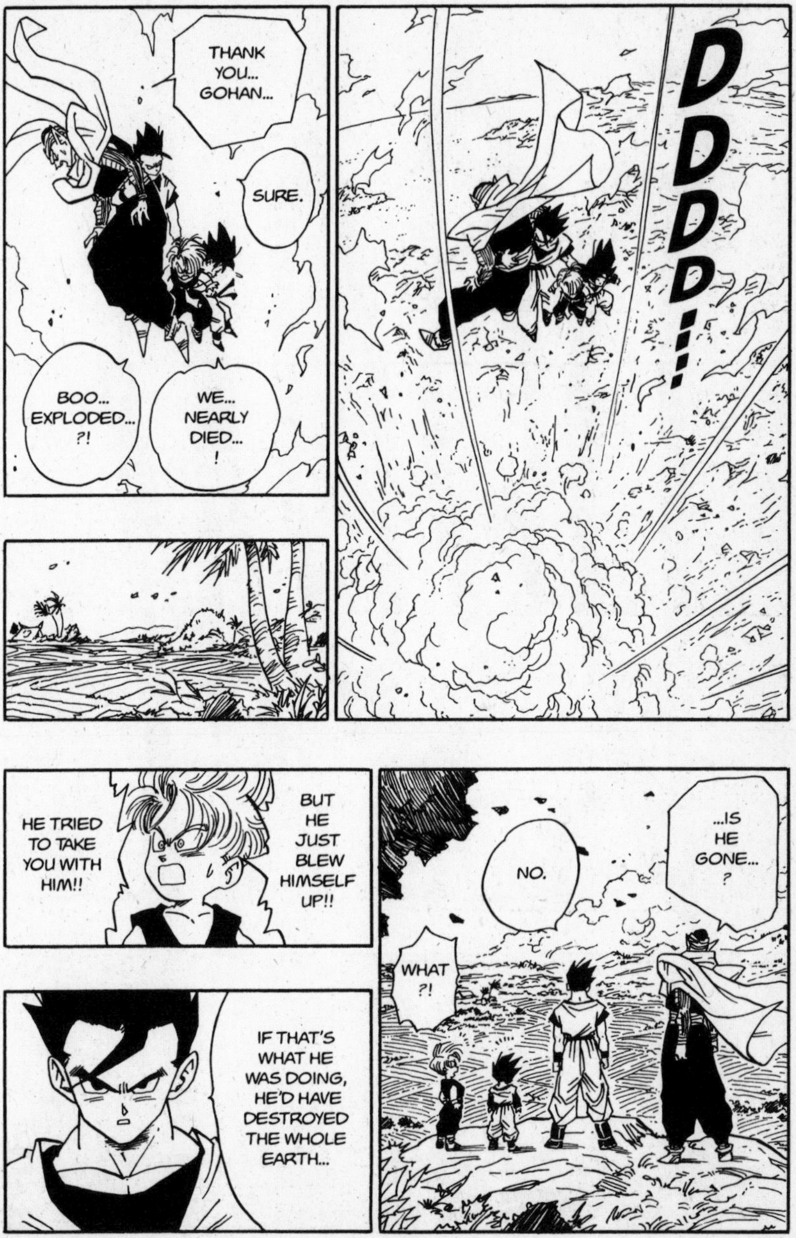
DDDD!!!
THANK YOU... GOHAN...
SURE.
WE... NEARLY DIED...!
BOO... EXPLODED...?!
...IS HE GONE...?
NO.
WHAT?!
BUT HE JUST BLEW HIMSELF UP!!
HE TRIED TO TAKE YOU WITH HIM!!
IF THAT'S WHAT HE WAS DOING, HE'D HAVE DESTROYED THE WHOLE EARTH...

READ THIS WAY

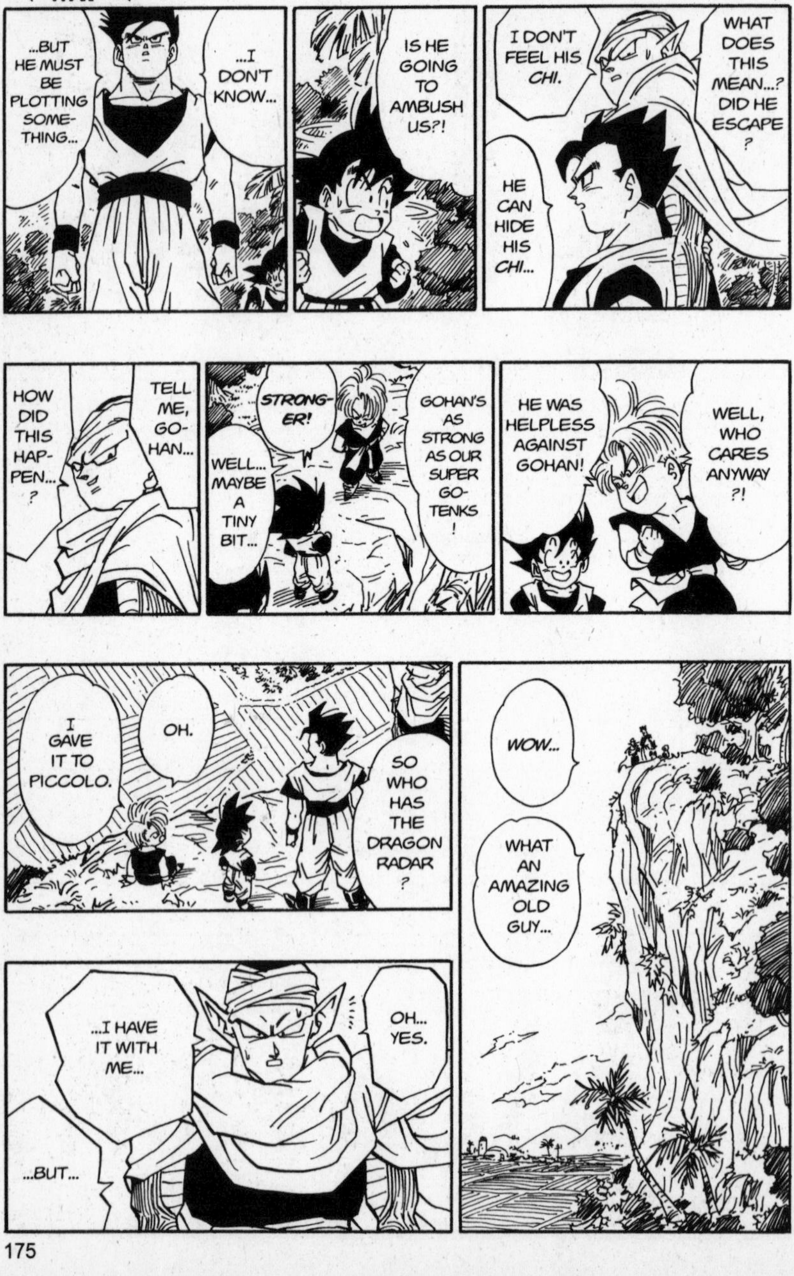
WHAT DOES THIS MEAN...? DID HE ESCAPE?
I DON'T FEEL HIS *CHI*.
HE CAN HIDE HIS *CHI*...
IS HE GOING TO AMBUSH US?!
...I DON'T KNOW...
...BUT HE MUST BE PLOTTING SOME-THING...
WELL, WHO CARES ANYWAY?!
HE WAS HELPLESS AGAINST GOHAN!
GOHAN'S AS STRONG AS OUR SUPER GO-TENKS!
STRONG-ER!
WELL... MAYBE A TINY BIT...
TELL ME, GO-HAN...
HOW DID THIS HAP-PEN...?
WOW...
WHAT AN AMAZING OLD GUY...
SO WHO HAS THE DRAGON RADAR?
OH.
I GAVE IT TO PICCOLO.
OH... YES.
...I HAVE IT WITH ME...
...BUT...

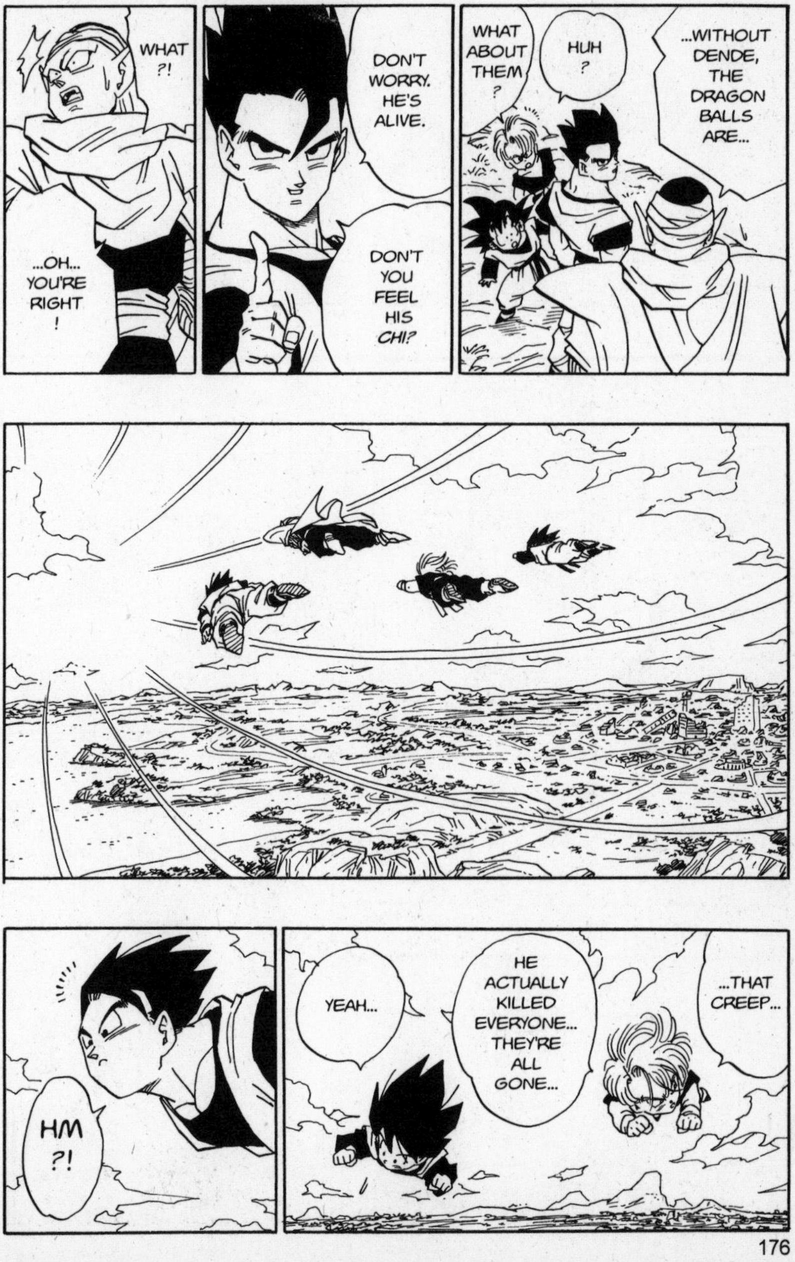
...WITHOUT DENDE, THE DRAGON BALLS ARE...
HUH ?
WHAT ABOUT THEM ?
DON'T WORRY. HE'S ALIVE.
DON'T YOU FEEL HIS CHI?
WHAT ?!
...OH... YOU'RE RIGHT !
...THAT CREEP...
HE ACTUALLY KILLED EVERYONE... THEY'RE ALL GONE...
YEAH...
HM ?!

READ THIS WAY

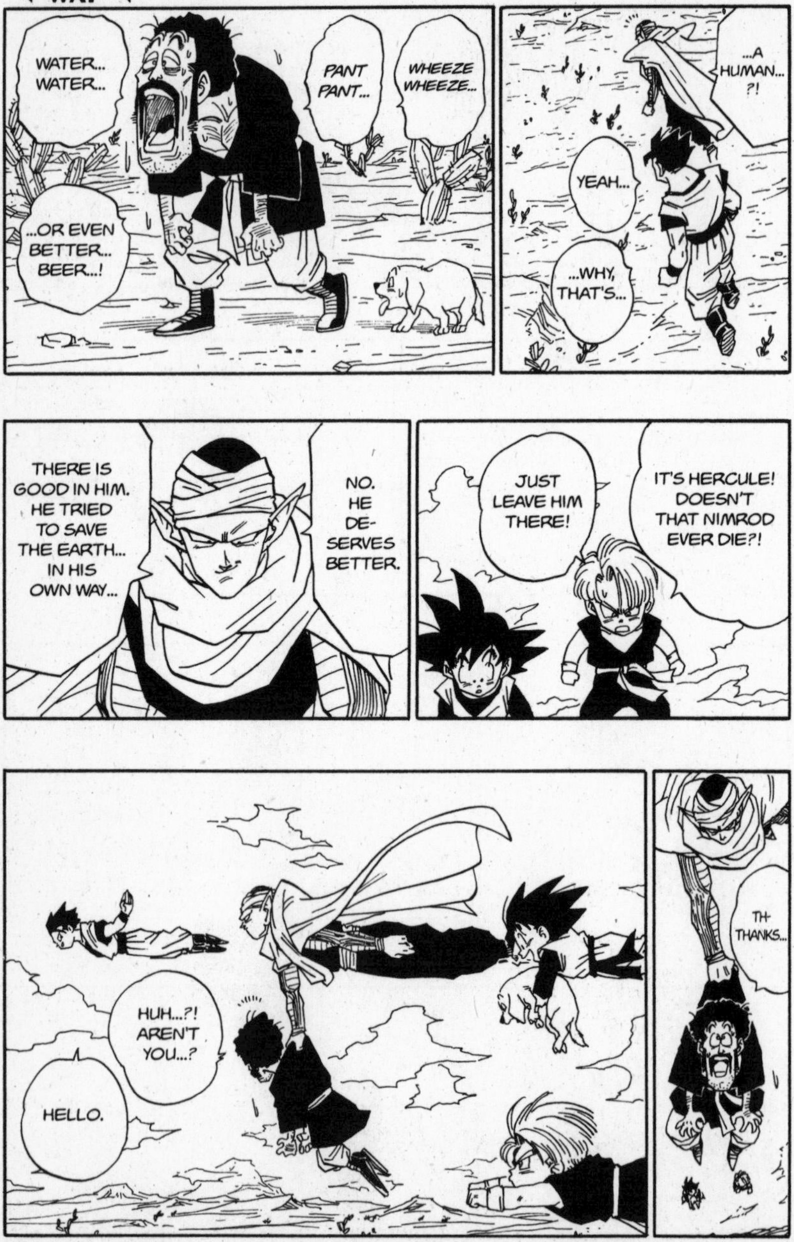
...A HUMAN...?!
YEAH...
...WHY, THAT'S...
WHEEZE WHEEZE...
PANT PANT...
WATER... WATER...
...OR EVEN BETTER... BEER...!
IT'S HERCULE! DOESN'T THAT NIMROD EVER DIE?!
JUST LEAVE HIM THERE!
NO. HE DE-SERVES BETTER.
THERE IS GOOD IN HIM. HE TRIED TO SAVE THE EARTH... IN HIS OWN WAY...
TH- THANKS...
HUH...?! AREN'T YOU...?
HELLO.

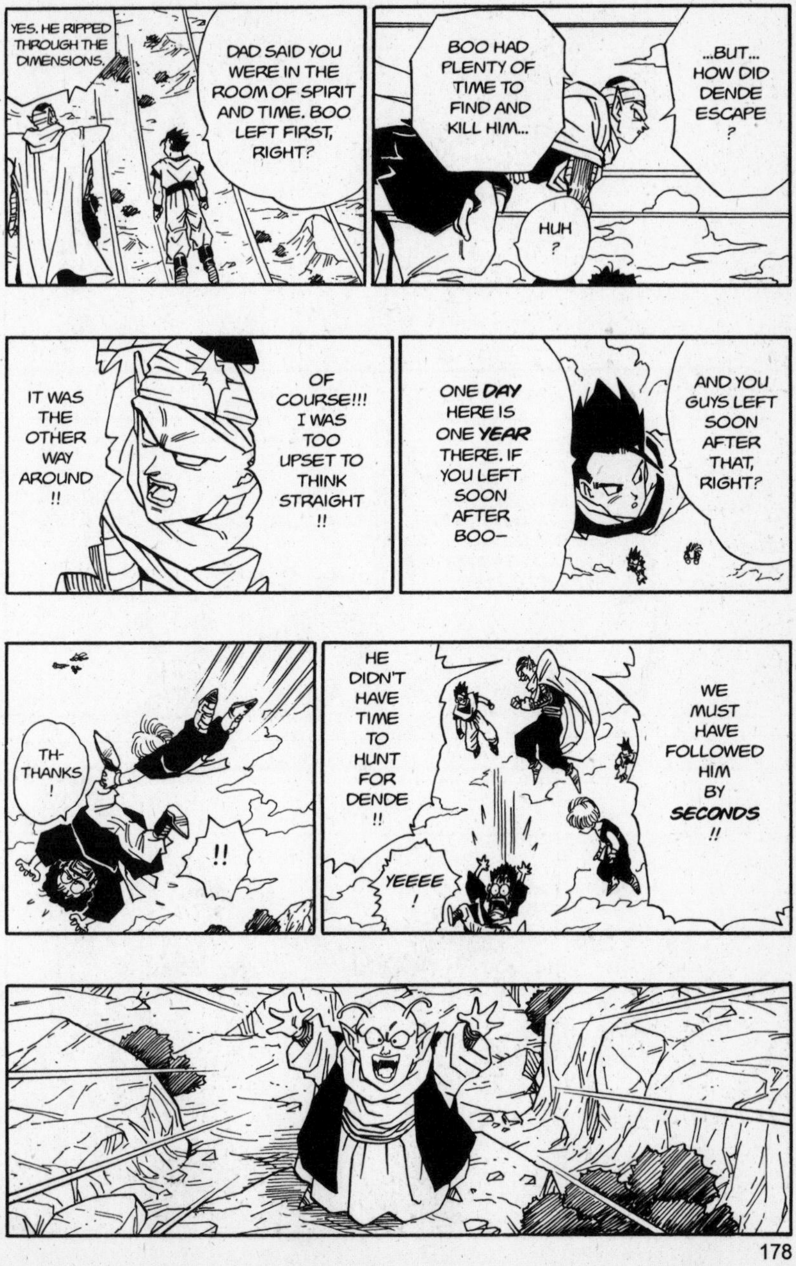
...BUT... HOW DID DENDE ESCAPE ?
HUH ?
BOO HAD PLENTY OF TIME TO FIND AND KILL HIM...
DAD SAID YOU WERE IN THE ROOM OF SPIRIT AND TIME. BOO LEFT FIRST, RIGHT?
YES. HE RIPPED THROUGH THE DIMENSIONS.
AND YOU GUYS LEFT SOON AFTER THAT, RIGHT?
ONE DAY HERE IS ONE YEAR THERE. IF YOU LEFT SOON AFTER BOO—
OF COURSE!!! I WAS TOO UPSET TO THINK STRAIGHT !!
IT WAS THE OTHER WAY AROUND !!
WE MUST HAVE FOLLOWED HIM BY SECONDS !!
HE DIDN'T HAVE TIME TO HUNT FOR DENDE !!
YEEEE !
!!
TH-THANKS !

READ THIS WAY

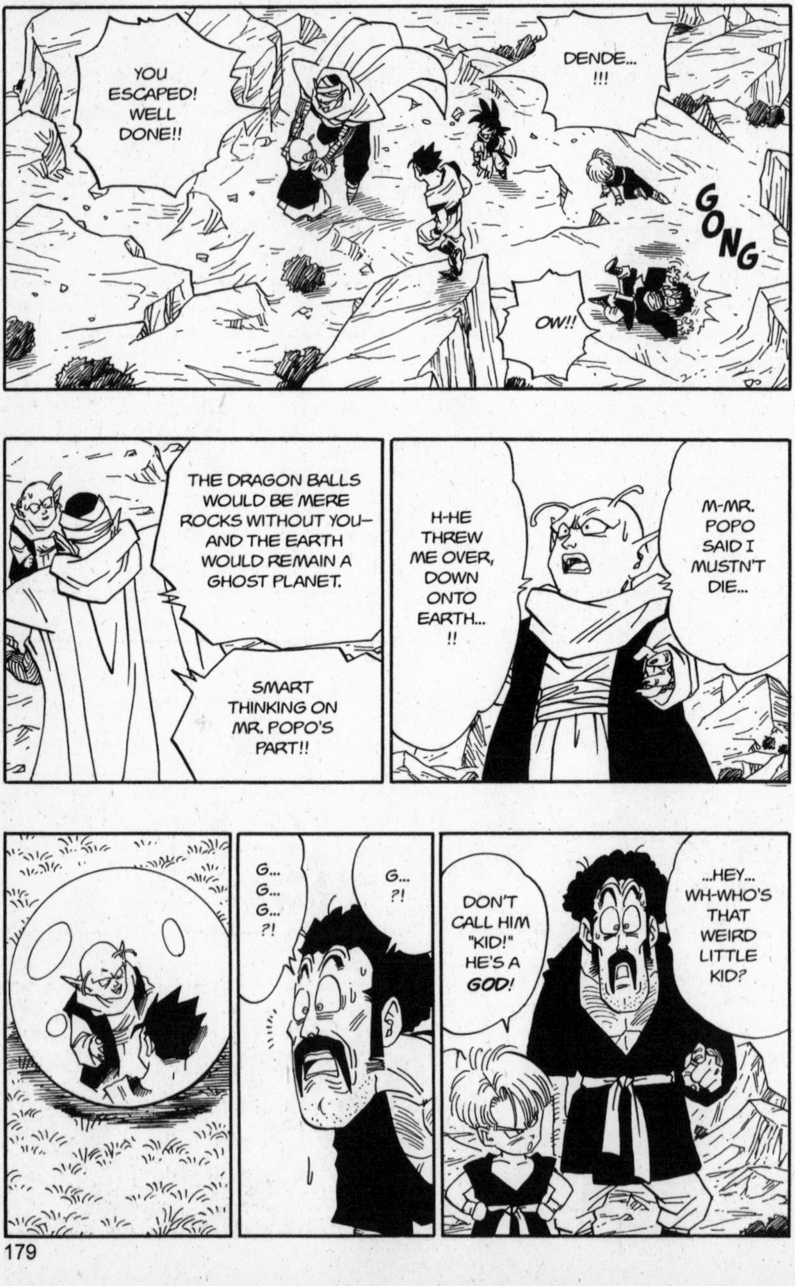

DENDE... !!!
GONG
OW!!
YOU ESCAPED! WELL DONE!!
M-MR. POPO SAID I MUSTN'T DIE...
H-HE THREW ME OVER, DOWN ONTO EARTH... !!
THE DRAGON BALLS WOULD BE MERE ROCKS WITHOUT YOU—AND THE EARTH WOULD REMAIN A GHOST PLANET.
SMART THINKING ON MR. POPO'S PART!!
...HEY... WH-WHO'S THAT WEIRD LITTLE KID?
DON'T CALL HIM "KID!" HE'S A *GOD*!
G... ?!
G... G... G... ?!

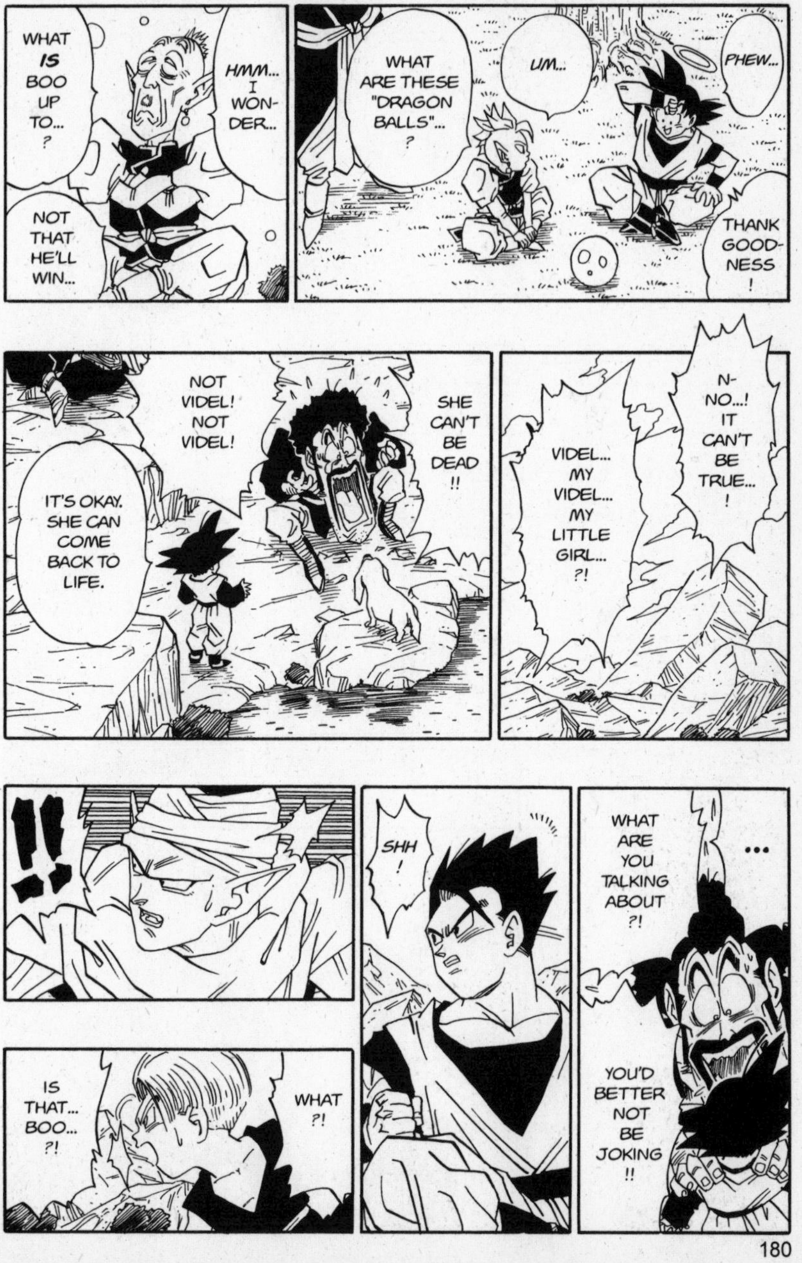
PHEW...
THANK GOODNESS!
UM...
WHAT ARE THESE "DRAGON BALLS"...?
HMM... I WONDER...
WHAT IS BOO UP TO...?
NOT THAT HE'LL WIN...
N-NO...! IT CAN'T BE TRUE...!
VIDEL... MY VIDEL... MY LITTLE GIRL...?!
SHE CAN'T BE DEAD!!
NOT VIDEL! NOT VIDEL!
IT'S OKAY. SHE CAN COME BACK TO LIFE.
...
WHAT ARE YOU TALKING ABOUT?!
YOU'D BETTER NOT BE JOKING!!
SHH!
!!
WHAT?!
IS THAT... BOO...?!

READ THIS WAY

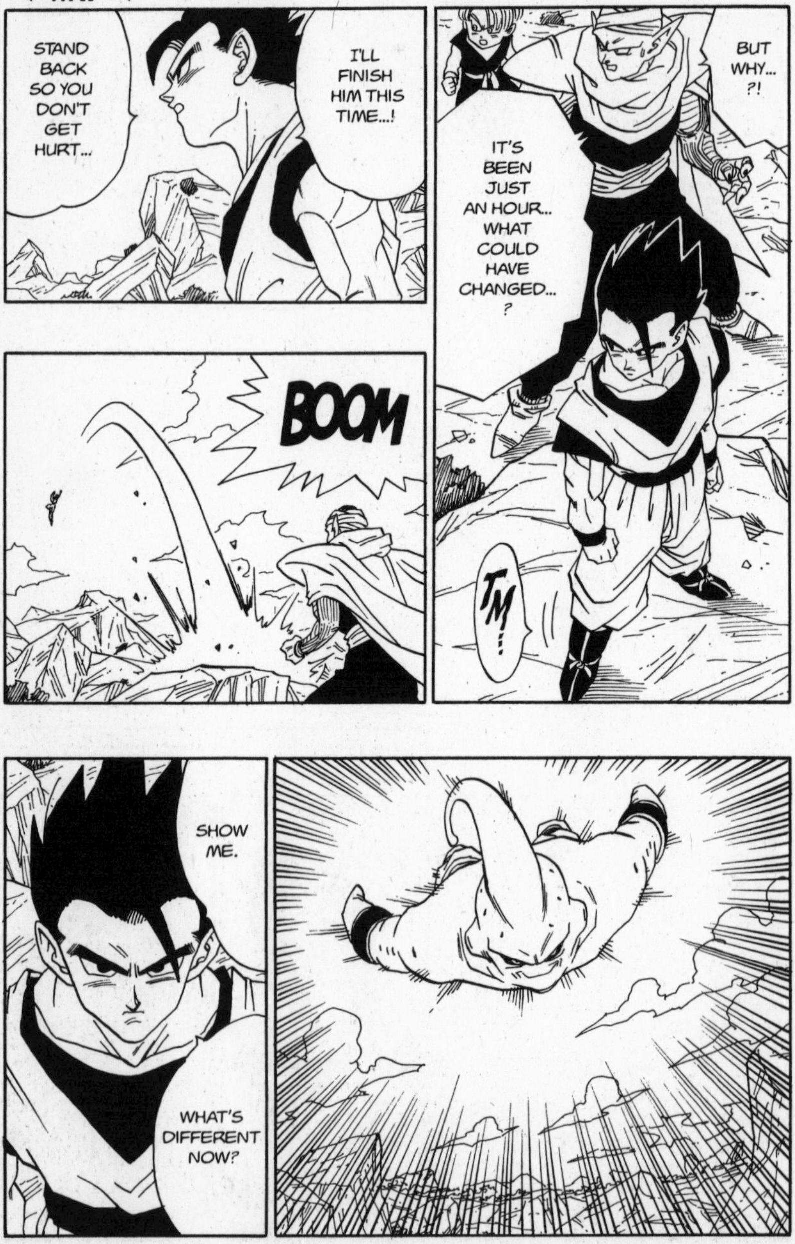

BUT WHY... ?!
IT'S BEEN JUST AN HOUR... WHAT COULD HAVE CHANGED... ?
TM...!
I'LL FINISH HIM THIS TIME...!
STAND BACK SO YOU DON'T GET HURT...
BOOM
SHOW ME.
WHAT'S DIFFERENT NOW?

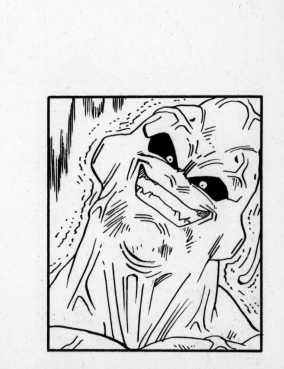

DBZ:305 · Ambush!

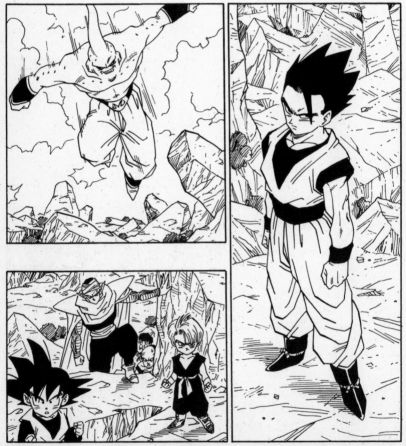

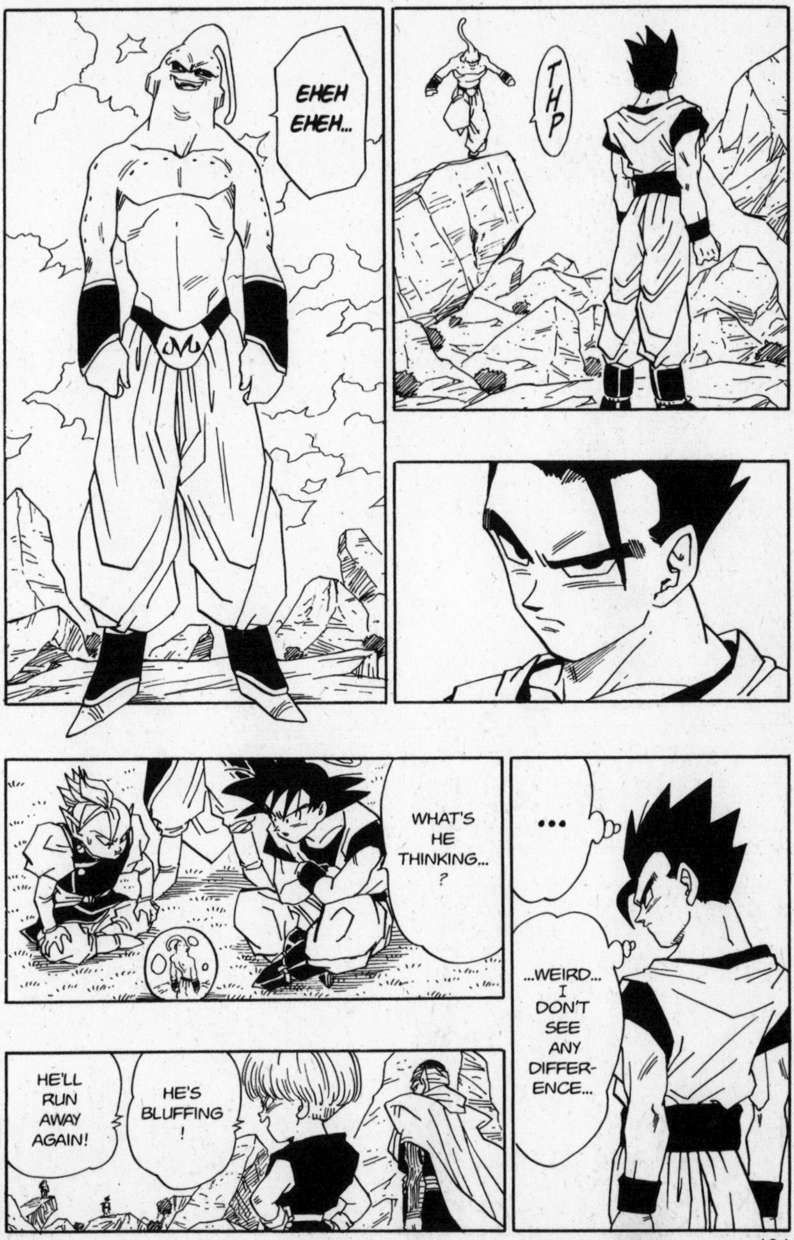
THP
EHEH EHEH...
...
...WEIRD... I DON'T SEE ANY DIFFER-ENCE...
WHAT'S HE THINKING...?
HE'S BLUFFING!
HE'LL RUN AWAY AGAIN!

READ THIS WAY

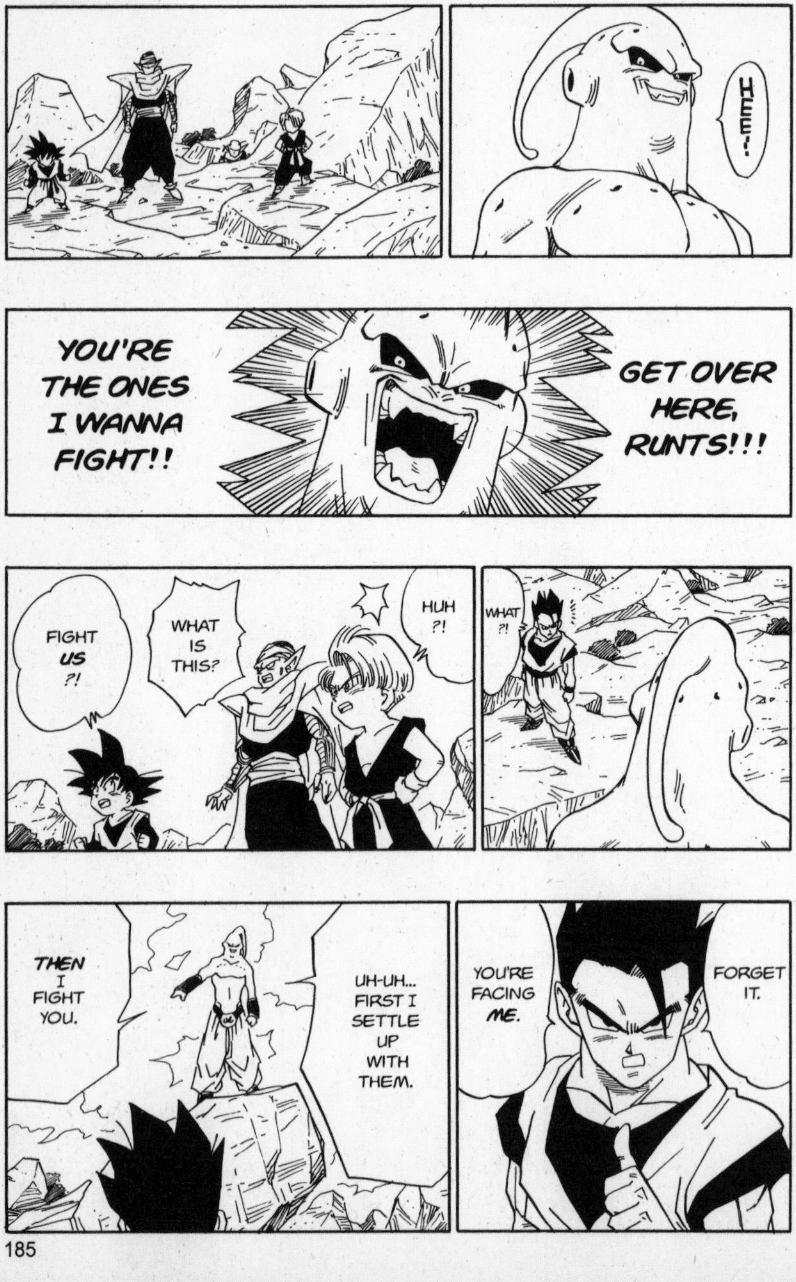

HEE!
GET OVER HERE, RUNTS!!!
YOU'RE THE ONES I WANNA FIGHT!!
WHAT ?!
HUH ?!
WHAT IS THIS?
FIGHT US ?!
FORGET IT.
YOU'RE FACING ME.
UH-UH... FIRST I SETTLE UP WITH THEM.
THEN I FIGHT YOU.

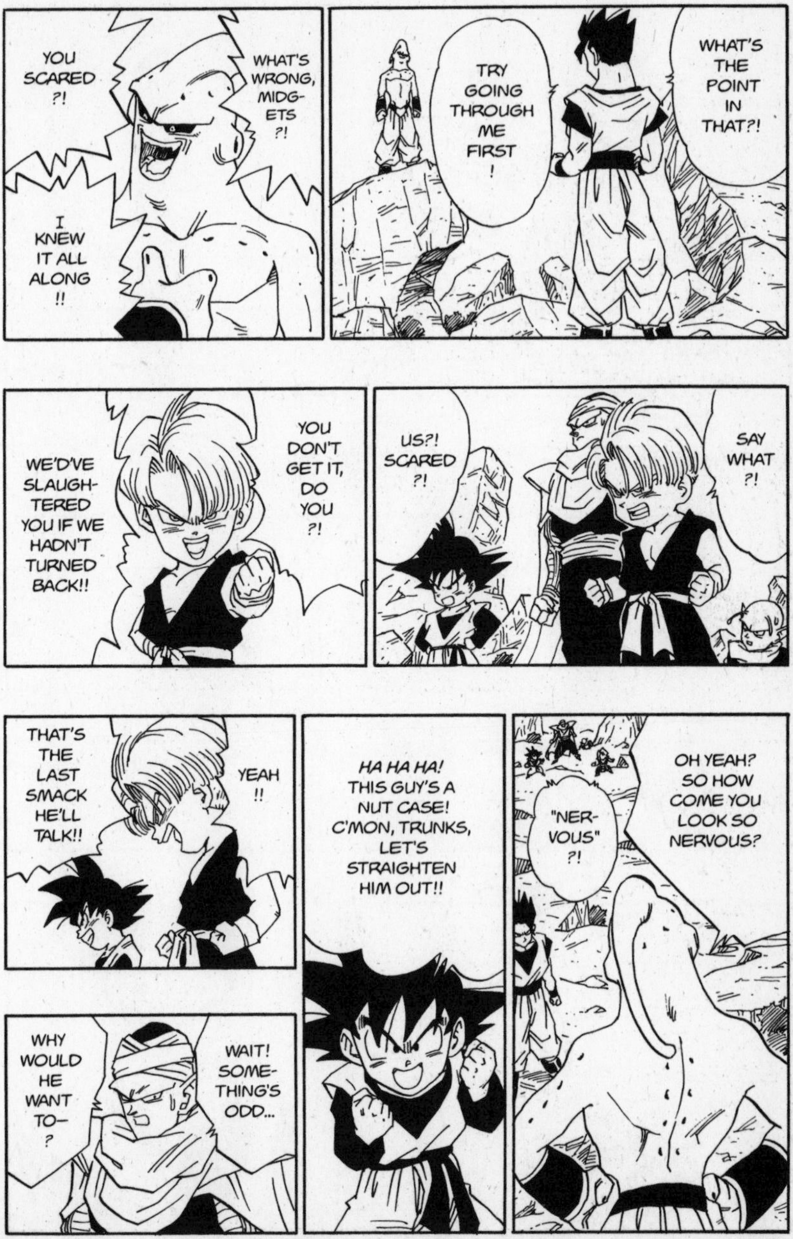
WHAT'S THE POINT IN THAT?!
TRY GOING THROUGH ME FIRST!
WHAT'S WRONG, MIDGETS?!
YOU SCARED?!
I KNEW IT ALL ALONG!!
SAY WHAT?!
US?! SCARED?!
YOU DON'T GET IT, DO YOU?!
WE'D'VE SLAUGHTERED YOU IF WE HADN'T TURNED BACK!!
OH YEAH? SO HOW COME YOU LOOK SO NERVOUS?
"NERVOUS"?!
HA HA HA! THIS GUY'S A NUT CASE! C'MON, TRUNKS, LET'S STRAIGHTEN HIM OUT!!
YEAH!!
THAT'S THE LAST SMACK HE'LL TALK!!
WAIT! SOMETHING'S ODD...
WHY WOULD HE WANT TO—?

READ THIS WAY

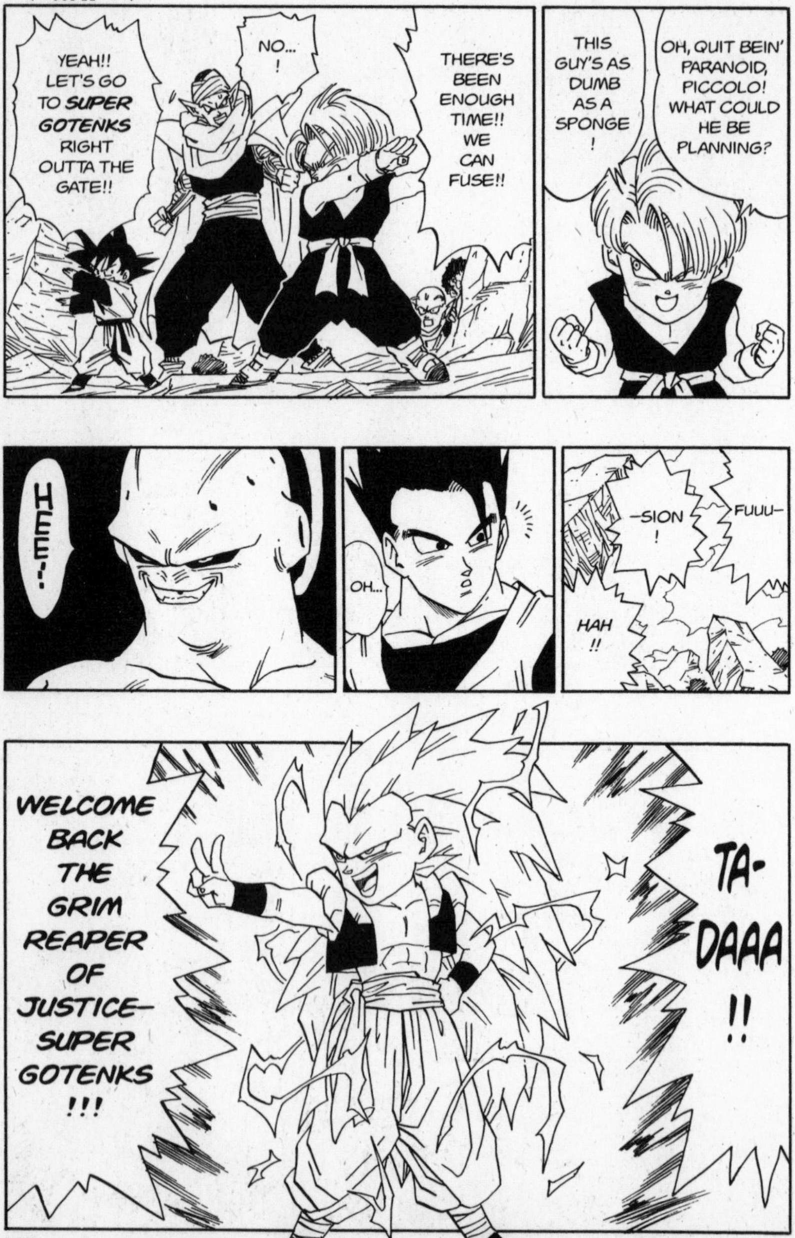

OH, QUIT BEIN' PARANOID, PICCOLO! WHAT COULD HE BE PLANNING?
THIS GUY'S AS DUMB AS A SPONGE!
THERE'S BEEN ENOUGH TIME!! WE CAN FUSE!!
NO...!
YEAH!! LET'S GO TO SUPER GOTENKS RIGHT OUTTA THE GATE!!
FUUU-
-SION!
HAH!!
OH...
HEE!!
TA-DAAA!!
WELCOME BACK THE GRIM REAPER OF JUSTICE— SUPER GOTENKS!!!

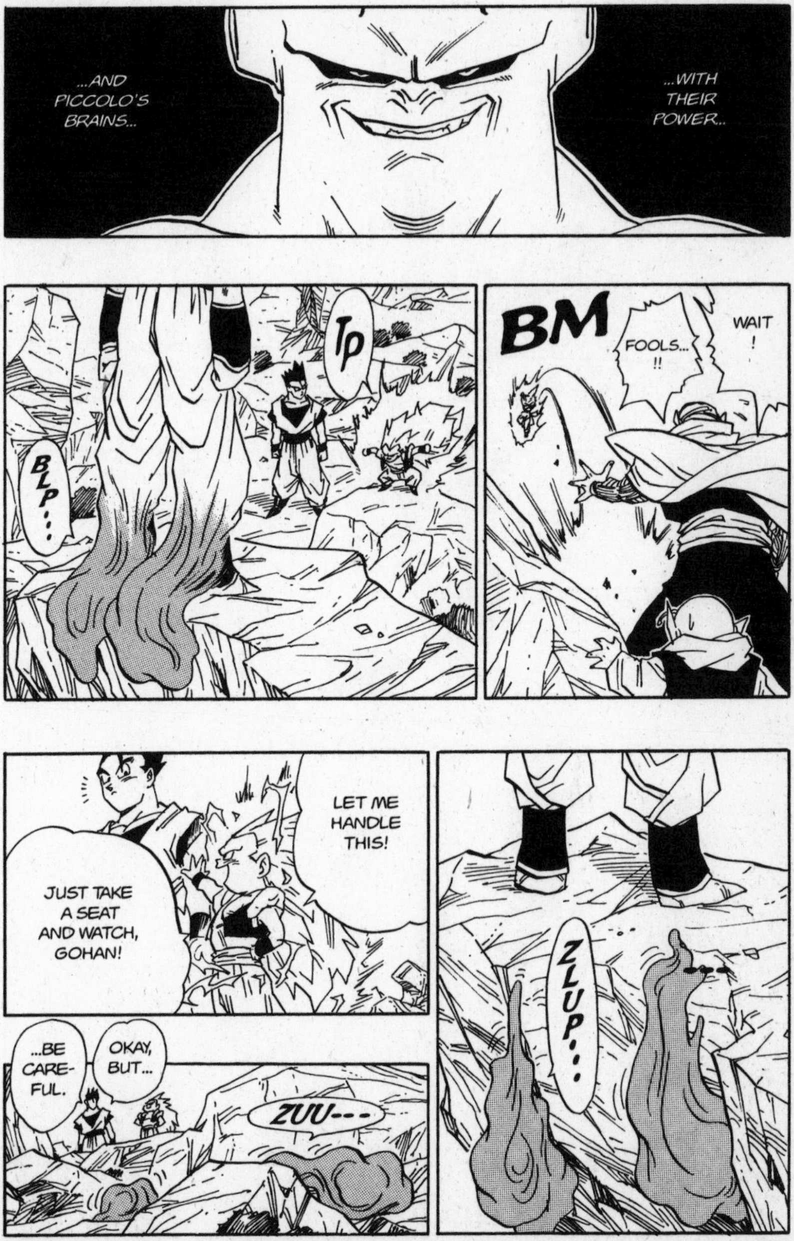
...WITH THEIR POWER...
...AND PICCOLO'S BRAINS...
WAIT!
FOOLS...!!
BM
TP
BLP...
ZLUP...
LET ME HANDLE THIS!
JUST TAKE A SEAT AND WATCH, GOHAN!
OKAY, BUT...
...BE CAREFUL.
ZUU---

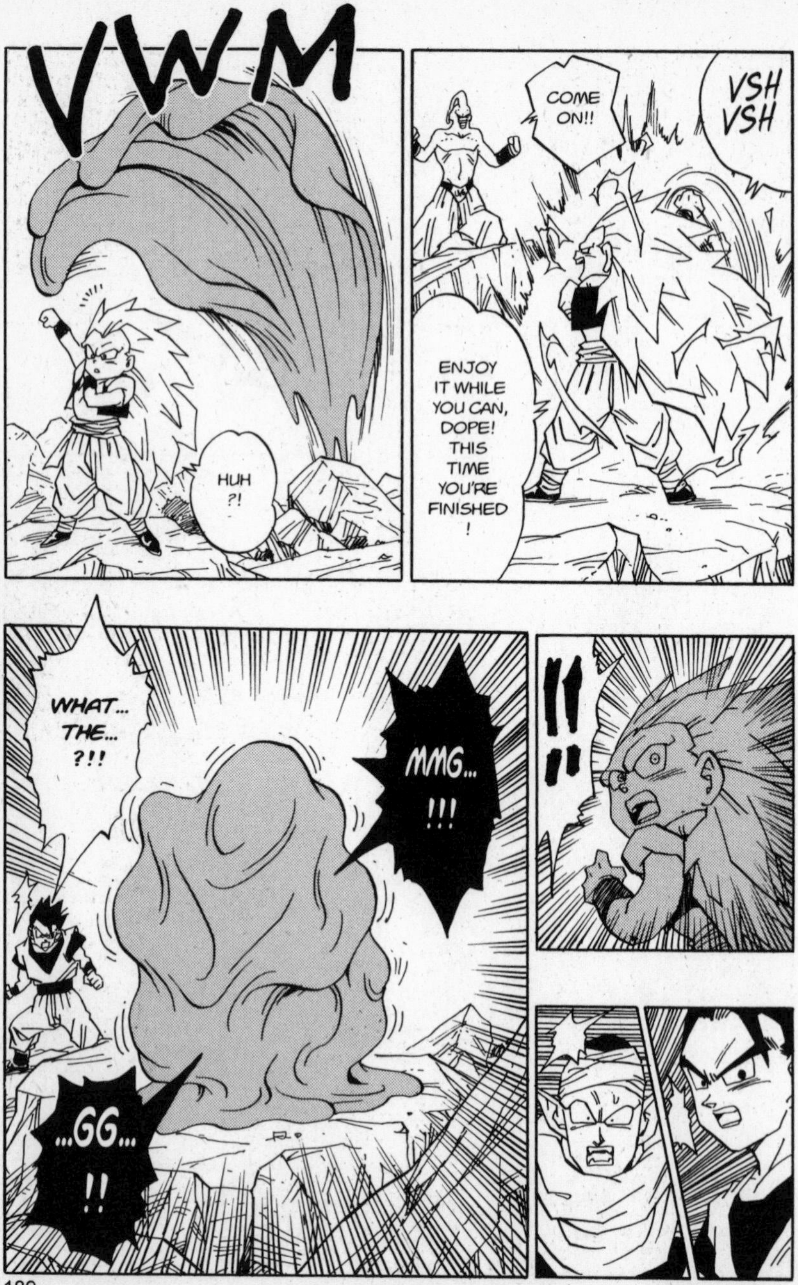
VSH VSH
COME ON!!
ENJOY IT WHILE YOU CAN, DOPE! THIS TIME YOU'RE FINISHED!
VWM
HUH ?!
!!
MMG... !!!
WHAT... THE... ?!!
...GG... !!

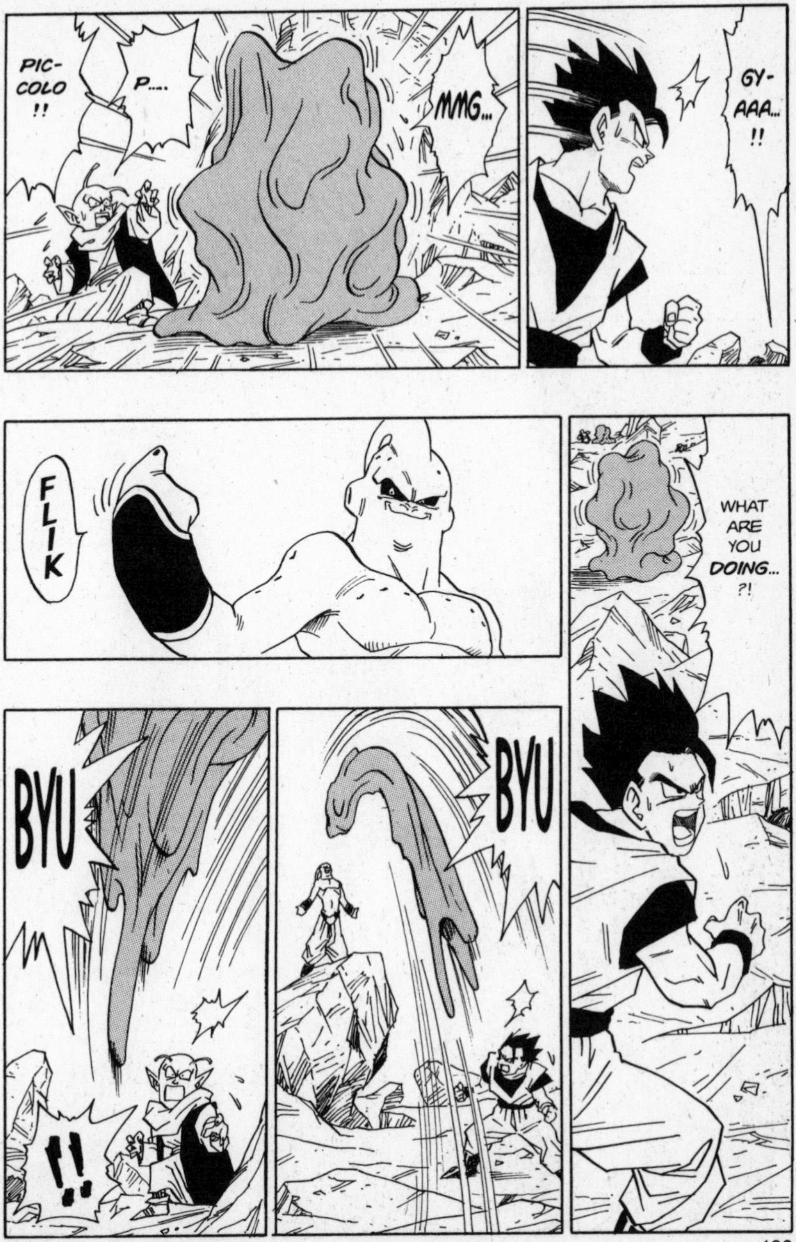
GY-AAA...!!
MMG...
P....
PIC-COLO!!
WHAT ARE YOU DOING...?!
FLIK
BYU
BYU
!!

READ THIS WAY

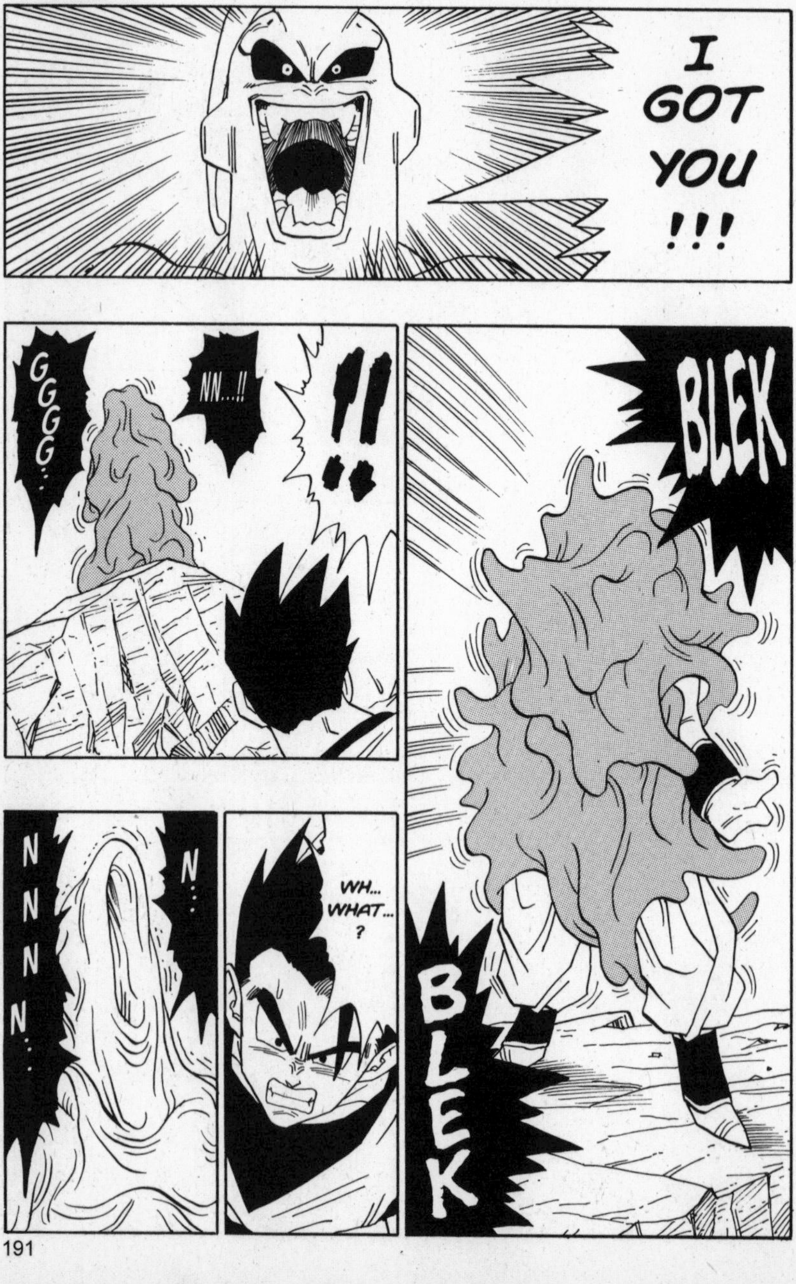
I GOT YOU!!!
BLEK
BLEK
!!
!!
NN...!!
GGGG...
WH... WHAT...?
N...
NNNN...

READ THIS WAY

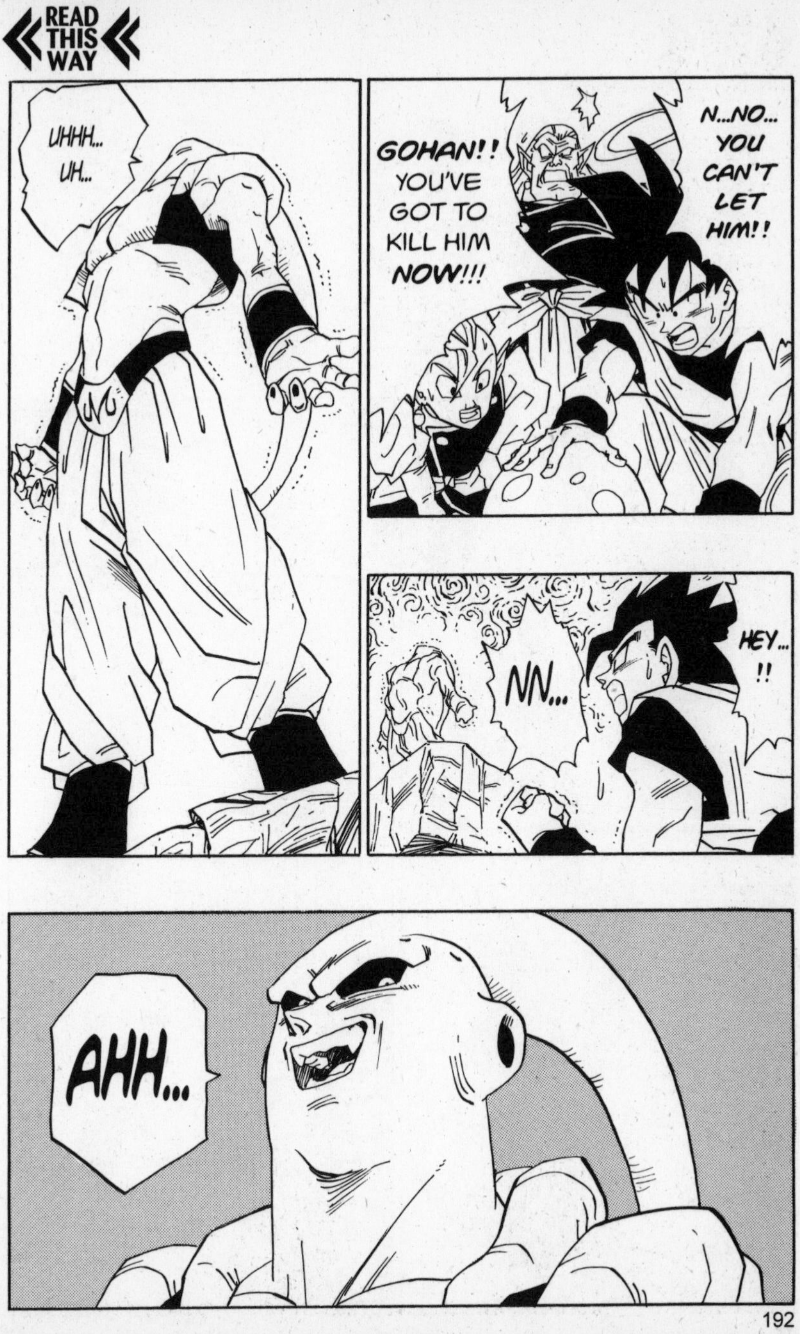
N...NO... YOU CAN'T LET HIM!!
GOHAN!! YOU'VE GOT TO KILL HIM NOW!!!
HEY... !!
NN...
UHHH... UH...
AHH...

READ THIS WAY

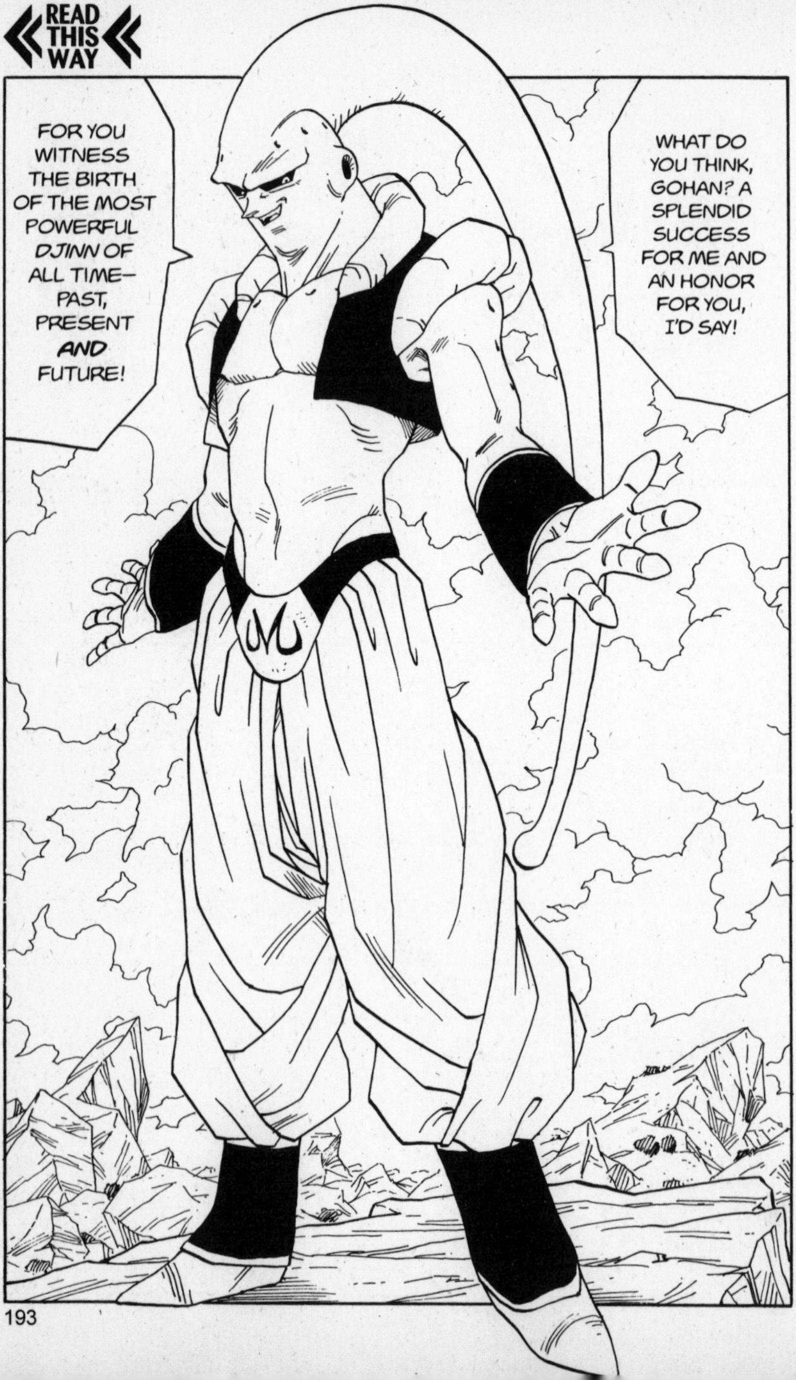
WHAT DO YOU THINK, GOHAN? A SPLENDID SUCCESS FOR ME AND AN HONOR FOR YOU, I'D SAY!
FOR YOU WITNESS THE BIRTH OF THE MOST POWERFUL DJINN OF ALL TIME—PAST, PRESENT *AND* FUTURE!

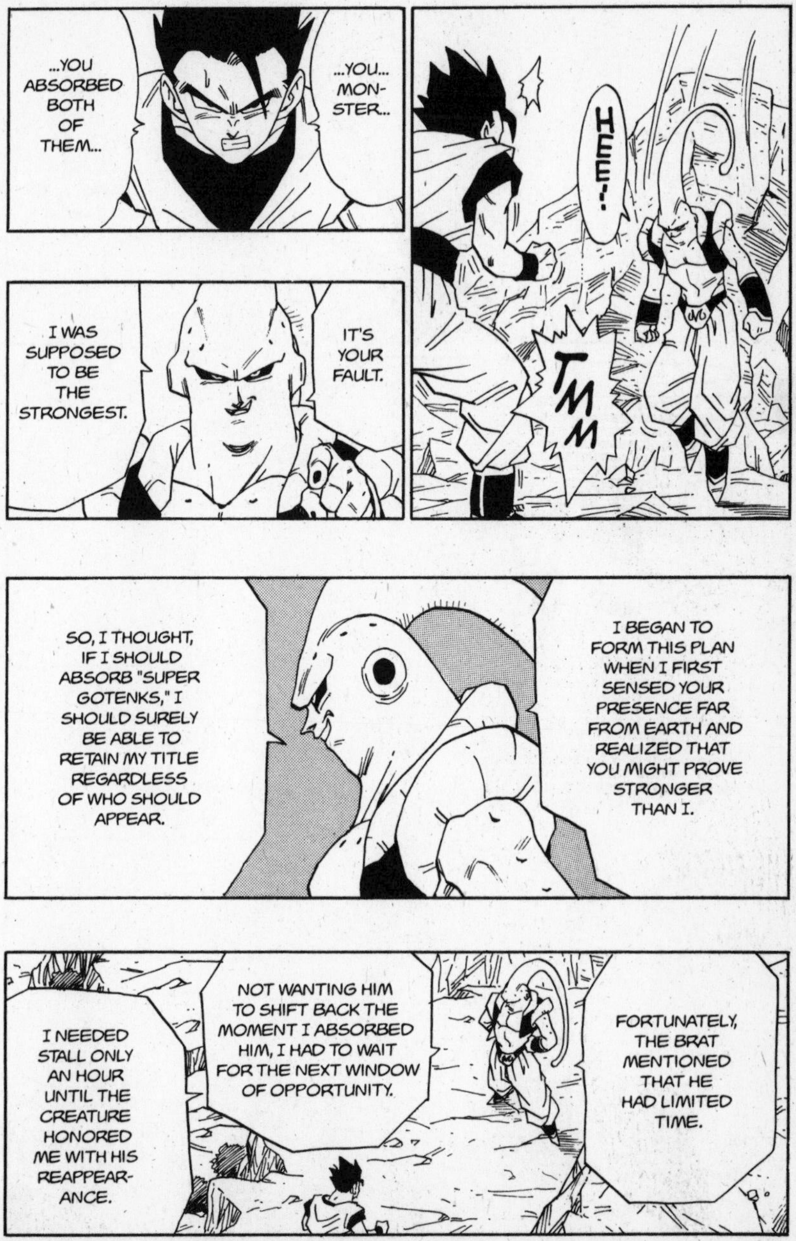
HEE!!
TMM
...YOU... MON-STER...
...YOU ABSORBED BOTH OF THEM...
IT'S YOUR FAULT.
I WAS SUPPOSED TO BE THE STRONGEST.
I BEGAN TO FORM THIS PLAN WHEN I FIRST SENSED YOUR PRESENCE FAR FROM EARTH AND REALIZED THAT YOU MIGHT PROVE STRONGER THAN I.
SO, I THOUGHT, IF I SHOULD ABSORB "SUPER GOTENKS," I SHOULD SURELY BE ABLE TO RETAIN MY TITLE REGARDLESS OF WHO SHOULD APPEAR.
FORTUNATELY, THE BRAT MENTIONED THAT HE HAD LIMITED TIME.
NOT WANTING HIM TO SHIFT BACK THE MOMENT I ABSORBED HIM, I HAD TO WAIT FOR THE NEXT WINDOW OF OPPORTUNITY.
I NEEDED STALL ONLY AN HOUR UNTIL THE CREATURE HONORED ME WITH HIS REAPPEAR-ANCE.

READ THIS WAY

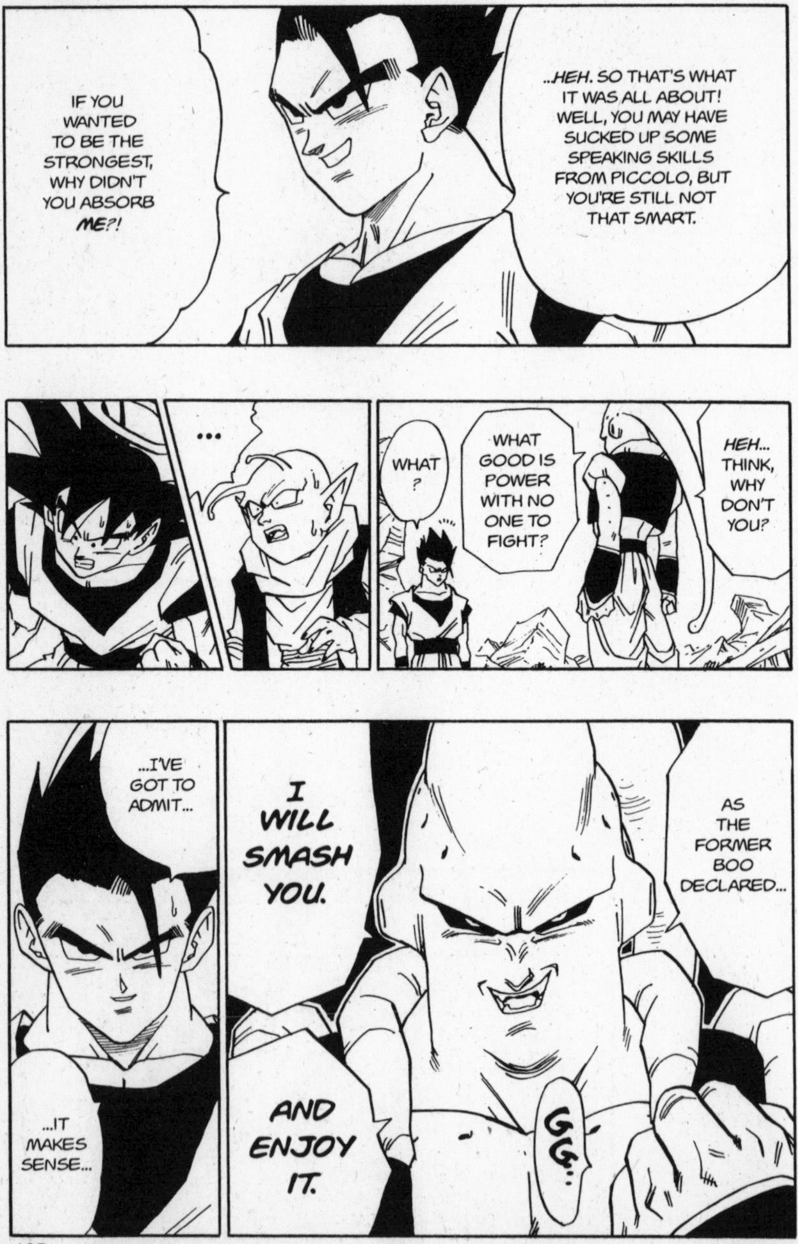

...HEH. SO THAT'S WHAT IT WAS ALL ABOUT! WELL, YOU MAY HAVE SUCKED UP SOME SPEAKING SKILLS FROM PICCOLO, BUT YOU'RE STILL NOT THAT SMART.
IF YOU WANTED TO BE THE STRONGEST, WHY DIDN'T YOU ABSORB *ME?!*
HEH... THINK, WHY DON'T YOU?
WHAT GOOD IS POWER WITH NO ONE TO FIGHT?
WHAT ?
...
AS THE FORMER BOO DECLARED...
I WILL SMASH YOU.
AND ENJOY IT.
GG..
...I'VE GOT TO ADMIT...
...IT MAKES SENSE...

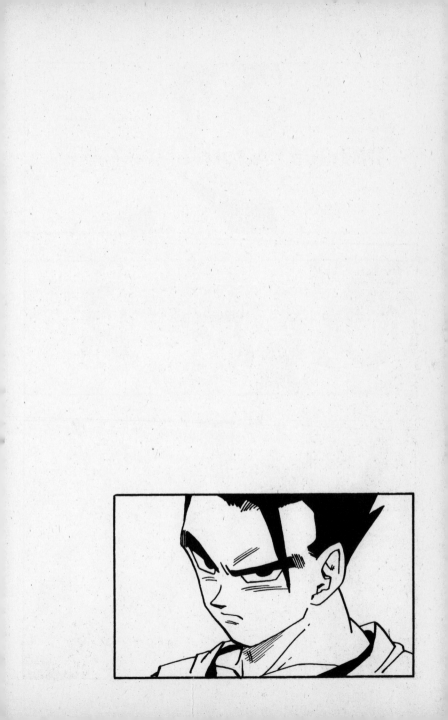

DBZ:306 • A Turn of the Tables

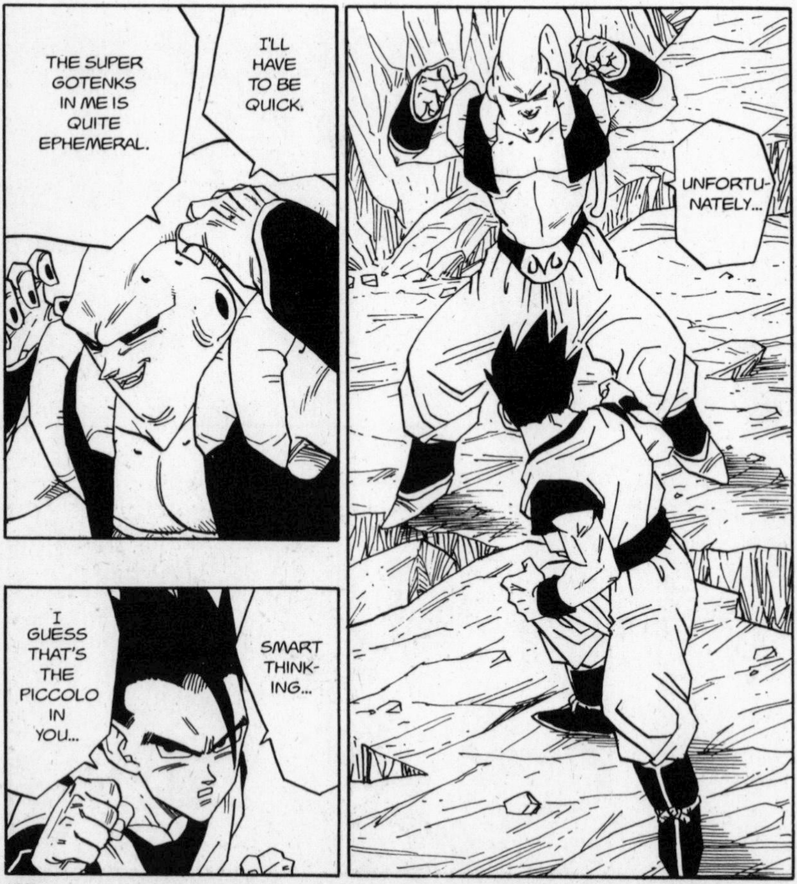
UNFORTUNATELY...
I'LL HAVE TO BE QUICK.
THE SUPER GOTENKS IN ME IS QUITE EPHEMERAL.
SMART THINKING...
I GUESS THAT'S THE PICCOLO IN YOU...

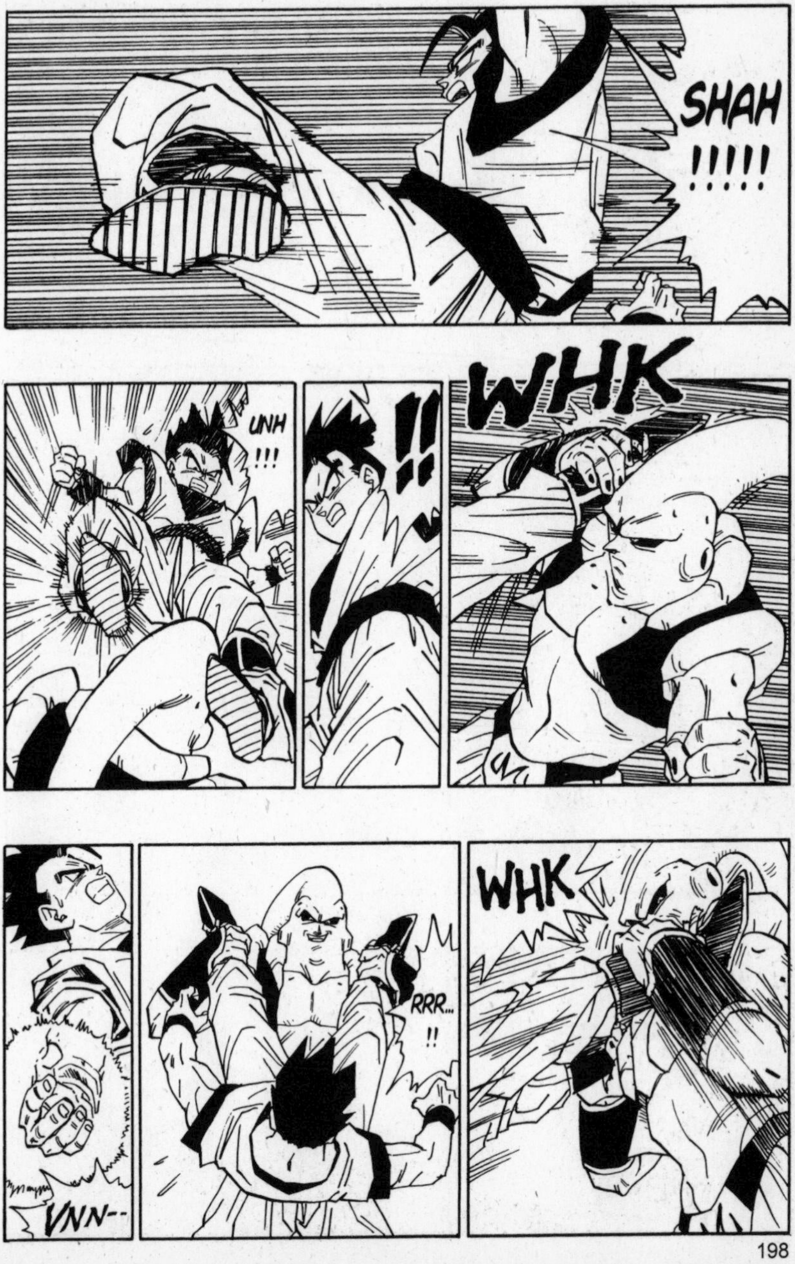
SHAH !!!!!
WHK
!!
UNH !!!
WHK
RRR... !!
VNN--

READ THIS WAY

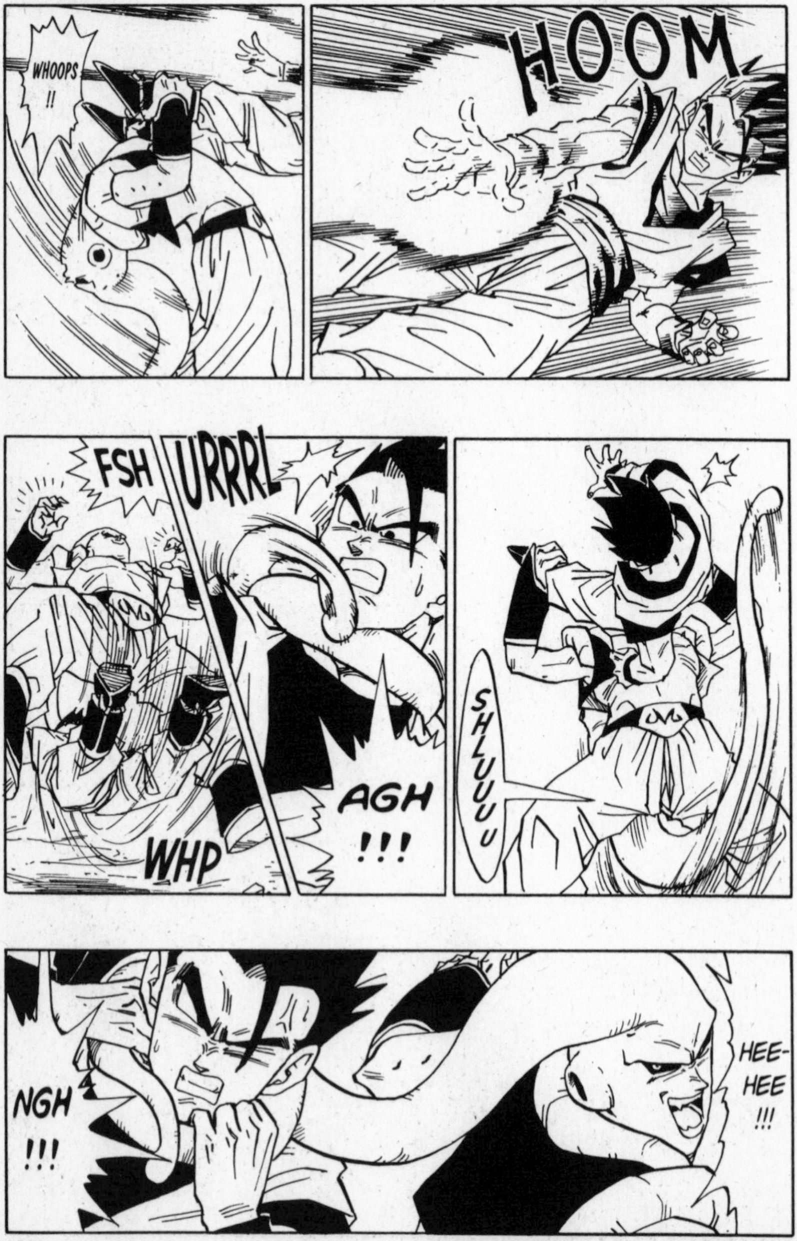
HOOM
WHOOPS !!
SHLUUUU
URRRL
AGH !!!
FSH
WHP
HEE-HEE !!!
NGH !!!

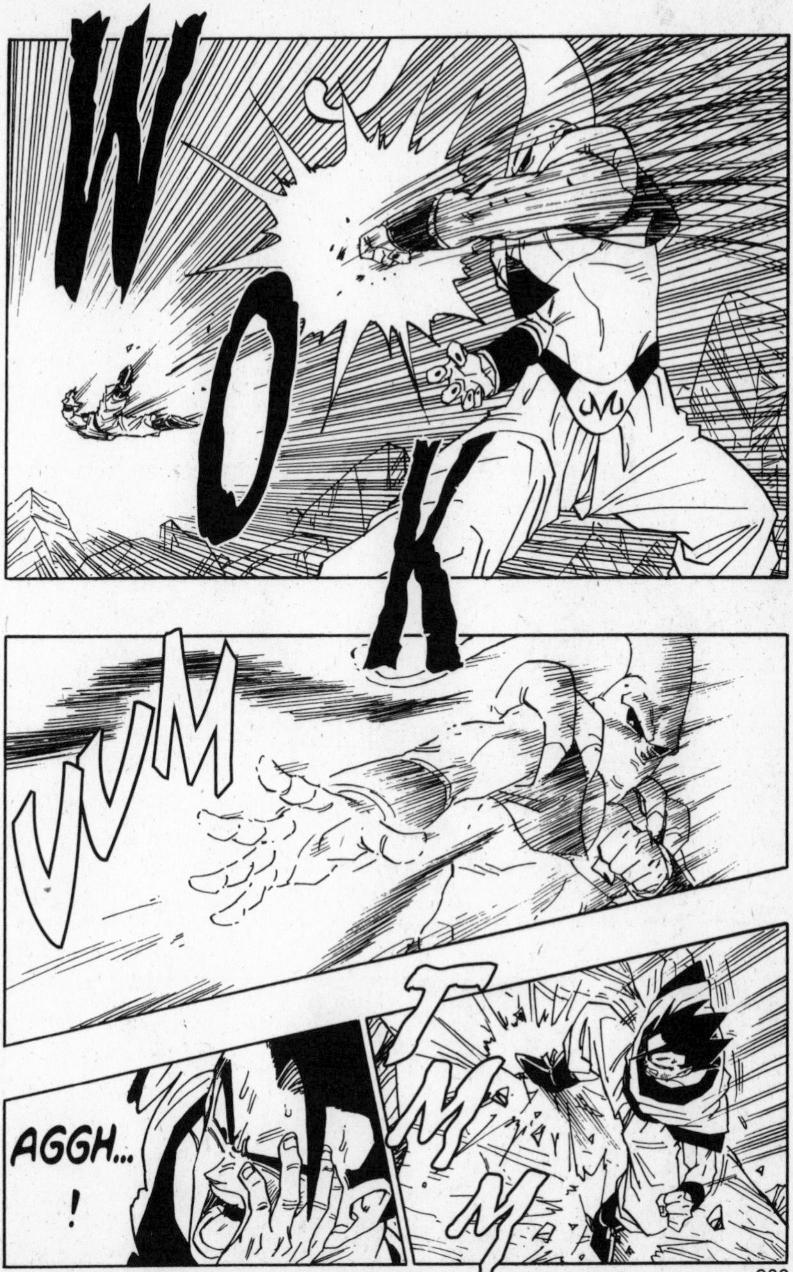
WOK
VUUM
TMM
AGGH...
!

READ THIS WAY

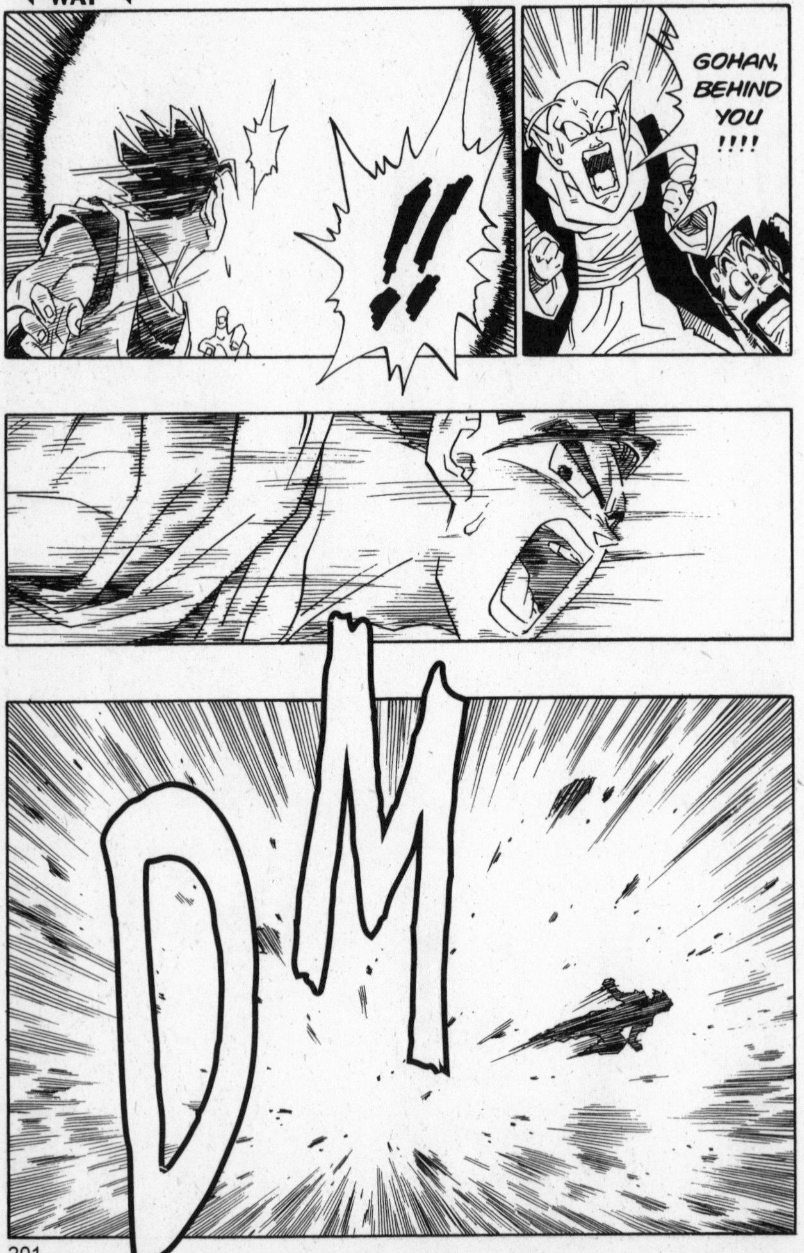
GOHAN, BEHIND YOU !!!!
!!
DM

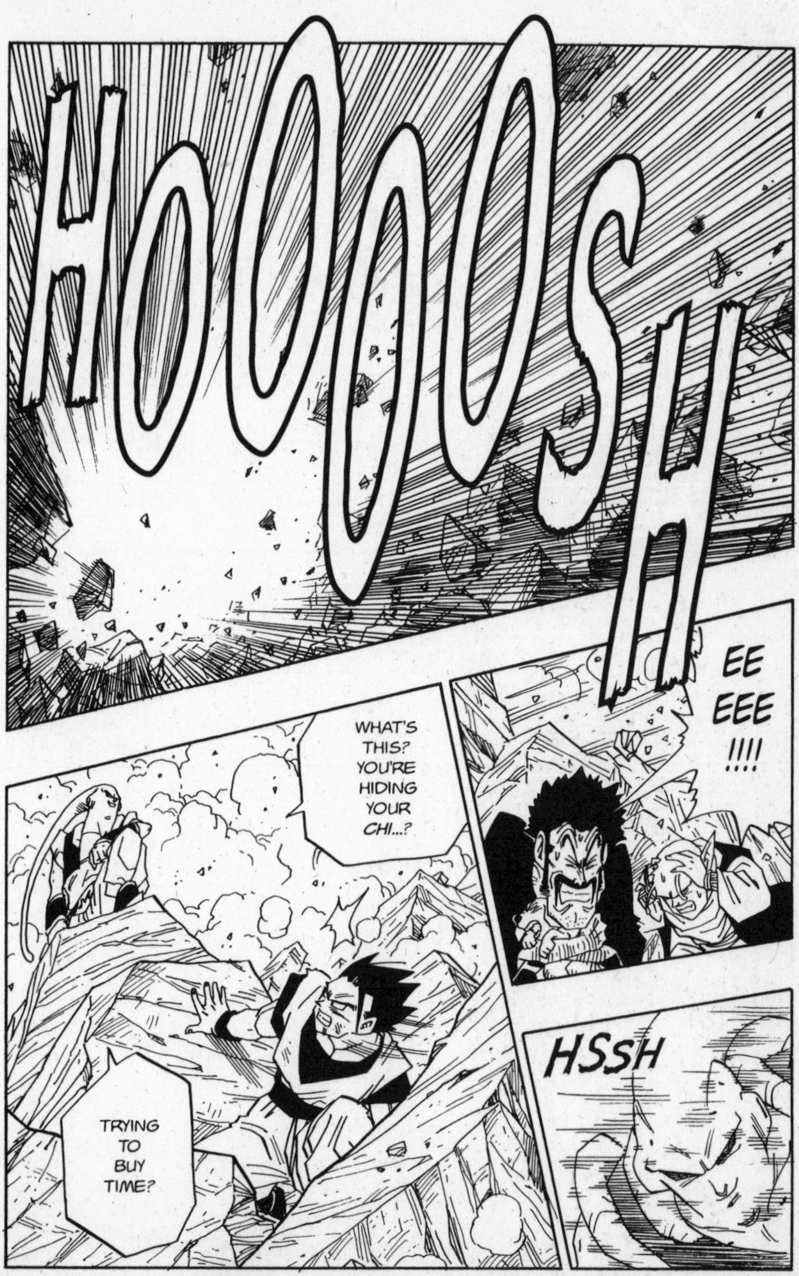
HOOOOSH
EE EEE !!!!
HSSH
WHAT'S THIS? YOU'RE HIDING YOUR *CHI*...?
TRYING TO BUY TIME?

READ THIS WAY

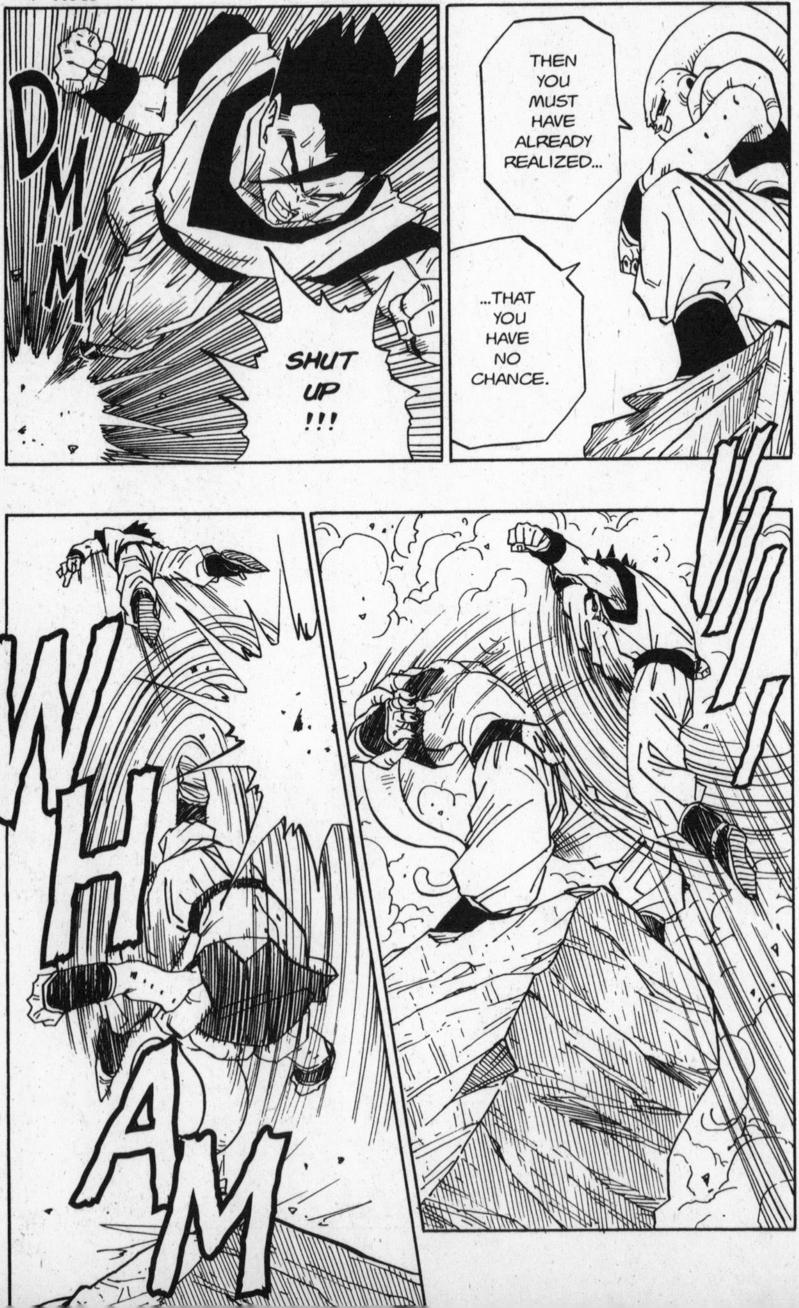
THEN YOU MUST HAVE ALREADY REALIZED...
...THAT YOU HAVE NO CHANCE.
DMM
SHUT UP!!!
WHAM

READ THIS WAY

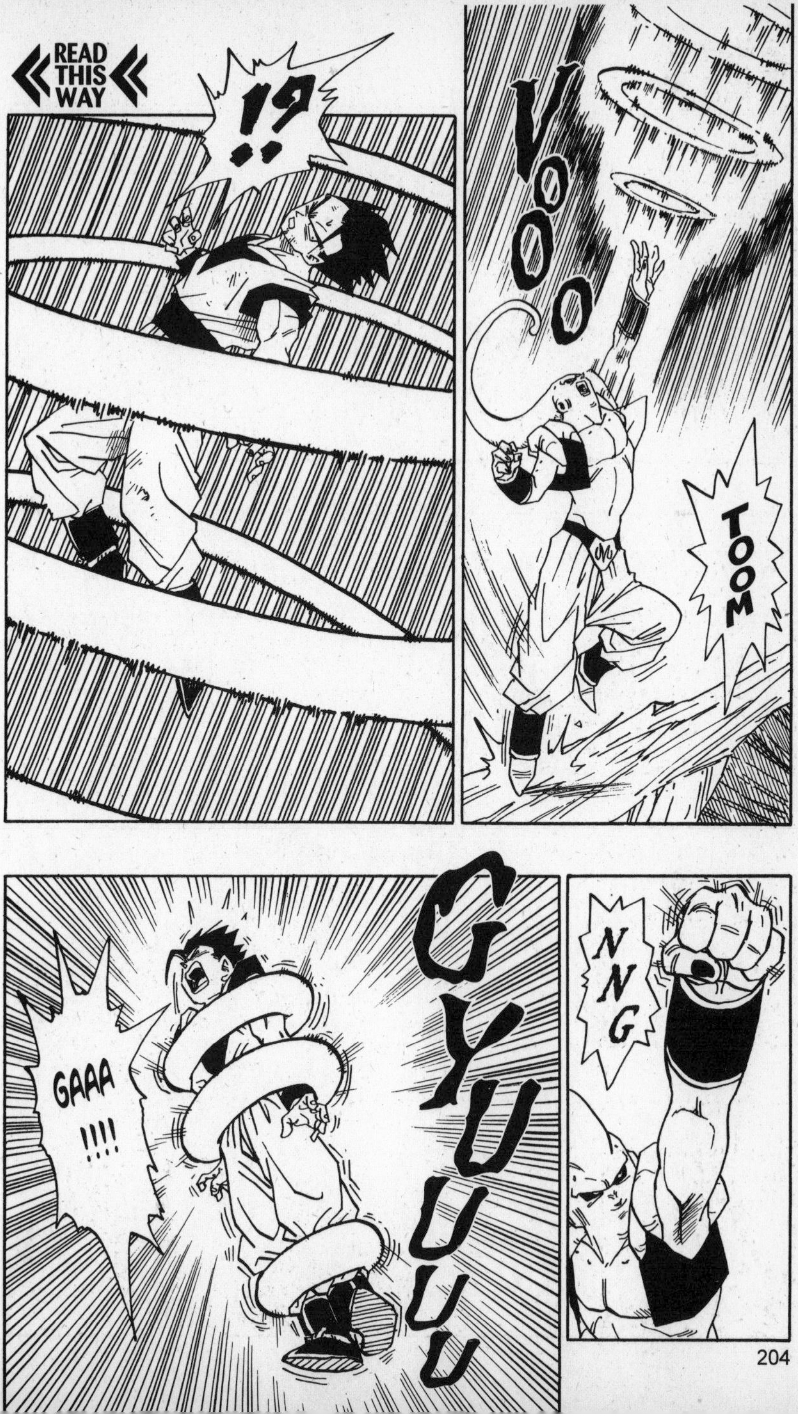
VOOOO
TOOM
!?
NNG
GYUUUU
GAAA !!!!

READ THIS WAY

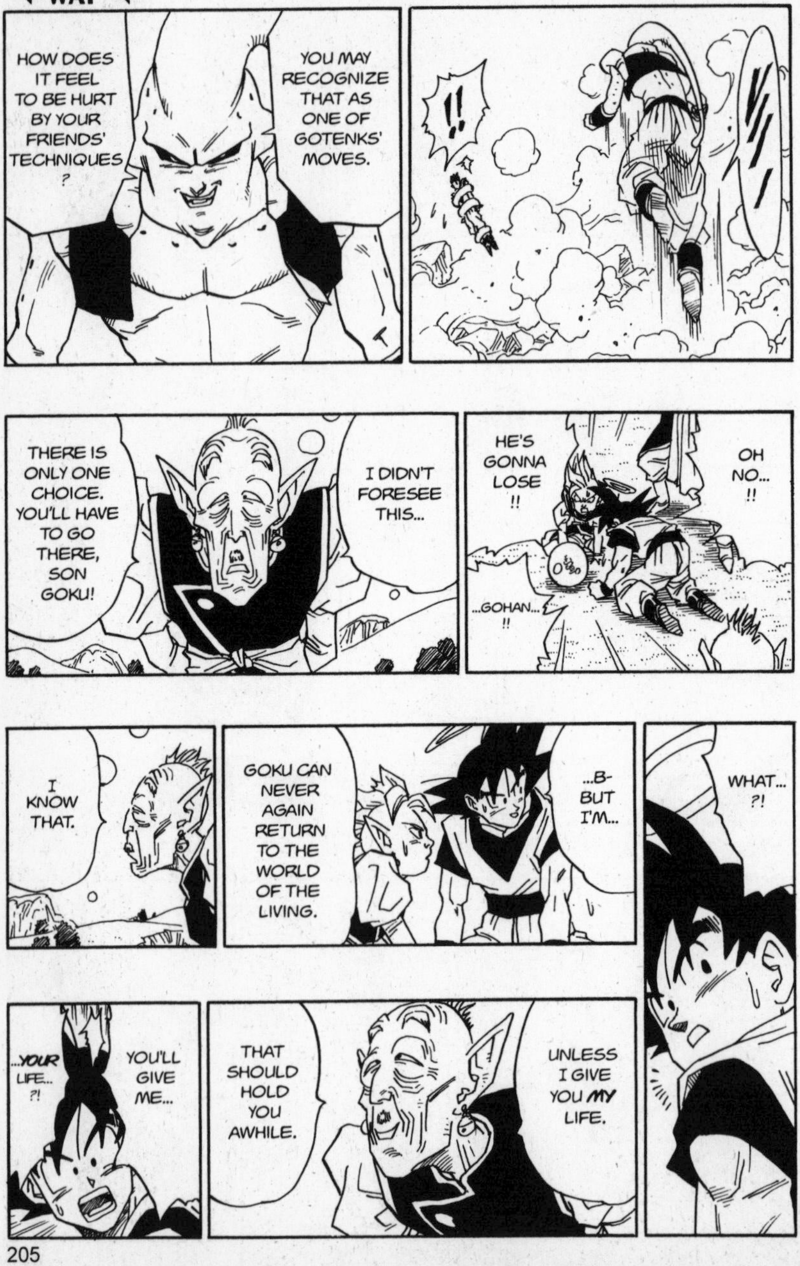

!!
YOU MAY RECOGNIZE THAT AS ONE OF GOTENKS' MOVES.
HOW DOES IT FEEL TO BE HURT BY YOUR FRIENDS' TECHNIQUES?
OH NO...!!
HE'S GONNA LOSE!!
...GOHAN...!!
I DIDN'T FORESEE THIS...
THERE IS ONLY ONE CHOICE. YOU'LL HAVE TO GO THERE, SON GOKU!
WHAT...?!
...B-BUT I'M...
GOKU CAN NEVER AGAIN RETURN TO THE WORLD OF THE LIVING.
I KNOW THAT.
UNLESS I GIVE YOU *MY* LIFE.
THAT SHOULD HOLD YOU AWHILE.
YOU'LL GIVE ME...
...*YOUR* LIFE...?!

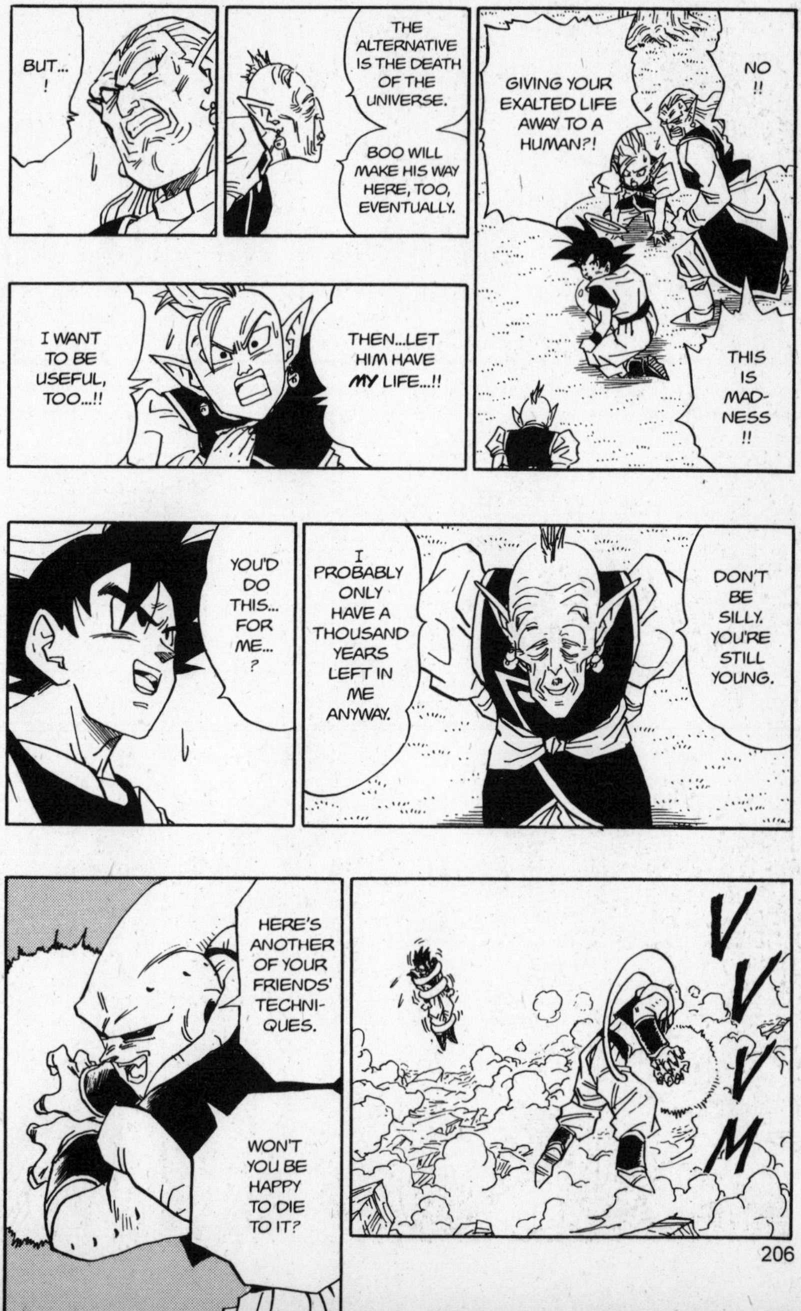
NO !!
GIVING YOUR EXALTED LIFE AWAY TO A HUMAN?!
THIS IS MADNESS !!
THE ALTERNATIVE IS THE DEATH OF THE UNIVERSE.
BOO WILL MAKE HIS WAY HERE, TOO, EVENTUALLY.
BUT... !
THEN...LET HIM HAVE *MY* LIFE...!!
I WANT TO BE USEFUL, TOO...!!
DON'T BE SILLY. YOU'RE STILL YOUNG.
I PROBABLY ONLY HAVE A THOUSAND YEARS LEFT IN ME ANYWAY.
YOU'D DO THIS... FOR ME... ?
VVVVM
HERE'S ANOTHER OF YOUR FRIENDS' TECHNI-QUES.
WON'T YOU BE HAPPY TO DIE TO IT?

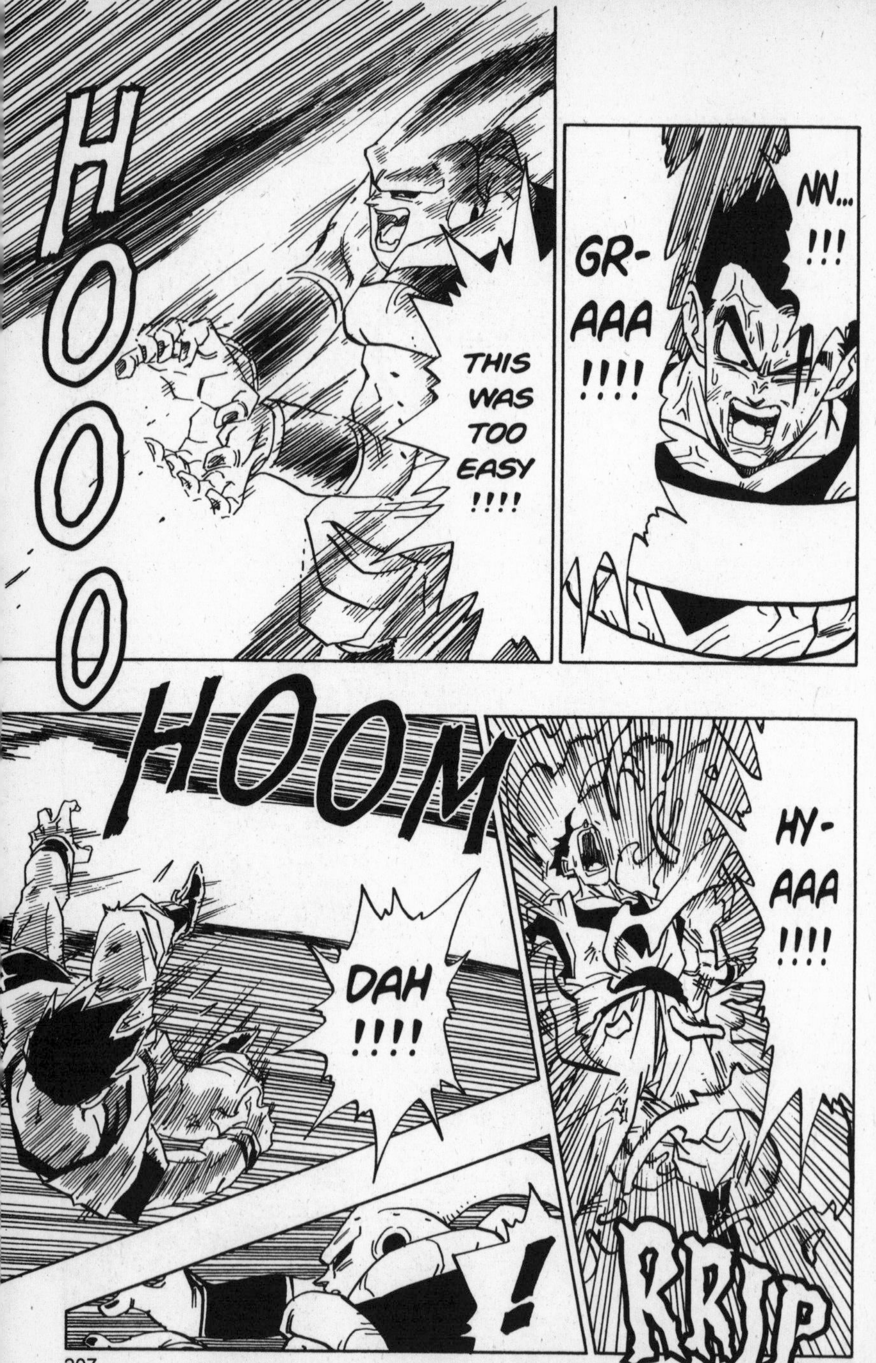
NN... !!!
GR-AAA !!!!
HOOOO
THIS WAS TOO EASY !!!!
HY-AAA !!!!
RRIP
HOOM
DAH !!!!
!

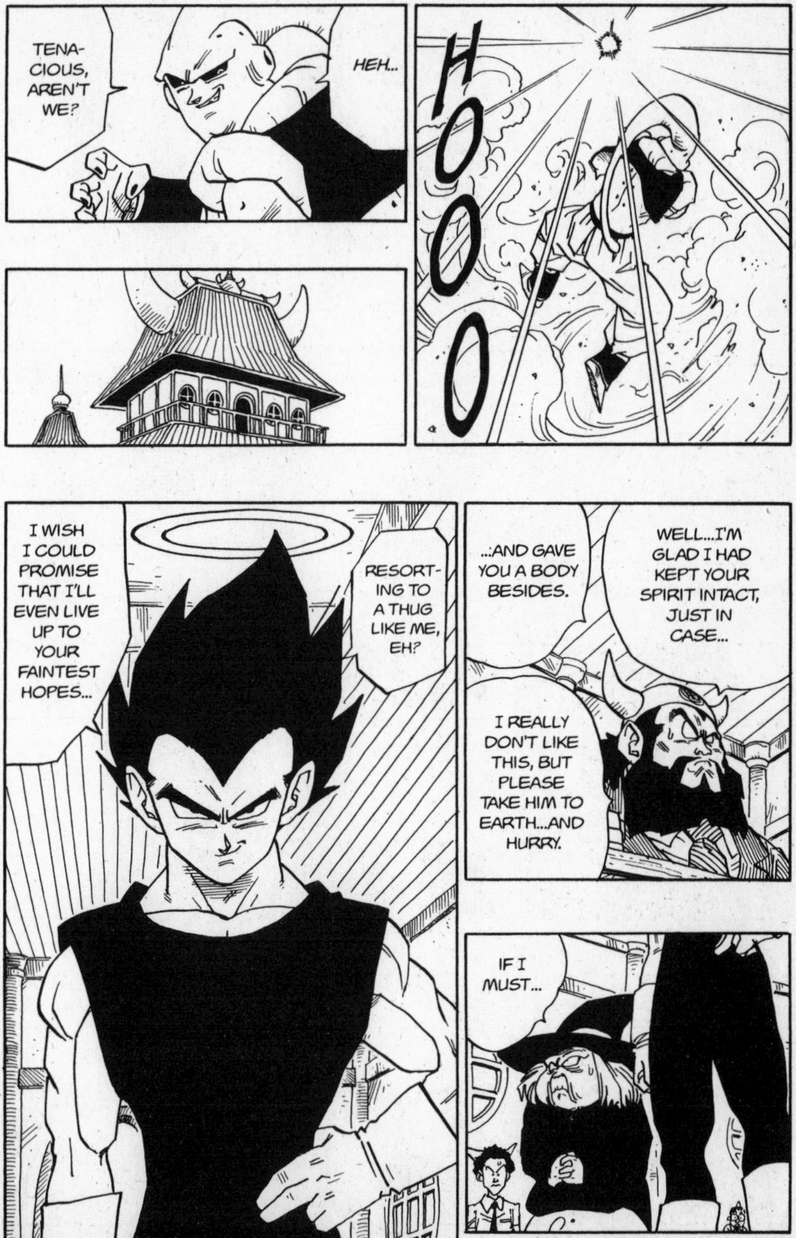
HOOOO
HEH...
TENA-CIOUS, AREN'T WE?
WELL...I'M GLAD I HAD KEPT YOUR SPIRIT INTACT, JUST IN CASE...
...AND GAVE YOU A BODY BESIDES.
I REALLY DON'T LIKE THIS, BUT PLEASE TAKE HIM TO EARTH...AND HURRY.
IF I MUST...
RESORT-ING TO A THUG LIKE ME, EH?
I WISH I COULD PROMISE THAT I'LL EVEN LIVE UP TO YOUR FAINTEST HOPES...

READ THIS WAY

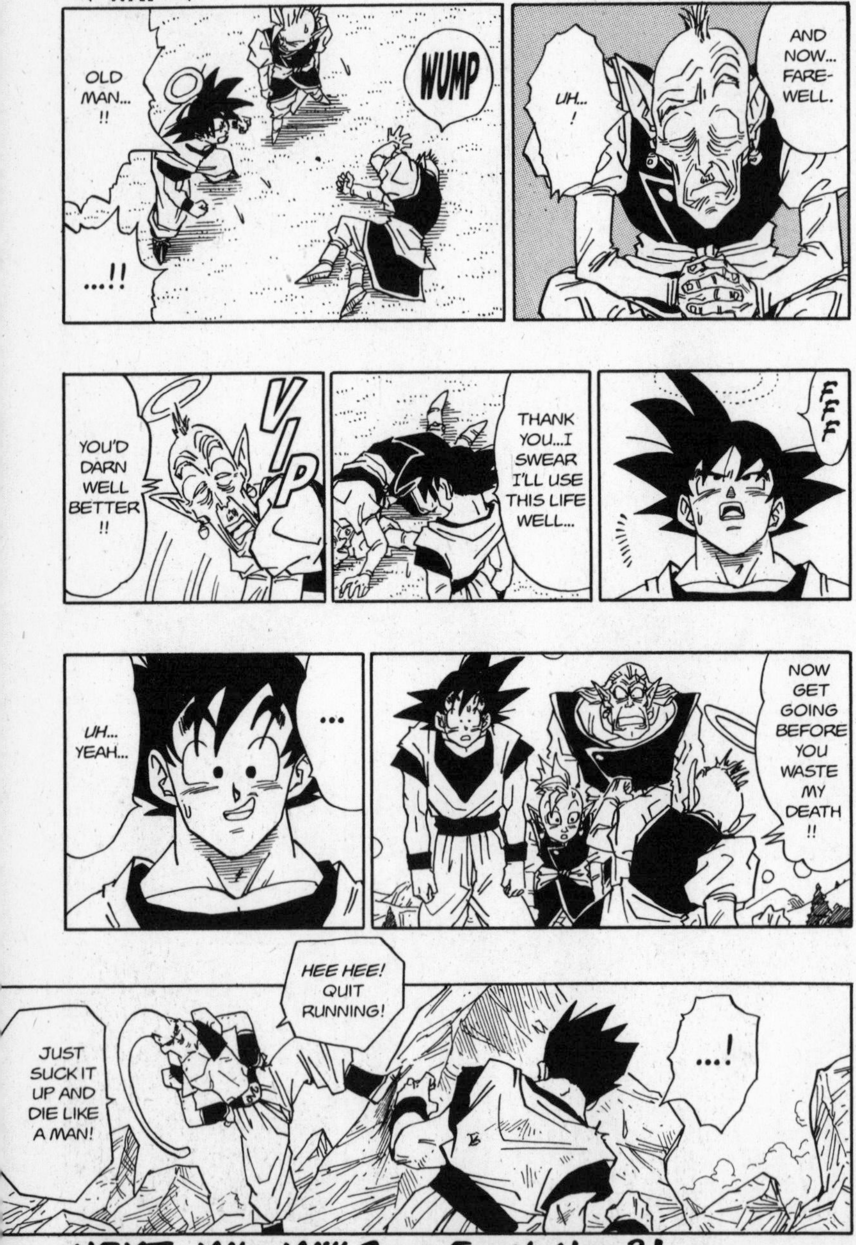
AND NOW... FARE-WELL.
UH... !
WUMP
OLD MAN... !!
...!!
EEE
THANK YOU...I SWEAR I'LL USE THIS LIFE WELL...
VIP
YOU'D DARN WELL BETTER !!
NOW GET GOING BEFORE YOU WASTE MY DEATH !!
...
UH... YEAH...
...!
HEE HEE! QUIT RUNNING!
JUST SUCK IT UP AND DIE LIKE A MAN!

NEXT: Who Will Save Earth Now?!

DBZ:307 · Enter a Savior?!

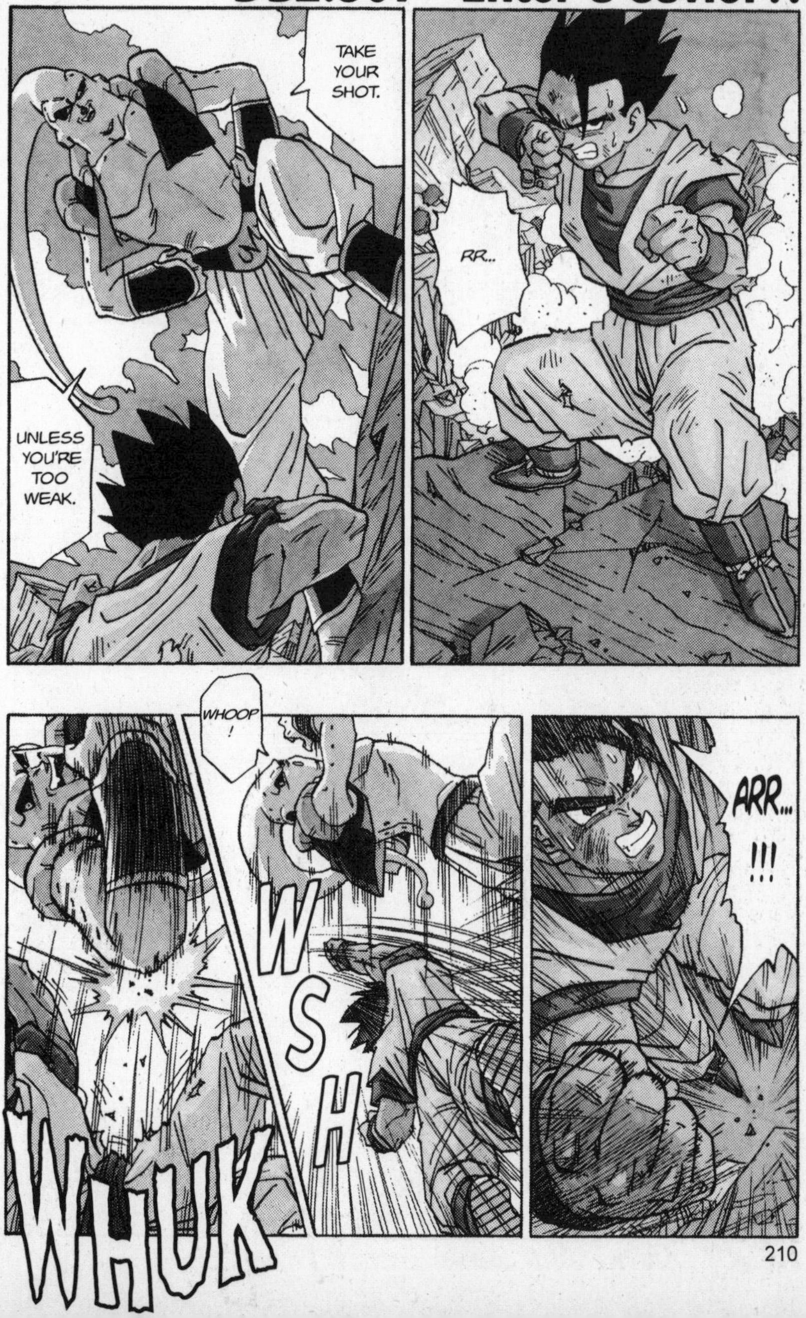
RR...
TAKE YOUR SHOT.
UNLESS YOU'RE TOO WEAK.
ARR... !!!
WHOOP!
WSH
WHUK

READ THIS WAY

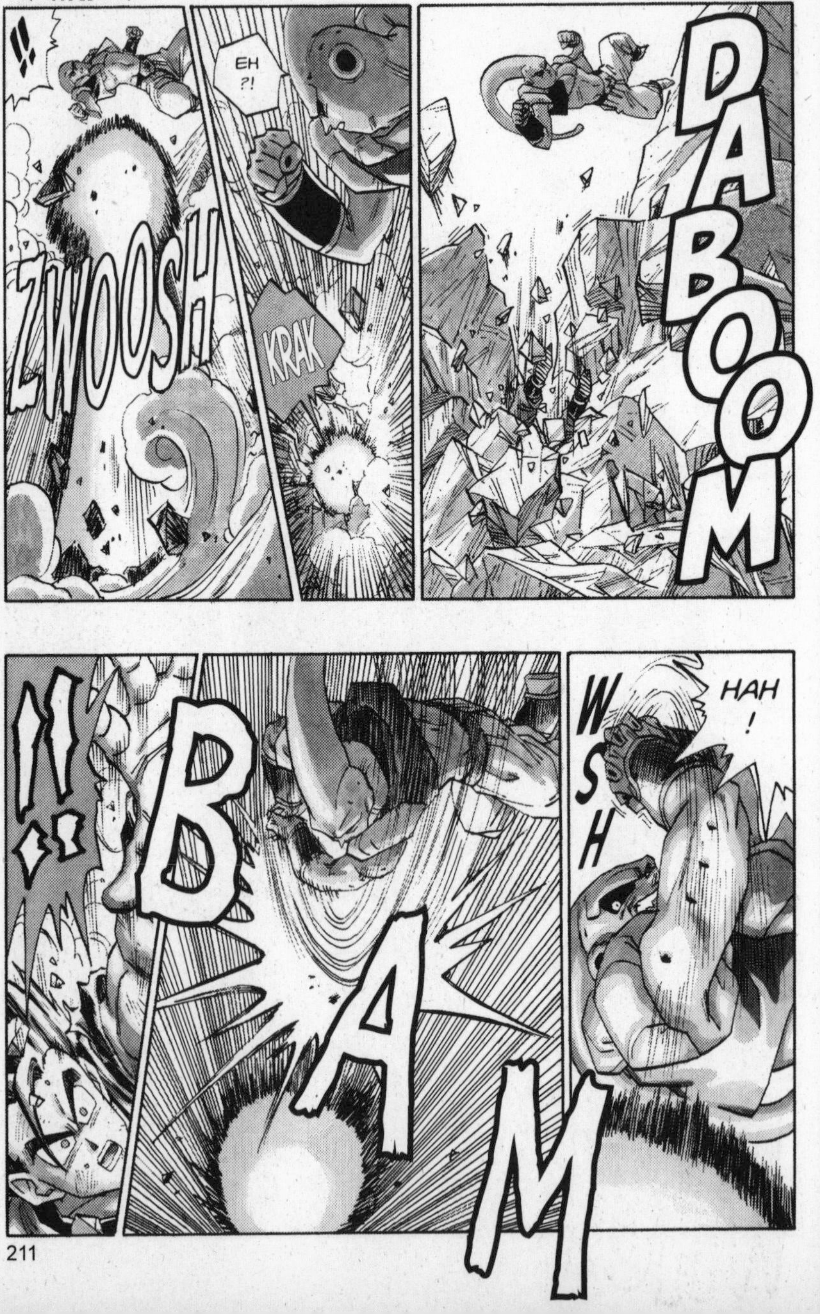
DABOOOM
EH ?!
KRAK
!!
ZWOOSH
HAH !
WSH
BAM
!!

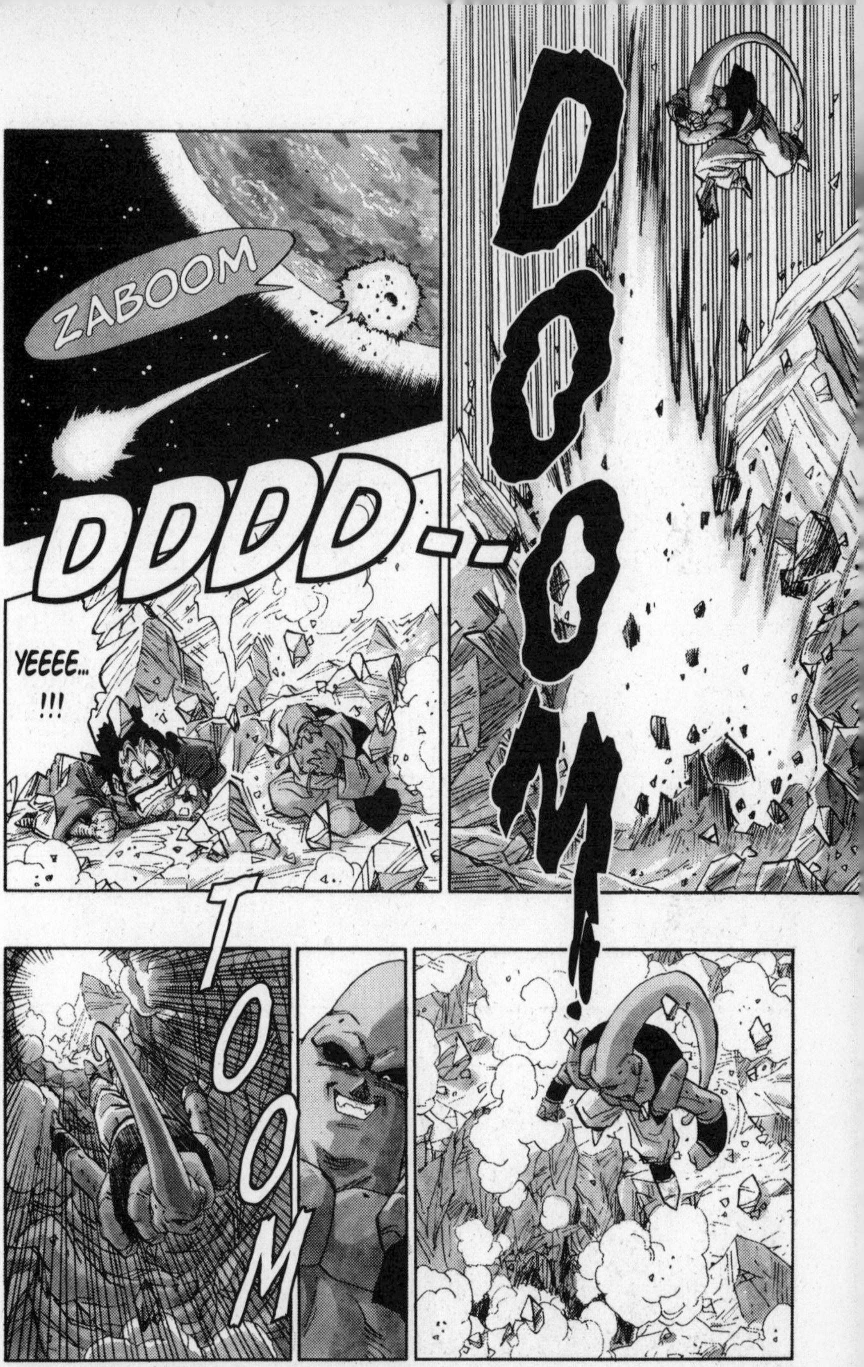
DOOOM!!
ZABOOM
DDDD..
YEEEE...
!!!
TOOOM

READ THIS WAY

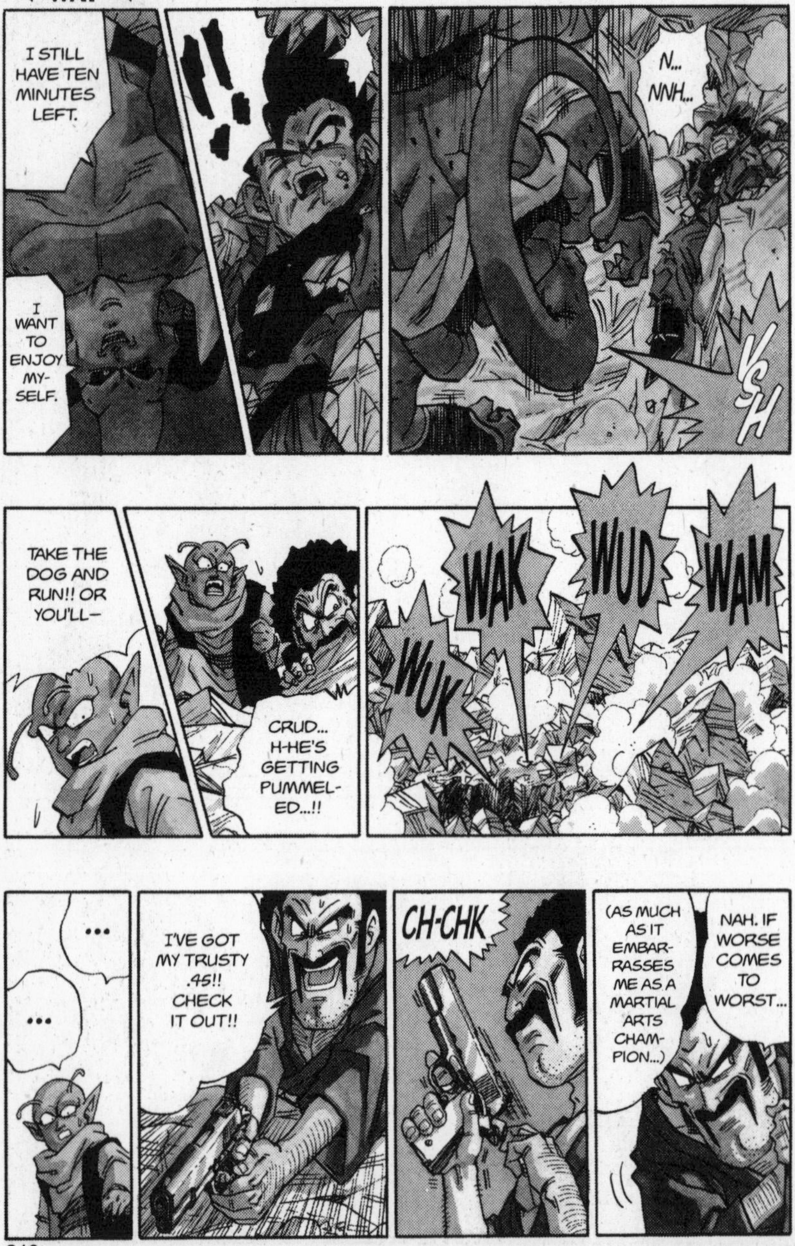
N...
NNH...
VSH
!!
I STILL HAVE TEN MINUTES LEFT.
I WANT TO ENJOY MY-SELF.
WAM
WUD
WAK
WUK
CRUD... H-HE'S GETTING PUMMEL-ED...!!
TAKE THE DOG AND RUN!! OR YOU'LL—
NAH. IF WORSE COMES TO WORST...
(AS MUCH AS IT EMBAR-RASSES ME AS A MARTIAL ARTS CHAM-PION...)
CH-CHK
I'VE GOT MY TRUSTY .45!! CHECK IT OUT!!
...
...

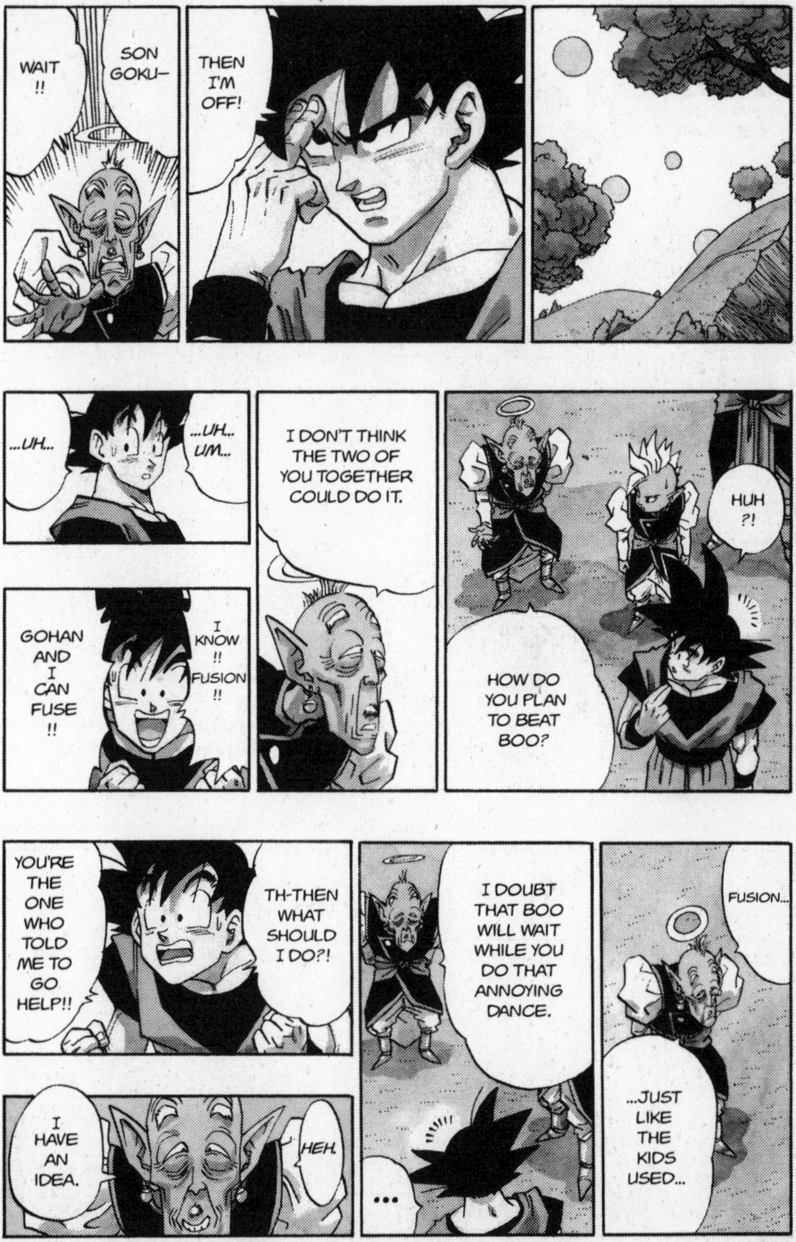
THEN I'M OFF!
SON GOKU—
WAIT !!
HUH ?!
HOW DO YOU PLAN TO BEAT BOO?
...UH.. UM...
...UH...
I KNOW !! FUSION !!
GOHAN AND I CAN FUSE !!
I DON'T THINK THE TWO OF YOU TOGETHER COULD DO IT.
FUSION...
...JUST LIKE THE KIDS USED...
I DOUBT THAT BOO WILL WAIT WHILE YOU DO THAT ANNOYING DANCE.
...
TH-THEN WHAT SHOULD I DO?!
YOU'RE THE ONE WHO TOLD ME TO GO HELP!!
HEH.
I HAVE AN IDEA.

READ THIS WAY

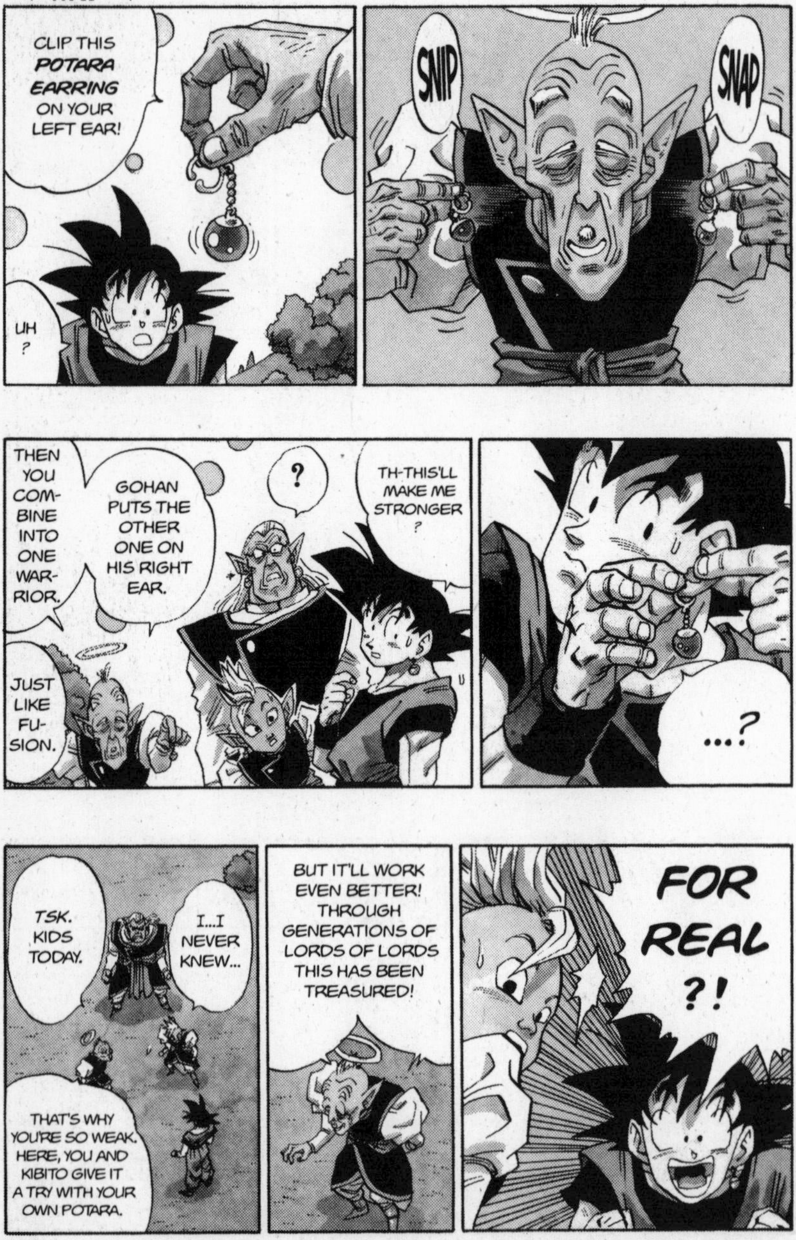
SNIP
SNAP
CLIP THIS *POTARA EARRING* ON YOUR LEFT EAR!
UH?
...?
TH-THIS'LL MAKE ME STRONGER?
?
GOHAN PUTS THE OTHER ONE ON HIS RIGHT EAR.
THEN YOU COMBINE INTO ONE WARRIOR.
JUST LIKE FUSION.
FOR REAL?!
BUT IT'LL WORK EVEN BETTER! THROUGH GENERATIONS OF LORDS OF LORDS THIS HAS BEEN TREASURED!
I...I NEVER KNEW...
TSK. KIDS TODAY.
THAT'S WHY YOU'RE SO WEAK. HERE, YOU AND KIBITO GIVE IT A TRY WITH YOUR OWN POTARA.

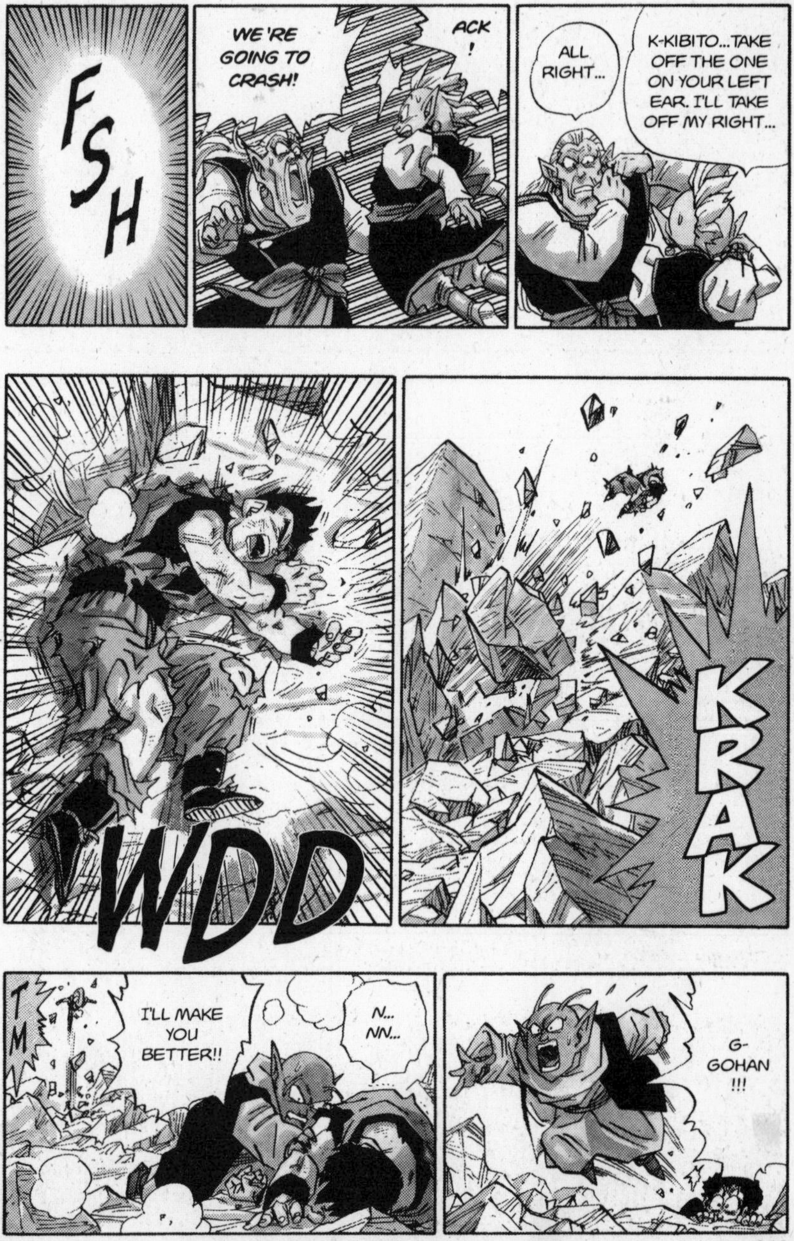
K-KIBITO...TAKE OFF THE ONE ON YOUR LEFT EAR. I'LL TAKE OFF MY RIGHT...
ALL RIGHT...
ACK !
WE'RE GOING TO CRASH!
FSH
KRAK
WDD
G-GOHAN !!!
N... NN...
I'LL MAKE YOU BETTER!!
TM

READ THIS WAY

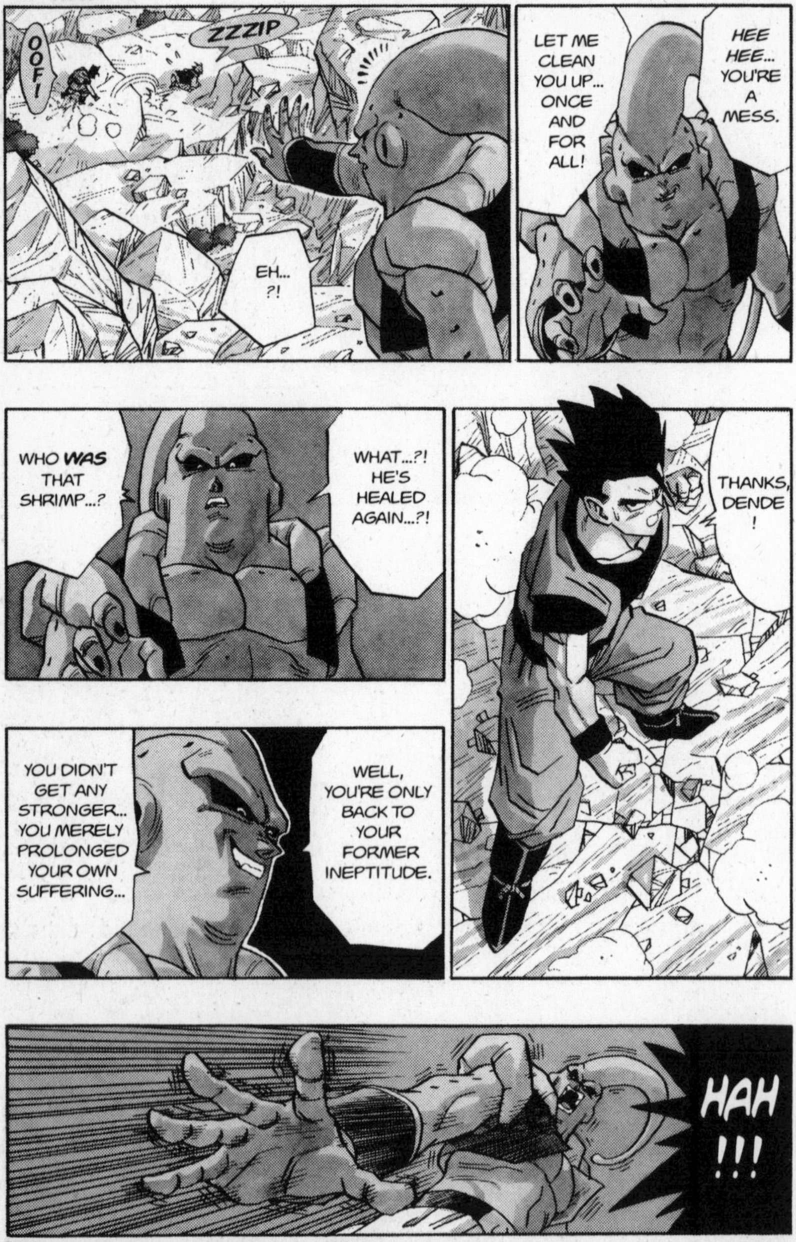
HEE HEE... YOU'RE A MESS.
LET ME CLEAN YOU UP... ONCE AND FOR ALL!
ZZZIP
OOF!
EH... ?!
THANKS, DENDE!
WHAT...?! HE'S HEALED AGAIN...?!
WHO **WAS** THAT SHRIMP...?
WELL, YOU'RE ONLY BACK TO YOUR FORMER INEPTITUDE.
YOU DIDN'T GET ANY STRONGER... YOU MERELY PROLONGED YOUR OWN SUFFERING...
HAH!!!

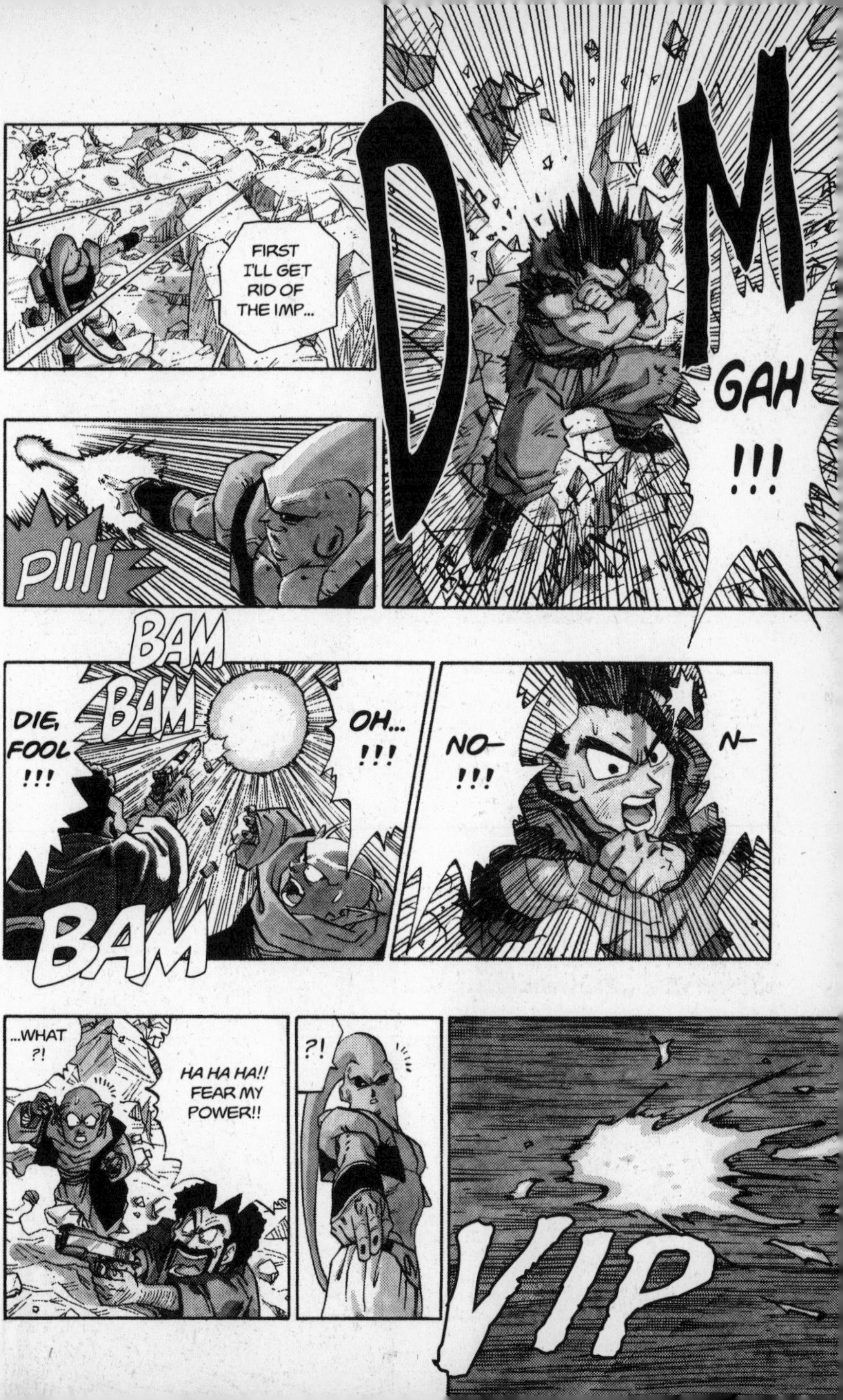
D M
GAH !!!
FIRST I'LL GET RID OF THE IMP...
PIIII
N—
NO— !!!
OH... !!!
BAM
BAM
DIE, FOOL !!!
BAM
VIP
?!
HA HA HA!! FEAR MY POWER!!
...WHAT ?!

READ THIS WAY

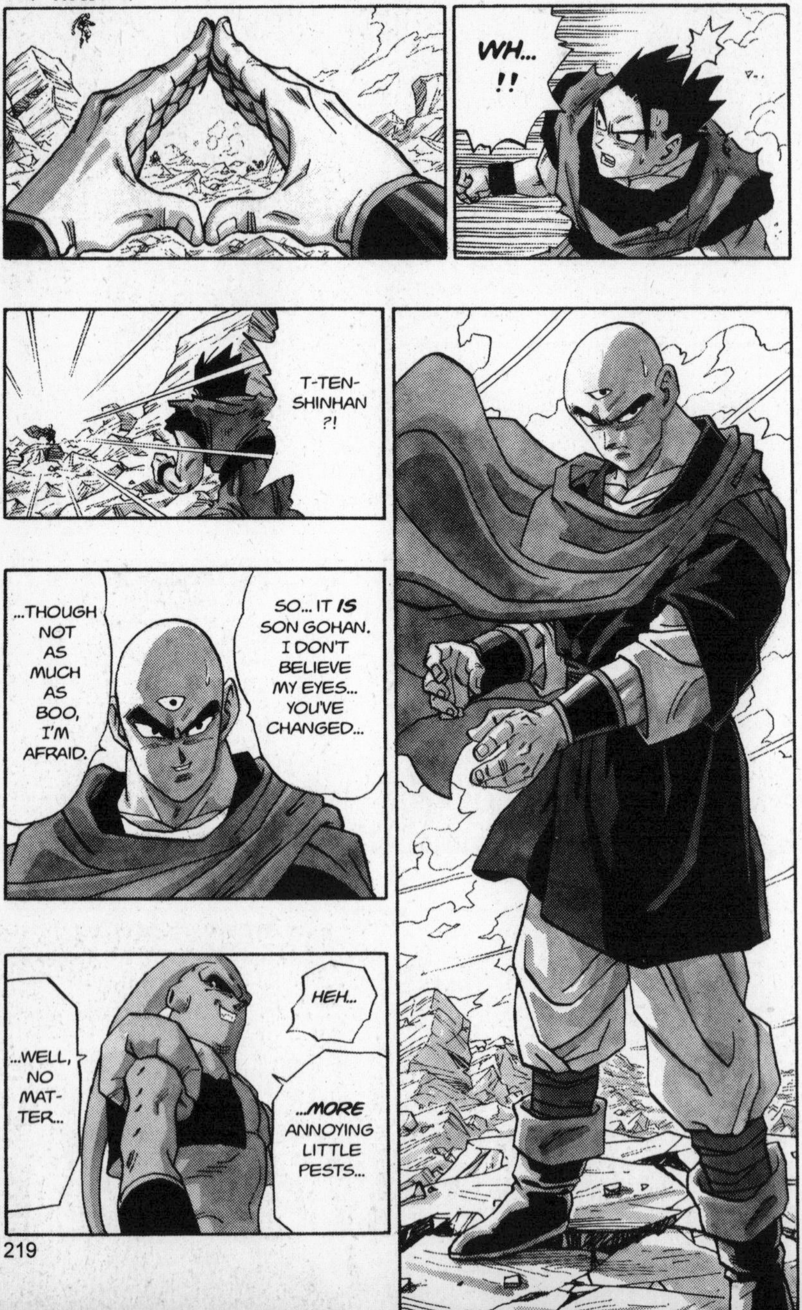

WH... !!
T-TEN-SHINHAN ?!
SO... IT **IS** SON GOHAN. I DON'T BELIEVE MY EYES... YOU'VE CHANGED...
...THOUGH NOT AS MUCH AS BOO, I'M AFRAID.
HEH...
...MORE ANNOYING LITTLE PESTS...
...WELL, NO MATTER...

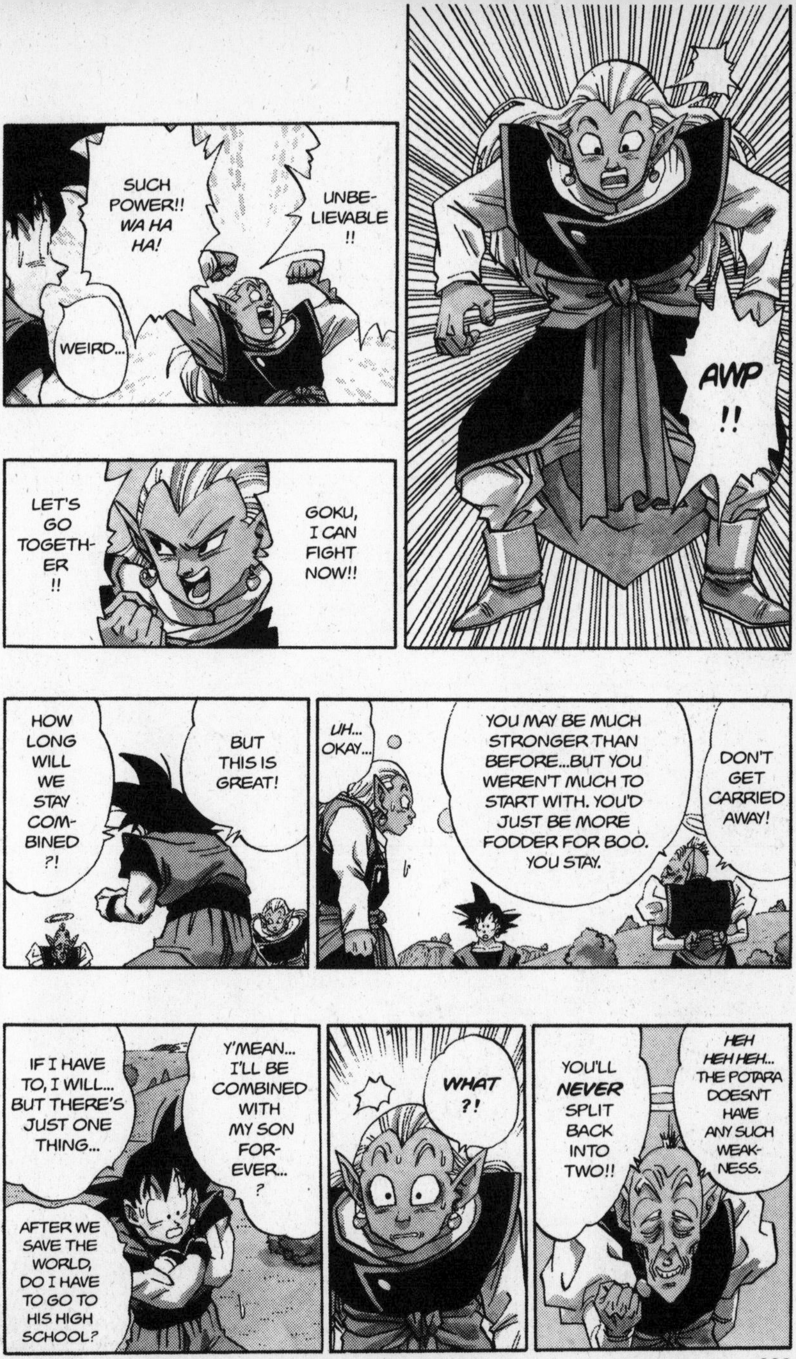
AWP !!
UNBELIEVABLE !!
SUCH POWER!! WA HA HA!
WEIRD...
GOKU, I CAN FIGHT NOW!!
LET'S GO TOGETHER !!
DON'T GET CARRIED AWAY!
YOU MAY BE MUCH STRONGER THAN BEFORE...BUT YOU WEREN'T MUCH TO START WITH. YOU'D JUST BE MORE FODDER FOR BOO. YOU STAY.
UH... OKAY...
BUT THIS IS GREAT!
HOW LONG WILL WE STAY COMBINED ?!
HEH HEH HEH... THE POTARA DOESN'T HAVE ANY SUCH WEAKNESS.
YOU'LL **NEVER** SPLIT BACK INTO TWO!!
WHAT ?!
Y'MEAN... I'LL BE COMBINED WITH MY SON FOREVER... ?
IF I HAVE TO, I WILL... BUT THERE'S JUST ONE THING...
AFTER WE SAVE THE WORLD, DO I HAVE TO GO TO HIS HIGH SCHOOL?

READ THIS WAY

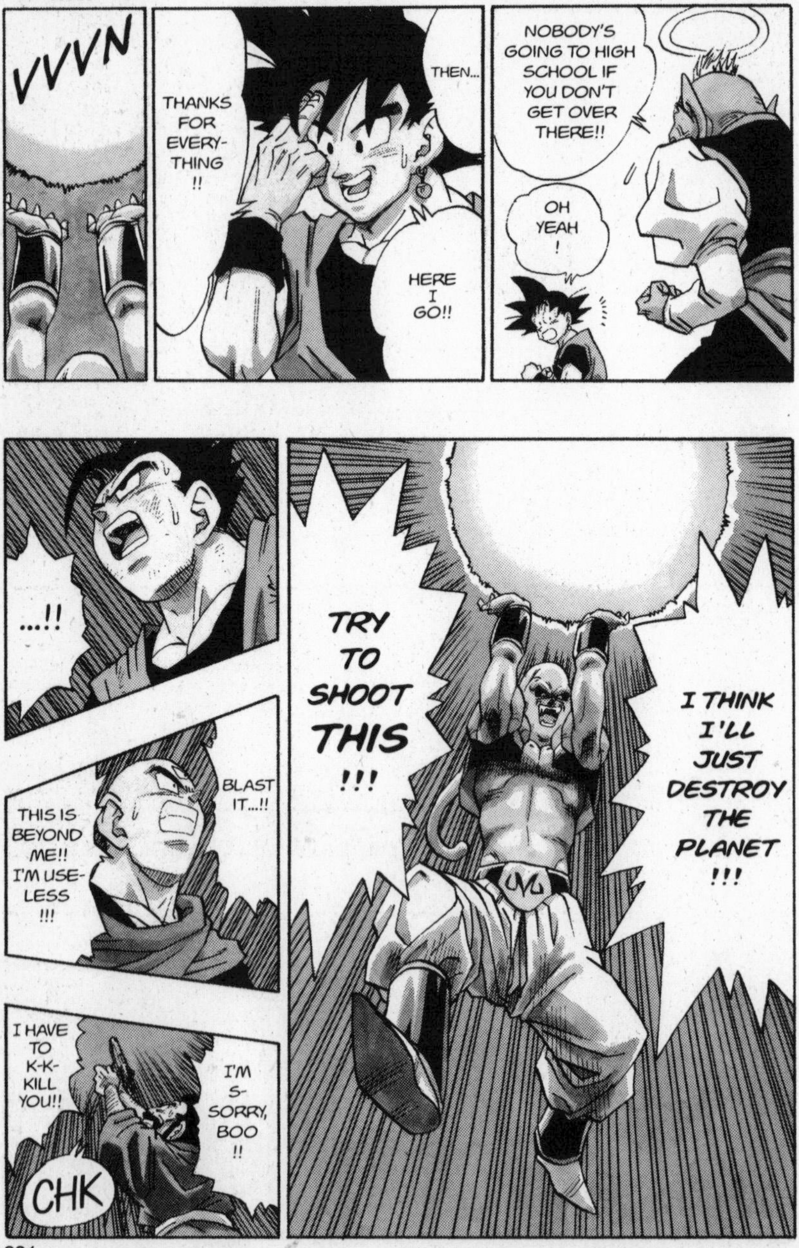
NOBODY'S GOING TO HIGH SCHOOL IF YOU DON'T GET OVER THERE!!
OH YEAH!
THEN...
THANKS FOR EVERYTHING!!
HERE I GO!!
VVVN
I THINK I'LL JUST DESTROY THE PLANET!!!
TRY TO SHOOT THIS!!!
...!!
BLAST IT...!!
THIS IS BEYOND ME!! I'M USELESS!!!
I'M S-SORRY, BOO!!
I HAVE TO K-K-KILL YOU!!
CHK

SNIP
SNAP

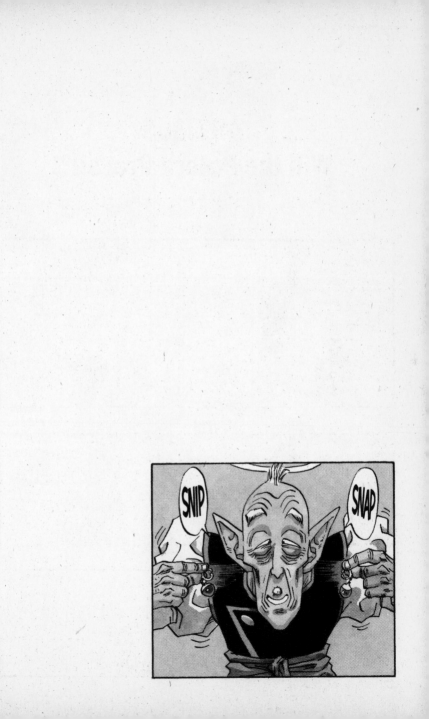

DBZ:308
Will the Potara Prevail?!

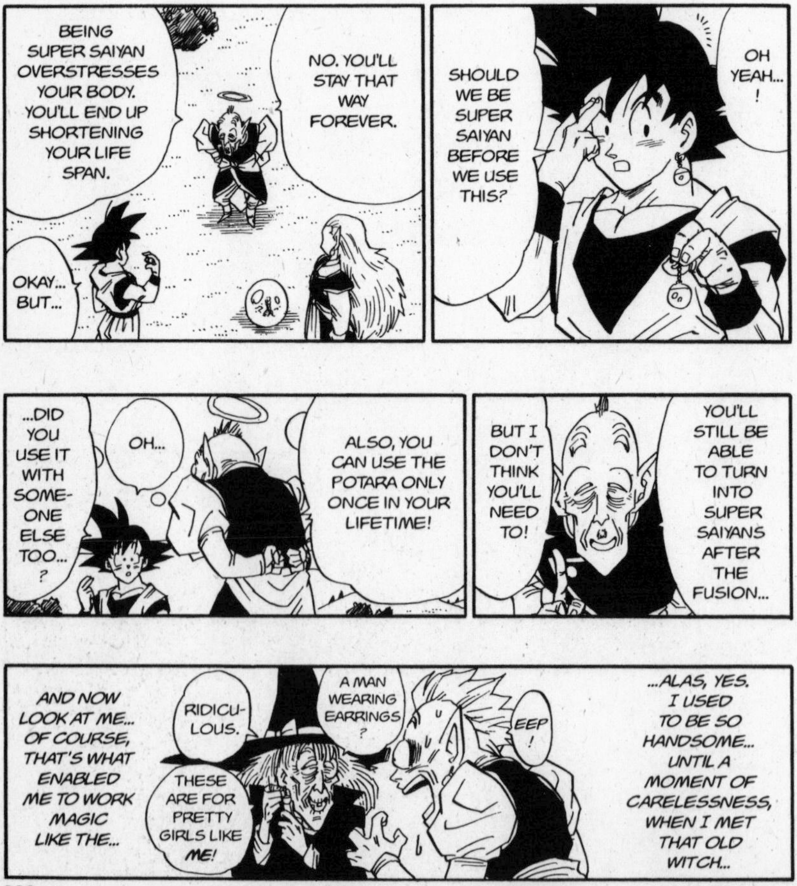
OH YEAH... !
SHOULD WE BE SUPER SAIYAN BEFORE WE USE THIS?
NO. YOU'LL STAY THAT WAY FOREVER.
BEING SUPER SAIYAN OVERSTRESSES YOUR BODY. YOU'LL END UP SHORTENING YOUR LIFE SPAN.
OKAY... BUT...
YOU'LL STILL BE ABLE TO TURN INTO SUPER SAIYANS AFTER THE FUSION...
BUT I DON'T THINK YOU'LL NEED TO!
ALSO, YOU CAN USE THE POTARA ONLY ONCE IN YOUR LIFETIME!
OH...
...DID YOU USE IT WITH SOME-ONE ELSE TOO... ?
...ALAS, YES. I USED TO BE SO HANDSOME... UNTIL A MOMENT OF CARELESSNESS, WHEN I MET THAT OLD WITCH...
EEP !
A MAN WEARING EARRINGS ?
RIDICU-LOUS.
THESE ARE FOR PRETTY GIRLS LIKE ME!
AND NOW LOOK AT ME... OF COURSE, THAT'S WHAT ENABLED ME TO WORK MAGIC LIKE THE...

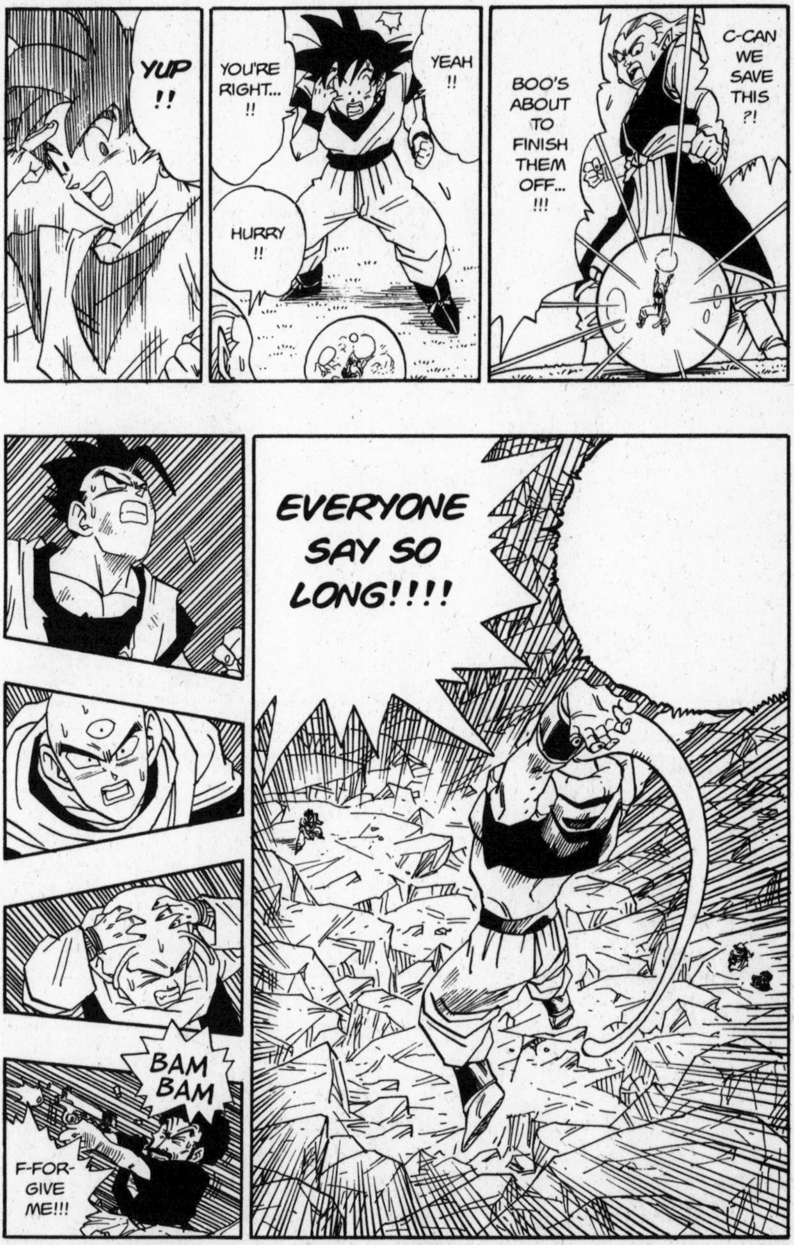
C-CAN WE SAVE THIS ?!
BOO'S ABOUT TO FINISH THEM OFF... !!!
YEAH !!
YOU'RE RIGHT... !!
HURRY !!
YUP !!
EVERYONE SAY SO LONG!!!!
BAM BAM
F-FOR-GIVE ME!!!

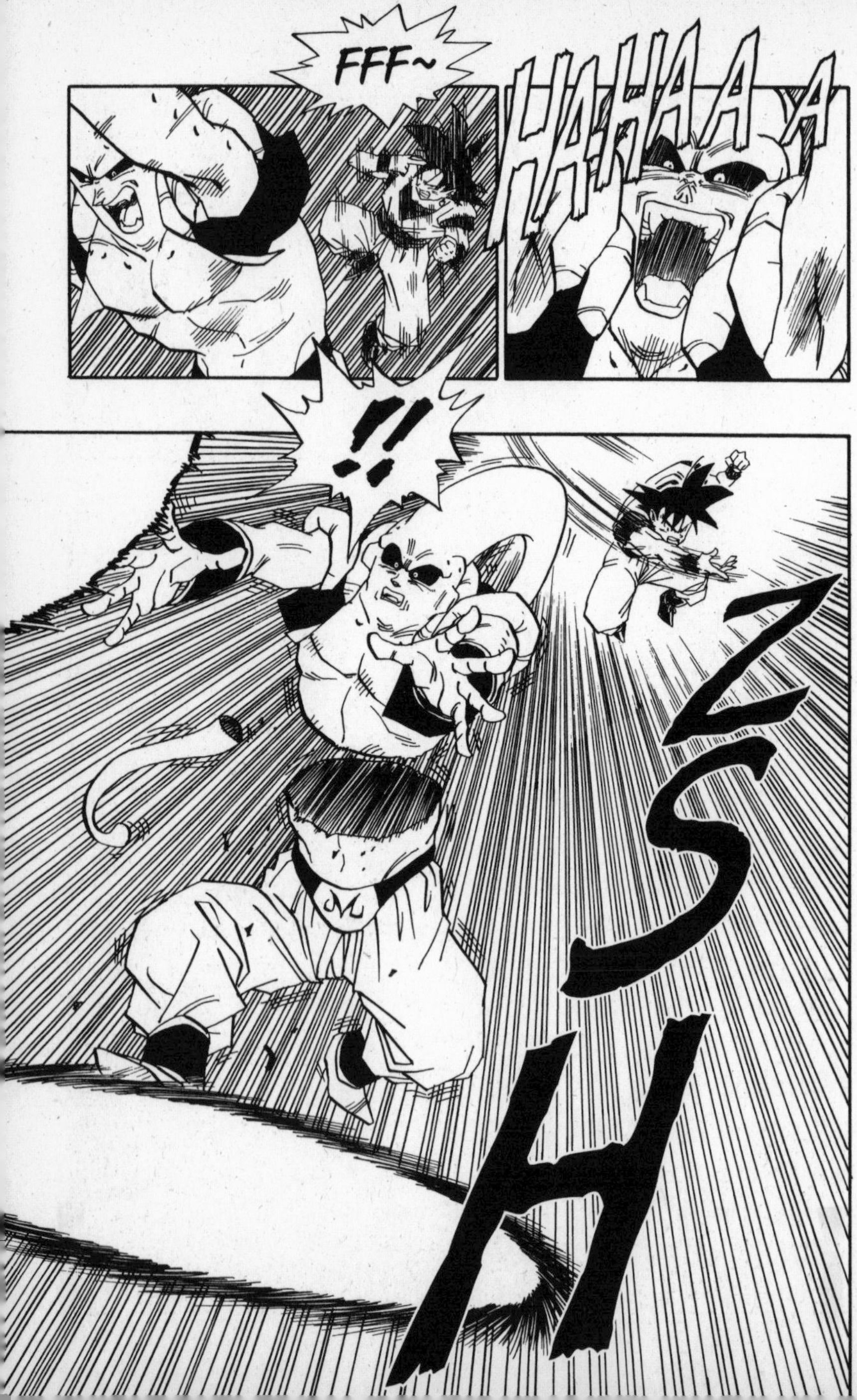
HAHAAA A
FFF~
!!
ZSH

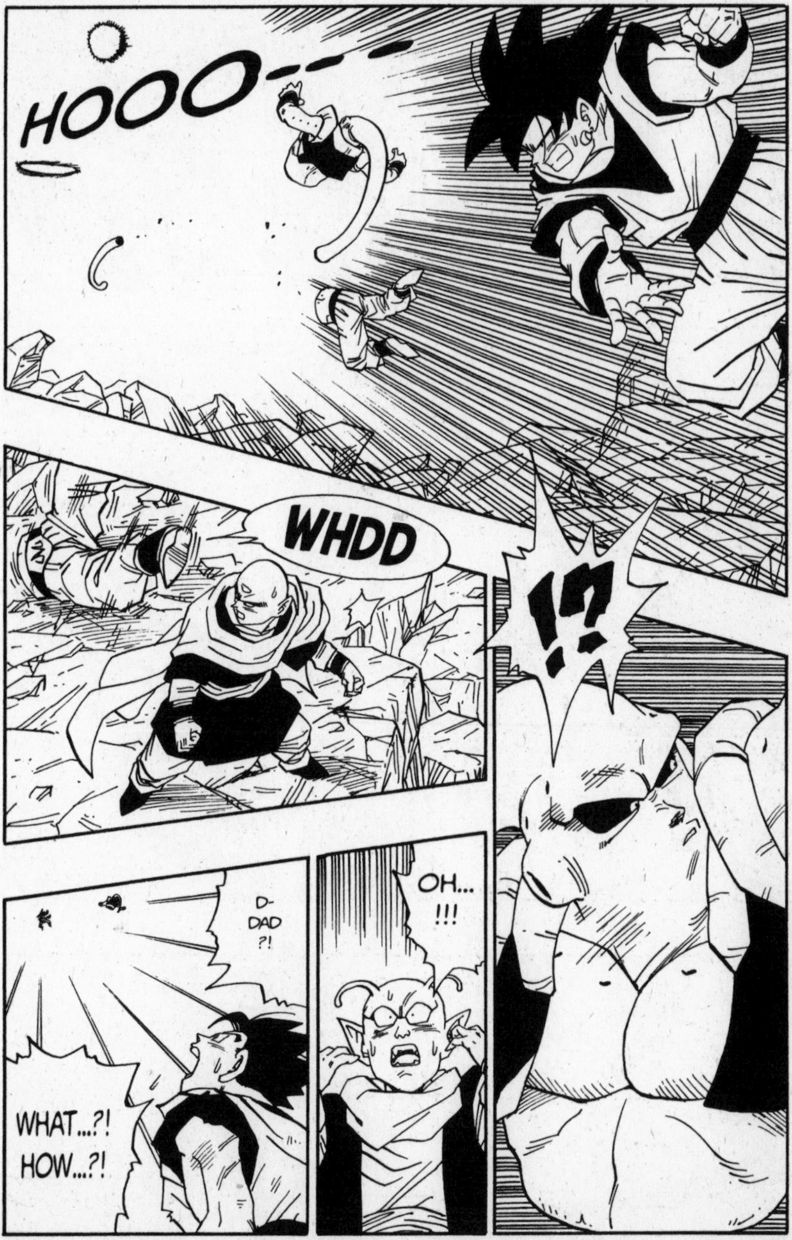

HOOO---
!?
WHDD
OH... !!!
D-DAD ?!
WHAT...?! HOW...?!

READ THIS WAY

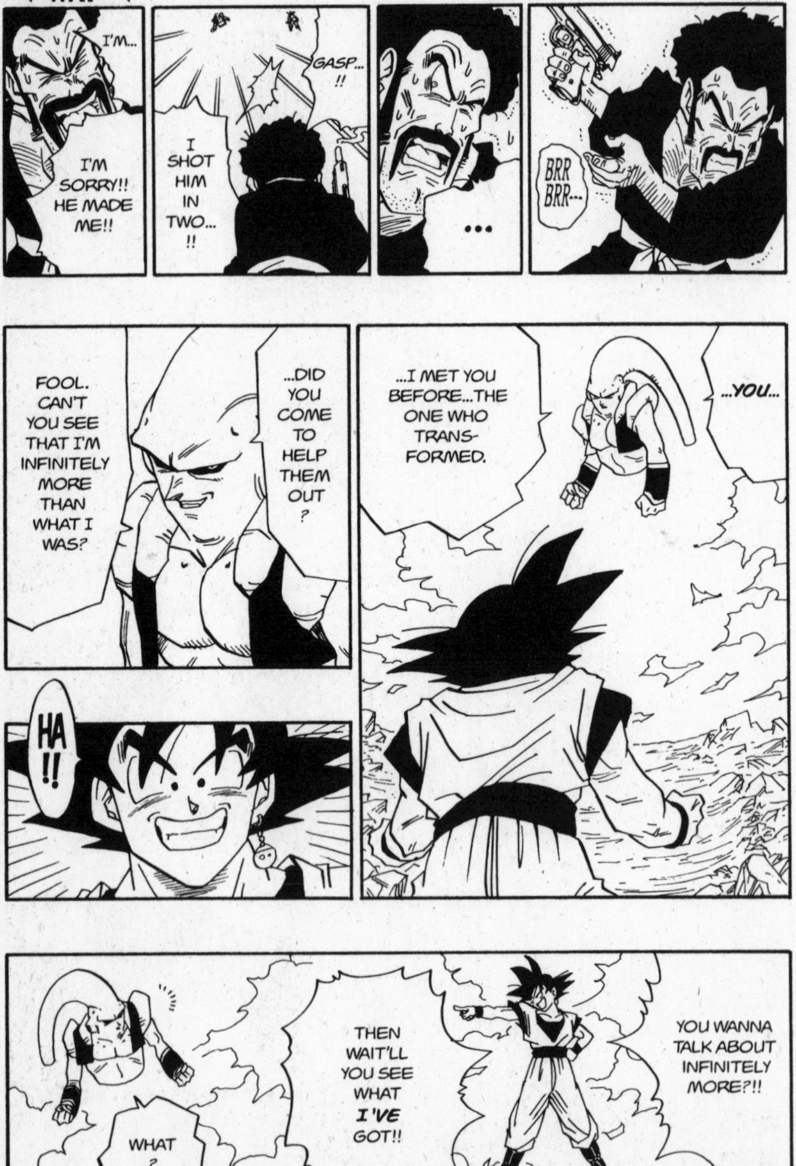
BRR BRR...
...
GASP...!!
I SHOT HIM IN TWO...!!
I'M...
I'M SORRY!! HE MADE ME!!
...YOU...
...I MET YOU BEFORE...THE ONE WHO TRANSFORMED.
...DID YOU COME TO HELP THEM OUT?
FOOL. CAN'T YOU SEE THAT I'M INFINITELY MORE THAN WHAT I WAS?
HA!!
YOU WANNA TALK ABOUT INFINITELY MORE?!!
THEN WAIT'LL YOU SEE WHAT I'VE GOT!!
WHAT?

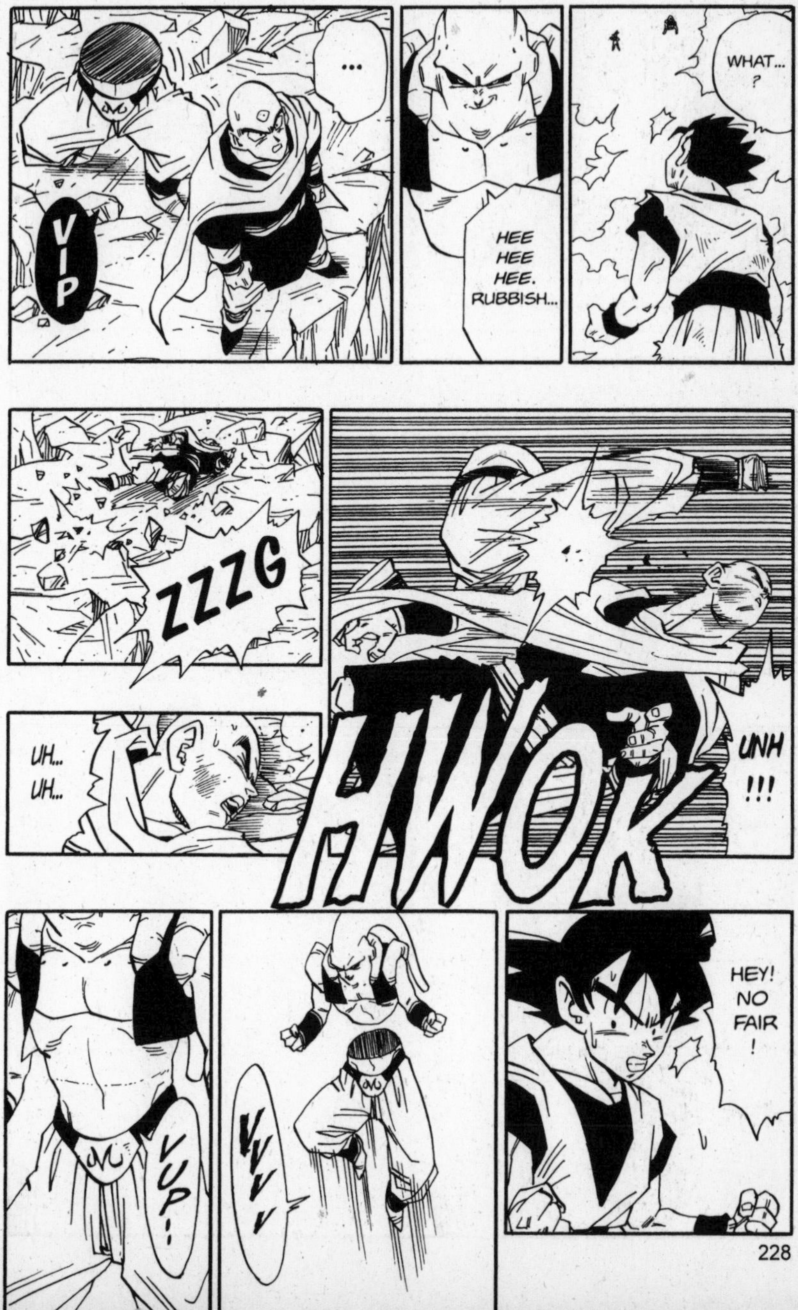
WHAT... ?
HEE HEE HEE. RUBBISH...
...
VIP
UNH !!!
HWOK
ZZZG
UH... UH...
HEY! NO FAIR !
VVVVV
VUP!

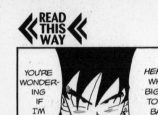

READ THIS WAY

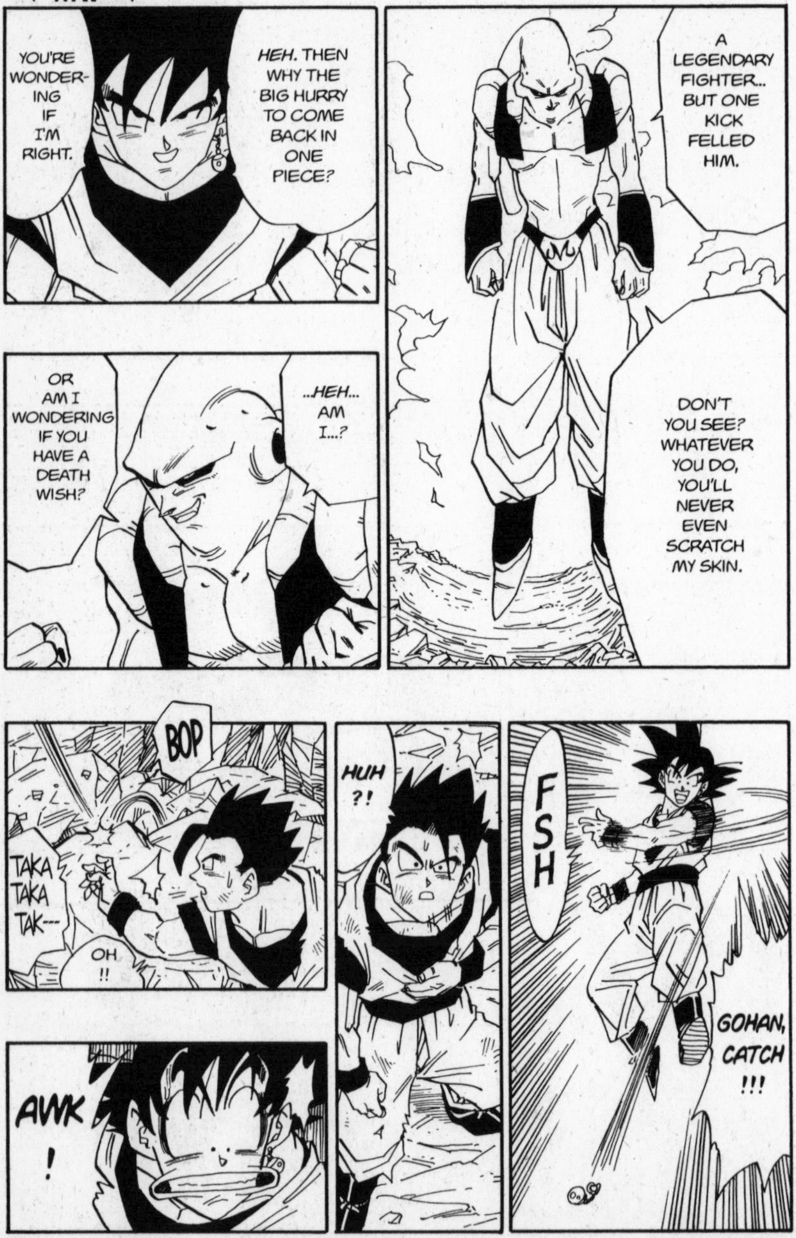
A LEGENDARY FIGHTER... BUT ONE KICK FELLED HIM.
DON'T YOU SEE? WHATEVER YOU DO, YOU'LL NEVER EVEN SCRATCH MY SKIN.
HEH. THEN WHY THE BIG HURRY TO COME BACK IN ONE PIECE?
YOU'RE WONDER-ING IF I'M RIGHT.
...HEH... AM I...?
OR AM I WONDERING IF YOU HAVE A DEATH WISH?
FSH
GOHAN, CATCH!!!
HUH?!
BOP
TAKA TAKA TAK---
OH !!
AWK !

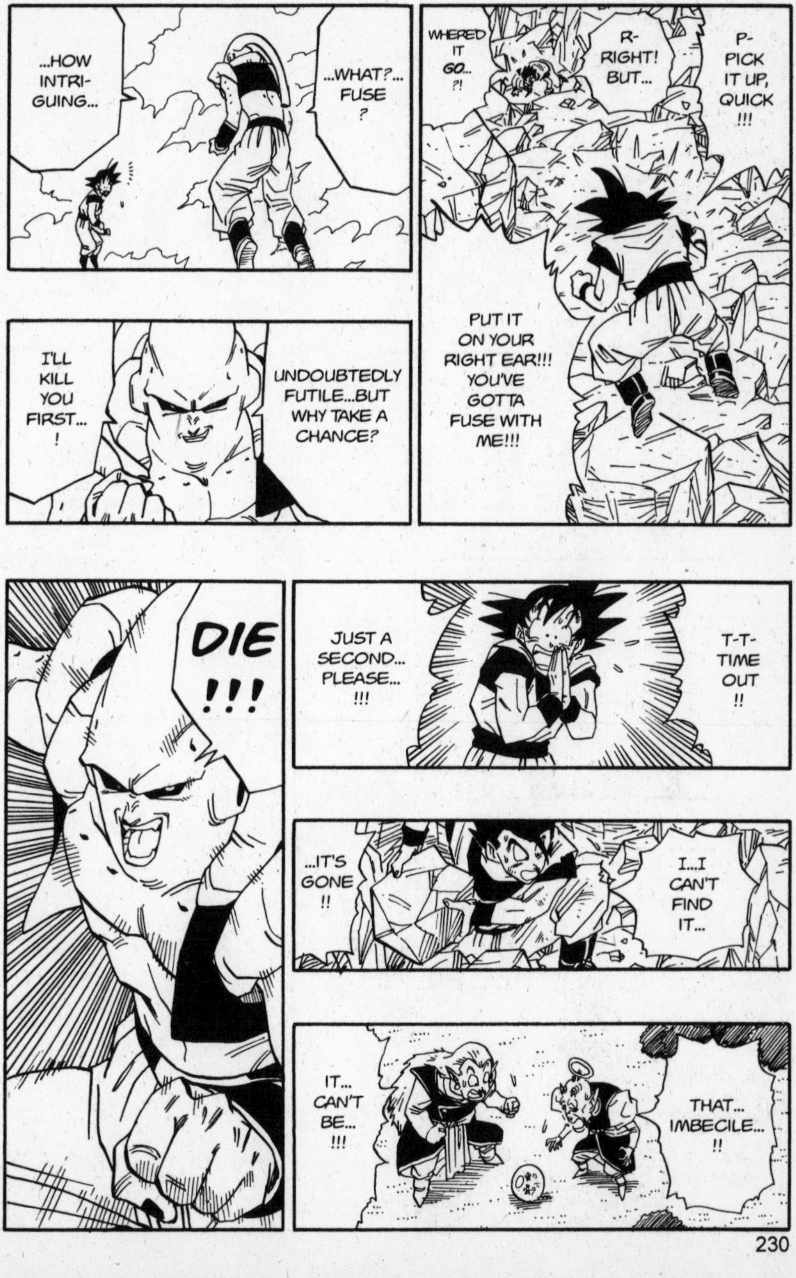
P- PICK IT UP, QUICK !!!
R- RIGHT! BUT...
WHERED IT GO... ?!
PUT IT ON YOUR RIGHT EAR!!! YOU'VE GOTTA FUSE WITH ME!!!
...WHAT?... FUSE ?
...HOW INTRI-GUING...
UNDOUBTEDLY FUTILE...BUT WHY TAKE A CHANCE?
I'LL KILL YOU FIRST... !
T-T-TIME OUT !!
JUST A SECOND... PLEASE... !!!
I...I CAN'T FIND IT...
...IT'S GONE !!
THAT... IMBECILE... !!
IT... CAN'T BE... !!!
DIE !!!

READ THIS WAY

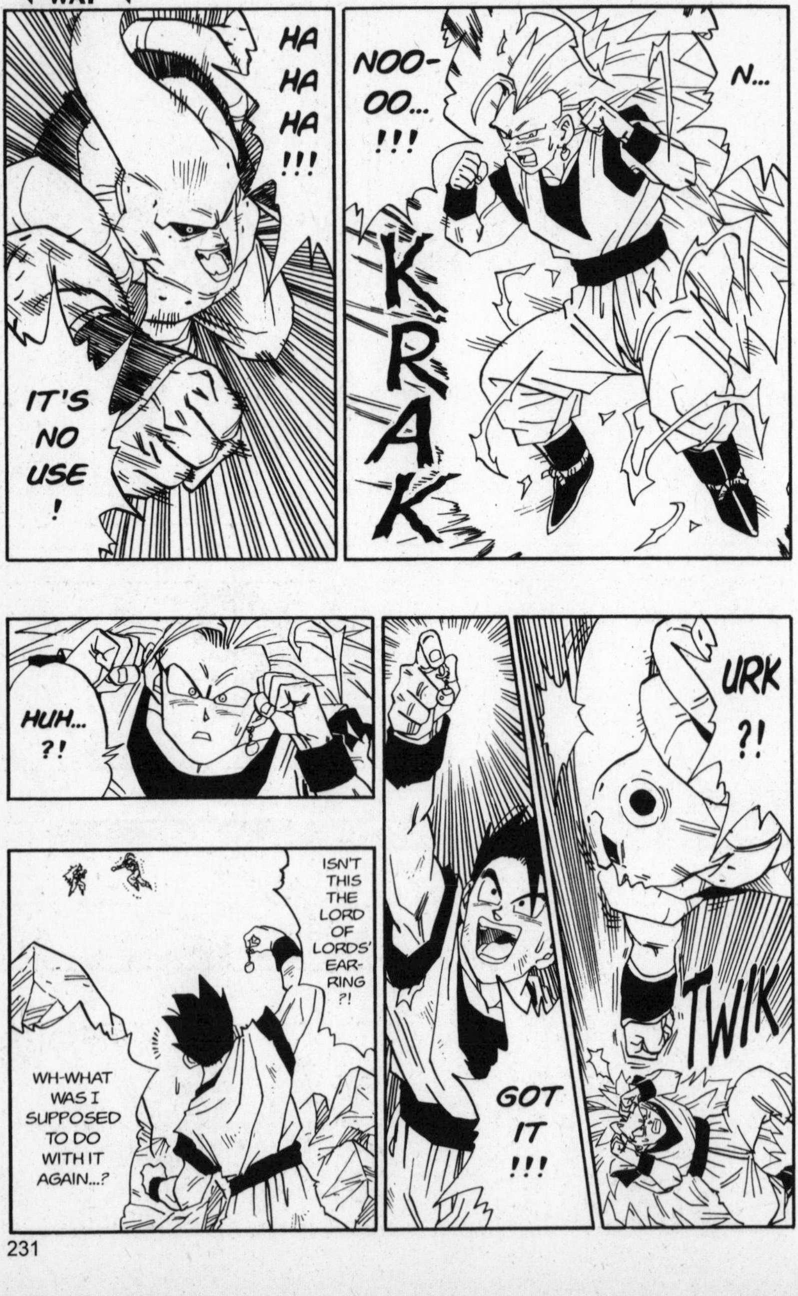
N...
NOO-OO...!!!
KRAK
HA HA HA!!!
IT'S NO USE!
URK?!
TWIK
GOT IT!!!
HUH...?!
ISN'T THIS THE LORD OF LORDS' EAR-RING?!
WH-WHAT WAS I SUPPOSED TO DO WITH IT AGAIN...?

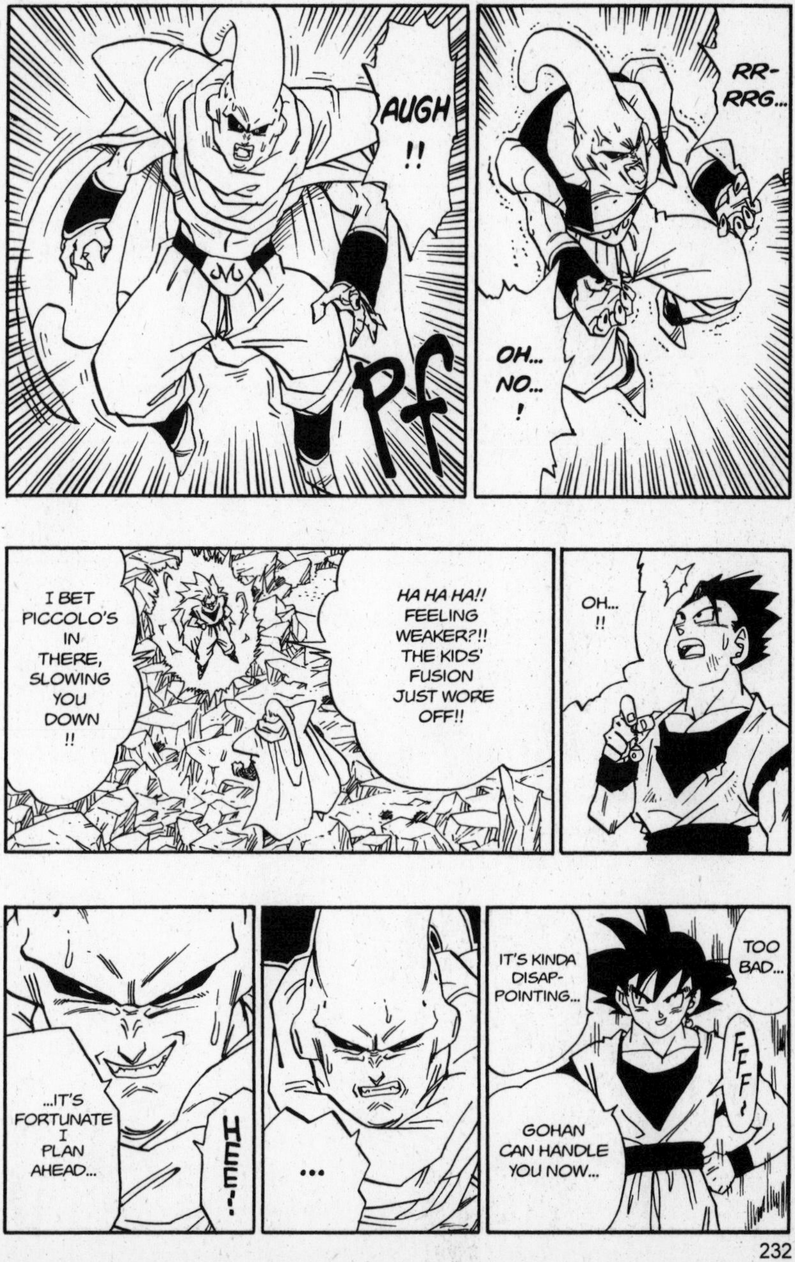
RR-RRG...
OH... NO...!
AUGH!!
Pf
OH...!!
HA HA HA!! FEELING WEAKER?!! THE KIDS' FUSION JUST WORE OFF!!
I BET PICCOLO'S IN THERE, SLOWING YOU DOWN!!
TOO BAD...
IT'S KINDA DISAP-POINTING...
FFF
GOHAN CAN HANDLE YOU NOW...
...
HEE!!
...IT'S FORTUNATE I PLAN AHEAD...

READ THIS WAY

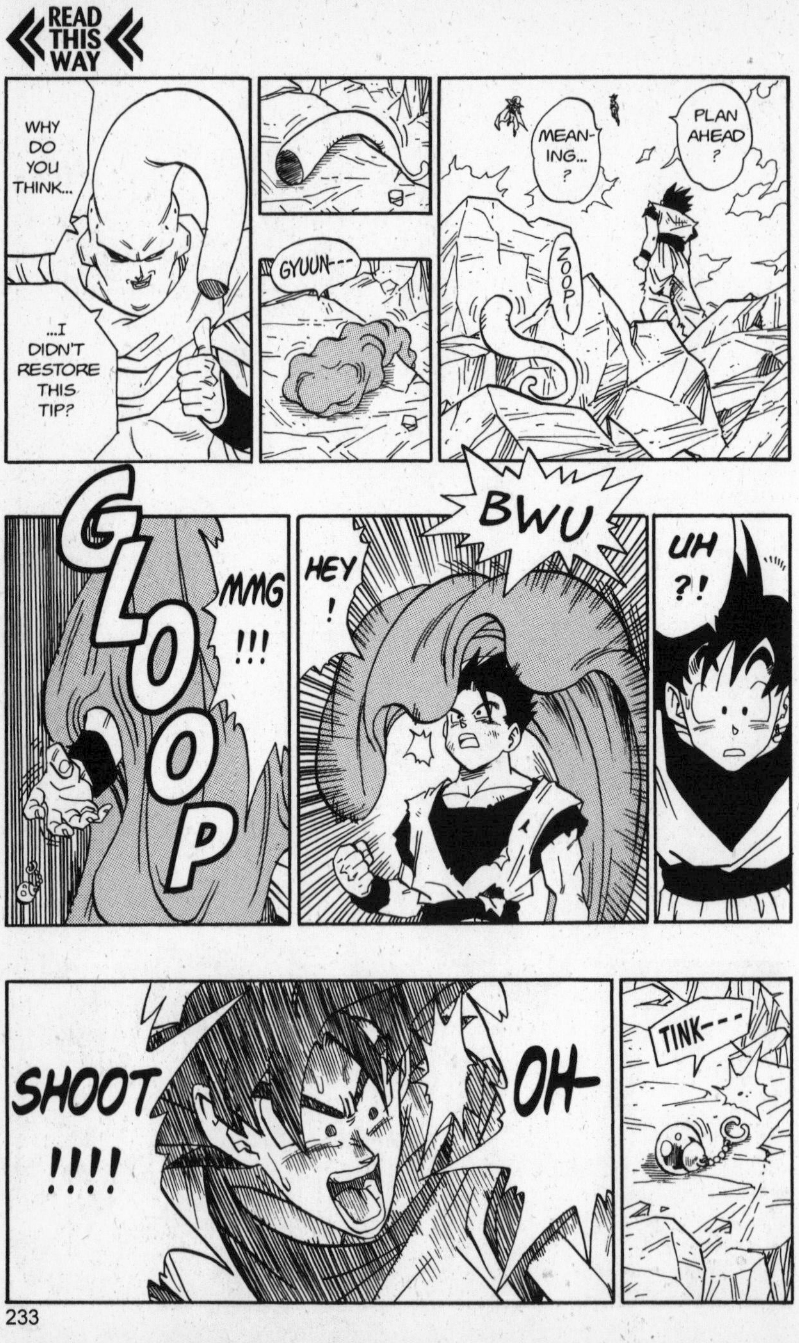

PLAN AHEAD ?
MEANING... ?
ZOOP!
GYUUN---
WHY DO YOU THINK...
...I DIDN'T RESTORE THIS TIP?
UH ?!
BWU
HEY !
MMG !!!
GLOOP
TINK---
OH
SHOOT !!!!

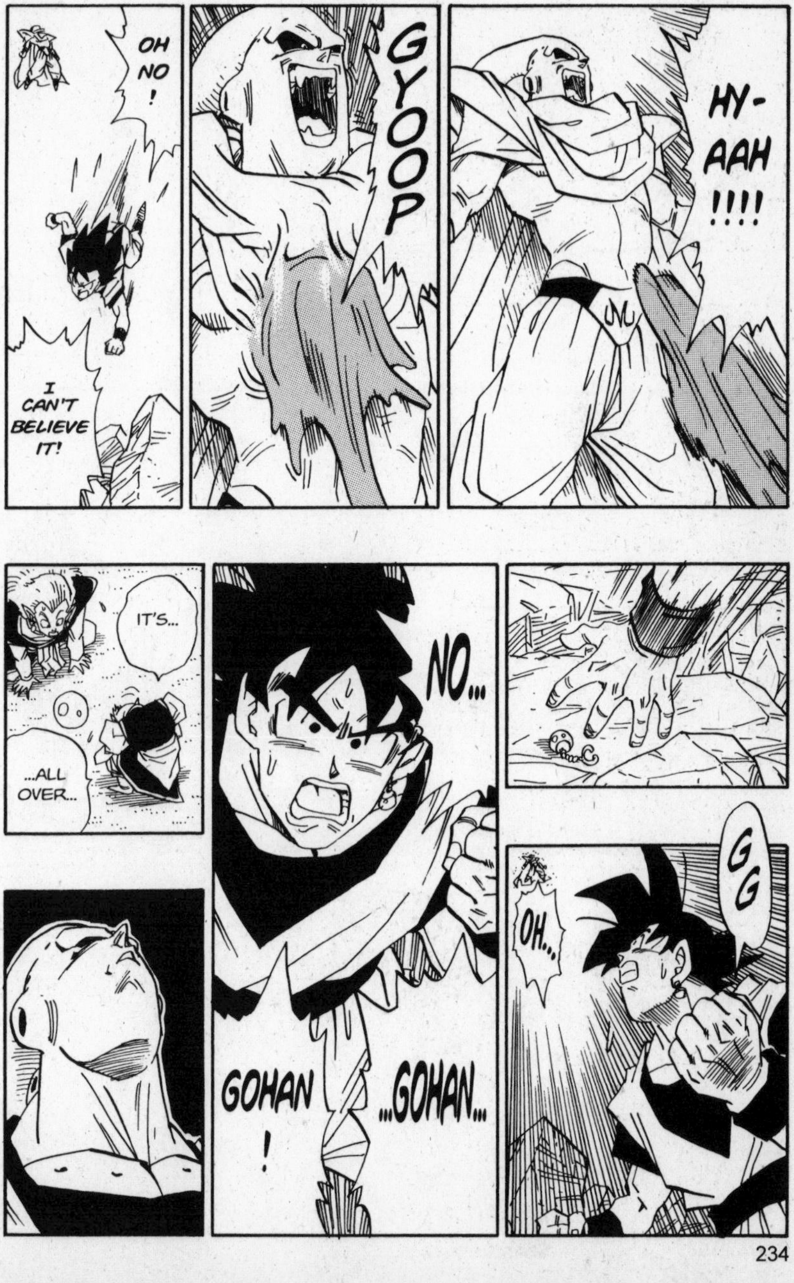
HY- AAH !!!!
GYOOOP
OH NO !
I CAN'T BELIEVE IT!
GG
OH...
NO...
...GOHAN...
GOHAN !
IT'S...
...ALL OVER..

READ THIS WAY

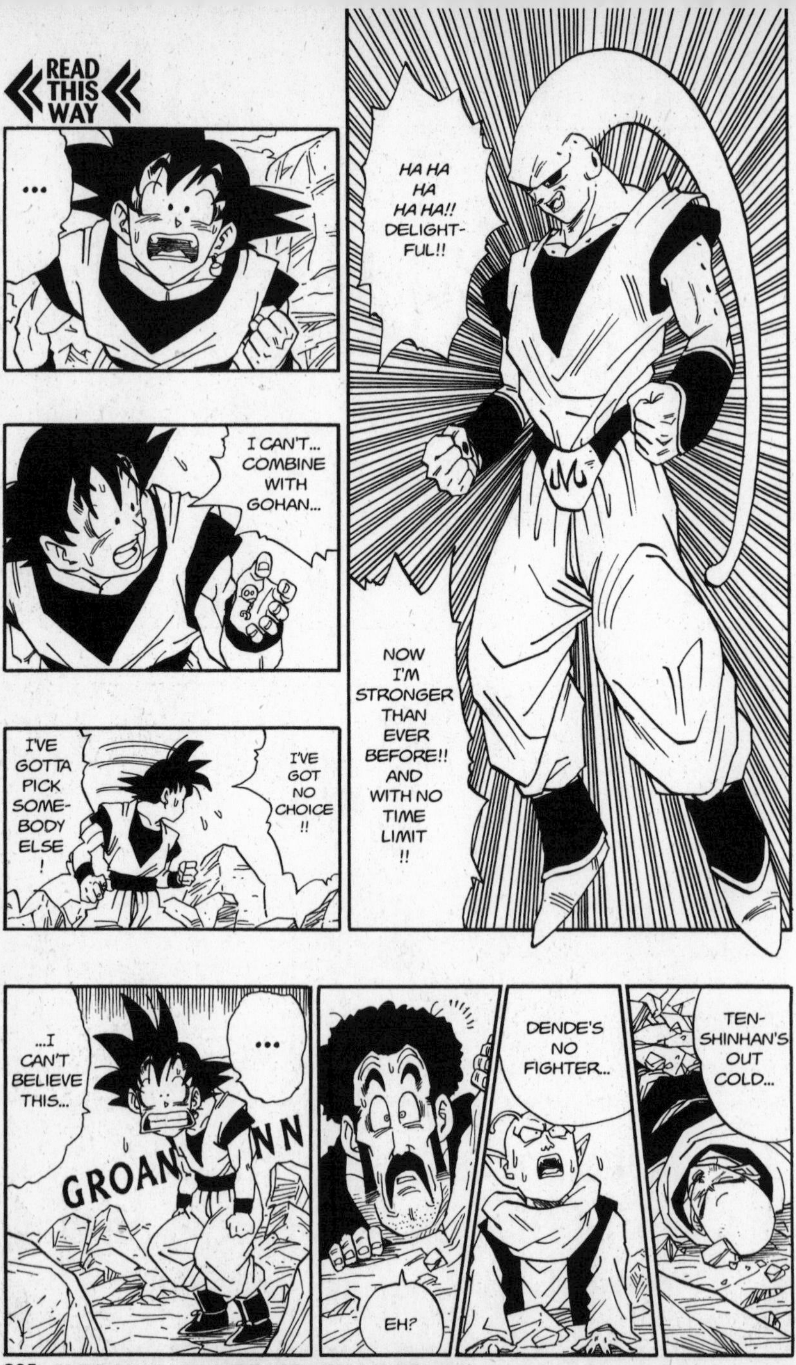

HA HA HA HA HA!! DELIGHTFUL!!
NOW I'M STRONGER THAN EVER BEFORE!! AND WITH NO TIME LIMIT!!
...
I CAN'T... COMBINE WITH GOHAN...
I'VE GOT NO CHOICE!!
I'VE GOTTA PICK SOMEBODY ELSE!
TEN-SHINHAN'S OUT COLD...
DENDE'S NO FIGHTER...
EH?
...
...I CAN'T BELIEVE THIS...
GROANNN

Title Page Gallery

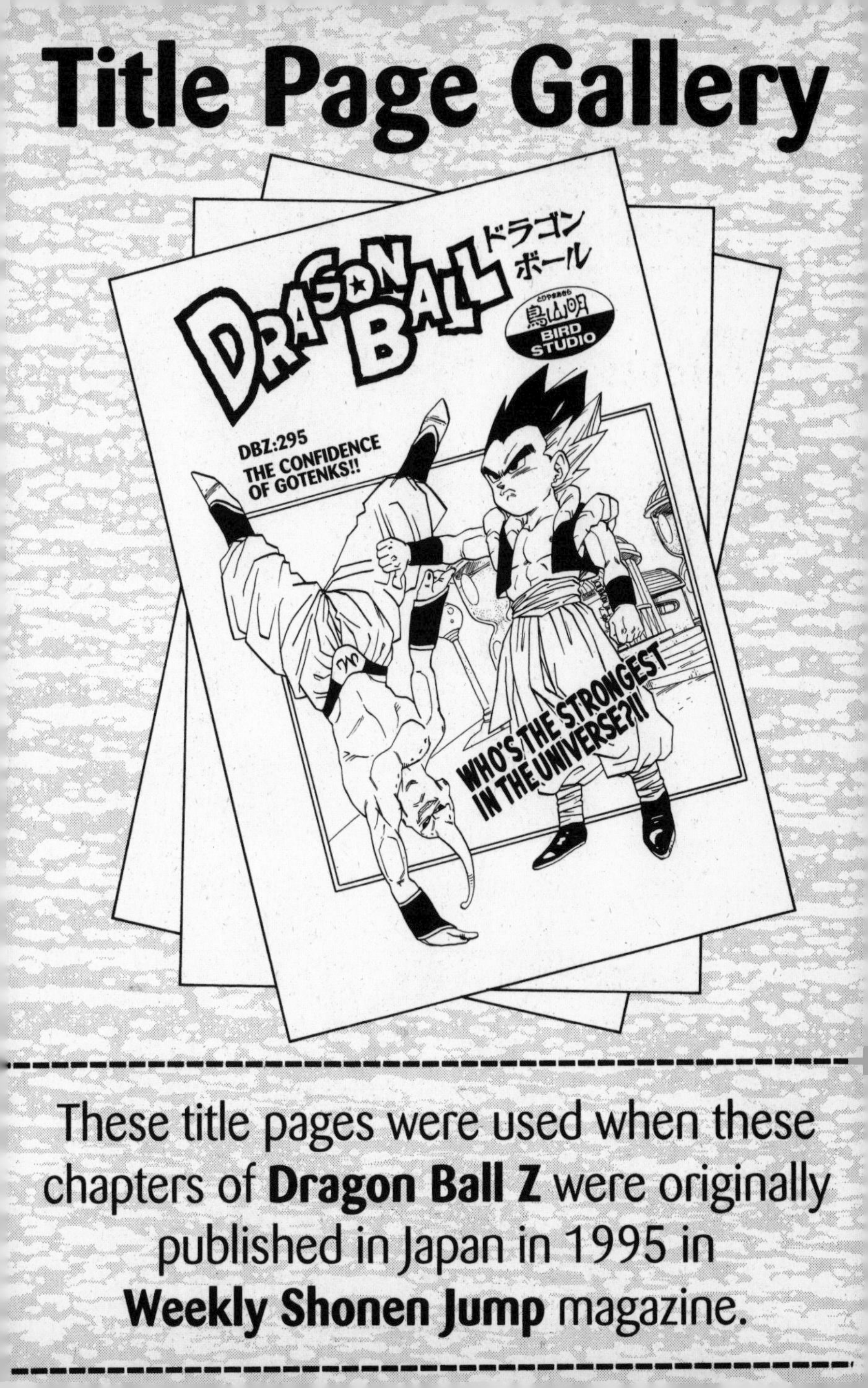
DRAGON BALL
ドラゴンボール
とりやまあきら
鳥山明
BIRD STUDIO
DBZ:295
THE CONFIDENCE OF GOTENKS!!
WHO'S THE STRONGEST IN THE UNIVERSE?!!

These title pages were used when these chapters of **Dragon Ball Z** were originally published in Japan in 1995 in **Weekly Shonen Jump** magazine.

DRAGON BALL

ドラゴンボール

DBZ:300
SUPER GOTENKS

とりやまあきら
鳥山明
BIRD STUDIO

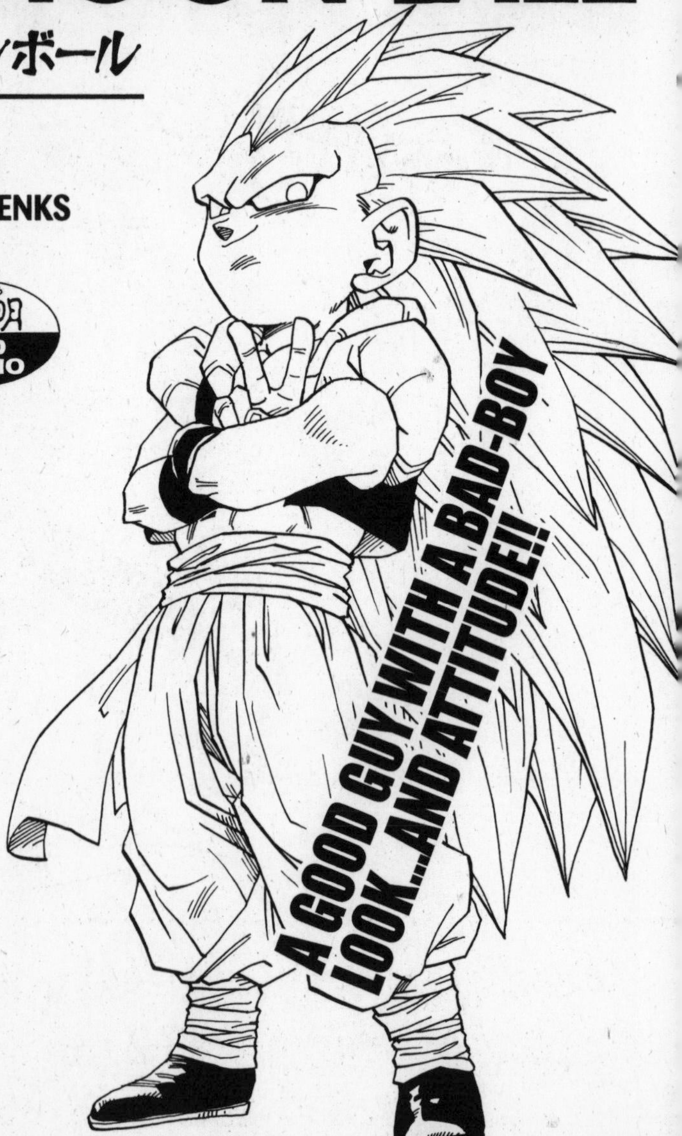
A GOOD GUY WITH A BAD-BOY
LOOK...AND ATTITUDE!!

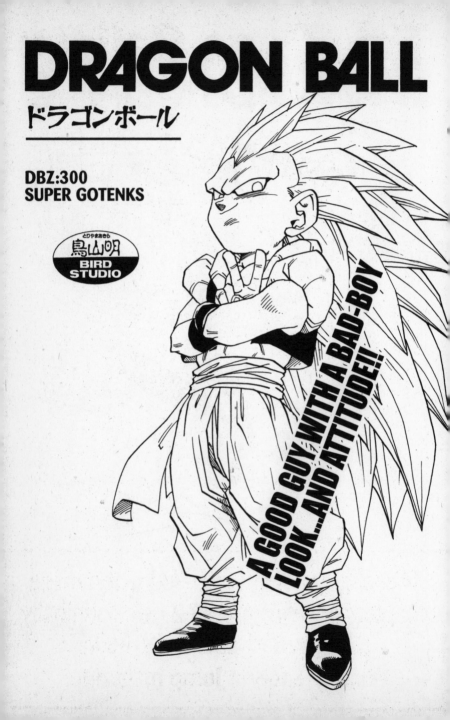

DRAGON BALL

ドラゴンボール

とりやまあきら
鳥山明
BIRD STUDIO

DBZ:303 · GOHAN'S COUNTERATTACK!!

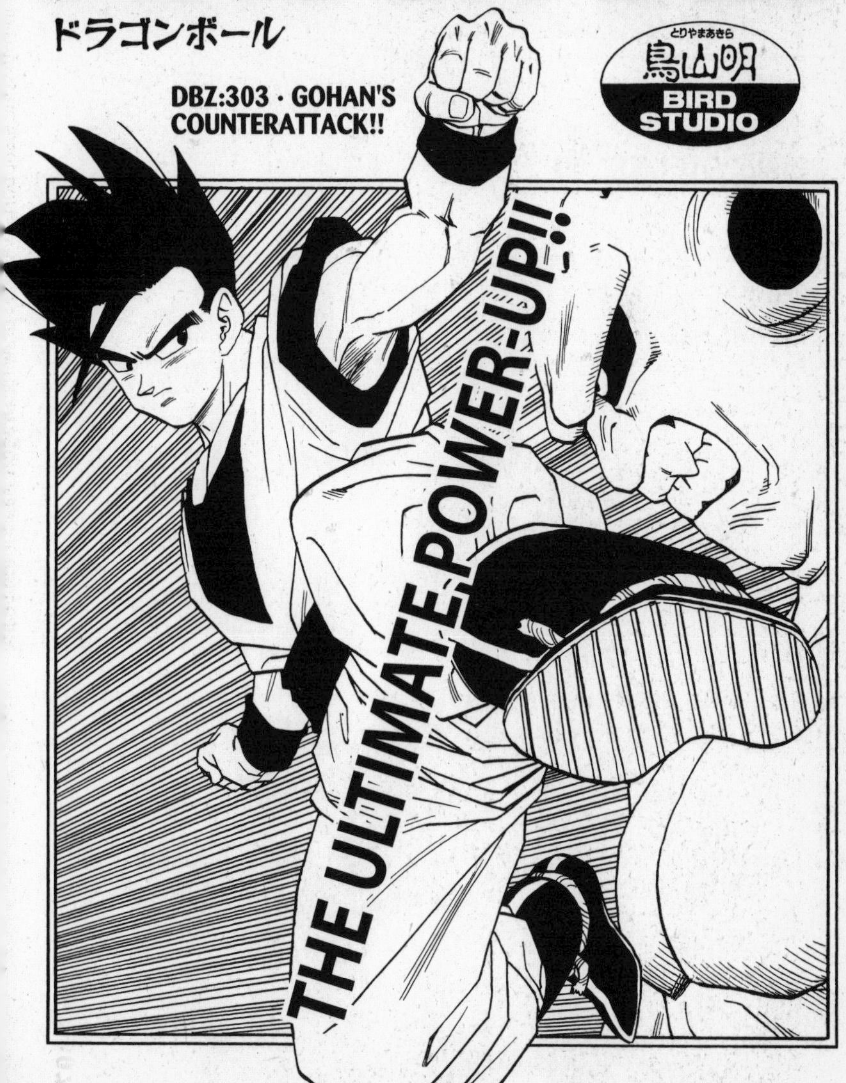
THE ULTIMATE POWER-UP!!

Thanks to everyone's support, I've been drawing **Dragon Ball** for ten years! In honor of the 501st chapter (counting from the beginning of **Dragon Ball**) we have special color pages for you!

DBZ:307
ENTER A SAVIOR?!

DRAGON BALL

———ドラゴンボール———

鳥山明
BIRD STUDIO

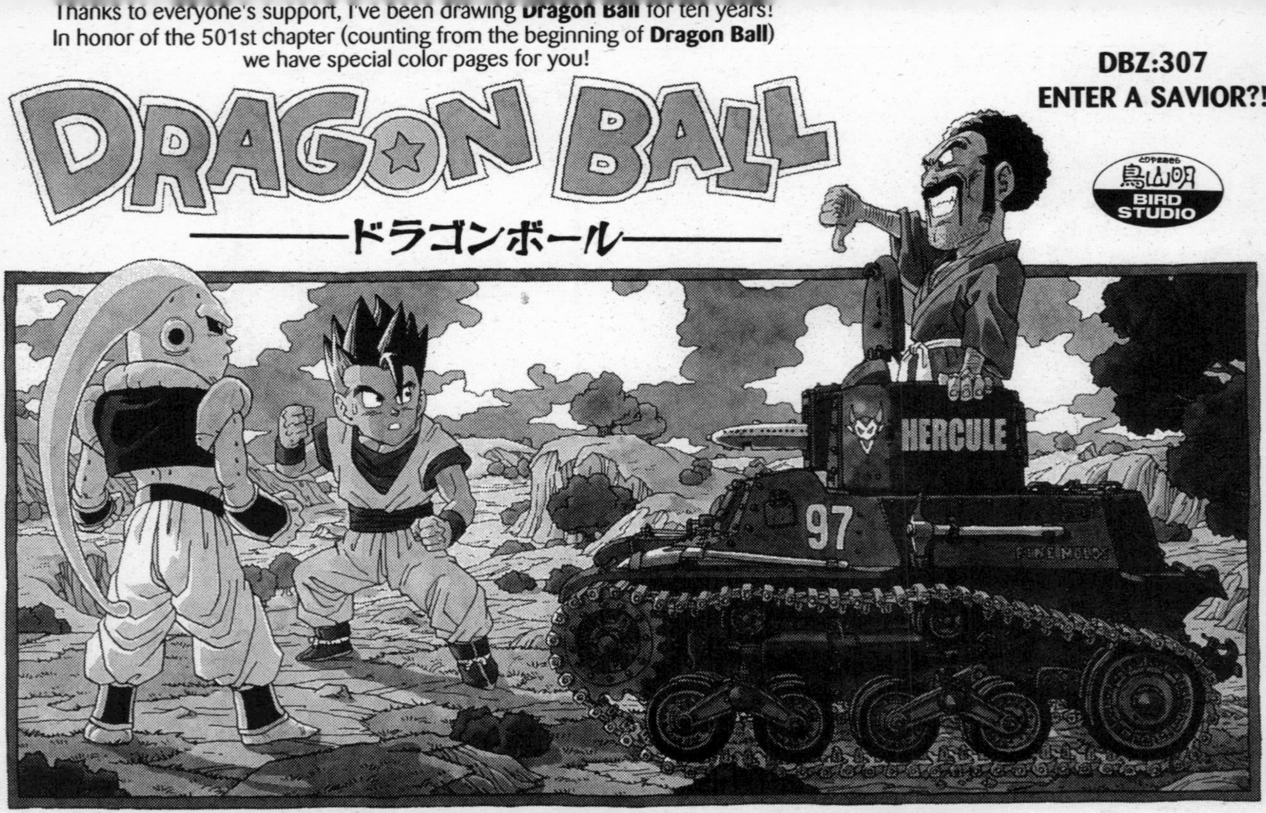
HERCULE
97

IT ALL COMES DOWN TO...HERCULE?!!

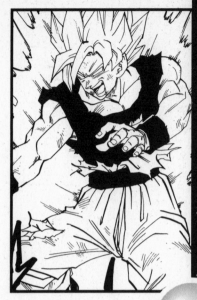

IN THE NEXT VOLUME...

The world's greatest heroes have fallen, absorbed by the ever more powerful Boo! Only Goku remains alive to fight...but even his strength will not be enough, unless he uses the Potara Earrings to permanently merge with another warrior! Whom will he choose...and when the dust has cleared, who or what will be the strongest fighter in the universe?

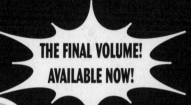

THE FINAL VOLUME!
AVAILABLE NOW!

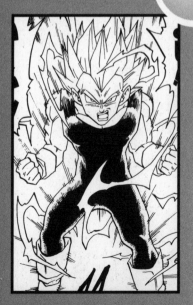

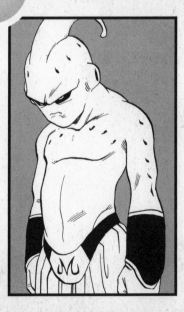

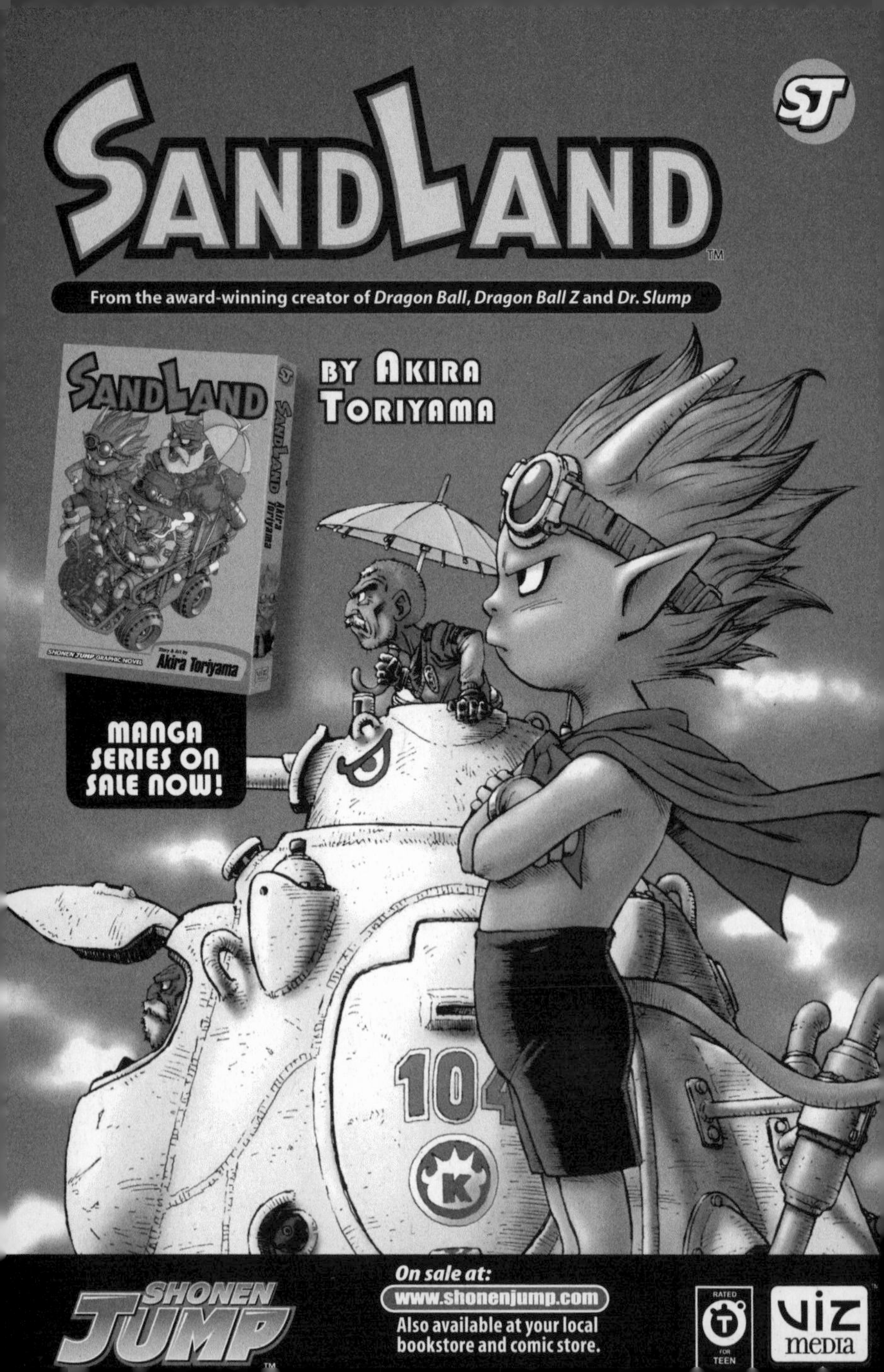
SJ
SANDLAND™
From the award-winning creator of *Dragon Ball*, *Dragon Ball Z* and *Dr. Slump*
SANDLAND
SHONEN JUMP GRAPHIC NOVEL
Story & Art by
Akira Toriyama
BY AKIRA TORIYAMA
MANGA SERIES ON SALE NOW!
104
K
SHONEN JUMP™
On sale at:
www.shonenjump.com
Also available at your local bookstore and comic store.
RATED T FOR TEEN
VIZ media

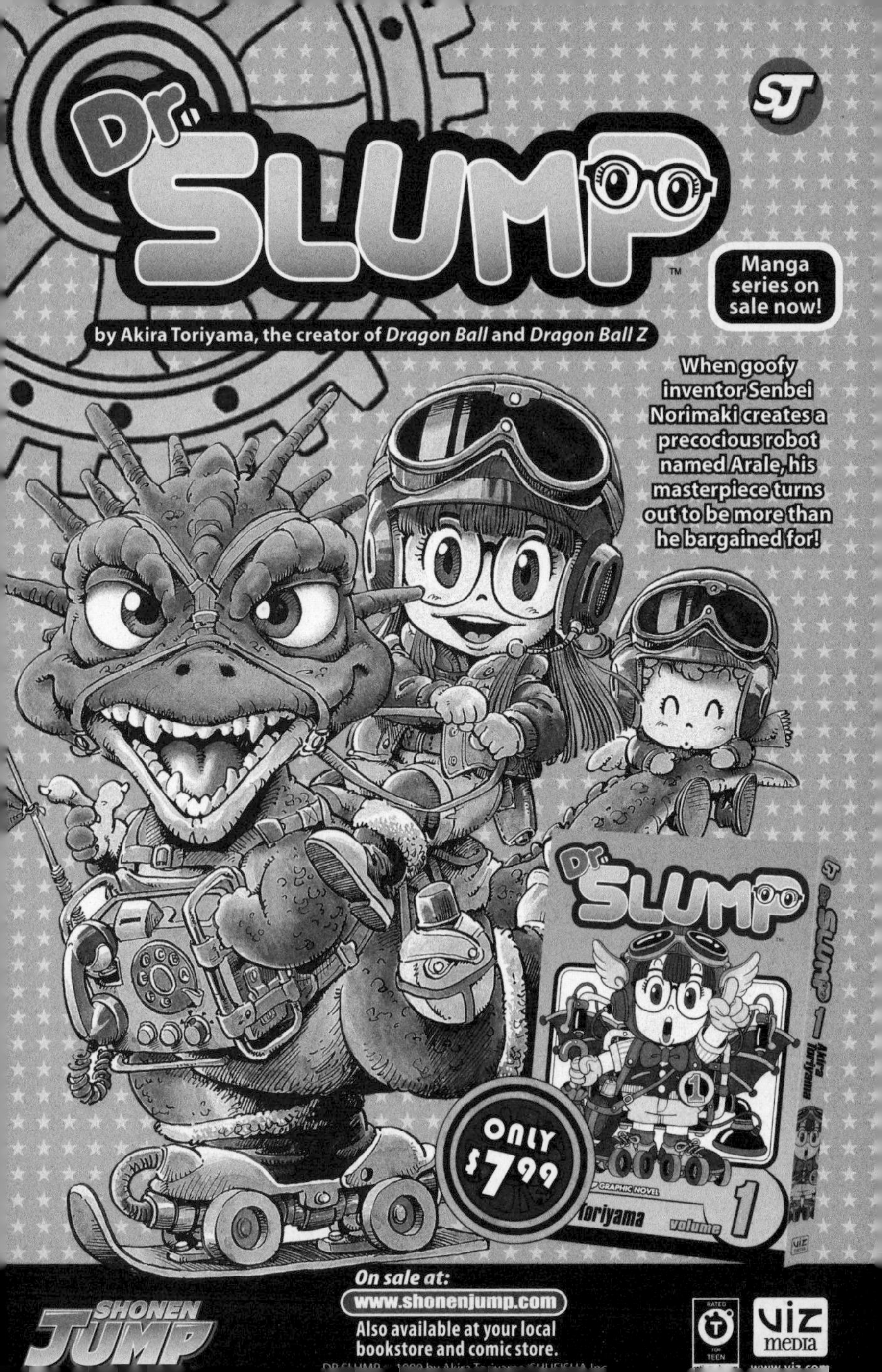
SJ
Dr. SLUMP™
Manga series on sale now!
by Akira Toriyama, the creator of *Dragon Ball* and *Dragon Ball Z*
When goofy inventor Senbei Norimaki creates a precocious robot named Arale, his masterpiece turns out to be more than he bargained for!
Dr. SLUMP™
GRAPHIC NOVEL
Toriyama
volume 1
ONLY $7.99
On sale at:
www.shonenjump.com
Also available at your local bookstore and comic store.
SHONEN JUMP
RATED T FOR TEEN
VIZ media

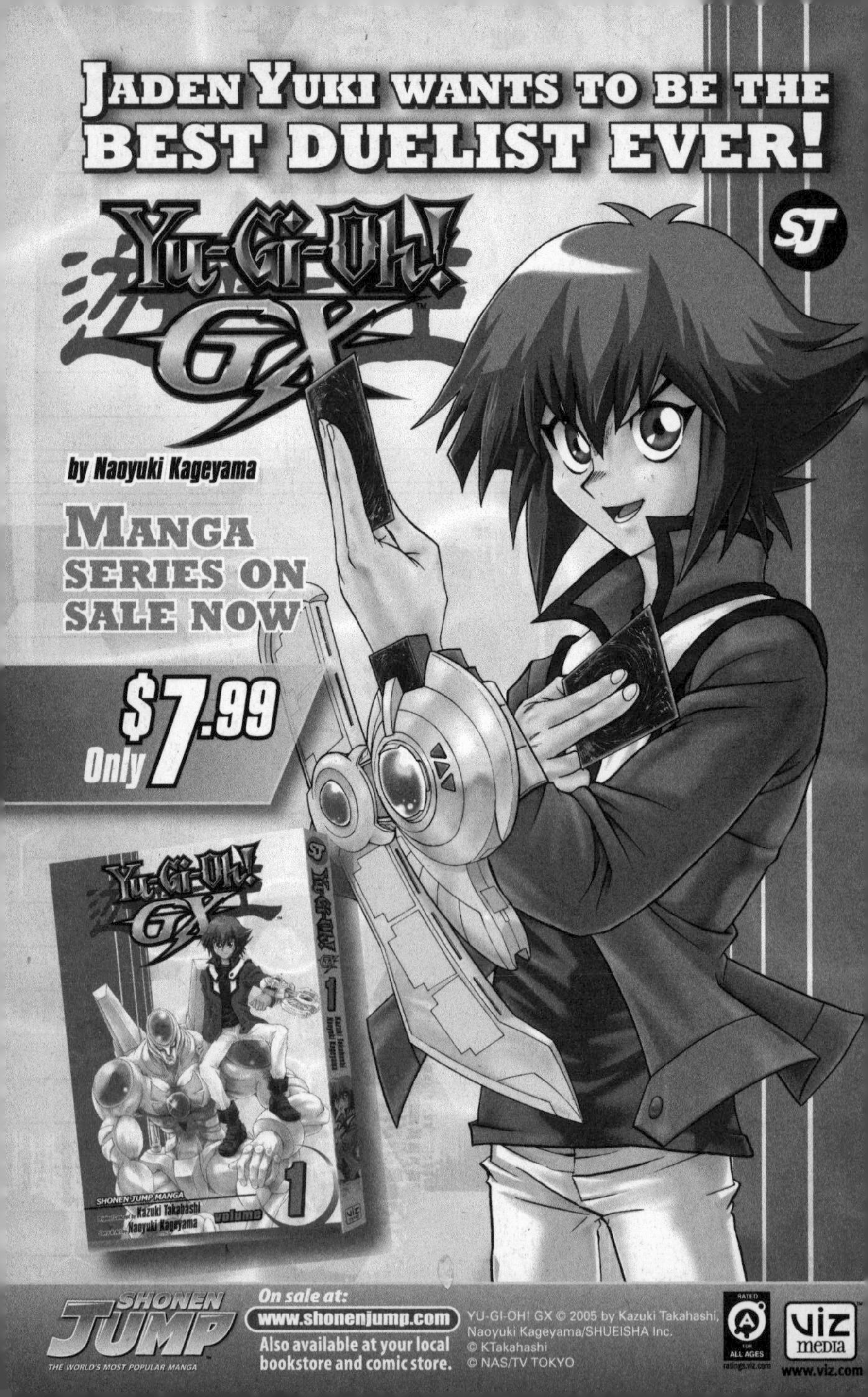

JADEN YUKI WANTS TO BE THE
BEST DUELIST EVER!
SJ
YU-GI-OH! GX™
by Naoyuki Kageyama
MANGA
SERIES ON
SALE NOW
Only $7.99
SHONEN JUMP MANGA
Kazuki Takahashi
Naoyuki Kageyama
volume 1
SHONEN JUMP
THE WORLD'S MOST POPULAR MANGA
On sale at:
www.shonenjump.com
Also available at your local
bookstore and comic store.
YU-GI-OH! GX © 2005 by Kazuki Takahashi, Naoyuki Kageyama/SHUEISHA Inc.
© KTakahashi
© NAS/TV TOKYO
RATED A FOR ALL AGES
ratings.viz.com
VIZ media
www.viz.com

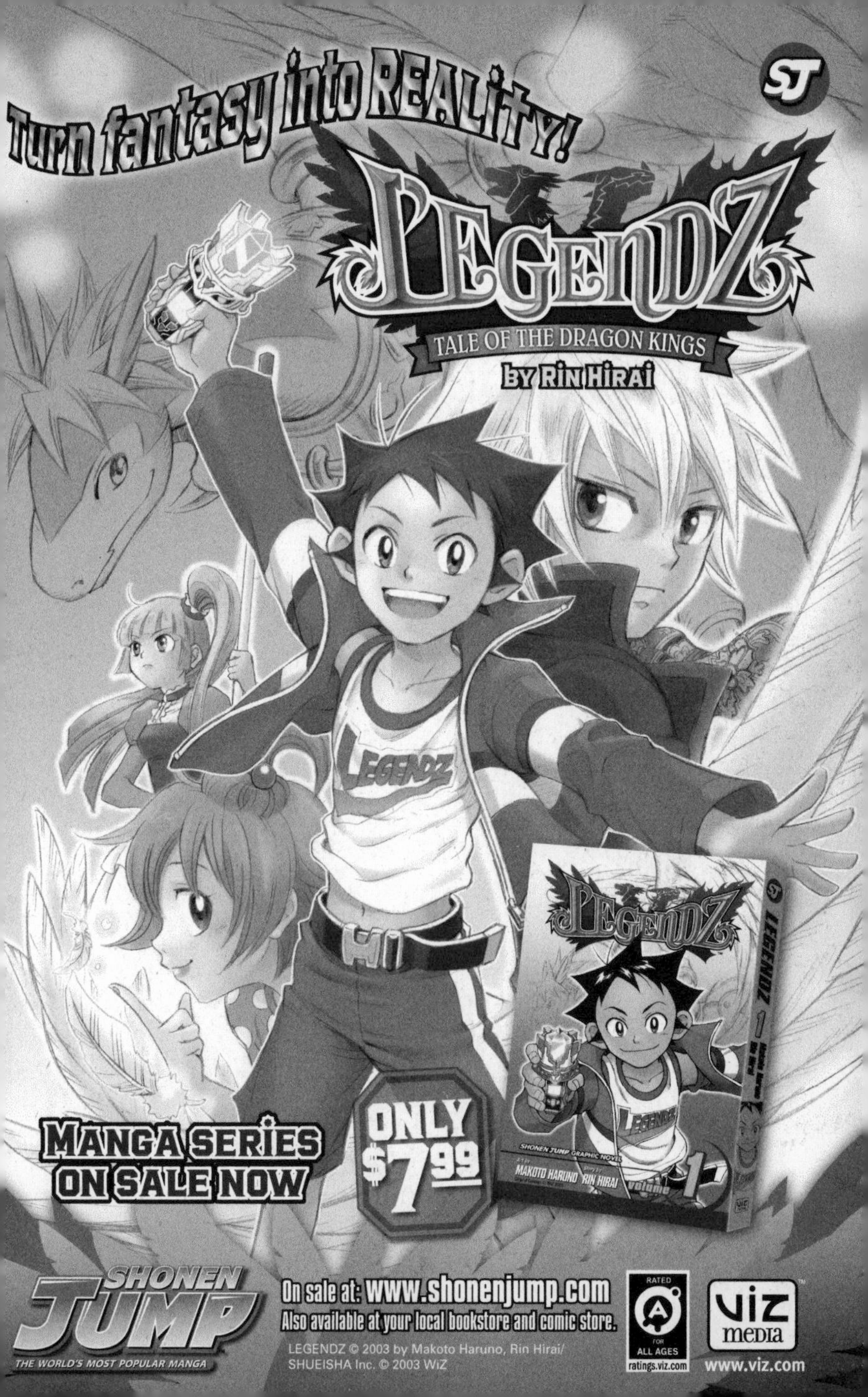

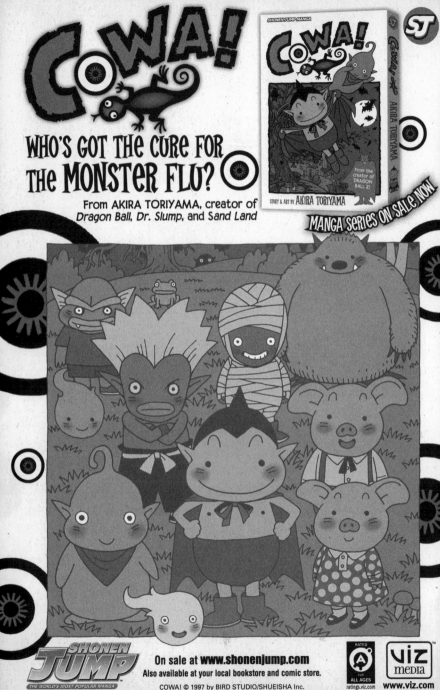

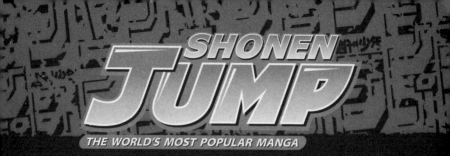

SHONEN JUMP

THE WORLD'S MOST POPULAR MANGA

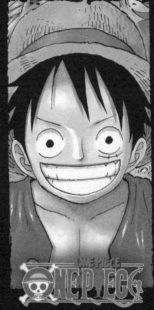

BLEACH

STORY AND ART BY
TITE KUBO

ONE PIECE

STORY AND ART BY
EIICHIRO ODA

Tegami Bachi
LETTER BEE

STORY AND ART BY
HIROYUKI ASADA

JUMP INTO THE ACTION BY TELLING US WHAT YOU LOVE (AND WHAT YOU DON'T)

LET YOUR VOICE BE HEARD!

SHONENJUMP.VIZ.COM/MANGASURVEY

HELP US MAKE MORE OF THE WORLD'S MOST POPULAR MANGA!

W9-BOM-330

RATED
T
TEEN
ratings.viz.com

VIZ
media
www.viz.com